DELINQUENCY
A SOCIOLOGICAL VIEW

DELINQUENCY
A SOCIOLOGICAL VIEW

Gary F. Jensen
UNIVERSITY OF ARIZONA

Dean G. Rojek
UNIVERSITY OF GEORGIA

D. C. HEATH AND COMPANY
Lexington, Massachusetts   Toronto

Dedication

To "Jense" and all others who care about kids.
Gary

To Gene — my friend, mentor, and advisor.
Dean

Acknowledgments

Picture Credits
1 Arthur Tress/Photo Researchers, Inc.; 21 Wayne Miller/Magnum Photos, Inc.;
49 © Frank Siteman 1979/The Picture Cube; 87 Jim Richardson/Black Star;
121 Van Bucher/Photo Researchers, Inc.; 155 © George W. Gardner; 191 Tony
O'Brien/Criminal Justice Publications; 227 Charles Gatewood; 253 Robert V.
Eckert, Jr./EKM Nepenthe; 289 Mary Ellen Mark/Magnum Photos, Inc.; 331
Tony O'Brien/Criminal Justice Publications; 367 Eric A. Roth/The Picture Cube.

Published simultaneously in Canada.

Printed in the United States of America.

International Standard Book Number: 0−669−00045−0

Library of Congress Catalog Card Number: 79−89481

PREFACE

The juvenile justice system is currently depicted to be in a state of tension, controversy, and change. This text was written to help the student make an honest assessment of this turmoil by presenting a succinct, comprehensive overview of adolescent lawbreaking and society's attempts to control it. Our perspective is primarily sociological, emphasizing social factors and influences, but does not ignore the role of psychological factors. Despite the short shrift that the study of juvenile delinquency has been given in the past, we feel that this subject deserves serious scholarly attention and concerted research efforts. The social forces that led to the emergence of the juvenile court, the myriad theories that attempt to explain delinquency, current research on adolescent misbehavior, and the dilemmas of juvenile court reform are all areas of study eminently suitable for sociological discussion.

We wrote this text for use in undergraduate and graduate delinquency courses. We wanted it to be reasonably short so that it could be used in combined crime and delinquency courses or in specialized courses. It can be used as a primary textbook, or used together with a book of readings, library assignments, or research monographs. We concentrated on those issues we found interesting and valuable to students. A considerable amount of research is summarized because students want to know what arguments seem to have found the best support in actual research. Students deserve the right to progress through the stages that so many critical criminologists progressed through in reaching what they considered to be the truth. If students find some "positivistic," "conservative," or "radical" phase of that process interesting or of personal relevance to them, that is their prerogative. In many areas, particularly the chapter on prevention, we challenge the student to formulate his or her own conclusions. Current conceptions of social policy are based on a variety of assumptions that need to be challenged. We want students to grapple with issues that are complex and to walk away from this text with questions as well as answers.

In Chapters 1 and 2 the subject matter of delinquency is put in perspective and the historical roots of the juvenile court are examined from a sociolegal viewpoint. Emphasis is given to the unique position of the juvenile court as a court of law and a social work agency. Chapters 3 and 4 focus on the multiple and often contradictory images of delinquency as gleaned from official statistics, victimization surveys, and self-report surveys. The explanations of delinquency, ranging from biological characteristics to social-cultural phenomena, are presented in Chapters 5 and 6. Each of the major theoretical perspectives is presented with a view toward theory testing as well as integrating these theories into common schools of thought. The varying contexts for adolescent socialization are discussed in Chapters 7 and 8. Surprisingly, many of these topics, such as the family, school, religion, and the media, have been almost totally ignored in the study of delinquency until the past few years. Chapters 9, 10, and 11 focus on society's reaction to delinquency. Specifically, we include consideration of deterrence and labeling, institutionalization and its alternatives, and the recent emphasis on diversion. Finally, the concluding chapter struggles with the dilemma of delinquency prevention. Despite the glib rhetoric normally accorded to prevention, any policy that seeks to "solve" the delinquency problem in America calls for radical, all-encompassing change. The question to consider is the degree to which we can embrace the logical consequences of a true prevention program.

It was our intent to write a clear, readable text at an appropriate level of sophistication for typical undergraduates. While jargon and "buzz" words have been minimized, we have tried to communicate many ideas that do require thinking and more than one reading. The reference section that follows each chapter represents a thorough review of the literature for that particular topic under discussion. The epigraphs, tables, displays, and even the cartoons were carefully chosen to supplement the material in each chapter.

We would like to thank Lane Akers and Phillip Hammond for convincing us to attempt the task and the Department of Sociology, University of Arizona, for support and use of their facilities. Thanks are owed to Renette Saunders and Carla Vassmer who did much of the proofing and Lois Tyndall and Kathy Williams who typed parts of early drafts. We would like to extend a special note of gratitude to Sandy Goers for all of the work she put into the manuscript. Her eye for errors and missing information saved us considerable work, and her typing provided us with an extremely clear and attractive manuscript.

Many of our teachers and colleagues had an impact on the text. Sociologists who had a particular impact were Ronald Akers, Herbert Costner, Maynard Erickson, Jack Gibbs, Travis Hirschi, and Malcom Klein. They provided the inspiration and knowledge that led us to write it.

Obviously our families deserve recognition. We would like to thank Kathy and Janet, Jennifer and Wendy, and Joel and Eric for their familyship, friendship, and faith.

Gary F. Jensen

Dean G. Rojek

CONTENTS

8. CONTEXTS FOR ADOLESCENT SOCIALIZATION: RELIGION, MEDIA, AND COMMUNITY   227

9. DETERRENCE AND LABELING   253

10. INSTITUTIONALIZATION AND ALTERNATIVES   289

11. DIVERSION   331

12. PREVENTION: DILEMMAS OF CHOICE, CHANGE, AND CONTROL   367

1.
DELINQUENCY
IN CONTEXT

Let any man that hath occasion either to walk or ride through the Out-parts of this City, (where mostly our poor people inhabit) tell but what he hath seen of the Rudeness of young Children, who for want of better Education and Employment, shall sometimes be found by whole Companies at play, where they shall wrangle and cheat one another, and upon the least Provocation, swear and fight for a Farthing, or else they shall be found whipping of Horses, by reasons of which, they sometimes cast their Riders, to the hazard or loss of their Lives or Limbs; or else they shall be throwing of Dirt or Stones into Coaches, or at the Glasses, insomuch that I have been a hundred times greatly troubled, to see the Rudeness and Misbehavior of the poorer sort of Children, (especially of late year) they having been generally so much neglected, that they have neither been taught their Duties either towards God or Man.

—A 17th Century English Philanthropist

AN ENDURING CONCERN

The subject of this text is juvenile delinquency, which is one dimension of the problem of crime in America. In a sense, juvenile delinquency is a relatively new dimension of the problem in that juvenile courts and legislation dealing exclusively with children are products of modern times. Illinois was the first state to pass a juvenile court act in 1899 and Wyoming the last to enact such legislation in 1945. In view of the long legal tradition that accompanies much of our civil and criminal law, juvenile statutes may thus be considered relatively recent additions to the American system of law.

On the other hand, despite the legal infancy of "juvenile delinquency" and the category of "delinquent," there has been a persistent concern with youthful misbehavior throughout history, along with a tendency to view the situation as progressively worse than in preceding generations. Consider, for example, the following anguished statement: "Youth is disintegrating. The youngsters of the land have a disrespect for their elders, and a contempt for authority in every form. Vandalism is rife, and crime of all kinds is rampant among our young people. The nation is in peril." Although this lament appears to be a contemporary critique of American youth, it actually dates back some four thousand years to a despondent Egyptian priest. During the "Golden Age" of Greece (500–300 B.C.), Socrates was quite disgruntled with the youth of his day, as evidenced by his claim that "children today love luxury. They have bad manners, a contempt for authority, a disrespect for their elders, and they like to talk instead of work. They contradict their parents, chatter before company, gobble up the best at the table, and tyrannize over their teachers."

The Code of Hammurabi, the oldest known code of laws, which dates back to 2270 B.C., prescribes specific punishments for children who disown, run away from, or strike their parents—for example, "If a son strikes his father, one shall cut off his hands" (Kocourek and Wigmore,

2

1951:427). Mosaic law prescribes even harsher penalties for children who strike or curse their parents: According to the Book of Exodus, such children should be put to death, while the Book of Deuteronomy decrees that any child accused of disobedience or rebellion should be stoned to death.

The image of the young as recalcitrant or incorrigible persists in contemporary American society, where crime is typically depicted as a problem of youth. For example, in the late 1960s the President's Commission on Law Enforcement and Administration of Justice (1967:169–170) concluded (1) that "enormous numbers of young people appear to be involved in delinquent acts," (2) that "youth is responsible for a substantial and disproportionate part of the national crime problem," and (3) that "America's best hope for reducing crime is to reduce juvenile delinquency and youth crime." The crimes and delinquencies of the young are viewed as an enormous social problem and as a major, if not *the* major, dimension of crime in the United States. The popular press (see Display 1–1) has depicted the problem even more dramatically, referring to the situation as the "youth crime plague" (*Time*, July 11, 1977:18).

"*Remember this, my child. The world is always in the biggest mess it's ever been in.*"

Illustration Reprinted from *Better Homes and Gardens* magazine.

DISPLAY 1–1   *The Youth Crime Plague*

Chicago. Johnny, 16, who had a long record of arrests for disorderly conduct, simple battery and aggravated assault, lured a motorist into an alley. He drew a .22-cal. pistol and shot the driver six times, killing him. Johnny was arrested yet again, but he was released because witnesses failed to show up in court. Today he is free.

New Orleans. Steven, 17, was first arrested for burglary when he was eleven and diagnosed as psychotic. But he kept escaping from the state hospital and was seized for 22 different crimes, including theft and attempted murder. Just four days after he was charged with robbery and attempted murder, he was arrested for raping and murdering a young nurse.

Hartford. Touché, 19, who earned his nickname by his dexterity with a switchblade, has been in trouble since he was eleven; he started fires, snatched pocketbooks, stole cars, burglarized homes, slashed and shot people. When a pal was locked up in Connecticut's Meriden Home for Boys, Touché broke in with a gun and freed him. Touché was placed in a specially built cell in Meriden because he had escaped from the institution 17 times.

Wilmington. Eric, 16, who had escaped conviction for a previous mugging charge, pleaded guilty to knocking down an 86-year-old woman and stealing her purse. Three months later, the woman is still hospitalized and is not expected to walk again. Eric was released into the custody of his father. Since then, he has been charged with three burglaries. Says Detective James Strawbridge: "He's going to kill somebody some day, and he's still out there."

Houston. Lawrence was 15 when he was charged with murdering two brothers in his neighborhood: Kenneth Elliott, 11, and Ronald Elliott, 12. Lawrence tied up Kenneth, castrated him and stabbed him twice in the heart. Then he cut off the boy's head, which he left about 50 feet from the body. He also admitted killing Ronald, whose body was never found, in similar fashion. Like all other offenders in juvenile facilities in Texas, Lawrence was released from prison when he turned 18.

People have always accused kids of getting away with murder. Now that is all too literally true. Across the U.S., a pattern of crime has emerged that is both perplexing and appalling. Many youngsters appear to be robbing and raping, maiming and murdering as casually as they go to a movie or join a pickup baseball game. A new, remorseless, mutant juvenile seems to have been born, and there is no more terrifying figure in America today.

Source: Reprinted by permission from *Time,* The Weekly Newsmagazine; Copyright © Time, Inc. 1977.

JUVENILES IN CONFLICT WITH THE LAW

It is a fact that a substantial proportion of young people have conflicts with the law before they reach adulthood. For instance, of all males born in Philadelphia in 1945, over one-third were found to have had recorded contacts with the police between their seventh and eighteenth birthdays (Wolfgang, Figlio, and Sellin, 1972:53–55). In similar research in nonmetropolitan Oregon (Polk, 1974), one-fourth of the males studied were found to have acquired official records with the county juvenile department by the time they were eighteen. Moreover, research has shown that race and socioeconomic status can have a pronounced relationship to conflict with the law. In the Philadelphia study, about 50 percent of the nonwhites, in contrast to nearly 30 percent of the whites, had acquired police records between ages seven and eighteen. In addition, nearly 90 percent of the nonwhite delinquents were of low socioeconomic status. Thus, conflict with the law is actually quite common among American youth and, under certain circumstances, is more the rule than the exception.

While a sizable proportion of American youth acquires an official record, an even greater proportion engages, without detection, in activities that are a *potential* source of conflict with the law. For example, in an interview study of delinquency in a representative national sample of youths thirteen to sixteen years of age, Jay Williams and Martin Gold (1972) found that although 88 percent of the youths had done something that could have resulted in trouble with the law, only 22 percent had ever had any contact with police and only 2 percent had been under judicial consideration. In similar research among high school students in upstate New York (Hindelang, 1973:474), 75 percent of the male subjects and 45 percent of the female subjects reported committing one or more of the six criminal acts studied in the survey.

Not only are such conflicts with the law quite common but, as the President's Commission indicated in its 1967 report, conflicts with the law also appear to be *disproportionately* common among the young. In Table 1–1 we have summarized the proportions of arrests accounted for by persons under eighteen, as reported in the *Uniform Crime Reports* of the Federal Bureau of Investigation (1977). Persons under eighteen made up about 30 percent of the population in 1977, which means that when they account for more than 30 percent of arrests they are *overrepresented* in the arrest statistics. Table 1–1 shows that in 1977 persons under eighteen accounted for more than 30 percent of arrests for robbery; burglary; larceny; motor vehicle theft; arson; receiving, buying, or possessing stolen property; vandalism; liquor law violations; and, of course, curfew, loitering, and runaway offenses (which are not offenses for adults). Since infants and young children account for very few arrests, some sources of statistics (for example, national juvenile court statistics) focus on the

TABLE 1–1 *Percentage of Arrests Accounted for by Persons under 18 in 1977 according to FBI Uniform Crime Reports*

All Offenses	24.0%		
Type of Offense	*%*	*Type of Offense*	*%*
Murder and nonnegligent manslaughter	9.7	Prostitution and commercialized vice	4.3
Manslaughter by negligence	11.1	Sex offenses (except forcible rape and prostitution)	23.2
Forcible rape	16.5	Narcotic drug laws	23.2
Aggravated assault	16.3	Gambling	4.2
Robbery	32.0	Offenses against family and children	5.9
Burglary	51.5	Driving under the influence	2.2
Larceny	42.9	Liquor law violations	37.3
Motor vehicle theft	53.0	Drunkenness	4.1
Arson	49.8	Disorderly conduct	19.4
Forgery and counterfeiting	12.8	Vagrancy	12.7
Fraud	10.3	All other offenses (except traffic)	20.8
Embezzlement	11.8	Curfew, loitering	100.0
Stolen property; buying, receiving, possessing	32.9	Runaways	100.0
Vandalism	60.3		
Weapons; carrying, possessing, etc.	16.0		

juvenile population aged ten through seventeen, which constitutes approximately 15 percent of the population. Thus, if 15 percent is used to assess over- and underrepresentation, then juveniles are overrepresented for many other offenses as well.

JUVENILE DELINQUENCY AND ADULT CRIME

All the foregoing observations—the enduring historical concern with the misbehavior of the young, the number of adolescents involved in illegal activities, and the disproportionate number of young people arrested for various crimes—have been the traditional justifications for devoting an extraordinary amount of attention to delinquency as a major aspect of crime in America. However, to put juvenile delinquency in proper perspective, we need to make some observations about juvenile crime in relation to the adult world and adult crime.

While the President's Commission and the popular press have dramatized the importance of addressing juvenile delinquency and youth crime as America's "best hope" for reducing crime in general, this point of view has certain shortcomings. For one thing, we need to recognize that within some categories of "serious" crime, juveniles are not overrepresented (assault and rape) and that within some, they are underrepresented (murder and manslaughter). These observations seem to contradict the imagery depicted in Display 1–1 ("The Youth Crime Plague"); however, it should be noted that the terms *youth, kids,* and *the young* are used rather loosely to encompass young adults as well as juveniles. The data in Table 1–1 are for the entire United States. In the United States as a whole, persons under eighteen are most distinctly involved in crimes against property. If the terms *youth, kids,* and *the young* are used to include young adults, then youth account for a disproportionate amount of arrests for all crimes. However, it is young adults who contribute most disproportionately to crimes of interpersonal violence (other than robbery). As we will note again in Chapter 3, more types of offenses peak at age twenty-one than at any other age.

A second point concerning juvenile delinquency in relation to adult crime is that our major body of statistics on crime in the United States presents a somewhat biased picture of the crime problem. The *Uniform Crime Reports* of the Federal Bureau of Investigation (FBI) provides the greatest detail on seven specific offenses—criminal homicide, forcible rape, robbery, aggravated assault, burglary, larceny, and motor vehicle theft. Together these offenses constitute the "serious-crime index." Four of the offenses included in the index (robbery, burglary, larceny, and motor vehicle theft) accounted for 90 percent of all index crimes in 1977. Larceny (theft) alone accounts for nearly *one-half* of the index crimes. In sum, the index is heavily weighted with offenses that are unusually common among juveniles.

Many crimes that are not included in indexes of serious crime—for example, consumer fraud, fraud, child abuse, drunken driving, drunkenness, gambling, prostitution, and vice—are more characteristic of adults than juveniles. These offenses are not included in the serious-crime indexes either because they are even more likely to go unreported than those that are included or because they are less reliably reported than other offenses. However, there are grounds for challenging the view that adult crimes are "less serious" than those that disproportionately involve juveniles. In terms of economic cost to the American public, the President's Commission (1967) estimated that the annual loss associated with consumer fraud alone is greater than that for all auto theft, burglary, larceny, and robbery in a given year. The Chamber of Commerce (1974) estimated that the cost of "white-collar" crimes in 1974 was at least $40 billion annually (see Table 1–2). The FBI's estimate for the four property-oriented crimes (burglary, larceny, motor vehicle theft, and robbery) was $3.2 billion for 1974, which is less than the loss due to the theft of securities and securities fraud. Some activities that are not even included as a category in crime data, such as price-fixing, have been estimated to

TABLE 1–2 *The Costs of White-Collar Crime (In Billions of Dollars)*

Bankruptcy, fraud		$ 0.08
Bribery, kickbacks, and payoffs		3.00
Computer-related crime		0.10
Consumer fraud, illegal competition, deceptive practices[a]		21.00
Consumer victims:	$ 5.5	
Business victims:	3.5	
Government revenue loss:	12.0	
Credit card and check fraud		1.10
Credit card:	0.1	
Check:	1.0	
Embezzlement and pilferage		7.0
Embezzlement (cash, goods, services):	3.0	
Pilferage:	4.0	
Insurance fraud		2.00
Insurer victims:	1.5	
Policyholder victims:	0.5	
Receiving stolen property		3.50
Securities thefts and frauds		4.00
	TOTAL (billions)	$41.78[b]

Source: Chamber of Commerce of the United States. *A Handbook on White-Collar Crime*, p. 6. Washington, D.C.: Chamber of Commerce of the United States, 1974.

Note: The dollar amounts pertain only to that aspect of each listed crime which is directed at, or committed by or within, business, industry, and the professions. These estimates do not include the cost involved in combating white-collar crime.

[a]Estimates related to price-fixing and industrial espionage are not included. Among the schemes or practices that victimize ethically run businesses are the following: advance fee, counterfeit products, illegal hiring of aliens, sweetheart contracts, etc. The figure for government revenue loss refers to business-related tax fraud, which has been reported as relatively prevalent among the self-employed (especially in the medical, legal, and accounting professions).

[b]This total is more than the $40-billion referred to in the text because the listed crime categories are not necessarily mutually exclusive. For example, a portion of the embezzlement figure is also part of the estimate for computer-related crime.

cost the public as much as $10 billion a year. Juveniles are rarely, if ever, in a position to engage in such costly forms of criminal activity.

Organized crime is another costly enterprise run by and profitable to adults. Yet, the activities of organized crime are not likely to enter into crime statistics, and those caught engaging in such activities are not likely to be those who profit the most. Organized crime is involved in a host of illegal pursuits that range from fraud and corruption to violence and murder—all of which are controlled by adults. Organized crime's involvement in gambling alone is estimated to result in greater economic loss than all seven of the "serious" crimes in the FBI's crime index. Moreover, organized crime uses the profits from the supply of illicit goods and services to gain control of other economic institutions and to corrupt the political system (Cressey, 1969). Syndicated criminal organizations are not the domain of juveniles. Juveniles are found within these criminal confederations only at the "street level," where profits and power are minimal.

It is easy to show that adult-controlled crimes result in far greater economic losses than juvenile crime. It is much more difficult, however, to assess the amount of misery, pain, and suffering that adult-controlled crime may generate. How many Americans have suffered as a result of fraudulent health devices and misrepresented drugs? How many have suffered because of price-fixing and its impact on everyday budgets? How much do we suffer when government and big business violate or circumvent laws governing their activities? The public tends to react most severely to crimes involving *direct, individual* threats and attacks against persons and property in which there are clearly defined victims and offenders. Yet, offenses that involve *indirect* and *collective* attacks against us all take a far greater toll.

To put juvenile delinquency in perspective, we also have to ask how fraud, corruption, and the violation of positions of trust affect attitudes toward law and authority. What are the feelings of frustration, rage, and despair among the millions of victims of such crime, *including the young?* In the early 1940s Edwin Sutherland (1940:1–12) argued that "white-collar" crime or crimes committed by persons in violation of their positions of trust not only are a serious form of crime in terms of financial loss but, even more important, they also contribute to distrust on a wide scale. Unethical and illegal practices are spread from person to person and from one business or occupational group to another, resulting in a general disrespect for the law by "noncriminals." Studies of occupational offenders indicate that while many feel *they* can violate the law with impunity ("business is business"), they also feel little shame in attributing the "crime problem" to others.

John Johnson and Jack Douglas have observed that in comparison to the thousands of studies of juvenile delinquency, social scientists have paid relatively little attention to business and professional deviance—despite the evidence that such adult-dominated crimes are "by far the most pervasive and massive forms of financial deviance in our society" (1978:1). They note that the traditional rationale of the social scientist in selecting delinquency as a research topic has been that "street crimes" and those offenses disproportionately involving "the lower part of our social-economic spectrum" (and we would add "the young") involve more violence and thus generate more public concern than business or professional crime. However, Johnson and Douglas firmly believe that in

Source: The *Milwaukee Journal,* October 24, 1975.

terms of human suffering and the total threat to personal safety and
human happiness, our attention has been misplaced.

With regard to the potential costs of organized crime, the President's
Commission on Law Enforcement and Administration of Justice (1967)
pointed out:

> In many ways organized crime is the most sinister kind of crime in
> America. The men who control it have become rich and powerful by
> encouraging the needy to gamble, by luring the troubled to destroy them-
> selves with drugs, by extorting the profits of honest and hardworking
> businessmen, by collecting usury from those in financial plight, by maim-

ing or murdering those who oppose them, by bribing those sworn to destroy them. Organized crime is not merely a few preying on a few. In a very real sense, it is dedicated to subverting not only American institutions, but the very decency and integrity that are the most cherished attributes of a free society. As the leaders of Cosa Nostra and their racketeering allies pursue their conspiracy unmolested, in open and continuous defiance of the law, they preach a sermon that all too many Americans heed: The government is for sale; lawlessness is the road to wealth; honesty is a pitfall and morality a trap for suckers. (Cressey, 1969:7)

Despite these observations we find "authorities" on crime in America continuing to assess the seriousness of types of crime in terms of direct threats and confrontations to people on the street and depicting the crime problem as a problem of youth. For example, Ramsey Clark (1970:83) minimized the problem of organized crime by asking, "What does it have to do with the juvenile offender who accounts for most of the increase in crime? . . . What does organized crime have to do with street crime— murder, rape, assault, mugging, robbery?" Such points of view ignore the indirect costs and broader social consequences of organized crime and assume that those whose crimes are most visible are the greatest threat to the nation.

Another type of crime that has been ignored by most sociologists and that only recently has begun to generate national concern is child abuse. The image of the delinquent juvenile preying on the weak and defenseless can be supported with numerous documented cases (see, for example, Display 1–1). However, there is increasing documentation of violent parents preying on their children. Despite that documentation, much of child abuse, like a considerable amount of youth crime, does not make its way into police statistics. In 1965 one researcher (Gil, 1970:59) estimated that between 2 and 4 million adults in the United States knew of families involved in incidents of child abuse. Some estimates put the number of abused children between 50,000 and 75,000 per year with 1 out of 4 ending in death (Leavitt, 1974:3). If the speculation that abused children become abusive parents is correct, then adults can become part of a vicious cycle in which violence breeds violence. Jerome Leavitt (1974:203) concluded that "the battered child syndrome is one of the most serious epidemic diseases in America."

In short, the traditional "nip-it-in-the-bud" philosophy suggests that by dealing with juvenile delinquency we are dealing with the roots of our crime problem. However, we can find as much justification for the position that an attack on adult-controlled criminal organizations and institutions would get at the roots of our crime problem in more ways than one. Delinquency and the transgressions of the young must be viewed in context. It is misleading to concentrate on the relatively powerless segments of American society when crime is intimately linked to institutions that adults control and to values and practices that are passed from one generation of Americans to the next. "The youth crime plague" is paralleled by "the adult crime plague," "the male crime plague," "the Watergate plague," "the business crime plague," "the computer crime plague," "the government crime plague," the "child abuse plague," and numerous other patterns of crime that are less amenable to dramatization than the offenses of persons under eighteen.

Dramatization and appeals to public opinion can be used to argue against our assessment of the relative seriousness of various types of crime. For example, in his book *Thinking about Crime,* James Q. Wilson excluded white-collar crime from his discussion on the grounds of his limited expertise on the subject and his conviction (which he believes to be the conviction of most citizens) "that predatory street crime is a far more serious matter than consumer fraud, antitrust violations, prostitution or gambling" (1975:xx). Adjectives such as *predatory* create the same type of imagery that is conveyed by the *Time* article in Display 1–1. However, *predatory* can be equally as well applied to consumer fraud, price-fixing, business crime, and child abuse.

John Conklin (1977) has observed that many students of crime cite a lack of public concern about white-collar crime but that the same students produce no real data to support such a contention. After reviewing evidence concerning public opinion toward crime in the business world, Conklin concluded that "the sparse evidence which is currently available indicates a much stronger condemnation of business crime than has been commonly thought to exist" (1977:32). He added, however, that the public is rarely indignant or militant in expressing that condemnation because of the complex and diffuse nature of business crime and the lack of continuing attention by the media.

In sum, it is understandable that indignation and concern are readily expressed about crimes in which there are clear-cut victims and offenders. Moreover, such crimes may be of particular concern to numerous "publics" when the offenders are young. However, the important point is that there are other criteria for assessing the "seriousness" of crime and a variety of reasonable arguments suggesting that juvenile delinquency may not be *the* most consequential dimension of the problem of crime in the United States.

WHY STUDY DELINQUENCY?

If we accept the argument that delinquency is not the major crime problem in the United States, then why should we pay attention to it? In the preceding discussion, we have tried to put delinquency in the context of other forms of crime. We have pointed out that there are grounds for arguing that crime involving adults is far more costly then crime involving juveniles and that delinquency qualifies neither as the most serious nor as the primary dimension of our crime problem. On the other hand, it is through the study of delinquency that we can begin to question popular images and conceptions of the crime problem and to put the problem of juvenile delinquency in proper perspective. Delinquency is *one* dimension of our overall crime problem—one that has generated considerable public and political concern. Moreover, a sizable proportion of us are involved in a legal system that views delinquency as a major problem.

In addition, delinquency is an illustrative subject matter for studying the social forces that affect our laws and for examining the social aspects of human behavior. The study of delinquency also gives us the opportunity to analyze the nature and consequences of different reactions to social "problems." Since the study of delinquency is the study of activities, conflicts, and experiences that are familiar to most of us, it is also a convenient subject matter for studying ourselves and the everyday social forces and experiences affecting our lives. Self-understanding and insight into the operation of our social world can be rewarding in their own right.

Of course, the most popular question in the study of delinquency has been "What can we do about it?" Whether the student of delinquency is radical, liberal, or conservative, he or she is likely to view delinquency as "a problem" in one sense or another. There are many different senses in which people consider delinquency to be a problem, and consequently there are many different opinions on appropriate solutions. For some people, the problem rests with the nature of the laws that define and sustain delinquency as a legal category. For others, the delinquent behavior and the people engaged in it are the crux of the problem. Others presume that delinquency is generated by social values, institutions, and structures and that these generating forces are the problem. Still others believe that our own everyday reactions and our system for reacting to youthful misbehavior are at fault.

Proposed solutions to such problems range from revolutionary change in our social-economic-political system to programs aimed at "early identification" and intensive treatment of individuals supposedly "predisposed" to crime. Whether we choose among alternative solutions or merely conclude that "something" ought to be done, we are making a moral decision. The study of delinquency thus forces us to consider our own moral and political preconceptions about the nature of delinquency within the context of scientific research. That research will not only provide us with justification for certain views and proposals but will also demonstrate that other forms of action are likely to be a total waste of time.

SOCIOLOGY AND THE STUDY OF DELINQUENCY

While people with a wide range of backgrounds contribute to the study of crime and delinquency *(criminology)* as an academic discipline and a traditional subject of study in American colleges and universities, criminology has been most intimately linked with sociology. Discourses on crime in society were among the earliest subject areas in sociology and have persisted as an integral part of sociological curriculum. Moreover, most of the textbooks and systematic research on crime and delinquency in the United States have been produced by persons who identify themselves as sociologists. Thus, students pursuing the study of crime or delinquency in an academic context are likely to encounter a sociological approach.

The sociological perspective on crime and delinquency can be differentiated from other perspectives and other "criminologies" by the unique coincidence of (1) a "social" conception of crime, (2) a concern for general patterns or regularities underlying individual events and cases, and (3) an insistence that claims concerning such patterns and regularities be backed with verifiable evidence. While the emphases on general patterns and verifiable evidence are characteristic of any discipline that claims to be "scientific," the emphasis on a social conception of crime reflects a commitment to a particular way of looking at the world and human behavior.

Sociologists have been interested in exploring the many senses in which crime can be considered a social problem, or—to avoid the moral connotations implicit in calling something a "problem"—a "social phenomenon." In fact, one of the best-known texts on the subject of criminology defines the field as the study of "the processes of making laws, of breaking laws, and of reacting toward the breaking of laws" (Sutherland and Cressey, 1974:3). Each of these areas is a source of public concern, and each may be studied with a view toward discovering and explaining regularities.

Lawmaking

Historically, the search for the causes, or etiology, of lawbreaking and for ways of changing lawbreakers (penology) has dominated criminological inquiry. The central questions have been: (1) "Why do some people become involved in crime or delinquency?" and (2) "What can we do about it either before or after the fact?" However, in the past decade there has been a growing concern with a third question: "Why do we have the laws we have?"

There are numerous spokesmen for the position that the crime problem is, at least in part, a problem of "overcriminalization" (that is, treating too many types of behavior as crime) and the proliferation of laws "creating" crime. For example, after an extensive analysis of the drug problem in the United States, Erich Goode (1972:181) concluded that our drug laws and their enforcement are primarily responsible for some of the most serious and harmful characteristics of the drug problem. The view that laws exist to prevent or solve problems and to protect society can be countered with rather convincing arguments that laws originally designed to cope with social problems may create new problems or may transform minor social problems into more serious ones (Rose, 1968: 33–43.)

Thus, at present, there appears to be widespread consensus that a comprehensive study of crime and delinquency requires consideration of the social forces and processes involved in the making, as well as the breaking, of laws. Our attempts to explain lawbreaking are often based on *implicit* theories and assumptions about the nature of criminal law and the relation of people in American society to those laws. Therefore, in considering the sources and causes of criminal behavior, we are often also advancing perspectives on the sociology of law.

Lawbreaking

There are several senses in which sociologists have been interested in lawbreaking as a "social" phenomenon. For example, we find some sociologists interested in explaining the emergence and persistence of certain types of "criminal behavior systems," such as "delinquent subcultures" or "delinquent gangs" (Sutherland and Cressey, 1974:274; Clinard and Quinney, 1973). Thus, it is possible to conceive of delinquency as a social phenomenon in the sense that some forms of delinquency can be viewed as organized systems or group phenomena themselves. Several major works on delinquency (for example, Cohen's *Delinquent Boys*, 1955, and Cloward and Ohlin's *Delinquency and Opportunity*, 1960) take as their main focus the emergence of a "delinquent subculture" or "types" of subcultures whose moral standards require certain forms of delinquent behavior. Consequently these works deal only indirectly with delinquent behavior.

The explanation of delinquent "behavior" has been a persistent concern in criminological inquiry, dominating much of the earliest work and much, if not most, of the research over the last decade as well. In pursuit of such an explanation, sociologists have examined the spatial and social distribution of officially recorded crime. Many of the most basic tenets about crime and delinquency grew out of attempts to explain such persistent regularities as (1) the concentration of certain offenses in slums and in the "transitional" areas of cities and (2) the disproportionate concentration of recorded crime in the "lower" classes and certain minority groups. Even those sociologists who have focused on subcultures or gang delinquency have taken such patterns into account in elaborating their perspectives.

There has been considerable interest in the "process" of becoming criminal or delinquent. Before the turn of the century, Charles Cooley (1896) and others posited that criminal and delinquent behavior are learned or acquired in interaction with others and that the processes involved are basically the same as those through which all social behavior and lifestyles are acquired. Detailed case histories and ethnographies carried out in the 1920s and 1930s (Thrasher, 1927; Shaw, 1930, 1931,

1938; Sutherland, 1937) supported such contentions, which have been repeatedly reaffirmed in more recent research. The view of criminal and delinquent behavior as a form of social behavior acquired in certain social and cultural settings became a key theme that is explicit or implicit in virtually all sociological analyses of crime and delinquency (Schur, 1969:118).

Reactions to Lawbreaking

We have already noted that delinquency is a social phenomenon in the sense that it is a legal concept created and interpreted by people and that a comprehensive analysis of delinquency requires that we examine both lawmaking and lawbreaking. In addition, we should note that the study of law is one aspect of a larger concern in sociology—that is, the study of "social control" or "reactions to deviance." As Jack Gibbs (1972:4) has pointed out, the most fundamental question in the study of social control is "What are the causes and consequences of variation in the character of reaction to deviance among social units over time?" The creation of laws or "legal norms" is one type of reaction to real or imagined problems and, hence, is a major aspect of the study of social control.

The dominant focus in the study of crime control has been *penology* — that branch of criminology concerned with the punishment and treatment of offenders and the administration of prisons (Fox, 1972). While the study of prisons and other "correctional" programs remains a vital concern in criminology, social scientists have been increasingly concerned with the administration of justice in general and have been extending the study of crime-control processes to include the police and the courts. Moreover, researchers have begun exploring the "community response to crime" and the sources of public attitudes, beliefs, and fears about crime and crime control (Conklin, 1975:373–385). Numerous observers and researchers have pointed out that the public plays a key role in the implementation (or lack of implementation) of formal control processes and that decisions to call the police, to press for action, and to provide testimony are problematic themselves (Black, 1970:733–738; Black and Reiss, 1970; Hawkins, 1973). Thus, the study of reactions to crime and delinquency has been extended to encompass not only the operation of the justice system but the causes of public reactions to crime as well.

ORGANIZING OUR INQUIRY

Our study of delinquency will be organized around the three basic issues outlined above: lawmaking, lawbreaking, and reactions to lawbreaking. In Chapter 2 we will consider lawmaking. By exploring the nature, origin, and changes in juvenile law and juvenile justice we can gain an understanding of the forces that shape and sustain delinquency as a legal category.

In Chapters 3 and 4 we will deal with *delinquent* and *delinquency* as labels applied to some juveniles and some behaviors by police and the courts. Given the existence of such a legal category as delinquency, how is it actually applied? Who gets labeled and why? Do data on officially labeled acts and persons give an accurate picture of the nature and distribution of delinquent activity? These are questions with which sociologists must deal as they attempt to assess the adequacy of certain bodies of data for reaching conclusions about delinquency. By seeking answers to these questions ourselves, we will find that we are forming images of delinquency that differ from the common stereotypes.

Not everyone engages equally in the types of activities that are defined as delinquency, and students of crime and delinquency have come up with a wide range of explanations for this variability. Sociologists focus on the social and cultural environment as sources of variation. Others have located the causes of variation in biological or genetic characteristics of individuals and groups. Yet others have searched for the causes of delinquency in the individual's personality. This text advocates a sociological point of view not out of blind faith, but in view of the greater explanatory power of research focusing on environmental variables. We try to present this case in Chapters 5 and 6 where we consider various explanations of delinquency, and in Chapters 7 and 8 where we consider different contexts for adolescent socialization.

No study of delinquency is complete without a consideration of reactions to delinquency. At present, the basic issue of dominant concern to criminologists is the consequence of alternative reactions to delinquency. Three specific issues have been receiving the bulk of recent attention. First, does official processing, labeling, and punishment deter juveniles from delinquency or help propel them into delinquent and criminal careers? Second, can community-based programs do a better job of preventing further delinquency than institutionalization of juvenile offenders? Third, what are the consequences of diverting juveniles from processing by the juvenile justice system? In Chapter 9, "Deterrence and Labeling," we will examine the first issue. The second will be the topic of Chapter 10, "Imprisonment and Alternatives," while Chapter 11, "Diversion," will concentrate on the final issue.

The concluding chapter will consider a much broader issue involving social policy and juvenile delinquency: "Prevention: Dilemmas of Choice, Change, and Control." There we will have to grapple with the really difficult aspects of the study of delinquency: What meaning does all the research to date have for policy? If broad-scale change is called for, how far can we go and how far are we willing to go in dealing with the delinquency problem? What changes in our perspectives, values, and goals are we willing to consider? We cannot even take it for granted that "something" must be done. Such decisions involve moral evaluations of delinquency and of the social arrangements that help produce delinquency.

SUMMARY

Although juvenile delinquency as a legal category is a relatively recent invention, there is a long history of concern for the misbehavior of the young, as well as an enduring tendency to view crimes of the young as the major dimension of the crime problem in the United States. The view that certain categories of juveniles are quite commonly involved in crime is supported by police and court statistics and by behavioral reports in surveys of juveniles. An inspection of the FBI's *Uniform Crime Reports* shows that juveniles are most distinct in their high arrest rates for offenses in which property is the target. However, they are underrepresented in numerous types of crime that cost Americans more economically and that many observers feel do more harm to individuals, institutions, and morale than the types of offenses for which juveniles are most commonly responsible. Delinquency is one dimension of the crime problem, but there are reasonable grounds for challenging the view that it is the most serious or primary dimension.

The study of delinquency as one dimension of our crime problem exposes us to an extensive literature of theory and research that can contribute to self-understanding and insight into the operation of our social world. That literature can also provide us with information relevant to personal and social decision making. A major proportion of criminological theory and research has involved sociologists who emphasize the social roots of crime and delinquency, the search for general patterns, and the importance of verifiable evidence. This sociological endeavor has come to encompass the study of social forces involved in lawmaking, lawbreaking, and reactions to lawbreaking. The text is organized to present the most central ideas, issues, and research concerning all three topics.

REFERENCES

Black, D. J. 1970. "Production of Crime Rates." *American Sociological Review* 35 (August):733–48.

Black, D. J., and A. J. Reiss, Jr. 1970. "Police Control of Juveniles." *American Sociological Review* 35 (February):63–77.

Chamber of Commerce of the United States. 1974. *A Handbook on White-Collar Crime.* Washington, D.C.: Chamber of Commerce of the United States.

Clark, R. 1970. *Crime in America.* New York: Simon & Schuster.

Clinard, M. B., and R. Quinney. 1973. *Criminal Behavior Systems*. New York: Holt, Rinehart and Winston.

Cloward, R. A., and L. E. Ohlin. 1960. *Delinquency and Opportunity*. New York: Free Press.

Cohen, A. K. 1955. *Delinquent Boys*. New York: Free Press.

Conklin, J. E. 1975. *The Impact of Crime*. New York: Macmillan.

———. 1977. *Illegal but Not Criminal*. Englewood Cliffs, N.J.: Prentice-Hall.

Cooley, C. H. 1896. "Nature v. Nurture in the Making of Social Careers." Proceedings of the National Conference of Charities and Corrections. Grand Rapids, Mich.

Cressey, D. R. 1969. *Theft of the Nation*. New York: Harper & Row.

Federal Bureau of Investigation. 1977. *Crime in the United States*. Washington, D.C.: U.S. Government Printing Office.

Fox, V. 1972. *Introduction to Corrections*. Englewood Cliffs, N.J.: Prentice-Hall.

Gibbs, J. P. 1972. "Social Control." New York: Warner Modular Publications, Module 1.

Gil, D. G. 1970. *Violence against Children: Physical Child Abuse in the United States*. Cambridge, Mass.: Harvard University Press.

Goode, E. 1972. *Drugs in American Society*. New York: Alfred A. Knopf.

Hawkins, R. 1973. "Who Called the Cops: Decisions to Report Criminal Victimization." *Law and Society Review* 7 (Spring):427–43.

Hindelang, M. J. 1973. "Causes of Delinquency: A Partial Replication and Extension." *Social Problems* 20 (Spring):471–87.

Johnson, J. M., and J. D. Douglas. 1978. *Crime at the Top: Deviance in Business and the Professions*. Philadelphia: J. B. Lippincott.

Kocourek, A., and J. H. Wigmore. 1951. *Source of Ancient and Primitive Law: Select Readings on the Origin and Development of Legal Institutions*. Boston: Little, Brown.

Leavitt, J. E., ed. 1974. *The Battered Child: Selected Readings*. Morristown, N.J.: General Learning Press.

Polk, K. 1974. *Teenage Delinquency in Small Town America*, Research Report 5. Center for Studies of Crime and Delinquency, National Institute of Mental Health, Rockville, Md.

President's Commission on Law Enforcement and Administration of Justice. 1967. *The Challenge of Crime in a Free Society*. Washington, D.C.: U.S. Government Printing Office.

Rose, A. M. 1968. "Law and the Causation of Social Problems." *Social Problems* 16 (Summer):33–43.

Schur, E. M. 1969. *Our Criminal Society*. Englewood Cliffs, N.J.: Prentice-Hall.

Shaw, C. R. 1930. *The Jack-Roller*. Chicago: University of Chicago Press.

———. 1931. *Natural History of a Delinquent Career*. Chicago: University of Chicago Press.

———. 1938. *Brothers in Crime*. Chicago: University of Chicago Press.

Sutherland, E. H. 1937. *The Professional Thief*. Chicago: University of Chicago Press.

———. 1940. "White Collar Criminality." *American Sociological Review* 5 (February):1–12.

Sutherland, E. H., and D. R. Cressey. 1974. *Criminology*. New York: J. B. Lippincott.

Thrasher, F. M. 1927. *The Gang.* Chicago: University of Chicago Press.

Time. 1977. "The Youth Crime Plague." *Time* (July 11):18–28.

Williams, J. R., and M. Gold. 1972. "From Delinquent Behavior to Official Delinquency." *Social Problems* 20 (Fall):209–29.

Wilson, J. Q. 1975. *Thinking about Crime.* New York: Vintage Books.

Wolfgang, M. E., R. Figlio, and T. Sellin. 1972. *Delinquency in a Birth Cohort.* Chicago: University of Chicago Press.

2.
THE ORIGIN AND DEVELOPMENT OF JUVENILE JUSTICE

The rights to a definite charge, counsel, a fair hearing, reasonably relevant and convincing evidence, and appeal are insured to a man on the most trivial issues of political administration, but not to the child. In a large proportion of specialized urban children's courts the child enters with what is in effect a presumption of his delinquency and, under the conditions of today's "chancery" procedure there, it is almost impossible for him to rebut that presumption, once a probation officer has found a personal problem in his history to work on. Who is to save the child from his saviors?
—Paul W. Tappan, *Juvenile Delinquency**

WHAT IS DELINQUENCY?

In the mid-1970s several thousand high school students were asked whether they ever thought of themselves as "delinquent" or whether other people ever thought of them as "delinquent" (Jensen, 1976). Overall, about half of the students indicated that at least occasionally they had considered themselves in this way. Nearly 60 percent felt that other people thought of them as delinquent. In short, a sizable proportion of adolescents seems to personally acknowledge the label. Yet, a question raised by students during the course of the survey was "What does *delinquent* mean?" Some thought it meant *juvenile.* A student's exposure to the term *juvenile* is quite often in association with the term *delinquent.*

The tendency for notions of delinquency and juvenile status to "blur" together is not surprising: the creation of delinquency as a legal category was closely associated with images of adolescence as a time of turmoil, stress, and conflict. Since "delinquency" refers to a legal status defined by age, its creation was necessarily related to the nature of the "age stratification" or "age grading" found in human societies. It may seem facetious, but it is nevertheless true, that before the legal category of "juvenile delinquent" could be devised, the "juvenile" had to be discovered. The creation of delinquency was preceded by the recognition and prolongation of childhood and the development of a specific age gradation encompassing the prolonged period between puberty and adult status, which we refer to as "adolescence."

THE DISCOVERY OF ADOLESCENCE

All societies are characterized by some form of differentiation based on age. However, the number of age gradations, the transition points for

moving from one age group to another, ceremonies surrounding transitions, and the expectations for persons in those groups—all are quite
variable from society to society. Four age stages are universally
recognized: infancy, childhood, adulthood, and old age (Linton, 1942;
Elder, 1968).

The interim status between childhood and adulthood, which we call
"adolescence," is not universally recognized. For example, in his examination of *Centuries of Childhood* (1962), Philippe Aries noted that in the
French language there were three age references throughout the seventeenth century—childhood, youth, and old age—with youth signifying
the prime of life. The common word for referring to children from birth
through their teens was *enfant*. Aries observed that the differentiation
between infancy and childhood in the French language did not occur until
the nineteenth century. Medieval texts did refer to an age category called
adolescence, but this period began with puberty and extended to persons
as old as thirty-five.

After analyzing art, literature, language, dress, and games over several
centuries, Aries concluded that with the prolongation of the life span,
new "tracts of life" such as childhood and adolescence, were "discovered." However, Aries also argued that following the sixteenth century,
the differentiation of childhood and adolescence as distinct, particular-
ized age categories was most prominent in middle-class and aristocratic
families and among boys:

> A new moral concept was to distinguish the child or at least the school-
> boy, and set him apart: the concept of the well-bred child. . . . [the concept]
> was the product of the forming opinions of an elite of thinkers and moral-
> ists who occupied high positions in Church or State. The well-bred child
> would be preserved from the roughness and immorality which would
> become the special characteristics of the lower classes. In France this well-
> bred child would be the little bourgeois. In England he would be the
> gentleman, a social type unknown before the nineteenth century, and
> which a threatened aristocracy would create, thanks to the public schools,
> to defend itself against the progress of democracy. (1962:327–28)

Aries tied the development or recognition of adolescence to the rise of an
emphasis on militaristic discipline in the schools and the preparation of
"boys of good family" for military careers. The adolescent was the young
would-be soldier. Thus, the idea of adolescence as a distinct age group
began in Europe and was related to the development of an educational
system designed to produce disciplined, well-bred children whose further
training in adolescence would prepare them for military careers.

Thus, Aries suggested that the differentiation of age grades between
infant and adult and the view of these stages as special and unique may
have reflected social and political developments of the seventeenth and
eighteenth centuries. In contrast, David Bakan (1971) has argued that
"the conversion of the idea of adolescence into a commonly accepted
social reality was largely associated with modern industrial life." Bakan's

claim is that "adolescence" took shape as a distinct socio-legal age category in the last two decades of the nineteenth century in the United States as a result of three major social movements. These movements were aimed at (1) compulsory public education, (2) child labor legislation, and (3) the establishment of a juvenile court. Through legislation, adolescence was defined as the period of time between puberty and the legal ages established for compulsory education, employment, and criminal procedure.

The social movements of the nineteenth century reflected the transformation of American society from a rural-agrarian economy to an urban-industrial one. The transformation took place as huge waves of immigrants poured into urban settings. Of particular importance for that transformation were the reactions of the established Protestant middle and upper classes. Those classes provided the social reformers and the leaders of the social movements. In New York in the early 1800s and Chicago in the late 1800s, upper- and middle-class reformers exhibited common concerns about establishing institutions and shaping policies to socialize the urban lower-class immigrant into their conceptions of the American way of life.

The drive for compulsory public education of the young reflected the reformers' perceived need to integrate and control the masses and to prepare them for work. The Panel on Youth of the President's Science Advisory Committee (1974) attributed the original impetus for child labor legislation to the push for compulsory education. To acculturate the new Americans, children had to be taken out of the labor force and put in school. The importance of public education was also reinforced by an increasing industrial need for skilled labor and by the efforts of labor unions to gain control over working conditions. Cheap, readily available child labor was an impediment to successful unionization, and labor leaders were opposed to it on economic, as well as social, grounds. Thus, a concern for creating special institutions that could socialize and control emerging problem populations preceded the development of a special legal status for certain age groups.

In summary, the prolongation of childhood and the delineation of adolescence as a distinct age grade were ultimately the products of social, economic, and technological change. Such change led to the increasing survival of children, the development of educational institutions for the children of the well-to-do, and the preparation of male youth for military careers. Industrialization, population growth, and urbanization resulted in the extension of education, originally limited to middle-class and aristocratic families, to an increasing proportion of the population. In the United States, adolescence was finally transformed into a bio-legal fact as social movements advocating compulsory education, child labor legislation, and a specialized system of juvenile justice resulted in the setting of transition points between one legal age status and another.

THE ORIGINS OF JUVENILE JUSTICE

Several historical studies in recent years have dealt with the evolution of juvenile justice in the United States and Canada (Platt, 1969a, 1969b; Finestone, 1976; Schlossman, 1977; Hagan and Leon, 1977). In these studies, there is disagreement on the sources or meaning of certain important developments in the processing of juveniles. For instance, a popular work by Anthony Platt focuses on the "child-saving" movement in the *late* 1800s as the factor that resulted in the establishment, in Chicago, of the first juvenile court. In their histories of juvenile justice, Steven Schlossman (1977) and Harold Finestone (1976) describe the crucial developments and court justifications that ultimately led to a separate justice system for juveniles as occurring quite *early* in the 1800s. Moreover, the forces of social class and religious conflict of the late 1800s upon which Platt focuses are quite similar to the forces Schlossman and Finestone identify as operating at earlier points in time. Schlossman and Finestone view the establishment of the juvenile court as partially a reflection of later developments in juvenile justice, rather than as purely an extension of the reformist ideology and the vested interests of certain groups reflected in the early development of separate institutions for juveniles. We will elaborate on these disparities in the pages that follow as we deal with the precedents and legal disputes involved in the development of the juvenile court.

Compulsory Education and Houses of Refuge

An important development in the early evolution of juvenile justice in the United States was the establishment of the "house of refuge" in the 1820s. Such institutions were prisonlike schools for juvenile offenders and impoverished children. Their development was intimately connected with the push for compulsory public education. Both compulsory education and the concept of the reformatory grew out of the efforts of middle- and upper-class reformers to deal with new problem populations through the extension of state control over children. In 1838, for example, a key court decision *(Ex parte Crouse)*, which concerned the constitutionality of incarcerating a child in a house of refuge without "due process of law," drew on the arguments that reformers used to advance compulsory education (Schlossman, 1977).

The 1838 case involved Mary Ann Crouse, who was committed to the Philadelphia House of Refuge on the basis of a complaint lodged by her mother. Her father did not find out about the action until after Mary was committed, and he subsequently sought to have Mary released on the grounds that her rights had been violated. The court decided that the Bill of Rights did not apply to children and that the house of refuge was merely a type of school for problem children. The notion that the state can act as parent or guardian of the child *(parens patriae)* was invoked as a legal precedent justifying the lack of attention to due process. Schlossman has summarized the view of supporters of the reformatory movement as follows:

> They urged the judges to place both types of facility, public school and reformatory, under the safeguard of the *parens patriae* doctrine, and to establish once and for all time that the state's provision of education for the poor was a legitimate exercise of its police powers.
>
> The court agreed entirely with [this] point of view. The reformatory, it insisted, was nothing but a residential school for underprivileged children, a horizontal expansion of the fledgling public school system. A reformatory was "not a prison but a school." Its objectives were in the broadest sense educational: to train children in industry, morality, the means to earn a living, and most importantly, to isolate them from the "corrupting influences of improper associates." The court went on: "As to the abridgment of indefeasible rights by confinement of the person, it is no more than what is borne, to a greater or less extent, in every school; and we know of no natural right to exemption from restraints which conduce to an infant's welfare." In sum, the court concluded, the government's right to incarcerate children who had not committed criminal acts was neither capricious nor vindictive, for the house of refuge was nothing but a residential public school for unfortunate youth. (1977:10)

This conception of reformatories was disputed in 1870 in Illinois in the case of *People* v. *Turner.* The case involved a boy who had been committed to the Chicago Reform School on vague charges that did not involve a definable crime. The state appellate court ordered the boy's release and questioned the analogy that had been drawn between reformatories and public schools, as well as the right of the state to intervene in violation of children's rights and parents' rights. However, as Schlossman has pointed out, this decision had little impact on the spread of reformatories or on subsequent court challenges. The movement to deal with problem populations through compulsory education and the extension of governmental control was too widely supported by reformers, industrialists, and the dominant ideology of the times to be overturned by a court decision.

In the mid-1800s reformers, drawing on European views of juvenile corrections, challenged the idea of the "schoollike" institution with its emphasis on discipline and work. The basic concept and practice of differential treatment of juveniles was accepted both in the United States and abroad, but the correctional model in Europe took the form of the "family reform school" (Schlossman, 1977:37). "Antiinstitutionalists"— such as Charles Loring Brace of New York and Samuel Gridley Howe of Massachusetts—opposed the use of prisonlike institutions and advocated a greater reliance on the "family" as a tool for changing behavior. They particularly advocated using rural, frontier, or farm families to provide foster homes for the "vagabond," the "wretched," and the "home-less."

However, this antiinstitutionalist point of view was influenced by the religious and class conflicts of the time. Brace founded the Children's Aid Society and, consistent with his philosophy concerning the family, established a program that sent orphaned children to foster families in the West. The program tended to send Catholic youth to Protestant homes. Between 1855 and 1880, Brace, who attributed the crime problem "to the cheapness of spirit and the multitudes of low Irish Catholics," sent an estimated 50,000 Catholic orphans to Protestant families in the West (Hawes, 1971).

The Juvenile Court

By the mid-1800s debates over houses of refuge in northeastern states had established the precedents for differential handling and processing of youthful "troublemakers" and problem children. As early as the 1880s some judges in New York were holding separate hearings for children, and a crude probation system had developed in Massachusetts (Schlossman, 1977:63–64).

The first bill establishing a distinct juvenile court was passed by the state legislature in Illinois in 1899. The legislation formally established a separate system of juvenile justice that was to be essentially noncriminal and oriented toward "treatment," rather than punishment, of juvenile offenders. The new juvenile court was not to be a mere extension of the jurisdiction of the criminal court, but rather an independent court system with complete jurisdiction over the affairs of juveniles.

Some observers view the motivation for the creation of the juvenile court as a product of the same conservative reformist concerns that resulted in the establishment of houses of refuge and reformatories. Anthony Platt described the conservative nature of reform during the late nineteenth century as follows:

> Contemporary programs of delinquency-control can be traced to the enter-prising reforms of the child-savers who, at the end of the nineteenth cen-tury, helped to create special judicial and correctional institutions for the labeling, processing, and management of "troublesome" youth. Child-saving was a conservative and romantic movement, designed to impose sanctions on conduct unbecoming youth and to disqualify youth from enjoying adult privileges. The child-savers were prohibitionists, in a gen-eral sense, who believed in close supervision of adolescents' recreation and leisure. The movement brought attention to, and thus "invented," new categories of youthful misbehavior which had been previously unappre-ciated or had been dealt with on an informal basis. Child-saving was heav-ily influenced by middle-class women who extended their housewifely roles into public service and emphasized the dependence of the social order on the proper socialization of children. (1969b:21)

Elsewhere in his writings (1974:356–89), Platt extended his analysis to argue that the middle-class reformers were supported by an upper-class and industrial elite who would benefit from industrial discipline and who were concerned with establishing stability and order in a rapidly changing urban environment. Thus, Platt views the creation of the juvenile court as an outgrowth of middle- and upper-class interests, fears, and concerns that promoted an increase in the scope of state control.

In contrast to Platt, Schlossman (1977) and Finestone (1976) believe that what was most distinctive or "progressive" about the idea of the juvenile court was its emphasis on probation and on the home and family as the target for treatment. According to Finestone (1976:46), "Since the formation of the juvenile court represented the culmination and response to almost fifty years of criticism of the institutionalized handling of juvenile delinquents, it was primarily concerned with treatment in the community." Thus, the emphasis was on probation and the probation officer as an "agent of the court in the community." In an analysis of the development of juvenile court legislation in Canada, John Hagan and Jeffrey Leon (1977:597) presented a similar interpretation. They argued that an emphasis on probation and the family as the locus of treatment was central to such legislation.

Whether the creation of the juvenile court was progressive or conservative or motivated by humanitarian concerns or class interests is a continuing source of controversy. However, there does appear to be agreement that the gap between the "promise" of the juvenile court and its actual implementation was considerable. Platt argued that treatment for lower-class youths took the form of "training schools" built as prisons and based on principles of reform through militaristic discipline and forced labor. The noncriminal nature of its proceedings gave the court greater control over the lives of juveniles in that it could deal with behavior that was not criminal but that was defined as "bad" by the reformers. In his analysis of the operation of the Milwaukee Juvenile Court in the early 1900s, Schlossman (1977:167) reported that (1) relations between the court and clientele "were generally hostile and always superficial," (2) the court showed little concern with fair proceedings, and (3) actual operations were infused with a view of youth (particularly lower-class immigrant youth) as threatening and perverse.

Overall, it appears that the establishment of the juvenile court represented a combination of humanitarianism and an antiinstitutional ideology that emphasized probation. However, its popularity, support, and implementation also reflected antiurban, anti-Catholic, and anti-lower-class biases—in short, a concern with gaining better legal control over threatening categories of people. Humanitarianism demanded that children be "saved" from the brutal realities of the adult criminal justice system, but at the same time many adults felt that they needed to be saved from the children of the "dangerous" classes. The criminal justice system was not controlling the young effectively. Judges were reluctant to deal with youth in the same fashion as adults and were releasing them back to the streets. Something had to be done. That something was the creation of a separate justice system for juveniles that encompassed a far wider range of offensive behaviors than the adult criminal justice system.

Parens Patriae and Due Process of Law

The move toward separate legal institutions for juveniles was justified as an "obvious" extension of a doctrine in English common law known as *parens patriae* ("parent of the land"). This legal concept is reflected in virtually all juvenile codes and serves as the legal rationale for both the form and substance of juvenile justice in the United States. The major consequence of applying this concept to juvenile justice is that the court, acting on behalf of the state, can become the legal guardian of all juveniles in its jurisdiction and can thereby limit and possibly terminate the guardianship and custody rights of the natural, or biological, parents.

The concept of *parens patriae* arose as part of the principle of "equity" or fairness in English law when the king began to act on behalf of children whose property rights needed protection. The king's protective power over children was used ostensibly to maintain the structure of feudalism and to assure the orderly transfer of feudal duties from one generation to the next. The passage of the Poor Law Act in 1601 by the English Parliament extended the original interpretation of *parens patriae* to infer the right of the state to remove children from destitute parents and apprentice them to others. This extended interpretation was based on the notion of the duty of the crown as parent to educate and care for children. However, the application of the legal doctrine of *parens patriae* in England seems relatively limited and specific when compared to the implementation of this concept in the United States.

Under the common law in England and the United States, a child under seven years of age could not be charged with a criminal offense, and between the ages of seven and fourteen, the child was normally not considered responsible for violations of criminal law. Exceptions could occur if it were shown that the child understood the nature of the offense and could distinguish between right and wrong. Thus, it is conceivable that under common-law principles juveniles between the ages of seven and fourteen could be found criminally responsible and sentenced to prison or execution as if they were adult offenders. However, the evidence is extremely weak that such punishments were actually carried out in England (Sanders, 1945) or in the United States (Platt, 1969).

Nonetheless, the possibility of indiscriminate punishment and imprisonment of the juvenile and hardened adult offender alike in the criminal justice system was often cited in the first efforts to establish houses of refuge in New York, Boston, and Philadelphia. The argument was used again in the crusade for the creation of the juvenile court later in the nineteenth century. The amplification of the *parens patriae* doctrine in the United States allowed the relaxation of procedural safeguards and allowed the juvenile court far greater discretion in dealing with juveniles.

Under the spirit of *parens patriae,* the American juvenile court emerged and spread to every state in the Union within a few decades (see Table 2–1). Between 1899 and 1909, thirty-four states had enacted some form of juvenile court law. All but two states (New York and Wyoming) had such legislation by 1919. Acting in its capacity of legal parent, the juvenile court was to reform and save the child from wayward or delinquent transgressions. Because juvenile proceedings were civil and not criminal, "due process of law," the procedural safeguards accorded to adult offenders, was not constitutionally required. The child was not to be contaminated with the criminal process as an adult offender. Instead, the juvenile court was to act in the best interests of the child as a kindly parent:

> The juvenile court, then, was born in an aura of reform and it spread with amazing speed. The conception of the delinquent as a "wayward child" first specifically came to life in April, 1899, when the Illinois legislature passed the Juvenile Court Act, creating the first statewide court especially for children. It did not create a new court; it did include most of the features that have since come to distinguish the juvenile court. The original act and the amendments to it that shortly followed brought together under one jurisdiction cases of dependency, neglect, and delinquency—the last comprehending incorrigibles and children threatened by immoral associations as well as criminal lawbreakers. Hearings were to be informal and nonpublic, records confidential, children detained apart from adults, a probation staff appointed. In short, children were not to be treated as criminals nor dealt with by the processes used for criminals.
>
> A new vocabulary symbolized the new order: Petition instead of complaint, summons instead of warrant, initial hearing instead of arraignment, finding of involvement instead of conviction, disposition instead of sentence. The physical surroundings were important too: They should seem less imposing than a courtroom, with the judge at a desk or table instead of behind a bench, fatherly and sympathetic while still authoritative and sobering. The goals were to investigate, diagnose, and prescribe treatment, not to adjudicate guilt or fix blame. The individual's background was more important than the facts of a given incident, specific conduct relevant more as symptomatic of a need for the court to bring its helping powers to bear than as prerequisite to exercise of jursidiction. Lawyers were unnecessary—adversary tactics were out of place, for the mutual aim of all was not to contest or object but to determine the treatment plan best for the child. That plan was to be devised by the increasingly popular psychologists and psychiatrists; delinquency was thought of almost as a disease, to be diagnosed by specialists and the patient kindly but firmly dosed. (President's Commission on Law Enforcement and Administration of Justice, 1967:3)

TABLE 2–1   *Year of First Statewide Enactment*
            of a Juvenile Court Law

State	Year	State	Year
Alabama	1907	Montana	1907
Alaska	1913	Nebraska	1905
Arizona	1907	Nevada	1909
Arkansas	1911	New Hampshire	1907
California	1903	New Jersey	1903
Colorado	1903	New Mexico	1917
Connecticut	1905	New York	1922
Delaware	1911	North Carolina	1915
Florida	1911	North Dakota	1911
Georgia	1908	Ohio	1904
Hawaii	1905	Oklahoma	1909
Idaho	1905	Oregon	1905
Illinois	1899	Pennsylvania	1903
Indiana	1903	Rhode Island	1909
Iowa	1904	South Carolina	1912
Kansas	1905	South Dakota	1909
Kentucky	1906	Tennessee	1905
Louisiana	1906	Texas	1907
Maine	n.a.	Utah	1905
Maryland	1916	Vermont	1912
Massachusetts	1906	Virginia	1910
Michigan	1905	Washington	1905
Minnesota	1905	West Virginia	1915
Mississippi	1916	Wisconsin	1901
Missouri	1907	Wyoming	1945

Source: Michael Gordon. *Juvenile Delinquency in the American Novel,*
1905–1965. Bowling Green, Ohio: Bowling Green University Popular
Press, 1971.

Early critics of the juvenile court questioned the concept of *parens patriae* as an adequate legal precedent. Because the notion had applied to protecting the property of children (Tappan, 1949:169–70), it was not a purely logical or automatic outgrowth of a legal tradition. Rather, the concept was extended by analogy as a legal defense of the court. The early critics challenged its constitutionality on the grounds that its application by the juvenile court violated notions of due process of law. However, because the juvenile court defined its procedures as civil rather than criminal, constitutional guarantees were not applicable.

Of course, the denial of due process was not entirely unique to the juvenile justice system. As Glen and Weber (1971:1) have pointed out: "State Court systems were relatively free to operate as they wished, bound only by their own constitutions and State Court interpretations." The autonomy of state courts allowed considerable variation in the extension of due-process guarantees to adults who were being processed for criminal offenses. Extension of guarantees of due process to minors began much later and is still in process. States have had considerable autonomy in the handling of juveniles, and in the 1940s and 1950s some began to extend due-process protections to juveniles (Glen and Weber, 1971). During those years, Wisconsin, Minnesota, Oregon, and California revised or rewrote their juvenile codes to extend greater due-process guarantees to juveniles.

JUVENILE JUSTICE AND THE SUPREME COURT

It was not until 1966 that the United States Supreme Court began making rulings that bore on the constitutionality and legal foundation of juvenile court proceedings. Between 1966 and 1975 the Supreme Court advanced five decisions relevant to the rights of juveniles in juvenile court proceedings: (1) *Kent* v. *United States*, 383 U.S. 541 (1966); (2) *In re Gault*, 387 U.S. 1 (1967); (3) *In re Winship*, 397 U.S. 358 (1970); (4) *McKeiver* v. *Pennsylvania*, 403 U.S. 528 (1971); and (5) *Breed* v. *Jones*, 421 U.S. 519 (1975). These cases represent the sum total of the Supreme Court's legal clarification of the meaning of due process for juveniles.

1. *Kent* v. *United States*. The *Kent* case is a most significant decision because it was the first time that the United States Supreme Court agreed to hear a case regarding a juvenile. As late as 1955 the Court refused to rule on the issue of due process of law for juveniles: "Since juvenile courts are not criminal courts, the constitutional rights granted to persons accused of crime are not applicable to the children brought before them" (*In re Holmes*, 109A, 2d 523). The Supreme Court argued that the juvenile court, operating under the doctrine of *parens patriae*, does not punish children but acts on their behalf. Due process of law does not apply to juveniles since the juvenile court is not a criminal court and the juvenile is not charged with committing a criminal act.

In 1966 the Court reversed its stand on the negation of due process in juvenile matters by ruling on the case of sixteen-year-old Morris A. Kent, Jr. The specifics of the case were as follows: (1) Kent, first arrested in 1959 at the age of fourteen for housebreaking, was freed on probation; (2) in 1961 during the investigation of a theft, Kent's fingerprints were found at the scene of the crime; (3) the juvenile judge, after considering the charges against Kent, decided to waive jurisdiction and transferred the case from juvenile to adult court without stating a reason to the youth or his parents; (4) Kent stood trial as an adult and received a sentence of thirty to ninety years in prison. If Kent had been tried in juvenile court, the maximum sentence for the sixteen-year-old boy would have been five years (the court's jurisdiction does not extend beyond age twenty-one).

The *Kent* case was appealed to the Supreme Court, and in 1966 the Court reversed the decision on the grounds that Kent's right of due process had been violated. In handing down its decision, the Supreme Court ruled that (1) a hearing must be given in juvenile court on the issue of remanding or transferring a juvenile case to an adult court; (2) the juvenile is entitled to counsel at the waiver proceeding; (3) counsel is entitled to have access to all the social records of the juvenile prepared by the staff of the court in presenting their decision to waive jurisdiction; (4) it is incumbent upon the juvenile court that a statement of reasons accompany the waiver order.

Although this 1966 decision is confined only to matters of waiver of jurisdiction, it marked the first significant step toward a review of the juvenile justice system. The Supreme Court appeared to open the door for further litigation by emphasizing the need for due process and fair treatment in the juvenile court. Mr. Justice Fortas added his personal observations to the *Kent* decision with the following statement:

> While there can be no doubt of the original laudable purpose of juvenile courts, studies and critiques in recent years raise serious questions as to whether actual performance measures well enough against theoretical purposes to make tolerable the immunity of the process from the reach of constitutional guarantees applicable to adults. There is much evidence that some juvenile courts, including that of the District of Columbia, lack the personnel, facilities and techniques to perform adequately as representatives of the state in a *parens patriae* capacity, at least with respect to children charged with law violation. There is evidence, in fact, that there may be grounds for concern that the child receives the worst of both worlds; that he gets neither the protection accorded to adults nor the solicitous care and regenerative treatment postulated for children. (383 U.S. 541–555–56, 1964)

This poignant statement added to the Supreme Court's concern that the right to representation is "not a grudging gesture to a ritualistic requirement" but is the essence of justice. The *Kent* ruling set the stage for the landmark *Gault* case that was acted upon the following year.

2. *In re Gault.* On June 8, 1964, the sheriff of Gila County, Arizona, arrested fifteen-year-old Gerald Gault. The sheriff was acting on a complaint from a neighbor, Mrs. Cook, that Gerald and another boy had made lewd and indecent remarks to her on the telephone. Gerald was taken to the local detention facility, and his parents, who were both at work, were not informed of the arrest until later that evening. On June 9 an adjudication hearing (basically a hearing at which guilt is assessed) was held, at which time Gerald and his parents were informed of the nature of the complaint. Mrs. Cook, however, did not appear. This hearing was conducted without any formal notice of charges, without legal counsel, without the presence of any witnesses, and without any record or transcript of the hearing. The dispositional hearing (a hearing at which the judge imposes a sentence or makes a final disposition of the case) was held on June 15, and the juvenile court reported that "after a full hearing

and due deliberation the Court finds that said minor is a delinquent child, and that said minor is of the age of fifteen years." The juvenile judge committed Gerald as a juvenile delinquent to an institution for boys "for the period of his minority"—that is, until Gerald was twenty-one years of age. As a juvenile, Gerald was sentenced to six years; had he been an adult, the maximum penalty would have been a fine of fifty dollars or a jail sentence of not more than two months.

Arizona law permitted no appeal in juvenile cases. Instead, a petition for a writ of habeas corpus was filed with the Supreme Court of Arizona on August 3, 1964. Such a writ, in effect, demands that reasons be given concerning the detention of any individual. The writ was based on an alleged denial of the following rights: (1) notice of the charges; (2) right to counsel; (3) right to confrontation and cross-examination; (4) privilege against self-incrimination; (5) right to a transcript of the proceedings; and (6) right to appellate review.

The Supreme Court of Arizona dismissed the writ and each of the six allegations. The court argued against the first allegation (denial of notice of charges) by stating that the Gaults knew of the nature of the charges against Gerald by virtue of their appearance at the two hearings. Furthermore, the court stated that specific written charges are not necessary because "the policy of the juvenile law is to hide youthful errors from the full gaze of the public and bury them in the graveyard of the forgotten past." The court rejected the second charge (denial of counsel) by arguing that "the parent and the probation officer may be relied upon to protect the infant's interests." In addition, the court maintained that the juvenile court has the discretion, but not the duty, to allow legal representation. The third and fourth charges were dismissed on the grounds that "the necessary flexibility for individualized treatment will be enhanced by a rule which does not require the judge to advise the infant of a privilege against self-incrimination." The final two charges concerning appellate review and a transcript of the proceedings were also denied. The court argued that Arizona law permitted no appeal of a juvenile court decision and that since juvenile proceedings are confidential, any transcript would have to be destroyed in due time. In its commentary on each of the six allegations, the Supreme Court of Arizona implicitly argued that since proceedings involving juveniles are civil and not criminal, the juvenile court is not subject to those standards that restrict the state when it seeks to deprive a person of his or her liberty.

The *Gault* case was then appealed to the United States Supreme Court, and on May 16, 1967, the Court reversed the decision of the Supreme Court of Arizona. The Court reexamined each of the six charges and found that the juvenile court's unbridled discretion "however benevolently motivated, is frequently a poor substitute for principle and procedure." Due process of law is provided for by the Constitution and "the condition of being a boy does not justify a kangaroo court."

The Supreme Court specifically stipulated: (1) Notice of charges must be given sufficiently in advance of juvenile court hearings to permit time to prepare for the court proceedings. (2) The probation officer cannot act as counsel for the child because he or she is in fact acting as the arresting officer. In any juvenile proceeding that may result in commitment to an institution, the juvenile and his or her parents must be notified of the child's right to be represented by counsel; if they are unable to afford counsel, the court must appoint an attorney to represent the juvenile. (3) Confrontation and sworn testimony by witnesses available for cross-examination are essential in delinquency hearings. Any order of commitment to a state institution cannot be sustained in the absence of these fundamental principles of the adversary process. (4) Although a juvenile hearing may in fact involve civil rather than criminal proceedings, the privilege of the right to remain silent as stipulated in the Fifth Amendment nonetheless applies in juvenile matters. The Constitution guarantees that no person shall be compelled to be a witness against himself when he or she is threatened with deprivation of liberty. The Supreme Court argued that juvenile proceedings that may lead to commitment to a state institution must be regarded as criminal hearings for the purposes of the privilege against self-incrimination.

The Supreme Court did not rule on the fifth charge—that is, denial of the right to a transcript at juvenile hearings. Although such a practice is desirable, particularly in reconstructing the record in an appeals process, the Court did not enforce this procedure. Finally, regarding the sixth charge (denial of the right to appellate review), the Supreme Court chose not to rule on the constitutionality of the Arizona statute that denied appeal in juvenile cases.

The importance of the *Gault* decision in the extension of juvenile rights cannot be minimized. Although it neither overturned the juvenile court system nor invalidated questionable procedures in dealing with the rights of juveniles, it did introduce the concept of due process of law into the juvenile court system. The Supreme Court heavily qualified the capacity of the doctrine of *parens patriae* to be the all-pervading philosophy of the juvenile court. The *Gault* decision also challenged the common assumption that juvenile court proceedings are noncriminal. In sum, this decision was not so much a culmination of the fight for juvenile rights as a call to arms in recognizing the dignity and respect that individuals under the age of majority must be accorded.

3. *In re Winship.* The third case regarding juvenile rights came before the United States Supreme Court in 1970. A twelve-year-old boy named Samuel Winship had been charged with stealing $112 from a woman's purse. This act, if committed by an adult, would constitute a crime of larceny, and the probable punishment would not be particularly severe. As a juvenile, however, Winship was ordered to be placed in a training

school for a period of six years. The judge in the juvenile court relied on a provision of New York state law that states that proof of the matter in a juvenile case need not be established beyond a reasonable doubt but simply that an adjudicatory hearing be based on a "preponderance of the evidence."

The case was appealed to the United States Supreme Court on the grounds that the essentials of due process had been violated. In addition, the appellant contended that when a juvenile is charged with an act that would constitute a crime if committed by an adult, proof must be established beyond a reasonable doubt. The Court ruled that proof of a criminal charge beyond a reasonable doubt is constitutionally required for juveniles, as well as adults. Further, the Court argued, despite the rhetoric of the juvenile court, a delinquency adjudication is a conviction, and its proceedings are criminal. "Civil labels and good intentions do not themselves obviate the need for criminal due process safeguards in juvenile courts." Thus, the *Winship* case became the third significant advancement in hammering out a platform of legal rights for juveniles.

4. *McKeiver* v. *Pennsylvania.* What appeared to be a steady progression of Supreme Court rulings in favor of extending the provisions of the Bill of Rights to juveniles received a temporary setback with the 1971 *McKeiver* ruling. The case involved a sixteen-year-old boy, Joseph McKeiver, who had been charged with three felonious acts in juvenile court. At the time of his adjudication hearing, a request made for a jury trial was denied, and McKeiver was adjudged delinquent and placed on probation. The case was appealed to the Supreme Court on the grounds that it violated the Sixth Amendment's guarantee of the right to an impartial jury and the Seventh Amendment's stipulation of the right to a trial by jury.

After a careful review of previous decisions relating to juvenile matters, the Court concluded that the right to a trial by jury in the juvenile court's adjudication stage is not a constitutional requirement. The precise reasons set forth entail the transformation of the juvenile proceeding into an adversary process that would jeopardize the "idealistic prospect of an intimate, informal protective proceeding." Mr. Justice Blackmun, who delivered the decision, stated: "If in its wisdom, any State feels the jury trial is desirable in all cases, or in certain kinds, there appears to be no impediment to its installing a system embracing that feature. That, however, is the State's privilege and not its obligation." The essence of this decision is the Supreme Court's refusal to equate juvenile proceedings with the proceedings of the adult criminal justice system. The Court believed that such an equation would negate "every aspect of fairness, of concern, of sympathy, and of paternal attention that the juvenile court system contemplates."

5. *Breed* v. *Jones.* In 1971 a seventeen-year-old Los Angeles juvenile was arrested on the charge of robbery with a deadly weapon. The juvenile was ordered detained pending adjudication on the delinquency petition. The juvenile court sustained the delinquency petition, finding that the juvenile had committed the robbery, and ordered that the proceedings be continued for a dispositional hearing. At this subsequent hearing, the juvenile court judge ruled that this juvenile was "not amenable to the care, treatment and training program of the juvenile court" and therefore remanded the juvenile to the adult criminal court for a new trial. Despite the defendant's objections that such an action would constitute double jeopardy, the juvenile was tried in the adult criminal court and found guilty of committing a felony.

A petition of habeas corpus was filed in the federal district court on the grounds that the juvenile hearing and the adult trial on the same criminal act had placed the defendant in double jeopardy. The district court denied the petition, stating that juvenile proceedings were civil and not criminal in nature and that if the juvenile court had to follow the rigorous rules and formalities regarding double jeopardy, it would be deprived of its ability to function. The case was then taken to the court of appeals, which ruled that the double jeopardy clause of the Fifth Amendment is fully applicable to juvenile court proceedings, and furthermore, that the application of the double jeopardy guarantee in the juvenile court would not interfere with that court's goal of rehabilitation. In 1975 the decision of the court of appeals was appealed to the United States Supreme Court. In a unanimous decision, the Court upheld the ruling of the court of appeals.

In handing down its decision, the Supreme Court broadened the concept of double jeopardy beyond its traditional meaning of double punishment to include the "potential or risk of trial and conviction." The Court argued that the juvenile was put in double jeopardy even though the juvenile hearings did not run their full course and did not arrive at a final disposition. Although sentenced for punishment only at the adult criminal trial, the juvenile was subjected to the burden of two trials for the same offense and twice had to marshal resources against the state. The effect of this ruling was to require that decisions about the transfer of jurisdiction be made before the juvenile or criminal proceedings are initiated.

Overview: The Extension of Juvenile Rights

With the 1966 *Kent* decision, the United States Supreme Court began extending to juveniles basic constitutional rights that the omnipotent authority of the juvenile court's *parens patriae* doctrine had tended to neglect or distort. Although the Court did not revolutionize the juvenile justice system, it did introduce the concept of due process of law at the juvenile level.

In all its decisions regarding the rights of juveniles, including its *McKeiver* ruling, the Court had expressed a growing disenchantment with numerous aspects of the juvenile justice system. Although the Court has not fully endorsed the procedural rights of juveniles regarding a criminal hearing (for example, the right to be released on bail, and right to a public or jury trial), it has seriously challenged the noncriminal nature of juvenile court proceedings. The Court has hesitated to negate what it feels is a unique function of the juvenile court system; it has not, however, specified the precise advantages of that system.

It is hazardous to predict what future constitutional rights will be extended to juveniles. Significant gains have been made, but the lack of procedural regularity in juvenile matters will inevitably produce legal difficulties in the future. Many questions pertaining to the rights of juveniles are as yet unanswered: the use of questionable search and seizure practices (Fourth Amendment rights); speedy and public hearings (Sixth Amendment rights); cruel and unusual punishments (Eighth Amendment rights); vague and ambiguous definitions of delinquency and the precarious balance between the social-work posture and the legal aspects of the juvenile court.

It should also be noted that the rights that the Court has extended to juveniles involve rules of evidence and due process at the *adjudicatory* level. Thus, when the juvenile stands accused he or she is now entitled to remain silent; to have an attorney (at state expense, if necessary); to be advised of his or her rights, notice of charges, and proceedings; and to subpoena witnesses. In addition, Court decisions suggest that rights to a transcript and appellate review are desirable. However, at the *dispositional* level the judge is not bound by the rules of evidence nor is the juvenile entitled to have an attorney. Some commentators on the juvenile court (Glen and Weber, 1971) view the dual character of the juvenile justice system (that is, different standards for the adjudication hearing and the disposition hearing) as a means of protecting the rights of juveniles and at the same time serving the treatment aims of the court. Others (Edwards, 1973) feel that the rights of children should be protected at all stages of the proceedings and advocate ensuring due process at points beyond the adjudication hearing.

We cannot assume that Supreme Court decisions have transformed the actual operation of the juvenile justice system into an adversary system in which defense attorneys battle with prosecutors to obtain a favorable verdict for their clients. The adult criminal justice system has been depicted (with considerable justification) as a system of "bargain-counter" justice in which notions of due process and the adversary roles of defense and prosecution are secondary to efficiency and mass production (Blumberg, 1970). Platt and Friedman (1968) found that in the Chicago Juvenile Court, private attorneys for juveniles, even after the *Gault* decision, tended to be small-fee lawyers who neither represented their clients in an adversary fashion nor negotiated or bargained for their clients. Similarly, public defenders appear to spend very little time on behalf of their juvenile clients (Platt, Schechter, and Tiffany, 1968). On the other hand, Spencer Cox (1967) reported that in Philadelphia the percentage of juveniles represented by counsel increased from 5 percent to 40 percent following the *Gault* decision. Cox noted that this increase had a number of consequences for the processing of juveniles: (1) a reduction in detention before hearings, (2) a drop in commitment to institutions, and (3) a staggering backlog of cases awaiting disposition.

In summary, the extension of certain rights to juveniles may have benefited juveniles in certain ways. Yet, the juvenile court, like the criminal court, is a mass-processing system with characteristics and practices that are dictated by concerns for the efficient processing of thousands of cases rather than by legal notions of due process of law.

CURRENT STATUTES AND JUVENILE JUSTICE

While due process and the procedural rights of juveniles are in a state of flux and the subject of legal battles, legal specifications of activities that can lead to adjudication of juveniles have been criticized for their lack of precision and their all-encompassing nature. Even the meaning of the term *delinquent* is questionable. For example, if we try to specify a legal definition of delinquent that would be generally applicable around the United States, all we can state is that a delinquent is a nonadult or a child who has been adjudicated for a "delinquent" act.

The definition of nonadult varies from state to state, with the most common cutoff point between adult and nonadult being age eighteen. In some states the cutoff point is as low as sixteen. In others it may extend to age twenty-one, with the criminal court sharing concurrent ("at the same time") jurisdiction with the juvenile court over persons aged eighteen to twenty-one. The lower age limits of children subject to the juvenile court's jurisdiction are rarely specified, but when they are, they range between ages seven and ten. Moreover, common-law traditions have in essence set an operational lower limit of eight years of age. A person younger than eight is presumed not to be responsible for his or her actions. In some states a child under eight years of age who enters the juvenile justice system may be dealt with as a "dependent," rather than a "delinquent," child. Finally, we should add that in some state   t may be dealt with by ("remanded" to) the adult criminal jus   f the judge deems it best for the community or the youth involved. In reality, such transfers are most likely to occur when a juvenile has committed a serious criminal offense that has generated moral indignation in the community.

Excerpts from the state juvenile court code for Arizona are presented below and reflect the basic characteristics of substantive juvenile law:

> "Juvenile court" means the juvenile division of the superior court when exercising its jurisdiction over children in any proceeding relating to delinquency, dependency or incorrigibility.

> "Delinquent act" includes an act by a child which, if committed by an adult, would be a public offense or any act that would constitute a public offense which could only be committed by a child or by a minor, including violation of any law of this state, or of another state if the act occurred in that state, or of the United States, or any ordinance of a city, county, or political sub-division of this state defining crime, or the failure to obey any lawful order of the juvenile court; provided, however, that any child remanded for prosecution as an adult shall not be adjudicated as a delinquent child for that same offense for which he was remanded.

> "Dependent child" means a child who is adjudicated to be: (1) in need of proper and effective parental care and control and has no parent or guardian, or one who has no parent or guardian willing to exercise or capable of exercising such care and control; (2) destitute or who is not provided with the necessities of life, or who is not provided with a home or suitable place of abode, or whose home is unfit for him by reason of abuse, neglect, cruelty, or depravity by either of his parents, his guardian, or other person having his custody or care; (3) Under the age of eight years who is found to have committed an act that would result in adjudication as a delinquent or incorrigible child if committed by an older child.

> "Incorrigible child" means a child adjudicated as one who refuses to obey the reasonable and proper orders or directions of his parent, guardian, or custodian, and who is beyond the control of such person, or any child who is habitually truant from school, or who is a runaway from his home or parent, guardian, or custodian, or who habitually so deports himself so as to injure or endanger the morals or health of himself or others. *(Arizona Revised Statutes)*

"Incorrigibility" is a broad category encompassing a wide range of "status" offenses—that is, acts that can result in arrest, court referral, and adjudication *only* if the persons committing them fall within the age status specified in the juvenile code. Delinquent acts include acts that are criminal regardless of age, as well as status offenses, such as drinking, smoking, and curfew violations. The distinction between delinquency and incorrigibility is not characteristic of all states. In fact, the National Center for Juvenile Justice, which compiles delinquency statistics for the United States as a whole, defines juvenile delinquency cases as "those referred for acts defined by the statutes of the State as the violation of a

state law or municipal ordinance by children or youths of juvenile court age, or for conduct so seriously antisocial as to interfere with the rights of others or to menace the welfare of the delinquent himself or of the community."

In other words, a "delinquent" may or may not be a person who has committed a criminal act in that the label can be applied to some status offenders. Moreover, a person committing a criminal act may or may not be labeled "delinquent" if he or she is under the age of eight. Depending on the type of status offense committed, a person may be legally classified as "incorrigible" (for example, because of a runaway offense) or as "delinquent." Thus, while we are likely to have formed an image in our minds of what a "delinquent" is and what a "delinquent" does, the actual legal situation may involve overlapping realms of status offenses, incorrigible actions, criminal acts, and certain categories of dependent children.

Although the distinction between delinquency and incorrigibility appears in statutes, the actual designation may have little effect on what happens to nonadults processed through the juvenile court. For instance, a report to the National Council on Crime and Delinquency concluded that while juvenile statutes increasingly include such a distinction, delinquency and incorrigibility continue to be handled similarly (Glen and Weber, 1971:6). The authors of this report stated in no uncertain terms that "the ostensible trend toward separation of criminal from noncriminal jurisdictional bases for dealing with children is a hoax."

A considerable volume of juvenile court cases deal with the broad category of status offender, whether incorrigible or delinquent. Table 2–2 was derived from a juvenile court report and illustrates the types of cases that a juvenile court handles. "Juvenile offenses" in this particular report include runaway, incorrigible, and curfew offenses, offenses against health, welfare, and morals, liquor offenses, tobacco offenses, and truancy. The table shows that such offenses constituted close to one-fourth of the total offenses for males (1,991 out of 8,200) and about one-half (1,304 out of 2,625 referrals) of the total offenses for females. Moreover, the rate at which these status offenders were detained by the court in this county (that is, held at juvenile court facilities pending further action or hearing) was actually twice as high as the rate of detention for juveniles committing acts that would be criminal for adults.

Along the same vein, Paul Lerman (1971) reported that status offenders were as likely as those accused of criminal offenses (if not more likely) to have a petition (that is, charges) filed against them, to be convicted, and to be placed in an institution or other program. Moreover, in a study of one Manhattan borough, Lerman found that the average length of imprisonment was eleven months for juvenile offenders committing criminal acts and sixteen months for status offenders.

In sum, a wide range of behaviors, problems, and conflicts are encompassed by juvenile law and the juvenile court. There is little evidence that

TABLE 2-2 *Reason for Referral to the Pima County Juvenile
            Court, 1976*

	Male	Female	Total
Juvenile Offenses:			
Runaway	917	971	1,888
Incorrigible	109	48	157
Curfew	193	43	236
Health, welfare, morals	321	173	494
Liquor offenses (status only)	410	64	474
Tobacco offenses	29	3	32
Truancy	12	2	14
Total Juvenile Offenses	1,991	1,304	3,295
Minor Personal Behavior	511	117	628
Major Personal Offenses	1,054	185	1,239
Offenses against Persons	492	100	592
Offenses against Property	4,232	919	5,151
Total Offenses	8,280	2,625	10,905

Source: Pima County Juvenile Court. *Pima County Juvenile Court
Statistics, Annual Report.* Tucson, Ariz.: Pima County Juvenile Court
Center, 1976.

it really matters whether a person is caught up in the system as delinquent, incorrigible, or status offender. The juvenile court operates as both
a social welfare agency and a court of law. Delinquency statutes reflect
the concept of the court as an agency that intervenes on behalf of the
state to enforce the law, to uphold certain moral standards, and to protect
children. No wonder the scope of the court has generated controversy and
concern.

CONTINUING CONTROVERSY

While it appears that more and more adult rights are being extended to
the young, it is not without resistance and concern from many quarters.
For example, a recent Gallup poll found that 45 percent of the public
believed that students have "too many" rights and only 10 percent felt
that students had too few rights. In the area of criminal justice, many
critics of Supreme Court decisions argue that there is too much emphasis
on the rights of "criminals" and not enough emphasis on the rights of
"victims." Politicians can always count on enthusiastic support from
much of the populace when they campaign against the "mollycoddling"
of juvenile thugs and young hoodlums. The periodic criticism of juvenile
judges who are too "soft" and police resentment of the lax treatment of
juvenile offenders attest to the ebb and flow of crusades for and against
juvenile rights.

As the Supreme Court changes, interpretations of the nature of one's "rights" and of "due process of law" also change. In reality, rights are not stable, constant, and unambiguous but are instead subject to human interpretation. Abraham Blumberg summarized the situation as follows:

> The legal concept of due process serves much the same function in the legal system as does the joker in a card game: it has a shifting meaning and application. Just as the structure of legal and judicial systems are a reflection of group structure and the individuals who comprise it, so the content of due process of law (whether at the Supreme Court or state level) may have a particular meaning, purpose, and character that mirror the unique angle or mission of a historical and social location. In a rational-legal society, the "rule of law" is invoked as a source of legitimacy. In dealing with a wrongdoer, the question is not guilt or innocence, but rather a demonstration of the "approved way" in which evidence can be used legitimately vis-à-vis a given individual. In American society the "approved way" means due process of law, which in essence refers to the normatively established, institutionalized recipes for invoking and using legal machinery. (1970:20)

Even if standards of due process are clearly defined and extended to minors who have committed criminal offenses, a significant proportion of adolescents—"incorrigible" youths and status offenders—will continue to be processed through the juvenile court system without having committed a criminal offense. Among juvenile court personnel there is growing support for the idea that as many cases as possible should be diverted away from judicial processing and that general community resources should be increasingly used in dealing with noncriminal problems. Thus, the position that the court cannot serve as a home, parent, school, welfare agency, and a court of law all at the same time is gaining popularity.

Edwin Lemert (1967) has advocated a position of "judicious nonintervention" for the juvenile court. In Lemert's view, local communities have placed an impossible burden on the juvenile court with expectations that it intervene in an overwhelming range of adolescent problems. His recommendation is that the juvenile court take a step backward in its involvement in such matters. Lemert envisions a juvenile court that operates much like an appeals court, hearing cases only after other avenues of resolution have been exhausted. The court's function would be "reduced to enforcement of the ethical minimum of youth conduct necessary to maintain social life in a high energy pluralistic society" (1967:97). Edwin Schur (1973) has argued that we should greatly restrict the jurisdiction of the juvenile court system in dealing with adolescent problems. His strategy is one of "radical nonintervention," its basic dictum being that we should "leave kids alone whenever possible" (1973:155).

Some radical critics of current policies for dealing with delinquency have argued that the only effective approach to the problem is to attack the economic and social *marginality* of youth directly. In other words, rather than developing programs that rely on such institutions as the court to cope with the *consequences* of the marginal position of youth, we should attack the "marginalization" itself (Schwendinger and Schwendinger, 1976). This radical approach to the problems of adolescence in the United States calls for major changes in our economy: the elimination of unemployment and subemployment through government control of industry and extensive public works programs. Although such approaches upset many people, they do direct our attention to the fact that the juvenile justice system was developed to deal with an age category that did not (and still does not) quite fit into the American economic system.

In chapters 10, 11, and 12, we will review a wide range of experimental programs for dealing with delinquency within the juvenile justice system. Unfortunately none of these programs has had a significant effect on either the prevention or inhibition of delinquent activity. Such pessimistic findings, together with the alleged failure of the juvenile justice system to cope with the delinquency problems, have led critics to seriously question whether modifications *within* the juvenile justice system can ever have any significant impact. Broad-scale change in the economy may make no difference either, but convincing arguments along these lines have been advanced by numerous scholars.

The sociological approach to delinquency requires that the behavior and attitudes of the young be understood in the context of a largely adult-controlled world. Children can easily become scapegoats for the grief and woes of modern industrial society. In America today, adolescents are seen as the cause of many of society's shortcomings. Crimes against persons and property, drug-related problems, lack of respect for authority, overweening ambition, and widespread apathy are interpreted as the unique problems of youth; in fact, they are as much, if not more so, the problems of society. In short, the problems of young people are very much a part of the problems facing the entire society.

SUMMARY

The terms *juvenile* and *delinquent* are commonly associated with one another, and, in fact, there are convincing arguments that the development of adolescence as a distinct age category was intertwined with the development of delinquent as a special legal category. In the United States, movements for compulsory public education, child labor legislation, and the establishment of separate institutions and courts for juveniles helped establish adolescence as a bio-legal age category encompassing the years between puberty and legal adulthood.

The legal groundwork and philosophical precedents for the creation of a juvenile court can be traced to the development of houses of refuge and schools for troublesome youth in the early and mid-1800s. The legal doctrine invoked in establishing such institutions was *parens patriae,* the concept that the state has the right to act as a parent. However, the establishment of houses of refuge and the later "antiinstitutionalist" movement did not flow automatically from legal precedents or reflect solely humanitarian concerns; both movements reflected the religious and class conflicts of the time as well.

There is an ongoing debate among scholars about the forces that shaped the original development of a separate juvenile justice system. Anthony Platt has interpreted the emergence of the juvenile court in the late 1800s as an extension of religious and class conflicts. In contrast, Schlossman and Finestone have argued that the emergence of the juvenile court reflected an antiinstitutional ideology that stressed probation and the home and family as targets of treatment. However, scholars do agree that there was and is a considerable gap between the professed aims cited in the creation of a separate juvenile justice system and its actual operation.

Although the first juvenile court was established in 1899, it was not until 1966 that the United States Supreme Court began ruling on the constitutionality of juvenile court proceedings. In a series of cases between 1966 and 1975, the Supreme Court extended several rights of "due process" to juveniles at the adjudicatory level. These rulings do not, however, apply to the dispositional level. Moreover, the Court has not addressed several of the constitutional protections extended to adults in terms of their applicability to juveniles. Whether the Court's decisions have made any significant difference to what happens to juveniles processed through the system is still a subject of dispute. The mass-processing, "bargain-justice" aspects of the administration of justice, whether for adults or for juveniles, may make such Court decisions irrelevant to the everyday operation of juvenile justice systems.

The creation of a separate juvenile court was more than a matter of instituting new procedures. It involved the extension of state control over a wider range of activities than criminal law had ever encompassed. An examination of current statistics shows several overlapping categories of activity or problems that can bring a juvenile to the attention of the juvenile court. Offenses alone do not automatically enable us to decide whether a youth is liable to categorization as delinquent, incorrigible, or dependent. Categorization may also depend on such factors as age, gender, past behavior, and community reaction. Moreover, while distinctions between categories are made in statutes, the relevance of these distinctions for the actual processing and ultimate disposition of cases has been challenged by studies of the treatment of status offenders. The emphasis at the present time is to make the distinctions between legal categories consequential by diverting youths who have not committed criminal offenses away from the juvenile court.

REFERENCES

Aries, P. 1962. *Centuries of Childhood.* New York: Vintage Books. Copyright © 1965 by Alfred A. Knopf, Inc.

Bakan, D. 1971. "Adolescence in America: From Idea to Social Fact." *Daedalus* (Fall):979–95.

Blumberg, A. S. 1970. *Criminal Justice.* Chicago: Quadrangle Books.

Cox, S. 1967. "Lawyers in Juvenile Court." *Crime and Delinquency* 13 (October): 488–93.

Edwards, L. 1973. "The Rights of Children." *Federal Probation* 37 (June):34–41.

Elder, G. 1968. "Age Groups, Status Transitions, and Socialization." Report for the Task Force on Environmental, Social Structural, and Cultural Aspects of Psycho-Social Deprivation. National Institute of Child Health and Human Development. Washington, D.C.

Finestone, H. 1976. *Victims of Change.* Westport, Conn.: Greenwood Press.

Glen, J. E., and J. R. Weber. 1971. *The Juvenile Court: A Status Report.* Washington, D.C.: Center for Studies of Crime and Delinquency.

Gordon, M. 1971. *Juvenile Delinquency in the American Novel, 1905–1965.* Bowling Green, Ohio: Bowling Green University Popular Press.

Hagan, J., and J. Leon. 1977. "Rediscovering Delinquency: Social History, Political Ideology and the Sociology of Law." *American Sociological Review* 42 (August):587–98.

Hawes, J. 1971. *Children in Urban Society.* New York: Oxford University Press.

Jensen, G. F. 1976. "Report to Pima and Cochise County Schools." Unpublished technical report for National Institute of Mental Health research project, "Community Tolerance and Measures of Delinquency."

Lemert, E. M. 1967. "The Juvenile Court—Quest and Realities." In *President's Commission on Law Enforcement, Juvenile Delinquency and Youth Crime.*

Lerman, P. 1971. "Child Convicts." *Trans-Action* 8 (July/August):35–45.

Linton, R. 1942. "Age and Sex Categories." *American Sociological Review* 7:589–603.

Pima County Juvenile Court. 1976. *Pima County Juvenile Court Statistics, Annual Report.* Tucson, Ariz.: Pima County Juvenile Court Center.

Platt, A. 1969a. *The Child Savers: The Invention of Delinquency.* Chicago: University of Chicago Press.

———. 1969b. "The Rise of the Child-Saving Movement: A Study in Social Policy and Correctional Reform." *Annals of the American Academy of Political and Social Science* 381 (January):21–38.

———. 1974. "The Triumph of Benevolence: The Origins of the Juvenile Justice System in the United States." In R. Quinney, ed., *Criminal Justice in America.* Boston: Little, Brown.

Platt, A., and R. Friedman. 1968. "The Limits of Advocacy: Occupational Hazards in Juvenile Court." *Pennsylvania Law Review* 116:1156–84.

Platt, A., H. Schechter, and P. Tiffany. 1968. "In Defense of Youth: A Case Study of the Public Defender in Juvenile Court." *Indiana Law Journal* 43:619–40.

President's Commission on Law Enforcement and Administration of Justice. 1967. *Task Force Report: Juvenile Delinquency and Youth Crime.* Washington, D.C.: U.S. Government Printing Office.

President's Science Advisory Committee, Panel on Youth. 1974. *Youth: Transition to Adulthood.* Chicago: University of Chicago Press.

Sanders, W. B. 1945. "Some Early Beginnings of the Children's Court Movement in England." *National Probation Association Yearbook* 39:58–70.

Schlossman, S. L. 1977. *Love and the American Delinquent.* Chicago: University of Chicago Press. Copyright 1977 by the University of Chicago Press.

Schur, E. M. 1973. *Radical Nonintervention: Rethinking the Delinquency Problem.* Englewood Cliffs, N.J.: Prentice-Hall.

Schwendinger, H., and J. R. Schwendinger. 1976. "Marginal Youth and Social Policy." *Social Problems* 24 (December):184–91.

Tappan, P. W. 1949. *Juvenile Delinquency.* New York: McGraw-Hill.

3.
IMAGES OF DELINQUENCY: POLICE AND COURT STATISTICS

In 1965 a majority of all arrests for major crimes against property were of people under 21, as were a substantial minority of arrests for major crimes against the person. The recidivism rates for young offenders are higher than those for any other age group. A substantial change in any of these figures would make a substantial change in the total crime figures for the Nation.
 —President's Commission, *The Challenge of Crime in a Free Society*

THE "FACTS" ABOUT DELINQUENCY

The image of delinquency projected by news media, entertainment programs, police, and politicians characterizes delinquent behavior as a growing threat to the very fabric of American society. During his long tenure as director of the Federal Bureau of Investigation, J. Edgar Hoover used the term *youthful criminality* rather than *juvenile delinquency* to underscore his assessment of the serious nature of juvenile offenses and to argue against the "coddling" of young criminals. Similarly, as we see in the quotation above, the President's Commission on Law Enforcement and Administration of Justice indicted young offenders as the major contributors to the national crime problem. The growing publicity received by delinquency and the massive amount of "factual" evidence cited to justify this concern have made the term *juvenile delinquent* synonymous with young criminals in the public's mind. But where do such "facts" about delinquency originate and can we accept the observations and information presented as "facts"?

People arrive at what they believe to be the "facts" or the "truth" about juvenile delinquency in several different ways. Quite often we form our opinions on the basis of our acquaintance with young people who have been in trouble with the law or who have done things that could get them in trouble with the law if proper authorities were informed. The problem with this method is that the people we meet during our lives are not likely to be a random, representative sample of all the different people in our society. The very nature of one's race or ethnicity, place of residence, socioeconomic status, and even one's preferences for food, entertainment, and retail stores excludes a great range of people and "biases" one's encounters with and knowledge of certain categories of people. Sometimes we form our ideas about delinquency on the basis of "expert" testimony or the opinions of those whose knowledge or contact with segments of the criminal justice system gives them a valuable awareness of the magnitude of the problem. The problem with this technique is that opinions based on "experience" or a "working knowledge in the field" may result from unusual, unique, or nonrepresentative encounters with youthful offenders. Expert testimony by those who "work with" offenders is derived from a knowledge of those offenders who are caught and processed by the juvenile justice system. Just what proportion of delinquents is caught is impossible to answer. We also cannot be sure what discretionary practices enter into the recording of juvenile delinquency. But how else can we reach conclusions about the nature of delinquency other than by relying on our own limited experiences and experiences of experts?

Although we may never arrive at absolute truth, we can certainly consider a number of different sources of information and the image of juvenile delinquency suggested by each. Armed with pieces of the total picture, we can begin to put the puzzle together, even though many pieces are lost or missing. In this chapter and the next, we focus on "images" of delinquency rather than "facts" about delinquency because the "facts" may differ depending on the source of information we consider. Statistics compiled by police and courts are one source of information about delinquency. Other sources are the reports of adolescents themselves concerning their own and others' involvement in delinquency and the reports of the victims of delinquency. The images presented by each source may differ because each may measure or tap more than involvement in delinquency. For example, government statistics on crime and delinquency reflect the behavior of the public and the police, as well as the characteristics and activities of offenders. Similarly, what people say they have been doing may reflect their desire to present certain images of themselves. Victims' reports on their experiences are affected both by their memory and their willingness to acknowledge such experiences. By considering different images and pondering over the disparities, we should end up with a less simplistic view of delinquency than that conveyed by most proclamations about the "facts" of delinquency.

THE OFFICIAL CREATION OF DELINQUENT EVENTS AND PERSONS

We are continually bombarded with statistical information about the state of society and our collective well-being. "The cost of living increased by 10 percent!" "The value of the dollar has declined 20 percent!" "Crime increased by 5 percent!" Moreover, during political campaigns we are likely to find various candidates using the same statistics to support very different positions. It is not surprising then that so many people believe that "one can say anything with statistics." However, the more detailed our knowledge about the collection and use of statistics, the better able we are to assess their meaning and differentiate between proper and improper interpretations.

Federal, state, and local governments in the United States regularly compile data on the number of events and persons that have come to the attention of police and courts as criminal or delinquent. Most events and persons that *could* enter into such agency statistics do not, either because they go undetected or because they are never reported. A major reason that many criminal victimizations never become crimes recorded by the police or the courts is that the public does not take the initial step of reporting the crime (see Chapter 4).

Most police activity is in response to public complaints. Therefore, the public's willingness to report crimes is a major factor affecting the chances that a potentially criminal or delinquent event will be officially recognized and will eventually become "a statistic." A household survey by a national crime commission in 1967 found that only 49 percent of criminal victimizations were reported to the police (President's Commission on Law Enforcement and Administration of Justice, 1968). The most common explanation for not reporting a crime was the belief that "nothing could be done about it" even if police were notified.

Potentially criminal or delinquent incidents are lost at other stages as well. The 1967 crime commission found that police responded to only 77 percent of the incidents reported. Of that 77 percent, police took further action on 75 percent. Thus, of 2,077 incidents reported in interviews at 10,000 households, only 580 made it to the point of being officially defined as offenses. Some incidents, such as auto theft and murder, were very likely to be officially recognized. Such events as rape and criminal fraud were less likely to be reported. For all incidents, only 116 (5 percent) resulted in an arrest. In short, the events and persons that make their way into government statistics are not necessarily a representative sample of crime, criminals, delinquent offenses, or delinquents.

Because the public decision to report an offense or offender has been found to play a key role in the creation of official statistics, there is growing interest in the way interaction between the public and the police affects the "production of crime rates." Donald Black (1970) has reported on a study of encounters between patrolmen and citizens in the cities of Boston, Chicago, and Washington, D.C.: In cases in which there was no suspect, police decided to take action on 72 percent of the most serious offenses (felonies) and 53 percent of the less serious offenses (misdemeanors). However, if the complainant did not want the police to take further legal action, the police abided by this wish in every encounter observed. On the other hand, if the complainant pressed for further action, the police were apparently influenced by other considerations besides the complainant's wish in deciding whether or not to comply. Police abided by such preferences more often when (1) the offense was a felony rather than a misdemeanor, (2) the suspected offender was a stranger to the complainant rather than an acquaintance, and (3) the complainant was respectful to the police rather than disrespectful. There was also some indication that for serious offenses, police were more likely to honor the preferences of middle-class complainants than those of working-class complainants. However, there was no evidence that white complainants received more preferential treatment than black complainants.

In another phase of this same study, Black and Reiss (1970) examined the circumstances leading to encounters between police and juveniles and to police decisions to arrest. They found that most arrest situations (78 percent) developed through citizen complaints rather than police initiative—that is, most contacts represented "reactive" rather than "proactive" police action. Furthermore, the police were found to be quite lenient, arresting only 57 percent of felony suspects and 48 percent of misdemeanor suspects. The probability of being arrested, however, was enhanced when (1) the offense was serious, (2) the suspect was a stranger to the complainant, and (3) the suspect was disrespectful. Black juveniles were more likely to be arrested than white juveniles, but the greater hazard for black juveniles was found to reflect a tendency for black complainants to press for arrest.

In sum, criminal or delinquent events and persons represent only a small proportion of events and persons that could be so labeled. Whether an event or a person *is* so labeled is a product of legal constraints, complainant preference, relationships between suspects and complainants, and the interaction between police, complainants, and suspects. We will deal with other research concerning the decision to arrest later in this chapter when we discuss the issue of discrimination. At this point we will examine two major sources of data on persons and events that make their way into government statistics as criminal or delinquent.

UNIFORM CRIME REPORTS
AND JUVENILE COURT STATISTICS

The Federal Bureau of Investigation amasses great quantities of crime information in the United States on an annual basis and publishes these crime statistics in a volume referred to as the *Uniform Crime Reports* (UCR). Approximately 13,000 law enforcement agencies, which cover 95 percent of the United States population, submit monthly and annual reports to the FBI on the number of offenses known to the police, arrest statistics, statistics on characteristics of persons arrested, and law enforcement employee data. Most Americans have encountered these statistics being used in one form or another in proclamations about "crime" in the United States. They are the source of such announcements in the news as, "Crime in the United States increased by 4.2 percent according to the latest FBI statistics!"

For the seven offenses that constitute the "serious-crime index," the annual report provides statistics on "crimes known to the police" (that is,

FIGURE 3–1   *Crimes Cleared by Arrest, 1977*

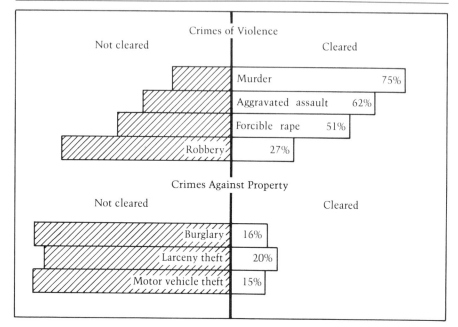

Source: Federal Bureau of Investigation. *Crime in the United States.*
Washington, D.C.: U.S. Government Printing Office, 1977 (released
October 1978).

offenses officially recognized by the police as crimes), as well as arrest
statistics. For other offenses, arrest data alone are provided. Only at the
point of arrest does the *Uniform Crime Reports* provide any information
on the age of the suspect. Since only a small percentage of most offenses
ever results in arrest (see Figure 3–1), arrest statistics do not necessarily
provide an accurate or representative picture of offenders in the United
States. Rather, they tell us who is being caught and arrested out of a much
larger universe of persons liable to arrest.

It is also important to note that arrest statistics generally refer to the
number of arrests by offense rather than the number of different people
arrested. A very high arrest rate for a particular grouping of people may
reflect heavy involvement of a few rather than common involvement of
the majority. This point is well illustrated in a recent study by Lyle
Shannon (1978). In an analysis of police-contact statistics for youths born
in Racine, Wisconsin, in 1949, Shannon found that around 5 percent of
the Anglo males accounted for over 38 percent of police contacts with
Anglo males and that 16 percent of the black males accounted for over 50
percent of police contacts with persons in that category. This disproportionate contribution of a few was found for females as well, with 8 percent of the black females accounting for 41 percent of all contacts with

TABLE 3-1 *Method of Handling Delinquency Cases Disposed of by Juvenile Courts, 1974*

Type of Court[a]	Total		Judicial		Nonjudicial	
	No.	%	No.	%	No.	%
Urban	776,600	100	442,600	57	334,000	43
Semiurban	375,800	100	166,900	44	208,900	56
Rural	100,300	100	58,200	58	42,100	42
Total	1,252,700	100	667,700	53	585,000	47

Source: National Center for Juvenile Justice. *Juvenile Court Statistics,* p. 14. Pittsburgh, Pa.: National Center for Juvenile Justice, 1974.

[a]Type of Court is determined by the percentage of population it serves that live in urban areas (as classified by the Bureau of the Census); for "urban courts," 70% or more; for "semiurban courts," 30–69%; for "rural courts," under 30%.

black females and 5 percent of Anglo females accounting for 44 percent of contacts with that grouping.

In addition to the arrest data presented in the *Uniform Crime Reports,* a second source of information on delinquency is the *Juvenile Court Statistics,* which is currently issued by the National Center for Juvenile Justice. This publication gives the total number of delinquency cases disposed of by juvenile courts with a breakdown by gender, location of the court, and method of handling cases. Information on the number, rate, and distribution of delinquency cases by type of court for the previous fifteen years is also presented in this report.

Unlike the *Uniform Crime Reports,* the *Juvenile Court Statistics* does not identify types of offenses, the reason being that the juvenile court does not convict a juvenile of a specific crime (see Chapter 2) but instead finds the individual to be "a juvenile delinquent." As Table 3–1 shows, nearly half of all delinquency cases are disposed of "nonjudicially," that is, without the filing of a petition. Once the case is brought to the juvenile court, it can be handled judicially in a delinquency hearing before the judge or in a more informal, "nonjudicial" fashion by having a member of the juvenile court staff "adjust" the matter.

Just as a small number of juveniles accounts for a sizable proportion of police contacts, a small number also contributes disproportionately to juvenile court cases. For example, a juvenile court report from Pima County, Arizona, shows that in 1976 there were 9,185 "referrals" but only 6,228 different children referred (Pima County Juvenile Court, 1977). Of these 6,228 different children, 3,311 were "new" cases referred to the court for the first time. The other 2,917 (47 percent) had been referred to the court in earlier years or more than once in 1976. Repeaters or "recidivists" account for a disproportionate amount of juvenile court referrals.

Most of the available data pertain to arrests or referrals, rather than to different people arrested or referred. In other words, most data are relevant to *incidence* rates rather than *prevalence* rates (Gordon, 1976:201–84). When dealing with *incidence,* the focus is on the proportion of a population appearing in police or court statistics during a given year or time period. When dealing with *prevalence,* the focus is on the proportion of a population that has *ever* made its way into such statistics by a certain age or time. Hence, in the annual juvenile court report summarized above, 53 percent of the children referred were "new" cases. The accumulation of such new cases over the years would add up to a considerable proportion of any given "cohort" (for example, all juveniles born in a particular year, such as 1952) of juveniles appearing in juvenile court statistics by the age of eighteen. In the juvenile court from Pima County, new cases represented between 2 and 3 percent of all persons under eighteen in that jurisdiction. If an additional 2 or 3 percent of the juvenile population appeared in the court statistics for the first time every year, then between their tenth and eighteenth birthdays, somewhere between 16 and 25 percent of the juvenile population in that jurisdiction would appear in court statistics.

There are no regularly collected nationwide data on the proportion of the juvenile population arrested or appearing in court in a given year (incidence rate) nor on the prevalence of such experiences for cohorts of juveniles (prevalence rate). However, judging from a review of existing studies in particular cities or regions (Gordon, 1976), it appears that between 15 and 25 percent of juveniles in the United States will acquire a juvenile court record by age eighteen, with males and blacks having much higher prevalence rates than females and whites, respectively.

PATTERNS BASED ON POLICE AND COURT STATISTICS

What do data on crime and delinquency show about variations or patterns over time, in different settings, and among different categories of people? It is hard to grow up in the United States without encountering observations relevant to this question. Most people believe that crime and delinquency have been increasing, that they are primarily urban problems, and that males, minority groups, and the disadvantaged account for an unusual amount of the criminal and delinquent activity in the United States. Such images can and have been supported by police and court statistics.

There are, however, contrasting points of view. Since police and court statistics on crime and delinquency reflect the behavior of the public, the police, the courts, and the offenders, there is obviously room for disagreement about how much each contributes to whatever patterns are observed. Changes in public willingness to report offenses or in police and court procedures can affect the volume and rate of recorded crime and delinquency. In addition, differences in public, police, and court response to crime and delinquency in different settings or among different categories of people can lead to differences in crime and delinquency statistics—differences that do not accurately reflect criminal and delinquent activity. Hence, the patterns outlined below can be given *several* interpretations and cannot be taken as conclusive statements of the "facts" about delinquent behavior in the United States.

Time

Crime and delinquency are generally viewed as *growing* social problems, getting worse year after year, and police statistics are typically cited in support of this observation. The major source of data on crime *over time* in the United States is the *Uniform Crime Reports.* The FBI's data on "crimes known to the police" are generally viewed as better than arrest statistics for assessing crime trends since they are not influenced by the contingencies affecting arrest. At the "crimes-known" level, the statistics merely refer to those incidents recognized by the police as crimes whether or not they are ever solved or ever result in an arrest. Because the age of the offender is not known, these statistics do not provide information specifically on crimes by juveniles. However, since male juveniles account for especially high proportions of some of these "crimes known to the police," these statistics are relevant to assessing trends in crimes commonly depicted as crimes of juveniles.

Figures 3–2 and 3–3 summarize crimes known to the police per 100,000 persons between 1933 and 1965. Rates for most crimes were declining or stable in the 1930s and early 1940s. Assault began climbing in the early to mid-1940s, as did burglary and larceny. Motor vehicle theft began its long upward climb in the early to mid-1950s. Robbery began a long upward trend in the late 1950s. Forcible rape increased gradually between 1933 and the early 1960s, after which it began to increase dramatically. Willful homicide rates were stable or declining during most of the years between 1933 and 1965 but started climbing in the mid-1960's.

Table 3–2 is reproduced from the annual report released by the FBI in 1978. It provides comparative data for 1977 and the preceding nine years. This table suggests either a leveling out or a decline of crime after 1975—a finding that is consistent with other data that we will summarize in Chapter 4. If we consider the crimes to which male juveniles make the most disproportionate contribution—the three property crimes (burglary, motor vehicle theft, and larceny) and robbery—we find that the rates in 1977 were lower than those in 1975 for all four offenses. In addition, the murder rate declined from its high of 9.8 per 100,000 persons in 1974 to 8.8 in 1977. Only the rates for forcible rape and assault were higher in 1977 than in the preceding two years. In sum, those crimes that have been most disproportionately common to juveniles (in terms of arrests) may have stabilized or even declined between 1975 and the late 1970s. Future data, however, may show this trend to be a temporary change. We do not know enough about the factors affecting these crime rates to make an accurate forecast of future rates.

FIGURE 3–2 *Index Crime Trends for Reported Crimes against
the Person, 1933–1965*

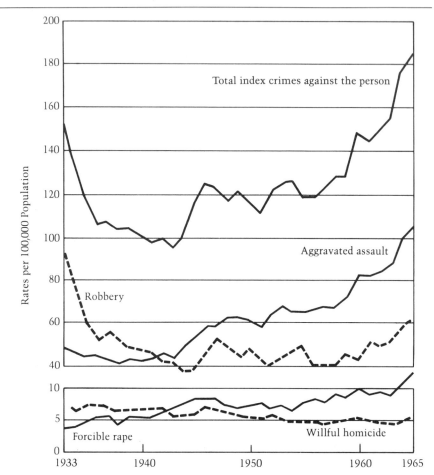

Source: President's Commission on Law Enforcement and Administration
of Justice. *Task Force Report: The Assessment of Crime,* p. 19.
Washington, D.C.: U.S. Government Printing Office, 1967.

In Table 3–3 we have summarized the changes in proportion of arrests
accounted for by males and females aged ten through seventeen between
1960 and 1968, between 1968 and 1973, and between 1973 and 1977, as
well as the changes in the proportion of the population accounted for by
those groups. Looking at Table 3–3, we see that between 1960 and 1968,
the proportion of the population made up of females ten through seventeen increased about 9 percent but that the proportion of arrests for which
they accounted increased between 31 percent for assault and 70 percent
for larceny. Between 1968 and 1973, the proportion of the population
made up of that age-sex group increased by around 3 percent, while
accounting for 9 to 59 percent greater proportion of arrests. Finally, for the

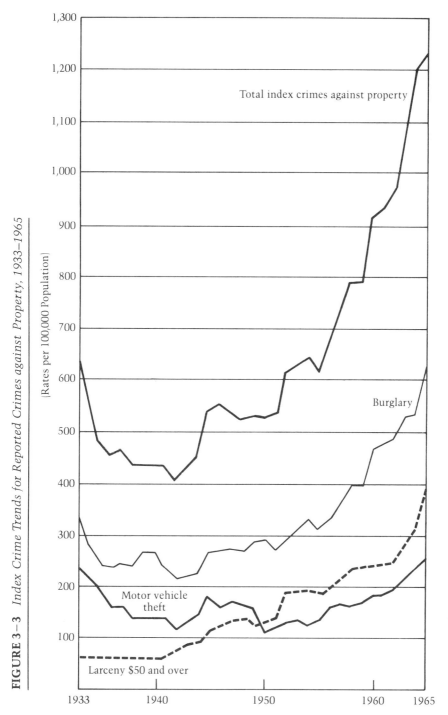

FIGURE 3–3 *Index Crime Trends for Reported Crimes against Property, 1933–1965*

(Rates per 100,000 Population)

Total index crimes against property

Burglary

Motor vehicle
theft

Larceny $50 and over

1933   1940   1950   1960   1965

Source: President's Commission on Law Enforcement and Administration of Justice. *Task Force Report: The Assessment of Crime,* p. 20. Washington, D.C.: U.S. Government Printing Office, 1967.

TABLE 3–2   *Index of Crime, 1968–1977 (Rate per 100,000 Inhabitants)*

Year	Crime Index Total	Violent[a] Crime	Property[a] Crime	Murder and Non-negligent Man-slaughter	Forcible Rape	Robbery	Aggra-vated Assault	Burglary	Larceny-Theft	Motor Vehicle Theft
1968	3,370.2	298.4	3,071.8	6.9	15.9	131.8	143.8	932.3	1,746.6	393.0
1969	3,680.0	328.7	3,351.3	7.3	18.5	148.4	154.5	984.1	1,930.9	436.2
1970	3,984.5	363.5	3,621.0	7.9	18.7	172.1	164.8	1,084.9	2,079.3	456.8
1971	4,164.7	396.0	3,768.8	8.6	20.5	188.0	178.8	1,163.5	2,145.5	459.8
1972	3,961.4	401.0	3,560.4	9.0	22.5	180.7	188.8	1,140.8	1,993.6	426.1
1973	4,154.4	417.4	3,737.0	9.4	24.5	183.1	200.5	1,222.5	2,071.9	442.6
1974	4,850.4	461.1	4,389.3	9.8	26.2	209.3	215.8	1,437.7	2,489.5	462.2
1975	5,281.7	481.5	4,800.2	9.6	26.3	218.2	227.4	1,525.9	2,804.8	469.4
1976	5,266.4	459.6	4,806.8	8.8	26.4	195.8	228.7	1,439.4	2,921.3	446.1
1977	5,055.1	466.6	4,588.4	8.8	29.1	187.1	241.5	1,410.9	2,729.9	447.6

Source: Federal Bureau of Investigation. *Crime in the United States*, Table 2. Washington, D.C.: U.S. Government Printing Office, 1977 (released October 1978).

Note: Crime rates calculated prior to rounding number of offenders.

[a]Violent crime includes offenses of murder, forcible rape, robbery, and aggravated assault. Property crime includes offenses of burglary, larceny-theft, and motor vehicle theft.

TABLE 3-3 *Changes in Proportion of Population and Arrests Accounted for by Males and Females Aged 10–17*

	% Change 1960–1968	% Change 1968–1973	% Change 1973–1977
Change in Proportion of Population Accounted for by Females	+ 9	+ 3	− 8
Change in Proportion of Population Accounted for by Males	+10	+ 2	− 8
Arrests of Females for Murder	+40	+29	0
Arrests of Males for Murder	+36	+ 5	− 9
Arrests of Females for Aggravated Assault	+31	+59	+ 4
Arrests of Males for Aggravated Assault	− 8	+48	+ 3
Arrests of Females for Robbery	+33	+25	+15
Arrests of Males for Robbery	+33	+ 2	− 5
Arrests of Females for Burglary	+64	+22	+32
Arrests of Males for Burglary	+26	−10	+ 4
Arrests of Females for Larceny (Theft)	+70	+20	+ 9
Arrests of Males for Larceny (Theft)	+ 6	−20	−10
Arrests of Females for Motor Vehicle Theft	+42	+ 9	+38
Arrests of Males for Motor Vehicle Theft	0	− 7	−10
Arrests of Males for Forcible Rape	+19	− 6	−10

period from 1973 through 1977, the proportion of the population consisting of females ten through seventeen actually fell off by around 8 percent, while they continued to account for an increasing proportion of every offense except murder. In sum, juvenile females have been accounting for a growing proportion of arrests, even though as a group they are still underrepresented in crime statistics.

While male juveniles are overrepresented for most of the FBI index crimes, their patterns of growth and decline are more complex than those of females. Between 1960 and 1968, males aged ten through seventeen grew as a proportion of the population by about 10 percent, but the proportion of murders, robberies, and burglaries for which they accounted increased between 26 and 36 percent. On the other hand, their contribution to arrests for aggravated assault, larceny, and motor vehicle theft did not keep pace with their increase as a segment of the United States population. Similarly, between 1968 and 1973, only in the categories of murder and aggravated assault did their increases outstrip their population growth. Their contribution to arrests for burglary, larceny, and motor vehicle theft actually declined. Beginning in 1973 with persons born during the post–World War II "baby boom" having reached adulthood, the proportion of the population made up of persons under eighteen began declining, with close to an 8 percent decline for both males and females. As noted above, female juveniles accounted for an increasing proportion of arrests despite this population decline. In contrast, the contribution of male juveniles to arrests decreased for murder (down 9 percent), larceny (down 10 percent), robbery (down 5 percent), and motor vehicle theft (down 10 percent). Arrests for aggravated assault and burglary increased despite the decline in "baby boom" youth as a segment of our population.

Thus, according to recent FBI reports, the stabilization of crime rates in the mid-1970s has been accompanied by some increases, some declines, and some instances of stability in the contribution of juveniles to arrest statistics. Juvenile females, although still underrepresented in arrest statistics, are accounting for a growing proportion of arrests for most index crimes, while juvenile males show a growing proportion of arrests for only two offenses.

Statistics for juvenile courts have also shown an increase in the rate at which these courts deal with delinquency cases (see Table 3–4). In 1957, with an estimated 22,173,000 persons ten through seventeen years of age, juvenile courts handled 440,000 cases which makes the rate about 20 cases per 1,000 juveniles. The rate hovered around 20 per 1,000 until 1962 when it started climbing. By the mid-1960s, it was around 25 per 1,000. The rate reached 30 per 1,000 by 1969 and 34 per 1,000 by 1971. The most recent year for which such statistics have been published (as of this writing) is 1974 when the rate was 37.5 per 1,000, or nearly double the 1957 rate. From the director of the National Center for Juvenile Justice, we have received unpublished information indicating a referral rate to the juvenile court system of 39.9 per 1,000 for 1975. However, consistent with the trend shown in FBI reports, forthcoming reports on juvenile court statistics supposedly show a leveling out or decline of referral rates in 1976 and 1977. That leveling out or decline may be a result of the national move to divert status offenders away from the juvenile justice system at the earliest possible stages (see Chapter 11). On the other hand, it may reflect a leveling out or decline of delinquency.

In considering the official statistics on juvenile delinquency and their changes over time, we should recognize that the rate may have been higher in the years before nationwide estimates were first compiled in the 1930s. It appears, for example, that the 1870s—the Reconstruction

TABLE 3-4 *Delinquency Cases Disposed of by Juvenile Courts,*
1957–1974

Year	Judicial		Nonjudicial	
	No.	%	No.	%
1957	239,000	54	201,000	46
1958	237,000	50	233,000	50
1959	250,000	52	233,000	48
1960	258,000	50	256,000	50
1961	257,000	51	246,000	49
1962	285,000	51	270,000	49
1963	298,000	50	303,000	50
1964	333,000	49	353,000	51
1965	327,000	47	370,000	53
1966	357,000	48	387,000	52
1967	382,100	47	428,900	53
1968	425,400	47	474,400	53
1969	433,300	44	555,200	56
1970	472,000	45	580,000	55
1971	475,000	42	650,000	58
1972	461,300	41	651,200	59
1973	522,000	46	621,700	54
1974	667,700	53	585,000	47

Source: National Center for Juvenile Justice. *Juvenile Court Statistics.*
Pittsburgh, Pa.: National Center for Juvenile Justice, 1974.

period of American history—may have been the most violent period in American history (National Commission on the Causes and Prevention of Violence, 1969). Even after the development of the *Uniform Crime Reports,* we find that the homicide rate in 1975 (9.7 per 100,000 population) was the same as in 1933 (9.6 per 100,000 population). The rate declined during the 1930s, leveled out in the late 1940s and 1950s at about 5 per 100,000 and began increasing in the early 1960s. A study of juvenile cases in an Ohio county found a rate of 66 per 100,000 in 1919, as compared to 21 in 1939 and 34 in 1957 (Teeters and Matza, 1959). Thus, juvenile court referral and arrest rates may have been higher at points in time when nationwide data were not available.

We should also note than an increase in the national delinquency rate does not mean that the rate is increasing in every jurisdiction and in every state. Increases in referral rates nationwide could be due to the expansion of juvenile referral facilities. Changes in police practices can also play a role in increasing referral and arrest rates. In a study of the processing of juveniles in two California communities—one with a "professional" police force and the other with a "fraternalistic" police force—James Wilson (1968) compared police contacts with juveniles that resulted in arrest. The "professional" force was one in which there were formally stated guidelines for handling cases, centralized control of the police, and close supervision and record keeping. On the other hand, the "fraternalistic" force was decentralized and had little supervision, few formally stated procedures, and little emphasis on record keeping. Of cases processed by the "professional" police force, 47 percent resulted in arrests or citations. Of cases processed by the "fraternalistic" department, 30 percent resulted in an arrest or citation. Thus, in the one jurisdiction there was a greater probability of a case resulting in arrest. As police jurisdictions move increasingly in the direction of the professional model, we would expect some increase in arrests because of changes in procedure. Similarly, as people move to urban centers with professionally run police departments, their behavior may become subject to a higher risk of official labeling. In contrast, the spread of programs designed to divert people away from the courts could have the opposite effect.

Changes at other points in the juvenile justice system can affect delinquency statistics as well. For example, in a study of delinquency statistics in Florida, Chilton and Spielberger (1971) found that a "meteoric" rise in delinquency in one county coincided with the construction of a new court building and increases in staff. If referral facilities do not exist, then police and the public may be more inclined to handle cases informally; inadequate facilities may have the same effect.

Space

Variation in delinquency rates from one area to another or in different areas of cities was the subject matter of the earliest sociological approaches to delinquency. As a result of studies begun in the 1920s, Clifford Shaw and Henry McKay (1942) observed that rates of officially recorded delinquency in the city of Chicago were characterized by a "gradient tendency," with the greatest rates occurring in the "transitional" (or "interstitial") zone surrounding the central business district. Successively lower rates occurred in areas more removed from that transitional zone. It did not appear that any unique property of particular racial or ethnic minorities accounted for such a gradient: the high-rate areas tended to remain high-rate areas even though different groups occupied the transitional zone over time. Thus, Shaw and McKay concluded that the causes of delinquency must be found in characteristics of communities and social settings:

> The high degree of consistency in the association between delinquency and other characteristics of the community not only sustains the conclusion that delinquent behavior is related dynamically to the community but also appears to establish that all community characteristics, including delinquency, are products of the operation of general processes more or less common to American cities. Moreover, the fact that in Chicago the rates of delinquents for many years have remained relatively constant in the areas adjacent to centers of commerce and heavy industry, despite successive changes in the nativity and nationality composition of the population,

> supports emphatically the conclusion that the delinquency-producing fac-
> tors are inherent in the community. (1942:435)

Of course, we must remember that official statistics reflect the behavior of victims and officials, as well as of offenders. Thus, variations by area of the city may reflect variations in reactions to delinquency, rather than variations in delinquent behavior.

Reporting on these same areas forty years later, McKay (1967) found that there had been a rather dramatic decline in delinquency rates in areas where the population had remained sufficiently stable to "make an adjustment to urban life." The areas of Chicago with the greatest decrease were the very areas that had had the highest rates in the early Chicago studies. The areas of the city characterized by increasing rates were areas that were experiencing the same sort of population changes and transitions associated with the high rates in the 1930s. Thus, the spatial distribution of officially recognized crime may change as the conditions associated with high rates change and redistribute themselves in different areas.

Other spatial patterns of interest to criminologists are the urban-rural difference and differences by community size. In 1977 in large metropolitan areas, which are defined as "standard metropolitan statistical areas" (SMSAs) by the Bureau of the Census, there were 12 times more robberies per 100,000 population reported to the police than in rural areas. There were 5 times more auto thefts reported, a 5.6 times greater larceny rate, a 2.4 times greater rape rate, 2.1 times more burglaries, 2.1 times more assaults, and 1.2 times more homicides. Similar patterns can be found in juvenile court statistics. For all courts reporting in 1971, there were 42 delinquency cases per 1,000 disposed of by juvenile courts in urban jurisdictions, as compared to 38 in semiurban courts and 21 in rural jurisdictions. However, the differences between rural jurisdictions and large cities seem to be declining. In 1967 the robbery rate was 30 times greater in SMSAs than in rural jurisdictions, as compared to 12 times greater in 1977. Overall, the rate of growth of "crimes known to the police" is greater in rural and suburban areas than in cities.

While there is a correlation between crime rates and such variables as city size and population density, several studies using official statistics have found that some small towns or rural areas have rates that are similar to or higher than those for more densely populated urban areas. For example, in his study of rural Oregon teenagers, Kenneth Polk (1974) found that his subjects got into trouble with the police just about as often as a similar cohort of urban boys in Philadelphia (Wolfgang, Figlio, and Sellin, 1972). Polk noted:

> In the days when the United States was primarily a country of farms and
> small towns, it was generally believed that teenage delinquency was
> almost entirely confined to cities. Even today many people think that

teenage boys who live outside metropolitan areas get into substantially less trouble than their city cousins, and that when they do, their scrapes are usually minor.

Perhaps surprisingly, studies made in recent years have shown that there is no basis for this common assumption—nonmetropolitan youth have just about as many run-ins with the law as metropolitan youths, and the causes of these confrontations are often of roughly equal seriousness in both towns and cities. (1974:1)

Sutherland and Cressey (1974:176–80) have observed that the crime rates in urban areas may be exceeded by crime rates in some types of rural or small-town settings. Crime rates appear to have been high in frontier cities, resort towns, and logging communities. Such communities may have developed what Sutherland and Cressey call "criminalistic traditions," resulting in their current crime rates being much greater than those of more densely populated, metropolitan settings.

Gender

Crime and delinquency are commonly thought of as male phenomena, and we have noted several times that FBI arrest statistics support such an image. In 1977 arrests of males under age eighteen for burglary exceeded juvenile female arrests by 15 times. For auto theft about 10 times more males were arrested. For robbery there were 11 times more males arrested. For murder, arrests of males under eighteen exceeded the rate for females under eighteen by about 12 times. For assault, the difference was about 6 to 1, while for larceny, males had nearly 3 times more arrests than females. Thus, the difference in arrests by sex is especially prominent for murder and the most serious property-oriented crimes and least prominent for less serious property-oriented crimes.

Juvenile court cases also disproportionately involve males, but this distinction is less prominent in recent statistics than it was during the 1950s and early 1960s. In 1957 male cases nationwide outnumbered female cases by about 4.4 times. By 1960 the ratio was 4 to 1. By 1965 it was 3.9 to 1, and by 1970 it was down to 3.2 to 1. During the 1970s the ratio reached 2.8 and has remained relatively constant at that level. This pattern is consistent with our computations of arrest rates for all offenses in the FBI reports. These computations suggest a decline in the overrepresentation of males relative to females from about 5.6 times higher an arrest rate for males to around 3.7 in the 1970s.

For *all* offenses taken together, female juveniles do not appear to be accounting for an ever increasing share of criminal and delinquent activities, as measured by arrests and referrals. On the other hand, if we consider only the FBI's *index crimes*, females exhibit impressive increases compared to males, particularly in the realm of major property crimes. For auto theft, burglary, and larceny, the disparities between male and female juvenile arrest rates in 1977 were less than half of what they had been in 1960. However, for murder and assault, females do not seem to be gaining on males.

Two particular types of offenses are often depicted as the domain of females—shoplifting and status offenses. For example, Edwin Schur (1969:177) noted that "women shoplifters greatly outnumber men." In *Sisters in Crime* (1975:89), Freda Adler expressed another common claim when she observed that "while boys tend to be arrested for offenses involving stealing and various sorts of mischief, girls are typically charged with sex offenses which are euphemistically described as 'delinquent tendencies,' 'incorrigibility,' or 'running away.'"

It is important, however, to recognize that several different ways of looking at male and female delinquency can shape our image of gender differences. For example, we can consider the *types of offenses* that bring female, as compared to male, offenders into police or court statistics. Table 3–5 summarizes the reasons for which both males and females appeared in a juvenile court. The table supports several observations concerning court referrals of juvenile females. A greater proportion of female referrals than male referrals were for such offenses as "runaway," "incorrigibility," and situations involving "health, welfare, and morals." Incorrigibility was not even among the ten most frequent offenses for males and, thus, was not included as a category for males in Table 3–5. In addition, a greater proportion of the female referrals were for shoplifting. The pattern of offenses for male offenders appeared more differentiated and varied than for female offenders.

However, looking only at the *proportions* of cases involving particular offenses can be misleading. For example, it would be easy to jump to the conclusion that the juvenile female population in the jurisdiction described in Table 3–5 had a higher court referral *rate* for shoplifting than juvenile males. This conclusion would be wrong. Examining Table 3–5 once again, we find that there were 834 referrals of males for shoplifting and 681 referrals of females. Similarly, there were 135 referrals of females for incorrigibility. Although the table does not include incorrigibility as a category for males, 229 males were referred for incorrigibility. In sum, there are more male cases of shoplifting and incorrigibility than are female cases. Thus, the data do not show females to have unusually high rates for these offenses as compared to those of males. What they do show is that females are referred so infrequently for other offenses (for example, 1,086 male burglaries as compared to 77 female burglaries) that juvenile or status offenses stand out as exceptions to the general pattern. The 681 cases of female shoplifting constitute nearly one-fourth of female offenses. Thus, shoplifting stands out in relation to females *not* because of a greater incidence of females being processed through the system as shoplifters, but because females are so unlikely to appear in court statistics for the wider range of offenses dominated by males.

TABLE 3-5   *Ten Most Frequent Offenses, by Sex*

Juvenile Males

Rank	Offense	% of All Offenses	No. of Offenses
1	Burglary	13.4	1,086
2	Runaway	11.0	888
3	Larceny: except shoplifting	10.6	858
4	Shoplifting	10.3	834
5	Malicious mischief	6.0	482
6	Dangerous drugs: marijuana	5.5	443
7	Liquor offenses	4.9	396
8	Trespassing	3.7	296
9	Health, welfare, morals (includes suicide)	3.3	270
10	Simple assault	3.2	262

Juvenile Females

Rank	Offense	% of All Offenses	No. of Offenses
1	Runaway	35.9	995
2	Shoplifting	24.6	681
3	Health, welfare, morals (includes suicide)	6.1	169
4	Incorrigible	4.9	135
5	Dangerous drugs: marijuana	3.2	89
6	Liquor offenses	3.0	84
7	Larceny: except shoplifting	2.9	80
8	Burglary	2.8	77
9	Simple assault	2.5	70
10	Malicious mischief	2.1	58

Source: Pima County Juvenile Court. *Pima County Juvenile Court Statistics, Annual Report,* p. 20. Tucson, Ariz.: Pima County Juvenile Court Center, 1975.

Race and Ethnicity

If asked what racial or ethnic category has the highest arrest rate, most people would answer that black Americans have the highest rates. However, arrest statistics in the *Uniform Crime Reports* show that the American Indian arrest rate for total offenses is higher than the rates for black, white, or Asian Americans (Jensen, Stauss, and Harris, 1977). However, this distinction is due primarily to alcohol-related offenses, which account for a large proportion of the total. For crimes against persons and property, the black rate exceeds the Indian rate in urban jurisdictions, while the Indian rate exceeds the black rate in rural jurisdictions. On the other hand, for alcohol-related offenses (driving under the influence, liquor law violations, and drunkenness), the Indian arrest rate exceeds the rates for blacks in both urban and rural jurisdictions. This overrepresentation occurs for both juveniles and adults and is supported by arrest data from Indian reservations with their own Indian police forces. In sum, FBI data on four racial or ethnic categories show Indian Americans to have the highest total rate, with black Americans second, white Americans third, and Asian Americans fourth.

At best, juvenile court reports provide only a breakdown for blacks, whites, and Mexican Americans. Searches of police and court data in several large cities show a higher rate of recorded conflict with the law for blacks than for whites. For example, in their study of nearly ten thousand males in the city of Philadelphia, Wolfgang, Figlio, and Sellin (1972) found that 35 percent of whites and 50 percent of blacks had acquired records by their eighteenth birthdays. A study in the San Francisco Bay area (Hirschi, 1969) found that 51 percent of the black adolescent males in their sample had police records, in comparison to 26 percent of the nonblacks. In Seattle another study (Nagasawa, 1965) found that 36 percent of the black subjects had been arrested, as compared to 11 percent of whites and only 2 percent of Japanese.

While several studies of arrest and referral data consistently depict high rates for Indian and black Americans and low rates for Asian Americans, few reports focus on the rates of Mexican Americans. One study in San Antonio, Texas, (Garcia and Weaver, 1975) found that the arrest rate for Chicano youth in 1973 was about 28 offenses per 10,000 as compared to 20 for Anglo youth and 58 for black youth. Juvenile court data summarized in Table 3–6 show the Chicano court referral rates in Pima County, Arizona, to be lower than rates for blacks and all other (non-Chicano, nonblack) youth. Another study (Shannon, 1978) has shown that among youths born in 1949 in Racine, Wisconsin, black males have a police contact rate over four times greater than whites, with Chicano males appearing in such statistics more than twice as often as whites. Although the scarcity of research on America's second largest minority group prevents firm conclusions, we are fairly safe in positing that the Chicano delinquency rate is lower than the black rate. The comparison with the white rate may vary in different settings and among Mexican Americans with different regional histories.

TABLE 3–6 *Referral Rates to Pima County Juvenile Court, 1972, by Sex and Ethnic Status*

	Male	Female
Chicano	38.6	14.5
Black	87.1	43.3
Other[a]	58.8	34.2
Total	53.6	28.3

Note: Rate is number of children referred to juvenile court in 1973 per 1,000 population under 18 in each category according to the 1970 census.

[a] Other is total minus Chicano and black.

Age

National crime statistics have persistently depicted the crime problem as a problem of the young. In fact, the overrepresentation of the young is so taken for granted that some sociologists identify the "peak" of crime in adolescence as a major theoretical issue in criminology (Glaser, 1978). But *does* crime peak in adolescence? *Are* the young overrepresented? To answer such questions, we have to consider what is meant by such terms as *crime, peak, adolescence,* and the *young.* In Figures 3–4 and 3–5 we have plotted the arrest rates for index crimes for each specific age category reported on in the FBI crime statistics, as well as the peak age of persons arrested. Thus, for murder, rape, and assault, the peak age is twenty-one and the average age between twenty-four (for rape) and twenty-nine (for murder). For property-oriented offenses, the averages and peaks occur at younger ages, with arrest rates for burglary, larceny, and motor vehicle theft peaking at age sixteen and robbery peaking at age seventeen. The average age for arrests for burglary was nineteen years, for motor vehicle theft twenty years, and for larceny and robbery twenty-two years. In short, according to FBI statistics, only some offenses peak in the preadult years. Others peak among young adults.

Of all thirty-two types of offenses for which arrest data are provided in the *Uniform Crime Reports,* thirteen peak in the under-eighteen age category. Two of those thirteen (runaway and curfew violations) are status offenses encompassing behavior that is only illegal for juveniles. The

FIGURE 3–4   *Arrest Rates for Crimes against Persons, by Age*

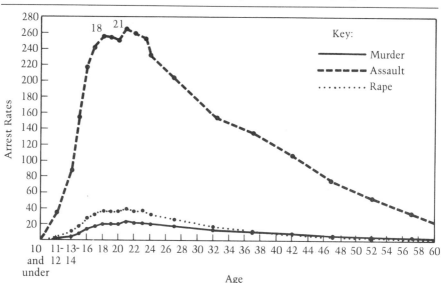

Source: Data from 1977 *Uniform Crime Reports* and Bureau of Census population estimates for 1977.

FIGURE 3–5 *Arrest Rates for Property-Oriented Crimes, by Age*

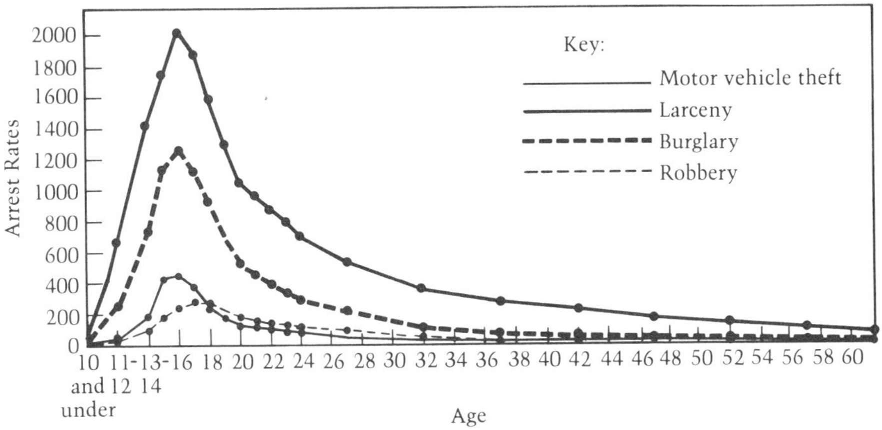

Source: Data from 1977 *Uniform Crime Reports* and Bureau of Census population estimates for 1977.

other nineteen offenses peak among adults. Table 3–7 indicates the ages at which the arrest rate for offenses of different types peak. In general, crimes involving elements of interpersonal conflict or sex peak at age twenty-one. Crimes against property tend to peak in the teenage years. Drug violations peak at age eighteen. Offenses involving drinking begin peaking at age seventeen with the violation of liquor laws. Other alcohol-related offenses peak among young adults (twenty-one to twenty-two). In the United States age twenty-one has historically been imbued with special sociological significance, and it is that age which constitutes the peak age for arrest for more types of crime than any other.

TABLE 3–7 *Peak Ages for Various Offenses*

Age	Offense
15	Arson, vandalism, runaway
16	Burglary, larceny, motor vehicle theft
17	Robbery, embezzlement, receiving stolen goods, liquor law violations
18	Illegal weapons, drug abuse, disorderly conduct, suspicion
19	Negligent manslaughter, "all other offenses" [a]
21	Murder and nonnegligent manslaughter, forcible rape, aggravated assault, other assaults, forgery, prostitution, sex offenses, driving under the influence
22	Offenses against family, drunkenness, vagrancy
24	Fraud
40–44	Gambling

Source: Data from 1977 *Uniform Crime Reports* and Bureau of Census population estimates for 1977.

[a] "All other" means all offenses other than the ones listed in the table.

Social Status and Social Class

Popular stereotypes, as well as scholarly works, have depicted delinquency (or, at a minimum, the most serious forms of delinquency) as a problem of "lower- or working-class" youth. However, while the *Uniform Crime Reports* provides breakdowns by race, sex, age, and community setting, it provides no nationwide data on crime by social class.

Even sociologists, who are most familiar with the concepts of social status and class, have been unable to agree on their meaning or measurement. For example, Richard Centers (1949) argued that the terms *social class* and *social status* are not synonymous. He maintained that a social class is subjective in character and emerges from a feeling of group membership or class consciousness. As such, "class" is a psychological phenomenon and may not necessarily conform to objective lines of cleavage, such as income, occupation, or education. In contrast, the concept of social status *is* based on objective criteria, including income, occupation, education, and place of residence. For ease of discussion, we will use the terms *social class* and *social status* interchangeably here.

Even if we agree that income is relevant to the measurement of social class, we still have problems of setting boundaries. What amount of money shall we establish as the maximum that a lower-class person can earn? The federal guidelines for poverty programs stipulate that the "poverty level" in the United States in 1978 for nonfarm residents is a yearly income of $2,800 or less for a single person and $5,500 for a family of four. For farm residents the poverty level is set at $2,400 for a single person and $4,680 for a family of four. Thus, if we use poverty level criteria to define social class, we would place approximately 10 percent of all families in the lowest category and somehow divide the other 90 percent between middle and upper classes.

Creating the boundaries for the middle class becomes even more problematic because both a ceiling and a threshold must be established. With the driving rate of inflation, reflected particularly in such basic needs as housing, food, and transportation, many middle-class families are experiencing the financial plight of lower-class families. Moreover, inflation makes it difficult to specify what income levels "middle class" should represent. Finally, the upper-class category is the most illusory of all because it incorporates moderately successful business persons or professionals earning upwards of $25,000 per year, as well as heads of corporations, eminently successful medical specialists, and popular entertainers whose earnings exceed $250,000.

Although there is no single recognized standard for measuring social class or social status, numerous studies relate indexes of parental income, education, and occupation to officially recorded crime and delinquency. A recent review of twenty-three such studies (Tittle and Villemez, 1977) reported that 65 percent of them found that crime or delinquency was

TABLE 3-8 *Delinquency by Social Class*

| | Social-Class Position | | | |
| | White-Collar | | Blue-Collar | |
Delinquency Status	No.	%	No.	%
Delinquent	81	16	80	17
Nondelinquent	441	84	386	83
Totals	522	100	466	100
Important delinquency	22	35	24	37
Nonimportant delinquency	41	65	41	63
Totals	63	100	65	100
One delinquency	53	65	51	64
Two or more delinquencies	28	35	29	36
Totals	81	100	80	100

Source: Dean E. Frease. "Delinquency, Social Class and the Schools."
Sociology and Social Research 57 (July 1973):445–46.

disproportionately common among persons categorized as of low status or class but that the differences between classes were not very great.

Table 3–8 summarizes the findings from a study that compared the delinquency status of sons of "blue-collar" and "white-collar" fathers (Frease, 1973). This study, which involved over 1,000 high school students in Marion County, Oregon, in 1964, could find no significant differences between the two groups in juvenile court referrals, referrals for serious offenses, or number of referrals. Similarly, a study based on a national survey of 847 teenagers, thirteen to sixteen years old, found: (1) a "negligible" relationship between social status and police contacts among both males and females, and (2) a significant relationship between social status and a police record only among white girls (Williams and Gold, 1972).

In contrast, the study of all boys born in Philadelphia in 1945 that we mentioned earlier (Wolfgang, Figlio, and Sellin, 1972) found that among both blacks and whites, boys of lower "socioeconomic status" (SES) had: (1) a greater likelihood of having acquired a delinquent record, (2) a greater likelihood of having committed more than one offense, and (3) a tendency to commit more serious offenses. The differences between SES categories were not huge. For example, 36 percent of the whites of lower SES had delinquent records by the time they were eighteen, as compared to 26 percent of the whites of higher SES. For blacks the comparable perentages were 53 percent and 36 percent. A study of official statistics in the San Francisco Bay area (Hirschi, 1969:74–75) reported similar results: The average number of officially recorded offenses for high school students of lower status was greater than the average number for students of higher social standing.

In sum, we can neither state that there is a definite relationship between social class or status and officially recorded delinquency nor can we claim that there is no such relationship. There are studies to support both conclusions. A recent review of the literature on the topic by Charles Tittle, Wayne Villemez, and Douglas Smith (1978) suggested the rather qualified conclusion that there is a *slightly disproportionate tendency* for youths of lower status to appear in police and court records more often than youths of higher status. However, it appears that studies done before 1950 were more likely to find a relationship between social class and criminality than were subsequent studies, with studies in the 1970s reporting the weakest association of all. While such change in observed relationships may reflect the use of different types of statistics, different samples, or other characteristics of research that can account for change over time, Tittle, Villemez, and Smith also noted that social class may have been more significant in differentiating among people in earlier decades than in more recent times. We have noted signs of convergence between males and females and between people living in rural and urban settings; it is conceivable that social class differences may be declining over the years as well.

DISCRIMINATION, STATISTICS, AND DELINQUENCY

Many critics of the system of justice in the United States vociferously argue that the lower classes and minority groups are sanctioned more frequently and more severely than middle- or upper-class white Americans and that their overrepresentation in statistics on crime and delinquency reflects enduring prejudice and discrimination. For many people, it is a foregone conclusion that black, Chicano, Puerto Rican, and other readily identifiable minority groups are harassed and intimidated by the police and that serious miscarriages of justice are inflicted upon the poor. While the rhetoric on this subject is hot and prolific, the scientific evidence to date supporting one side or another yields no consistent conclusion. To be sure, minority groups have suffered grave injustices in American society, but to what degree the biases of the police, courts, and prisons contribute to their plight is not clear. We should not gloss over allegations that racial, ethnic, or class considerations enter into the processing of criminal or juvenile delinquency cases, but we should recognize that the evidence concerning these allegations is more complex than is generally assumed.

Data from the *Uniform Crime Reports* (Federal Bureau of Investigation, 1975) on police disposition of cases show that the police refer about

53 percent of juvenile offenders to a juvenile court and a very small percentage to welfare agencies (1.4 percent), other police agencies (1.9 percent), or adult courts (2.3 percent). The remainder, about 42 percent, are handled by police departments and then released. Police and the courts are obviously making decisions and exercising discretion and, in that sense, are "discriminating" among juveniles in the processing of offenders. Moreover, the basic philosophy of juvenile justice has been that the disposition or treatment of a case *should* vary depending on factors other than the specific legalities of the case—factors such as the nature of the offense and a suspect's offense history. The juvenile court is *supposed* to take a juvenile's background and home life into account.

The controversy concerning discrimination centers around *acceptable* criteria for the differential processing of cases. The most vociferous attention has been devoted to discrimination on the basis of race, but there has been increasing concern over the influence of social class, gender, age, and other attributes on decision making. There are no easy answers to questions about what criteria should be used in the disposition of cases. For example, coming from a broken home may affect a juvenile court disposition, and the way a youth interacts with the police—his or her "demeanor"—may make a difference for the probability of arrest. To the police and the court, such considerations may seem completely legitimate, while to others they may appear completely arbitrary and "unfair." That the law should treat girls differently than boys may seem mandatory to some and totally discriminatory to others. In the United States today, the word *discrimination* implies differential treatment of people on the basis of characteristics that have been deemed irrelevant to differentiation by law or by vocal special-interest groups. Our review of discrimination against juveniles will concentrate on three particular background characteristics that have been studied in the context of unfair bias—race, social class, and gender. Having already examined police and court statistics pertaining to these groups, our question now is to what degree the patterns observed are a result of biases for and against certain juveniles in official labeling. To what degree are police and court statistics a reflection of differential legal response to different categories of people?

Differential Treatment by Race

Nathan Goldman (1963) conducted a study on police decisions to refer apprehended juvenile delinquents to court in Allegheny County, Pennsylvania, in the late 1940s. Goldman's study did point toward racial bias in processing. He found that in contrast to the 65 percent of black juveniles who were referred to court, only 34 percent of white juveniles were referred. Although for more serious offenses there was no evidence of a race differential, black offenders were more likely to be referred to juvenile court for minor offenses, such as property damage, status offenses, and malicious mischief.

Similarly, in tracking boys in Philadelphia who were ten years of age in 1955 until they were eighteen, Terence Thornberry (1973) found significant racial differences in processing. Seriousness of the offense was positively related to severity of disposition by the police, court intake procedures, and final disposition by the juvenile court. However, even with seriousness of the offense and prior juvenile record taken into account, racial differences were still very apparent. A greater proportion of black youths than whites were sent to court and more were committed to institutions.

Theodore Ferdinand and Elmer Luchterhand (1970), using a random sample of 1,525 teenagers in six inner-city neighborhoods in a city they called "Easton," found that black youths who were first offenders were referred to the juvenile court disproportionately more often than their white counterparts. The harsher dispositions received by black youths could not be explained as a result of type of offense, age, or gender. Although Ferdinand and Luchterhand concluded that black offenders in general are not more antisocial or more aggressive than white offenders, they did find evidence that black youths are more rejecting of public authority. That factor might have precipitated a greater number of police arrests.

Irving Piliavin and Scott Briar (1964) examined juvenile encounters with the police and found that the police had a wide latitude of discretion in dealing with minor offenses. Approximately 10 percent of the offenses were serious crimes, such as robbery, aggravated assault, rape, and auto theft, and these cases were dealt with uniformly for black and white youth. However, in the other 90 percent of police encounters in which the infractions involved minor offenses, the police searched for "clues" to the personal character of the offender, defining some offenders as "good boys" and others as "bad boys." The character assessment made a difference for whether the disposition was an arrest, informal reprimand, or outright release. Thus, in addition to previous record, the youth's demeanor affected the probability of arrest. When the youth's demeanor was assessed as being uncooperative, the probability of an arrest was extremely high. On the other hand, when a youth was seen as a cooperative "good guy," he was very likely released. Black youths were typically seen as "would-be tough guys," or "punks," who fully deserved the sanction of arrest because of their hostile demeanor toward the police. Piliavin and Briar noted that police routinely patrol the inner-city areas to a greater extent than other areas. What may result from that action is a vicious cycle of patrol activities producing resentment, leading to low respect for the police, and ultimately culminating in higher arrest rates.

There is not only considerable evidence that young blacks are less likely to respect the police than are other categories of people (Wilson, 1975:111–16), but there is also evidence that such attitudes may account for a higher risk of arrest. In his research on the social organization of arrest, Donald Black (1971) found that a black youth had a higher probability of being arrested than a white youth. However, Black found that this difference reflected the suspect's conduct in interacting with the police. Rather than responding specifically to race, the police appear to respond to indications of disrespect, which are in turn associated with race. The end result may be the same (that is, higher arrest rates for blacks), but the interpretation is different (that is, the police respond more severely to hostile suspects, whether black or white, and more blacks are hostile toward police).

While the studies mentioned above suggest racial bias, other studies indicate essentially legalistic treatment of juveniles regardless of race. Norman Weiner and Charles Willie (1971) examined decision making by juvenile officers of specialized youth bureaus in Washington, D.C., and Syracuse, New York. Although the police contact rate was greater for areas of lower social status within each city, the ratio of court referrals for blacks and whites did not vary markedly within residential areas. Weiner and Willie hypothesized that whereas the "cops on the beat" may exercise their own racial biases, specialized juvenile officers function in a different institutional environment with different expectations, which results in relatively unbiased arrest and referral decisions. Similarly, in examining the cases of over nine thousand juveniles who came into contact with the police in Racine, Wisconsin, Robert Terry (1967) found that seriousness of the offense and the number of prior offenses accounted for differences in arrest by race and socioeconomic status. Terry found no evidence of racial or ethnic discrimination by the police.

The observational studies of police interaction with the public have introduced some interesting new considerations for understanding the differential risks in official processing. For example, a study by Black and Reiss (1970) delineated the social circumstances surrounding an arrest and showed the probability of a juvenile arrest to be very low: Only about 15 percent of contacts with juvenile suspects resulted in an arrest. However, the probability of arrest was found to increase with the legal seriousness of the juvenile's offense. This finding may appear to be a fairly obvious point, but it tends to be discarded far too quickly when arrest statistics reflect a racial bias. Black and Reiss also found that the presence of a complainant greatly enhanced the chances of a black youth's being arrested. When the police officer acted on his own initiative without the presence of a complainant, the black-white arrest rates were quite similar: 14 percent of black youths and 10 percent of white youths were arrested. However, when a complainant participated in the arrest process, the differentials were considerably greater—21 percent for black youths and only 8 percent for white youths. Thus, the presence of a complainant greatly increased the probability of an arrest for a black youth. Moreover, black complainants were more likely than white complainants to press for police action.

Yet another study has suggested that the organization of police departments can play a major role in facilitating or inhibiting arbitrary discretion against black juveniles. James Q. Wilson (1968) examined the police departments in two California cities, which he called "Western City" and "Eastern City." "Western City" had a highly bureaucratic, "professionalized" police department, while "Eastern City" had an informal, "fraternal" police department. The standards and procedures in Western City resulted in the recruitment of officers who were better educated, less moralistic, and more rule-oriented than officers in Eastern City. The difference in organizational milieu was associated with dramatically different results in the handling of juveniles. Western City processed more than twice as many juvenile offenders as Eastern city, indicating that the greater the aura of professionalism and formalized structure, the greater the arrest rate and the less discretion in the field by the police officer. On the other hand, in Eastern City where the police force was highly decentralized and the opportunity for police discretion much greater, discriminatory arrest practices were apparent. Wilson found that in Eastern City approximately three times as many blacks as whites were taken to court, whereas in Western City the black-white differentials were very small.

Differential Treatment by Social Class

In our review of the relationship between social class and police and court records of delinquency, we noted that several studies found no relationship between social class and the probability of appearing in police or court statistics. We also noted that in those studies that did find differences, the differences reported were generally small. Nevertheless, since nearly two-thirds of the studies did report some differences by social class, the issue of discrimination by class merits our consideration.

The situation involving bias by social class is as complex as that involving race. Terry (1967) found no class differences when prior offense record and seriousness of offense were taken into account. Arnold (1971) reported racial bias but no class differences in the southern city he studied. In contrast, Thornberry (1973) found racial differences in the severity of treatment, as well as harsher treatment of lower-class males.

In an attempt to resolve such inconsistencies, Lawrence Cohen and James Kluegel (1978) studied the dispositions of juvenile cases in Denver and Memphis. Since these two jurisdictions differed in regional location and operating philosophies, the researchers felt that the comparison might yield different findings concerning bias. However, they concluded that their analysis "uncovered no evidence of race or class bias" working to the disadvantage of minority youth or youth from low-income families. In fact, they found that the effect of parental income was contrary to common predictions. Although the differences were small, Cohen and Kluegel's findings showed that the higher the income of a youth's parents, the more severe the treatment. In keeping with most research findings, the nature of the offense and the existence of a previous record were found to be the major determinants of dispositions. Cohen and Kluegel concluded that their findings challenge the view that racial bias and class discrimination "permeate the juvenile justice system" (1978:174).

Differential Treatment by Gender

Most of the research on discrimination or bias in law enforcement has concentrated on the effects of race and social class among males. Information about the treatment of females vis-à-vis that of males is relatively scarce. However, there are strongly stated claims that females receive lenient treatment, as well as strong claims that treatment for females is harsher than for males. One of the classic works on female criminality is Otto Pollak's book *The Criminality of Women* (1950). Pollak challenged the assumption that women commit fewer crimes than men, arguing that the crime rate is lower for women because (1) the types of offenses they commit go unreported (for example, shoplifting); (2) their roles allow crimes to go undetected (for example, poisoning); and (3) they are treated more protectively by the criminal justice system.

Rita Simon (1975) noted that an alternative to the preferential treatment model is the view that women receive more punitive treatment than males because their criminal behavior is more "out of line" with social expectations than male crime. In other words, involvement in crime and delinquency is a greater departure from ideals of how a woman *should* act than it is from ideals of how a man should act. If we were to accept this hypothesis, we would assume that girls who violate the law and are caught receive harsher treatment than their male counterparts.

On examining data on the conviction of *adult* female offenders, Simon found some support for the argument that females receive preferential treatment. She concluded that "women as recently as 1972 seem to be receiving some preferential treatment at the bar of justice" (1975:67). On the other hand, a report by the Female Offender Resource Center (1977) cited evidence of discriminatory treatment of female *juveniles* when they are arrested. This report noted that female status offenders were more likely to be confined than male status offenders and that a disproportionate number were sent to training schools.

In his study of discrimination in the handling of juvenile offenders, Terry (1967) reported that the police released 85 percent of the females and 90 percent of the males. The biggest disparity in release rates stemmed from the fact that police referred about 7 percent of the females to social or welfare agencies, rather than releasing them outright. In general, boys who were not released were referred to the county probation department; they were rarely (0.8 percent) referred to social or welfare agencies. Over 70 percent of referrals to such agencies were for status offenses; hence, female offenders had a lesser chance of outright release because of the inclination of police to refer female status offenders to social and welfare agencies.

Terry found that a greater proportion of males than females was referred to juvenile court or criminal court by the probation department, largely because the males' offenses were more serious. On the other hand, once a female reached the point of a juvenile court disposition, her chances of being committed to an institution of some kind were actually greater than a male's chances. Terry reported that females were more likely to be severely sanctioned than males even though males had more extensive previous records. One of the reasons for such severity was found to be the harsh punishment given for offenses concerning relations with the opposite sex and involvements with adult offenders, both of which were more common among female juvenile offenders than among males.

Other studies have also suggested differential treatment of some female offenders as compared to that accorded their male counterparts. For instance, in a study of police dispositions in Philadelphia, Thomas Monahan (1970) found that police treated girls somewhat more leniently than boys in cases involving acts that would be criminal for adults, but more harshly when sexual offenses were involved. In a similar study in Honolulu, Meda Chesney-Lind (1974) found that girls accused of their first status offense were actually more likely to be referred to the juvenile court than other girls charged with their first criminal offense. In a study using Los Angeles police records, A. W. McEachern and Reva Bauzer (1967) observed that in cases involving what they called "juvenile offenses," boys were less likely than girls to have petitions requested (comparable to having charges filed) but were more likely to have them requested in cases involving acts that would be crimes if committed by adults.

SUMMARY

Proclamations about the problem of juvenile delinquency typically cite a body of "facts" about youth crime or "facts" about delinquency. It is more appropriate to discuss "images" of delinquency since there are multiple sources of information that may or may not yield divergent observations. Many criminologists have questioned whether police and court statistics can give us the real or true facts about delinquency in that these statistics are the outcome of numerous behaviors and decisions by the public and by agents of the law. Thus, such data are affected by a wide range of factors other than the behavior of juveniles. Whether an event is recorded as a crime is a product of both public and police action and the interaction between the two. Whether suspects become statistics as criminals or delinquents depends on such contingencies as the offense committed, offense history, complainant preference, and the way suspects and complainants interact with the police. Despite these complexities, the image of delinquency suggested by police and court data is in many ways consistent with public stereotypes. However, when we examine this image in detail, we encounter numerous qualifications. The major observations suggested by the research and statistics examined in this chapter, together with important qualifications, are summarized below:

1. Crime and delinquency as recorded in police and court statistics have been increasing in the last several decades, *but* there is evidence that the rates may have been much higher before the collection of statistics nationwide. In addition, FBI data suggest a leveling off of reported crime in the mid-1970s. We do not know whether this is a temporary trend or the beginning of a stabilized or declining crime rate.

2. For several decades, juveniles have accounted for a growing proportion of arrests in national crime data, *but* the proportionate contribution of males under eighteen may have stabilized or declined for some offense categories in the mid-1970s, while the contribution of females under eighteen to major property crimes continued to grow.

3. Rates of crime and delinquency appear to be high in areas experiencing population changes and transitions, and in cities as compared to rural settings, *but* the differences between rural and urban settings appear to be declining. Moreover, many small towns and nonmetropolitan areas have rates greater than or comparable to those of large metropolitan communities.

4. Males are more likely than females to appear in arrest and court statistics, *but* the disparity was much greater in past decades than it is now; the disparity is not as great for shoplifting and status offenses as for more serious offenses; and females actually outnumber males for some status offenses, such as running away from home.

5. Persons aged ten through seventeen are disproportionately represented in arrests for the FBI's "serious" offenses, *but* the highest arrest rates for persons under eighteen are for crimes against property; crimes involving interpersonal conflict and violence tend to

peak in the young adults years; and arrests rates for more offense categories peak at age twenty-one than at any other age.

6. Of those racial categories used by the FBI, Indian Americans have the highest overall arrest rate, followed in order by blacks, whites, and Asian Americans, *but* in urban jurisdictions blacks have higher rates for crimes against persons and property. Moreover, the high Indian rate relative to blacks is most distinct in arrests for alcohol-related offenses.

7. Lower-class youths disproportionately contribute to police and court statistics, *but* numerous studies have found no relationship between social class and officially recorded delinquency. In studies that have noted such a relationship, the differences observed were small. Moreover, there is some indication that the relationship between social class and delinquency may have been greater in earlier decades than in the 1960s and 1970s.

8. No simple conclusion can be reached concerning discrimination against black American youth by police and courts. There is evidence that differentials in arrest and processing are generated by the seriousness of the offense committed and the offense history of the suspect; by the preferences of complainants who, if black, are more likely to press for police action; and by the nature of the suspect's interaction with police. Several studies have indicated greater risks of arrest and more severe dispositions for blacks than whites even when prior record and nature of the offense are taken into account.

9. Studies of the processing of lower-class youths suggest that legal criteria (offense seriousness and prior record) explain disproportionate representations in police and court statistics, *but* as observed above, there is not always a disproportionate representation to explain.

10. Females may receive either preferential or harsher treatment than males, depending on the offense. Males appear to be treated more severely than females for offenses that are crimes for adults, *but* this differential has been found to reflect the more serious nature of male offenses. On the other hand, females are treated more severely than males for noncriminal or status offenses involving sexual relations even when prior record is taken into account.

The tendency of social scientists to "qualify everything" is upsetting to politicians, students, and the general public. People like simple, direct, unambiguous, and straightforward answers. One of the authors of this book was once interviewed for a local news program and asked: "Why is the crime rate increasing?" The answer was supposed to fit in a twenty-second spot on the six o'clock news. Such questions cannot and, we would argue, *should not* be answered in twenty seconds. The observations and qualifications that we have made in this chapter may have to be revised on the basis of further evidence and challenges by other criminologists. We have attempted to simplify a wealth of complex data and to provide the type of supporting detail that a questioning student should demand of anyone who makes observations about delinquency. When such detail is provided, we learn something new and end up with observations that often challenge everyday beliefs and proclamations about juvenile delinquency.

REFERENCES

Adler, F. 1975. *Sisters in Crime.* New York: McGraw-Hill.

Arnold, W. R. 1971. "Race and Ethnicity relative to Other Factors in Juvenile Court Dispositions." *American Journal of Sociology* 77 (September):211–17.

Black, D. J. 1970. "Production of Crime Rates." *American Sociological Review* 35 (August):733–48.

———. 1971. "The Social Organization of Arrest." *Stanford Law Review* 23 (June):1087–111.

Black, D. J., and A. J. Reiss, Jr. 1970. "Police Control of Juveniles." *American Sociological Review* 35 (February):63–77.

Centers, R. 1949. *The Psychology of Social Class.* Princeton, N.J.: Princeton University Press.

Chesney-Lind, M. 1974. "Juvenile Delinquency: The Sexualization of Female Crime." *Psychology Today* (July):44–46.

Chilton, R., and A. Spielberger. 1971. "Is Delinquency Increasing? Age Structure and the Crime Rate." *Social Forces* 47:487–93.

Cohen, L. E., and J. E. Kluegel. 1978. "Determinants of Juvenile Court Dispositions: Ascriptive and Achieved Factors in Two Metropolitan Courts." *American Sociological Review* 43 (April):162–76.

Federal Bureau of Investigation. 1975. *Crime in the United States.* Washington, D.C.: U.S. Government Printing Office.

———. 1977. *Crime in the United States.* Washington, D.C.: U.S. Government Printing Office.

Female Offender Resource Center. 1977. *Little Sisters and the Law.* Washington, D.C.: American Bar Association.

Ferdinand, T. N., and E. G. Luchterhand. 1970. "Inner-City Youths, the Police, the Juvenile Court, and Justice." *Social Problems* 17 (Spring):510–27.

Frease, D. E. 1973. "Delinquency, Social Class, and the Schools." *Sociology and Social Research* 57 (July):443–59.

García, N. G., and C. N. Weaver. 1975. "Some Approximate Comparisons of the Arrest Rate of Mexican-American Juveniles." Paper presented at Southwestern Social Science Association annual meeting. San Antonio, Tex.

Glaser, D. 1978. *Crime in Our Changing Society.* New York: Holt, Rinehart and Winston.

Goldman, N. 1963. *The Differential Selection of Juvenile Offenders for Court Appearance.* New York: National Council on Crime and Delinquency.

Gordon, R. A. 1976. "Prevalence: The Rare Datum in Delinquency Measurement and Its Implications for the Theory of Delinquency." In M. W. Klein, ed., *The Juvenile Justice System*, vol. 5. Beverly Hills, Calif.: Sage.

Hirschi, T. 1969. *Causes of Delinquency.* Berkeley: University of California Press.

Jensen, G. F., J. H. Stauss, and V. W. Harris. 1977. "Crime, Delinquency, and the American Indian." *Human Organization* 36 (Fall):252–57.

McEachern, A. W., and R. Bauzer. 1967. "Factors Related to Disposition in Juvenile Police Contacts." In M. W. Klein, ed., *Juvenile Gangs in Context.* Englewood Cliffs, N.J.: Prentice-Hall.

McKay, H. D. 1967. "A Note on Trends and Rates of Delinquency in Certain Areas in Chicago." In President's Commission on Law Enforcement and Administration of Justice, *Task Force Report: Juvenile Delinquency and Youth Crime.* Washington, D.C.: U.S. Government Printing Office.

Monahan, T. 1970. "Police Dispositions of Juvenile Offenders in Philadelphia 1955 to 1966." *Phylon* 31 (2):134.

Nagasawa, R. H. 1965. "Delinquency and Non-Delinquency: A Study of Status Problems and Perceived Opportunity." M.A. thesis. University of Washington.

National Center for Juvenile Justice. 1974. *Juvenile Court Statistics.* Pittsburgh, Pa.: National Center for Juvenile Justice.

National Commission on the Causes and Prevention of Violence. 1969. *Violence in America: Historical and Comparative Perspectives.* Washington, D.C.: U.S. Government Printing Office.

Piliavin, I., and S. Briar. 1964. "Police Encounters with Juveniles." *American Journal of Sociology* 70 (September):206–14.

Pima County Juvenile Court. 1975. *Pima County Juvenile Court Statistics, Annual Report.* Tucson, Ariz.: Pima County Juvenile Court Center.

———. 1977. *Pima County Juvenile Court Statistics, Annual Report.* Tucson, Ariz.: Pima County Juvenile Court Center.

Polk, K. 1974. *Teenage Delinquency in Small Town America,* Research Report 5. Center for Studies of Crime and Delinquency, National Institute of Mental Health.

Pollak, O. 1950. *The Criminality of Women.* Philadelphia: University of Pennsylvania Press.

President's Commission on Law Enforcement and Administration of Justice. 1967. *Task Force Report: The Assessment of Crime.* Washington, D.C.: U.S. Government Printing Office.

———. 1968. *The Challenge of Crime in a Free Society.* New York: Avon Books.

Schur, E. M. 1969. *Our Criminal Society.* Englewood Cliffs, N.J.: Prentice-Hall.

Shannon, L. W. 1978. "Predicting Adult Criminal Careers." Iowa Urban Community Research Center, University of Iowa. Mimeographed.

Shaw, C. R., and H. D. McKay. 1942. *Juvenile Delinquency and Urban Areas.* Chicago: University of Chicago Press. Copyright 1942 by the University of Chicago Press.

Simon, R. J. 1975. *Women and Crime.* Lexington, Mass.: D. C. Heath.

Sutherland, E. H., and D. R. Cressey. 1974. *Criminology.* Philadelphia: J. B. Lippincott.

Teeters, N., and D. Matza. 1959. "The Extent of Delinquency in the United States." *Journal of Negro Education* 28 (Summer):200–13.

Terry, R. M. 1967. "Discrimination in the Handling of Juvenile Offenders by Social Control Agencies." *Journal of Research in Crime and Delinquency* 4 (July):218–30.

Thornberry, T. 1973. "Race, Socioeconomic Status and Sentencing in the Juvenile Justice System." *Journal of Criminal Law and Criminology* 64 (March):90–98.

Tittle, C. R., W. J. Villemez, and D. A. Smith. 1978. "The Myth of Social Class and Criminality." *American Sociological Review* 43 (October):643–56.

Weiner, N. L., and C. V. Willie. 1971. "Decisions by Juvenile Officers." *American Journal of Sociology* 77 (September):199–210.

Williams, J. R., and M. Gold. 1972. "From Delinquent Behavior to Official Delinquency." *Social Problems* 20 (Fall):209–29.

Wilson, J. Q. 1968. "The Police and the Delinquent in Two Cities." In S. Wheeler, ed., *Controlling Delinquents.* New York: John Wiley.

Wolfgang, M. E., R. Figlio, and T. Sellin. 1972. *Delinquency in a Birth Cohort.* Chicago: University of Chicago Press.

4.
IMAGES OF
DELINQUENCY:
SURVEY DATA

The juvenile delinquent leans against the lamppost, cigarette in hand and leer on face. His gang controls this part of the black ghetto, so he is, for the moment, safe. He and his buddies plan their crimes carefully, for crime gives them kicks and macho points. The boy's parents don't know or care what he does out on the streets; his father ran out years ago, and his weary mother has lost control of the boy.

We all know this juvenile delinquent. His image has been drummed into us from Hollywood movies, Government commissions, scholarly reports. In one sense it is handy to have a commonly accepted image; it provides a symbol for people to hurl accusations at or to rally around. There is only one thing wrong. Despite all the care and ink lavished on him by so many for so long, the delinquent is a myth.

—Bill Haney and Martin Gold, "The Juvenile Delinquent Nobody Knows" *

THE DELINQUENT AS MYTH

"The delinquent is a myth." For most of us, those are startling and disturbing words. If we refer back to Display 1–1 ("The Youth Crime Plague"), we will see that they certainly do not fit with the imagery and examples presented in that article. How could anyone possibly reach the conclusion that the delinquent is a myth? The complete answer to that question involves a recognition that for decades criminologists have been criticizing the use of dramatic examples and official statistics as the basis for developing an accurate, representative picture of crime and delinquency in the United States. The examples used in the mass media are meant to dramatize and arouse and are not necessarily a reflection of the "typical" or the "average" or the "ordinary." Moreover, as Haney and Gold (1973) go on to point out in their discussion of "the delinquent nobody knows," the profile of the criminal or the delinquent that emerges from police and court statistics is a profile based on those caught. As we noted in Chapter 3, statistics about persons who are caught reflect the behavior of the police, the public, judges, and attorneys, as well as characteristics of offenders and offenses. Criminologists widely recognize the possibility that those people who are caught are not necessarily representative of the total population of people who have done things for which they *could* have been arrested and punished. In scientific terms, the issue is one of *sampling bias:* Are the cases that appear in police and court statistics a *representative* or a *biased* sample of lawbreakers?

While Haney and Gold are concerned about the delinquent nobody knows, there is also a growing concern about "the *victim* nobody knows." The statistics on crime rates discussed in Chapter 3 can be viewed in two different senses. For all the "serious" crimes in the FBI's crime index, there are both *offenders* and *victims*. Thus, the crime rate in those instances can be viewed as both an offense rate and a victimization rate. However, just as police and court data do not measure the total amount of offenses, neither do they measure the total extent of victimization. We noted in Chapter 3 that a large proportion of offenses or victimizations is never reported to the police, that police do not respond to some victimizations as criminal events, and that the probability that a victimization will become an officially recognized crime is contingent on the seriousness of the offense and a variety of aspects of the relationships and interaction among complainants, suspects, and the police. Hence, those events or victimizations that make their way into police and court statistics may not be representative of all events that could be included.

Because official statistics reflect far more than criminal or delinquent activity, sociologists and other researchers have tried to develop alternative sources of data that eliminate public and police reaction from measures of lawbreaking. Such attempts have taken two major forms: *self-report* surveys and *victimization* surveys. Self-report surveys attempt to measure offense behavior through interviews or questionnaires dealing with the individual's *own involvement* in crime or delinquency. Victimization surveys attempt to measure the extent of certain types of crime through interviews or questionnaires dealing with the individual's experiences as the *victim* of a crime. Although these techniques for assessing the extent and correlates of crime and delinquency have been criticized, they do overcome some of the criticisms of police and court statistics. By considering several different kinds of information, even though each has its own limitations, we can begin to formulate a fuller, more accurate image of delinquency. Moreover, the *inconsistencies* associated with using different methods of assessment have helped generate new ideas about the nature of crime and delinquency in our society. Exposure to research on "the delinquent nobody knows" forces us to recognize that we actually knew him all along.

SELF-REPORTS OF DELINQUENCY

The most widely used alternative to police and court statistics in the study of delinquency is the self-report survey in which people are asked to report on their own delinquent activity. Such surveys were first used by Austin Porterfield (1946) in a study of Texas college students and by Murphy, Shirley, and Witmer (1946) in a study of boys in a counseling program. F. Ivan Nye and James F. Short, Jr., (1957), who began challenging conventional assumptions about social class in relation to delinquency during the mid-1950s, were particularly influential in the development of this method of studying delinquency. From a technique reported on in only a trickle of publications in the late 1940s and early 1950s, the self-report survey had, by 1970, become sociology's most popular method for studying the causes of delinquency.

Self-report surveys have taken two basic forms, each with its own advantages and disadvantages. One form is the *interview* in which the subject is questioned about his or her background, opinions, and delinquent activities. The second is a *checklist* or *questionnaire* that the subject fills in or completes. The interview method is thought to reduce error since the interviewer can explore a respondent's answers and gather more detail when needed. On the other hand, the interview makes it more difficult to assure the respondent of anonymity since he or she can be identified by the interviewer. Interviews are also more costly than surveys that can be administered to large groups of people all at once. The questionnaire method is useful both for gathering information from huge samples and for assuring anonymity, but it does not allow for the probing of answers or explanation of difficult questions. Questionnaires also assume that subjects can read reasonably well and can follow written directions. The anonymous questionnaire has been the more common of the two procedures in recent years. Examples of each type of self-report survey are presented in displays 4–1 and 4–2.

CRITICISMS OF SELF-REPORT SURVEYS

Although the self-report method emerged in the attempt to find measures of criminal and delinquent behavior that would be more valid and reliable than police and court statistics, the validity and reliability of self-reports have in turn also been challenged. The issues of validity and reliability are very complex, and we cannot deal with all their complexities here. Rather, we will concentrate on the most central issues.

When challenging the *reliability* of a measurement technique, the basic issue is whether repeated measurements would yield consistent results. If repeated measures using a particular technique yield inconsistent results (when there is no reason to believe that the phenomena being measured have changed), then that technique is likely to be viewed as unreliable. The basic issue in assessing *validity* is whether the technique or instrument being used measures what it claims to measure. Even though the self-report technique has been extremely popular, several critics of the method feel that its reliability and validity are not certain enough to justify such popularity (Reiss, 1975; Bidwell, 1975).

A number of studies have tested the reliability of the self-report technique by comparing the results of measurements at different points in time, by examining the results of different ways of measuring the same thing, and by scrutinizing the consistency of responses to different questions in the same survey. Such tests suggest that in terms of prevailing

DISPLAY 4-1 *Example of a Self-Response Questionnaire*

PART II

Please indicate how often you have done each of the following *in the last 12 months.*

If you have not engaged in a particular activity, put __0__ and go on to the next.	If you have, put the number of times.

REMEMBER: YOUR ANSWERS ARE PRIVATE SO YOU CAN ANSWER HONESTLY.

During the last 12 months, how many times did you:

1. Break into a place to do something illegal? _____

2. Take something from a store on purpose without paying for it ("shoplifting")? _____

3. Steal something worth more than $100 (*not counting shoplifting*)? _____

4. Steal something worth less than $100 (*not counting shoplifting*)? _____

5. Beat up or hurt someone on purpose? _____

6. Get into any fist fights or brawls (not counting the times you beat up or hurt someone on purpose)? _____

7. Ruin, break, or damage someone else's property on purpose? _____

8. Take a car without the owner's permission? _____

9. Take money or something by threatening someone with a weapon (gun, knife, etc.)? _____

10. Take money or something by threatening someone without a weapon? _____

Source: Excerpted from a high school survey used in research by M. L. Erickson, J. P. Gibbs, and G. F. Jensen as part of a National Institute of Mental Health study entitled "Community Tolerance and Measures of Delinquency."

standards for assessing reliability, self-reports yield consistent, reliable data on delinquency (Hirschi, 1969). A number of researchers argue, however, that interviews provide more reliable data than questionnaires (Erickson and Empey, 1963; Gold, 1970). Even some researchers who choose not to use self-reports have concluded that the problem of their statistical reliability "has in fact largely been settled and it now seems clear that with few exceptions it is possible to devise relatively reliable questionnaires" (Savitz, Lalli, and Rosen, 1977:4).

DISPLAY 4-2   *Example of an Interview Schedule and Instructions*
                   for Interviewers

Now I'd like to turn to a different topic. Young people sometimes do things that are against the law or things that would get them into trouble if they were caught. On each card in this stack is a sentence about something like that—such as, "skipped a day of school!" or "took something that didn't belong to you." I'd like to know which of the things on these cards you have done in the last three years whether you were caught or not. If you think that you can't tell me about this kind of thing honestly, then it is better that you don't try to answer at all.

Let me remind you at this point that everything you tell me is completely confidential; no one will ever see your name together with your answers.

Shall we go ahead?

| 1. YES | | 5. NO |

TURN TO P. 33

Here are three cards to mark the stacks (PUT EACH RESPONSE CARD ON THE TABLE AS YOU READ IT): "never in the last three years," "once in the last three years," and "more than once in the last three years." Put each card in this stack (ITEM CARDS) under the card on the table that tells how often you have done what it says on the card.

When you are finished, I'd like to ask you some questions about the things you've done.

Here are the cards. Tell me if you have any questions.

The validity of self-reports as measures of delinquent behavior has been a more controversial issue than their reliability. Do people give accurate, honest answers to questions about their involvement in delinquency? This question is very difficult to answer for the simple reason that if we had the information needed to assess whether self-reports "really" measure delinquent behavior, we would not need self-reports. In other words, that other information would itself be providing us with valid, reliable data. The self-report methodology emerged in the attempt to measure *behavior* independent of police and court statistics.

Direct observation or measurement of phenomena is preferred in all of the sciences but is rarely achieved. Instruments are designed to measure the unobservable or to measure more precisely and systematically those phenomena that we can observe. Self-report methods represent an effort to measure the occurrence of events that are not recorded or observed in police and court statistics, as well as those that are, and to measure both "hidden" and public events. In their attempts to provide accurate, valid

60. Ran away from home.
61. Hit one of your parents.
62. Skipped a day of school without a real excuse.
63. Purposely damaged or messed up something not belonging to you.
64. Tried to get something by lying about who you were or how old you were.
65. Tried to get something by lying to a person about what you would do for him.
66. Took something not belonging to you, even if returned.
67. Hurt or injured someone on purpose.
68. Threatened to hurt or injure someone.
69. Went onto someone's property when you knew you were not supposed to.
70. Went into a house or building when you knew you were not supposed to.
71. Drank beer, wine, or liquor without your parents permission.
72. Smoked marijuana.
73. Used any drugs or chemicals to get high or for kicks, except marijuana.
74. Took part in a fight where a bunch of your friends were against another bunch.
75. Carried a gun or knife besides an ordinary pocketknife.
76. Took a car without the permission of the owner even if the car was returned.

Source: M. Gold and D. J. Reimer. "Changing Patterns of Delinquent Behavior among Americans 13 to 16 Years Old, 1967–1972," pp. 31–32. Report no. 1 of the National Survey of Youth, 1972. Institute for Social Research, University of Michigan, 1974.

measures of delinquent behavior, self-report methods assume: (1) that the behavior in question can be clearly and precisely described, (2) that people will remember their transgressions, and (3) that they will give honest answers to queries about their behavior. Grave doubts have been expressed regarding all three assumptions.

Researchers concerned with measuring behavior that is in violation of the law are confronted with the fact that laws are imprecise and ambiguous. For example, the question in Display 4–1 "During the last twelve months, how many times did you take a car without the owner's permission?" was intended to measure events that could end up in police statistics as motor vehicle thefts. However, circumstances of "who took it from whom, for what reason, and for how long" would affect which events made their way into motor vehicle theft statistics and which did not. Similarly, disobeying or defying parents can be the legal basis on which a juvenile is processed as "incorrigible," but the law does not specify at what point defiance and disobedience qualify a juvenile for the label, and the vast majority of such events do not have such a consequence. In short, while behavioral events described in self-reports are often imprecise and may encompass activities that have little chance of causing police or court action, the laws defining activities that can result in legal action are also broad and imprecise.

People may not remember their transgressions and may therefore underreport delinquency; or they may remember activities that occurred before the period in question and may overreport crime for that time period. They may also conceal their activities or exaggerate them, depending on the image they want to project. Interviews are viewed as superior to questionnaires for accurate recall since answers can be probed during the interview. Whether interview techniques elicit more truthful responses than questionnaires has not been established as of this writing. Researchers who use interview methods argue that their probing questions eventually elicit admissions to many activities that the subject would otherwise have been able to conceal.

Since most researchers cannot validate their measurement of delinquency by direct observation of the delinquent behavior, how can the validity of self-reports be assessed? In his study of delinquency in Flint, Michigan, Martin Gold (1970:19–24) assessed the validity of his self-report survey by interviewing the teenaged acquaintances of his respondents, who were most likely to have information about the respondents' delinquent behavior. Thus, Gold could compare what the respondents in his study admitted with what the informants indicated about them. He found that his self-report interviews underestimated delinquent behavior by about 30 percent, but that there were no marked differences in concealment across categories of sex, race, and social status. Although the self-reports underestimated delinquency, they did so to such comparable degrees for different groups that differences among groups could be plausibly interpreted as reflecting real differences in delinquent behavior, rather than differences in honesty or memory.

Involvement in delinquency as measured by self-reports is related to extent of contact with the police, courts, and institutions (Nye, 1958; Erickson and Empey, 1963; Hirschi, 1969; Elliott and Voss, 1974). Of course, scientists always differ in their definitions of an acceptable level of validity, and the debate over the validity of self-report measures will no doubt continue. Those using such methods and favoring their use over police and court statistics acknowledge that the measures can be criticized and that efforts should be directed toward improving their reliability and validity as measures of delinquency.

The use of self-reports has been attacked on other grounds as well. For instance, in a recent study, "City Life and Delinquency," Leonard Savitz, Michael Lalli, and Lawrence Rosen presented the following argument:

> Self-report instruments, almost without exception, have produced no "new" variables or new relationships among variables relating to delinquency not uncovered by the use of official statistics. The basic rationale

> for the use of self-report has been to eliminate a presumptive bias of class and/or race in official statistics. In point of fact, the weight of evidence from self-report instruments has not clarified or solved the problem of racial and class biases. Indeed, greater ambiguity has been produced by self-report instruments on the relationship of class to delinquency than has occurred with the use of official statistics. (1977:4)

There are several problems with this argument. We never know in advance whether a technique will show new variables or new relationships among variables as being relevant to delinquency. But what is even more important, the failure to do so has no bearing on the value of the technique. For example, we could argue that criminological analyses of police and court statistics are consistent with public stereotypes and impressionistic evidence on delinquency; why bother, then, to analyze such data to tell us what we already knew? The answer is that social scientists prefer more systematic, representative, and quantitative data on delinquency. People have raised questions about using police and court statistics to make claims about delinquent *behavior*. Hence, self-report methodologies were developed to try to get a closer measurement of that behavioral phenomenon. If the results of self-reports coincide with police and court statistics, then there is a greater chance that what we have found is really there. If the results are inconsistent, then we will have to seek an explanation for such variation. Multiple techniques for studying a phenomena increase the chances of divergent findings, but the sciences have always pursued them as preferable to reliance on a single technique, especially when there are questions raised about prevailing methods. *Both* self-reports and police and court data are indirect measures of delinquent behavior, and *both* can suggest differences or similarities in behavior that are an artifact of the method, rather than a reflection of the realities of delinquent behavior.

Savitz, Lalli, and Rosen have expressed another common criticism of self-report surveys:

> Furthermore, the more widely used standardized scales have, for the most part, been concerned with the incidence of rather trivial misbehaviors (talking back to parents, stealing items of small value, smoking cigarettes, drinking wine, etc.) and as a result usually fail to discriminate between the serious delinquent (those committing acts involving serious physical harm and property loss) and the mildly errant boy. In effect, they may permit statements to be made, with considerable caution, on delinquencies beyond those known to authorities (self-perceived delinquencies) but they have not dealt any more adequately than have official statistics with the universe of all delinquencies committed. (1977:4)

There are problems with this criticism of the self-report technique as well. First, a considerable volume of self-report research specifically limits its scales to offenses that are included in the FBI's serious-crime index. Moreover, it is quite common for researchers using the self-report technique to create indexes that weight offenses by seriousness.

Second, "trivial" offenses make up a sizable proportion of arrests in FBI arrest statistics and juvenile court referrals. We have seen that nearly half of the offenses in the FBI's serious-crime index are larcenies, which include both petty and major thefts. Stealing items of small value is petty larceny. Moreover, stores and many Americans view any kind of shoplifting as a serious problem. Teenaged drinking is a status offense, but it appears in FBI arrest statistics under the guise of liquor law violations, drunkenness, and driving under the influence. Self-reports attempt to measure activities that the law defines as delinquent, activities that *can* result in legal processing. The realm is quite large and encompasses trivial, as well as more universally condemned, behavior. The most serious offenses constitute a small proportion of activities that juveniles self-report; however, such offenses also account for a small proportion of total criminal and delinquent activity in arrest and court statistics.

Finally, while self-report research is criticized for lumping the trivial with the serious, analyses using police and court statistics quite commonly divide juvenile populations into "delinquent" and "nondelinquent," with the categorization of delinquent based on contact with the police or court, regardless of offense, guilt, or disposition. It is ironic that Savitz, Lalli, and Rosen should challenge the self-report method for making crude distinctions and lumping the serious with the not so serious since they themselves categorize a youth as delinquent if he or she "has been apprehended by the police and comes within the purview of the Philadelphia Police Department Juvenile Aid Division, where an official (JAD) record is made of the action" (1977:17). They opt for using a recorded police contact rather than arrest, referral, or adjudication as the basis for categorization because such contact is "least affected by differential case mortality." If case mortality is justification for using the earliest point at which persons can become an official statistic as the basis for classifying them as delinquent, then why *not* use even earlier stages in the transformation of a delinquent event into a recorded offense? Why *not* try to measure delinquent behavior by asking *people* what they have done instead of asking police records? In sum, the very rationales used to justify the "police-statistics" approach to the study of delinquency have been the justifications for exploring alternative, survey methodologies.

PATTERNS BASED ON SELF-REPORTS

Both police and court statistics and self-reports have their limitations, and we will encounter different people accepting or rejecting the "facts" suggested by each method, depending on the weights that they assign to those limitations and the fit of the facts with their own preconceptions.

Theoreticians committed to the assumption that social status is an important correlate of delinquency are more likely to doubt the results of self-report research than are those committed to theories that do not assume such a correlation. Theoreticians who argue that the justice system discriminates against minorities are more likely to accept results that seemingly minimize real behavioral differences among groups. However, in certain areas, both self-report data and police and court statistics yield comparable observations. The disparities between studies using self-reports and studies using police and court data are typically less disparate than they seem, and data produced by both types of studies yield a surprising number of comparable findings. When different ways of measuring a phenomena yield similar patterns, then we tend to have greater confidence that the patterns are real and not merely artifacts of our methodology. We will now examine self-report surveys in terms of the same variations or patterns over time, space, and among various sociodemographic categories that we considered in relation to police and court statistics in Chapter 3.

Time

Since there is no nationwide self-report data on delinquency comparable to the FBI's *Uniform Crime Reports* or the *Juvenile Court Statistics*, we can say very little about self-reported delinquency over time. One study, conducted by the National Survey of Youth under the direction of Martin Gold at the Institute for Social Research (University of Michigan), is an ongoing attempt to monitor the self-reported behavior of nationwide samples of American youths over time. After comparing data gathered in 1967 and in 1972, Gold and Reimer noted:

> The most important result emerging from our comparison of delinquent behavior among 13 to 16 year olds from 1967 to 1972 is not that the amount of delinquency has changed, but that the style has changed. Boys in that age cohort in 1972 reported less delinquent behavior than their peers in the 1967 survey did; but they admitted to markedly different frequencies of certain offenses. Specifically, more of the '72 male respondents reported more frequent use of illicit drugs—mostly marijuana—than the 1967 resondents did, and less larceny, threatened assault, trespassing, forcible and non-forcible entry, and gang fighting. The girls in '72 also reported greater use of drugs—mostly marijuana but including alcohol—than girls did in '67, while reporting less larceny, property destruction, and breaking and entering. But the decline of the latter kinds of offenses among the girls in 1972 does not balance their greater use of drugs, so the girls in '72 reported more delinquent behavior overall. (1974:43)

Whether the decline in certain kinds of delinquency that Gold and Reimer observed is an exception limited to the 1967–1972 comparison or a reflection of a longer-term trend is unknown. When the results of the most recent replication (1977) are reported, we will have a much better image of trends.

In Chapter 3 we noted a leveling of the FBI index crime rate in the mid-1970s, a possible leveling of the juvenile court referral rate in 1976 or 1977, and a leveling of the arrest rate for males under age eighteen in the mid-1970s. However, the period from the mid-1960s through the early 1970s was one of increasing crime and delinquency. From 1967 to 1972, the overall arrest rate for persons under eighteen increased, and juvenile court referral rates increased from 26.3 per 1,000 persons aged ten through seventeen to 33.6 per 1,000. In sum, police and court statistics for that time period suggest increases, while Gold and Reimer's self-report survey shows a decline.

Police data coincide with the self-report data in one regard. According to the *Uniform Crime Reports,* the arrest rate for drug violations of persons ten through seventeen years of age increased some 270 percent from 45 per 100,000 in 1967 to 167 per 100,000 in 1972. Moreover, Gold and Reimer's observation of increases in drinking coincide with FBI statistics showing a slight increase in arrests for drunkenness during the same period. Thus, although there are some consistencies between the two bodies of data, they occur in the context of inconsistencies.

Space

In our discussion of official delinquency rates in Chapter 3, we noted two aspects of the spatial distribution of delinquency that are of interest to criminologists: the distribution of delinquency in areas of cities and differences among communities of different size. We also noted that in their explanation of variation in official delinquency rates, Shaw and McKay argued that rapid change or succession in racial or ethnic composition of a neighborhood prevented or disrupted the development of conventional institutions or organizations in the area and that the resulting social disorganization facilitated a high delinquency rate. This explanation fit their information on the distribution of officially recorded delinquency.

Although no self-report research exactly parallels studies of the spatial distribution of delinquency that are based on police and court data, a recent study (Kapsis, 1978) has been concerned with the distribution of delinquency in different neighborhoods. Focusing on black adolescent males in the San Francisco-Oakland metropolitan region, Robert Kapsis examined rates of self-reported and official delinquency in three neighborhoods that were at varying stages of racial change. Kapsis found that according to both measures of delinquency, the delinquency rate was highest for males living in neighborhoods with the highest racial succession and lowest in the most stable neighborhoods. Moreover, this pattern held true even when measures of socioeconomic status, family structure, and educational performance and commitment were taken into account.

Several studies have examined self-reported delinquency in communities of different size. One such study, by James F. Short, Jr., and F. Ivan Nye (1958), focused on high school students in three western cities of 10,000 to 30,000 and in three smaller midwestern communities. Out of twenty-one offenses, Short and Nye found nine significant differences between the western and midwestern boys, with midwestern boys higher in self-reported delinquency for eight of the nine. For girls, there were five significant differences, all involving higher rates of self-reported delinquency for midwestern girls. In sum, when differences occurred, they tended to involve higher rates for the smaller communities. However, the range of cities in terms of population size was quite small.

Clark and Wenninger (1962) found that although the rural farm community they studied tended to rank lowest in self-reported delinquency, there was actually very little overall difference between adolescents in a rural farm community and adolescents in urban settings. Compared with youth in an industrial city of 35,000, in a lower-class urban neighborhood, and in a wealthy Chicago suburb, rural youth ranked fourth for fourteen of thirty-eight offenses studied. However, for those fourteen offenses, the average percentage difference between the rural youth and each of the three urban samples was only 4.7 percent. The greatest urban-rural differences involved sneaking into theaters, curfew violations, major theft, borrowing money without intending to pay it back, drinking, using slugs in vending machines, and truancy. Major theft was the only serious offense for which the average difference between the rural youth and the three urban samples exceeded 10 percent. For violent offenses, arson, many forms of vandalism, trespassing, breaking and entering, and hanging around or entering adult-only establishments, the rural sample ranked first or second.

In their 1967 national survey of youth, Gold and Reimer (1974) found that central-city youths reported an average of 8.6 delinquent offenses during the three years preceding the interview, as compared to 7.5 for suburban youths, 5.9 for youths residing in small cities and towns, and 6.5 for rural youths. In 1972 the comparable rate was 7.8 for central-city youths, 6.0 for suburban youths, 7.1 for youths in small cities and towns, and 4.5 for rural youths. Overall, the differences by residence were small and varied between the two years of Gold and Reimer's study. However, the differences did show higher average delinquent involvement among central-city youths than among youths in smaller communities.

Finally, a study of youths in metropolitan areas and small towns in southern Arizona (Jensen and Erickson, 1977) reported that the highest rates of self-reported delinquency occurred among high school students in a small mining town of about 7,500 population. Youths from another small town (about 1,200 in population) ranked next highest, followed by high school students in Tucson (population 450,000). Students attending high school in a ranching and farming area had the lowest rates of self-reported delinquency. The Arizona study, together with the studies summarized above, suggests that other characteristics of communities besides their size (such as their economy, stability, and history) affect their rates.

Is the disparity between delinquency rates in rural and urban settings decreasing over time, as indicated in our discussion of official statistics in Chapter 3? Judging from the averages for all delinquent offenses reported in Gold and Reimer's national survey, we would have to answer no. In the 1967 survey, the average for central-city boys was 1.3 times greater than the average for boys living in rural settings (that is, 8.6 divided by 6.5), and in the 1972 survey the ratio was 1.7 (that is, 7.8 divided by 4.5). The same conclusion is supported by Gold and Reimer's index of serious delinquency. However, the one group that did report more frequent and more serious delinquency on the average in the 1972 survey than in the 1967 survey were boys living in "small cities and towns" (population 2,500 to 50,000). The decrease in self-reported delinquency among central-city and suburban boys, coupled with an increase for boys in small cities and towns, resulted in more nearly comparable averages in 1972 for central-city and small-city boys. Thus, while the rural versus urban difference did not decline between the 1967 and 1972 surveys, the urban versus small-town difference did appear to do so.

Gender

Several studies have focused on gender differences in delinquency. All suggest the same conclusion: Girls self-report significantly less delinquency than do boys. For example, after analyzing data collected in the early 1960s, Martin Gold (1970) concluded that girls in Flint, Michigan, engaged in much less delinquent behavior than boys and that the differences were not likely to reflect greater concealment of offenses by girls. Nancy Wise (1967) also found that, with few exceptions, the girls in her study reported significantly less delinquency than boys. Michael Hindelang (1971) described a similar finding in his study of youths in rural New York, while Jensen and Eve (1976) identified sex differences in self-reported delinquency among both black and nonblack youths in California.

In the southern Arizona project referred to earlier (Jensen and Erickson, 1977), the boys had higher rates than females in every town included in the study, and the pattern of differences was the same as that suggested by juvenile court statistics: The more serious the offense, the greater the sex difference in delinquency. As was the case with court statistics, self-reports of males and females showed more nearly similar rates for status offenses and shoplifting. For more serious offenses, males greatly outnumbered females.

Is the disparity between the delinquency of male and female youths narrowing over time according to self-reports? While a definitive answer is not possible given the limited amount of relevant research, the data from Gold and Reimer's national survey of youth indicate that the disparity between male and female frequency and seriousness of delinquency was lower in 1972 than 1967 for central-city, suburban, and rural youth, but not for small-town youth. The disparity between small-town males and females, which was actually greater in the 1972 survey than in the 1967 one, was a result of the unusual increase in reported delinquency among small-town boys.

Race and Ethnicity

A few studies have compared the rates of self-reported delinquency with the rates of police contact among different racial groups. For example, a study carried out in Seattle (Nagasawa, 1965) reported that 36 percent of the black, 11 percent of the white, and 2 percent of the Japanese youths in the sample had been arrested. In contrast, 53 percent of blacks and 52 percent of whites self-reported delinquent acts of one kind or another. Only 36 percent of Japanese youths self-reported any delinquent activity.

Hirschi (1969) reported that black adolescent males in his California study were more likely than nonblacks to have a record (51 percent as compared to 26 percent) but were not more likely to self-report delinquent activity. A further analysis of that data (Jensen and Eve, 1976) found that whites tended to have higher rates of self-reported delinquency for minor property theft, but that black teenagers tended to have higher rates than whites for major theft, fighting, and vandalism (see Table 4–1). In their national survey of youth, Williams and Gold (1972) reported similar findings: White males were as likely to report delinquent offenses as blacks, but black males scored higher on a measure of seriousness. However, even then, the differences were slight, with 42 percent of the whites "high" on the seriousness scale as compared to 53 percent of the blacks.

Very few studies have encompassed other minority groups, such as Asian, Chicano, or Indian Americans. Available information suggests that Asian Americans have lower rates of self-reported delinquency than do blacks or whites (Chambliss and Nagasawa, 1969; Gould, 1969). In an Arizona study, Indian-American youths appeared to have higher rates than whites or Chicanos for some kinds of offenses, while Chicano youths tended to have rates similar to those of white youths (Jensen, Stauss, and Harris, 1977).

TABLE 4-1 *Percentage Reporting Delinquency, by Race and Sex*

	Black		White	
	Male	Female	Male	Female
Theft under $2.00	47%	24%	53%	31%
Theft $2–$50	24	6	19	8
Theft over $50	12	2	6	1
Car Theft	13	4	11	4
Vandalism	32	13	25	8
Fighting	46	29	42	15

Source: Reprinted from "Sex Differences in Delinquency: An Examination of Popular Sociological Explanations" by Gary F. Jensen and Raymond Eve from *Criminology* 13, no. 4 (February 1976):434, by permission of the publisher, Sage Publications, Inc.

Age

In our summary of police and court records in Chapter 3, we noted that arrest rates for the types of offenses that disproportionately involve juveniles tend to peak during middle adolescence and that the more serious offenses tend to peak at later ages. Self-report studies of delinquency have tended to suggest a similar pattern with regard to overall involvement. Hirschi (1969) found the greatest proportion of youths self-reporting delinquent acts in grades nine and ten. In a national survey of youth (Williams and Gold, 1972) that encompassed only the years thirteen through sixteen, self-reported delinquency was found to be more frequent and more serious the older the age category of the respondent.

In their study of self-reported criminality in a sample of persons aged fifteen and older residing in three different states, Tittle and Villemez (1977) presented data that are essentially consistent with the view that young persons account for a disproportionate share of most offenses. Data from that study show the highest rates occurring among persons fifteen through twenty-four years of age for four offenses (minor and major theft, assault, and marijuana use) out of the six examined. Gambling and admissions of cheating on one's income tax were most common among persons aged twenty-five through forty-four. For all six offenses, persons over sixty-five had the lowest rates. For all age groups and offenses, males tended to report more criminality than females.

Social Status and Social Class

Since the advent of self-reported surveys some thirty years ago, the relationship between social status and delinquent behavior has been one of the most studied relationships in delinquency research. In the mid-

1930s Sophia M. Robison (1936) investigated "hidden" delinquency in New York City. On the basis of self-reported data, Robison argued that juvenile court statistics were unduly biased toward lower-class children; that the differentials between lower-class youths and middle- and upper-class youths reflected the greater availability of noncourt resources for more affluent children. A few years later Edward Schwartz (1945) conducted a similar study in Washington, D.C., and found far more delinquency in the middle and upper classes than was recorded in official statistics.

In his pioneering study of college students in Fort Worth, Texas, Porterfield (1946) found that despite the self-reports of a great number of delinquent offenses, virtually none of them had been brought to the attention of the police or the court. Porterfield interpreted his findings as the result of a differential application of the law that works against lower-class youths. He suggested that adolescents from economically deprived areas or families are observed more closely than juveniles from higher-status backgrounds. Porterfield also concluded that juveniles from lower-socioeconomic strata are dealt with in a more punitive manner than upper-class youth.

The research conducted by James Short, Jr., and F. Ivan Nye in the late 1950s was a major contribution to the study of hidden delinquency. These investigators measured delinquency by using a delinquency list of twenty-three items, with offenses ranging from driving without a license to grand larceny and drug use. The data were gathered with anonymous questionnaires in high schools and in correctional training institutions in several western and midwestern communities. Short and Nye found that nearly all of the institutionalized youths were from the lower-socioeconomic strata, in contrast to only 53 percent of the total high school population. However, when the high school samples were analyzed, the overall results showed essentially no consistent relationship between delinquency and social class. In a few instances some differences were found to be significant: Western lower-class boys had more "heterosexual relations"; midwestern upper-class male and female youth were involved in more offenses of purposeful damage or destruction to property; and upper-class girls reported more "running away from home." However, out of a total of 756 tests for differences by socioeconomic status, only 33 were found to be significant. The researchers concluded that juvenile delinquency is not linked to class and that much middle- and upper-class delinquent behavior is underreported. Short and Nye also dramatized the conceptual distinction between *official* delinquency and delinquent *behavior*. Simply stated, delinquent behavior is lawbreaking behavior that, *if* detected by an appropriate authority, could result in some form of legal sanctioning. Official delinquency represents the identification and response to delinquent behavior by the juvenile justice system.

Martin Gold (1970), using a sample of 522 adolescents between the ages of thirteen and sixteen in Flint, Michigan, found no reliable relationship between delinquent behavior and social status among girls. For white males he found that the lowest-status category accounted for more delinquency in terms of frequency of acts committed and the seriousness of the acts. The same pattern existed among black males. Although low-status black youths appeared to commit fewer delinquent acts than low-status white males, the acts they did commit were more serious in nature. Still, the differences Gold found by social status were quite small.

Empey and Erickson (1966) examined the question of a relationship between delinquent behavior and social status in four subsamples of white males: (1) high school students who had never been arrested, (2) offenders who had been to juvenile court once, (3) offenders who were on probation, and (4) offenders who were incarcerated. Overall, these researchers found little evidence of any status differences. The slight relationship that did exist reflected a lower rate of delinquency among upper-status boys, but delinquency rates for low- and middle-status adolescents appeared very similar.

The study cited earlier of students in the San Francisco Bay area (Hirschi, 1969) found essentially no relationship between social status and self-reported delinquent behavior. Hirschi used the father's occupation and father's education to measure social status. Both measures resulted in similar findings. Sons of white-collar workers were more likely to commit one or more delinquent acts, while sons of professionals or executives, as well as sons of unskilled laborers, were among the least delinquent groups in the sample. Similarly, father's education as a measure of social status yielded no significant findings regarding a relationship between socioeconomic status and the commission of delinquent acts.

Using data from a random sample of adolescents thirteen to sixteen years old residing in the forty-eight contiguous states, Williams and Gold (1972) attempted to resolve the issue of a relationship between delinquency and social class. When they examined their entire sample of black and white youths, they found virtually no relationship at all. Looking at the seriousness scale only for white males, Williams and Gold found a slight positive relationship between social status and delinquency that indicated more serious delinquency for higher-status white males than for lower-status youth. Looking at per capita offenses of white males for theft, joyriding, assault, and vandalism by social status, these investigators found higher-status youths tending to report more offenses than the lower status-youths, although the strength of the association was not particularly strong.

Several reviews of the body of self-report research have noted that most studies show little or no relationship between social status and delinquency. In the mid-1960s Ronald Akers (1964) reported that his own research, as well as most earlier studies, suggested that social class or social status was not an important determinant of delinquent behavior. A more recent review by Tittle and Villemez (1977) reaffirmed Akers' observation. Tittle and Villemez observed that while 65 percent of the studies of social status and official delinquency statistics reported higher delinquency for the lower-status categories, the comparable figure for self-report studies was 35 percent. Moreover, Tittle and Villemez observed no consistent relationship between social status and self-reported criminality.

In short, neither self-report research nor research based on official statistics has shown a consistent relationship between social status and delinquency. However, the self-report research is far less likely to support traditional beliefs than research that uses official statistics. Of course, the source of variation in research findings on the issue of social status and delinquency is not known. Disparate findings within the body of self-report research could reflect differences in definitions and measurements of social status and delinquency, differences in populations sampled, or differences over time. Similarly, the disparity between studies using official statistics and studies using self-reports could reflect problems with either or both bodies of data. Underreporting in self-reports may minimize group differences, and researchers are currently investigating just such a possibility. On the other hand, official statistics, reflecting police attitudes, complainant behavior, or the demeanor of juvenile suspects, may exaggerate certain group differences.

VICTIMIZATION SURVEYS

The victimization survey is another alternative to using police and court statistics for measuring the extent and nature of crime in the United States. Whereas the self-report survey asks people to report their own involvement in criminal and delinquent activity, the victimization survey asks people to report on their experiences as victims of such activity (see Display 4–3). Following exploratory efforts in the mid-1960s to measure victimization in a national sample of households in a few cities (Ennis, 1967), the technique grew rapidly in popularity. Since 1972 the Bureau of the Census has been conducting two sets of national crime surveys for the Law Enforcement Assistance Administration (LEAA). In one national crime survey (NCS), the Bureau of the Census has selected a national sample of households and has interviewed and reinterviewed respondents at six-month intervals. The Bureau of the Census has also been conducting a number of city surveys aimed at estimating the nature and extent of victimizations against persons, households, and commercial establishments during the twelve months preceding the interview (Garofalo, 1977). By the late 1970s victimization surveys had also been conducted to measure the extent of victimization of juveniles both at school and in the community (Savitz, Lalli, and Rosen, 1977; Boesel et al., 1978).

Whereas the anonymous, self-response questionnaire has been the most common technique in self-report research on delinquency, the most common technique in victimization surveys has been the in-person interview. This technique has been preferred because (1) it yields a high response rate from representative samples of households and commercial establishments, (2) victimization surveys seek a great deal of specific information from victims, and (3) interviewers can probe answers and clarify questions (Garofalo, 1977:20–21).

Because the in-person interview technique is quite costly (about thirty dollars per household in the NCS city surveys), telephone interviews and mail questionnaires have been considered as alternatives. Since over 90 percent of households have telephones, it is possible to obtain a fairly representative sample of households by means of "random-digit" dialing. Using this method, the interviewer or a machine dials the three digit prefixes listed for a given area and dials the remaining four digits at random. Thus, all possible numbers for a particular area become the population from which a sample is drawn. This method also eliminates the problems caused by unlisted numbers. In his review of different techniques, Garofalo concluded that the results of exploratory efforts show random-digit telephone interviewing to be "a promising, relatively low-cost technique for conducting victim surveys" (1977:23).

The mail questionnaire is less expensive than the in-person interview and may have some advantages, such as greater privacy and greater time for responding. However, victimization researchers feel the mail questionnaire technique results in less reliable and less valid information than the interview because it produces lower response rates and because it does not allow for probing and clarification of questions.

We have noted that self-report surveys have several problems; most apply to victimization surveys as well. Savitz, Lalli, and Rosen (1977:11) have summarized the problems of victimization surveys as follows:

   1. Memory decay (the respondent forgets personal or familial victimization experiences or thinks that they occurred before or after the study year, while in fact they occurred within the research period).

   2. Lack of knowledge by respondent (head-of-household respondent never knew of some or all of the victimizations experienced by other household members).

   3. Deliberate exaggeration and deliberate failure to admit victimization (the respondent, in effect, lies and recites events that did not take place or consciously fails to reveal victimization which had occurred).

   4. Telescoping of criminal events into the study period (the respondent states that a specific crime took place within the research year when, in fact, it occurred before or after the period being investigated).

   5. Victimization not a criminal event (the act thought to be, and described as a crime, upon close examination, is found not to be a legal offense.)

DISPLAY 4–3   *Example of a Victimization Survey*

Now I'd like to ask some questions about crime. They refer *only to the last 12 months.*

Household Screen Questions	*How Many Times*
1. Did anyone break into or somehow illegally enter your house, apartment, garage, or other building on your property?	_____
2. Other than the incidents just mentioned, did you find any signs of an *attempted* break-in?	_____
3. Was anything stolen that is kept outside your home or happened to be left out, such as a bicycle or garden hose?	_____
4. Did anyone steal, *try* to steal, or use without permission a motor vehicle belonging to you or any member of your household?	_____

Individual Screen Questions	*How Many Times*
1. Did you have your pocket picked/purse snatched?	_____
2. Did anyone take something else directly from you or *try* to rob you by using force or threatening to harm you?	_____
3. Did anyone beat you up, attack you with a weapon, or hit you with something, such as a rock?	_____
4. Did anyone *threaten* to beat you up or *threaten* you with a knife, gun, or other weapon, *not* including telephone threats, or *try* to attack you in some other way?	_____
5. Other than in incidents already mentioned, was anything stolen from you or did you find any evidence that someone attempted to steal something from you?	_____
6. Did you call the police to report something that happened to you that you thought was a crime? (Do not count calls about incidents already mentioned.) What happened? _____	
7. Did anything happen to you that you thought was a crime, but did *not* report to the police (other than incidents already mentioned)? What happened?	

Source: Adapted from Law Enforcement Assistance Administration. *Criminal Victimization in the United States.* Washington, D.C.: U.S. Government Printing Office, 1974.

DISPLAY 4-3 *Example of a Victimization Survey (continued)*

Household Screen Questions

29. Now I'd like to ask some questions about crime. They refer only to the last 12 months —

    between ____ 1, 197__ and ____, 197__.
    During the last 12 months, did anyone break into or somehow illegally get into your (apartment/home), garage, or another building on your property?

    □Yes —How many times?
    □No
    _____

30. (Other than the incident(s) just mentioned) Did you find a door jimmied, a lock forced, or any other signal of an ATTEMPTED break-in?

    □Yes —How many times?
    □No
    _____

31. Was anything at all stolen that is kept outside your home, or happened to be left out, such as a bicycle, a garden hose, or lawn furniture? (other than any incidents already mentioned)

    □Yes —How many times?
    □No
    _____

32. Did anyone take something belonging to you or to any member of this household, from a place where you or they were temporarily staying, such as a friend's or relative's home, a hotel or motel, or a vacation home?

    □Yes —How many times?
    □No
    _____

33. What was the total number of motor vehicles (cars, trucks, etc.) owned by you or any other member of this household during the last 12 months?

    0 □None —
        SKIP to 36
    1 □ 1
    2 □ 2
    3 □ 3
    4 □ 4 or more

34. Did anyone steal, TRY to steal, or use (it/any of them) without permission?

    □Yes —How many times?
    □No
    _____

35. Did anyone steal or TRY to steal part of (it/any of them), such as a battery, hubcaps, tape-deck, etc.?

    □Yes —How many times?
    □No
    _____

36. The following questions refer only to things that happened to you during the last 12 months —

    between ____ 1, 197__ and ____, 197__.
    Did you have your (pocket picked/purse snatched)?

    □Yes —How many times?
    □No
    _____

37. Did anyone take something (else) directly from you by using force, such as by a stickup, mugging or threat?

    □Yes —How many times?
    □No
    _____

38. Did anyone TRY to rob you by using force or threatening to harm you? (other than any incidents already mentioned)

    □Yes —How many times?
    □No
    _____

39. Did anyone beat you up, attack you or hit you with something, such as a rock or bottle? (other than any incidents already mentioned)

    □Yes —How many times?
    □No
    _____

40. Were you knifed, shot at, or attacked with some other weapon by anyone at all? (other than any incidents already mentioned)

☐Yes —How many times?
☐No

_____

41. Did anyone THREATEN to beat you up or THREATEN you with a knife, gun, or some other weapon, NOT including telephone threats? (other than any incidents already mentioned)

☐Yes —How many times?
☐No

_____

42. Did anyone TRY to attack you in some other way? (other than any incidents already mentioned)

☐Yes —How many times?
☐No

_____

43. During the last 12 months, did anyone steal things that belonged to you from inside any car or truck, such as packages or clothing?

☐Yes —How many times?
☐No

_____

44. Was anything stolen from you while you were away from home, for instance at work, in a theater or restaurant, or while traveling?

☐Yes —How many times?
☐No

_____

45. (Other than any incidents you've already mentioned) was anything (else) at all stolen from you during the last 12 months?

☐Yes —How many times?
☐No

_____

46. Did you find any evidence that someone ATTEMPTED to steal something that belonged to you? (other than any incidents already mentioned)

☐Yes —How many times?
☐No

_____

47. Did you call the police during the last 12 months to report something that happened to you which you thought was a crime? (Do not count any calls made to the police concerning the incidents you have just told me about.)

☐No —_SKIP to 48_
☐Yes —What happened?

_____
_____
_____

Look at 47. Was HH member 12 + attacked or threatened, or was something stolen or an attempt made to steal something that belonged to him?

☐Yes —How many times?
☐No

_____

48. Did anything happen to you during the last 12 months which you thought was a crime, but did NOT report to the police? (other than any incidents already mentioned)

☐No —_SKIP to Check Item E_
☐Yes —What happened?

_____
_____
_____

Look at 48. Was HH member 12 + attacked or threatened, or was something stolen or an attempt made to steal something that belonged to him?

☐Yes —How many times?
☐No

_____

Do any of the screen questions contain any entries for "How many times?"

☐No —_Interview next HH member. End interview if last respondent, and fill item 13 on cover._
☐Yes —_Fill Crime Incident Reports._

Victimization researchers have been aware of these problems and have tried to cope with them by limiting the time period covered by the survey (for example, the NCS chose the preceding six months to help avoid memory decay and telescoping); by carefully describing criminal victimizations; and by cross-checking reports by different members of households.

Attempts have been made to study the validity of victimization data, the relation of victimization data to police data, and possible sources of divergence between the two measures of crime. Wesley Skogan (1974) examined the relation between victimization survey crime rates and the rates given by the *Uniform Crime Reports* for auto theft and robbery in ten major American cities. He found definite correlations between the two measures of crime, but with considerable variation by offense. Since auto theft is the property victimization most likely to be reported to police, there was a very high correspondence between survey and official rates for that offense. For robbery the correlation was much smaller. However, the correlations were sufficiently strong for Skogan to suggest that both victimization surveys and official statistics measure an "actual" crime rate (1974:38). Similarly, in a study of police reports and victimization surveys for San Jose, California, M. Katherine Howard (1975:433) reported that both police robbery reports and victimization survey data appear to be "representative of the same population of robberies."

Efforts to understand why victimizations go unreported show such decisions to be quite rational. Skogan (1976) found the seriousness of the victimization to be the major determinant of whether a citizen reported a crime: The more serious the loss, threat, or harm, the greater the probability a citizen would report the victimization to the police. Skogan also reported that women were slightly more likely than men to report victimizations of all kinds and that the young (ages twelve through nineteen) were less likely to report victimizations than were older Americans. In addition, people were slightly more likely to report victimizations by strangers than victimizations by nonstrangers. Other researchers (Block, 1970; Hawkins, 1973; Smith and Hawkins, 1973) have concluded that attitudes toward the police do not affect citizens' reporting of victimizations. Overall, citizens' decisions to report crime appear to be based on considerations of loss, threat, and harm, rather than on more subtle considerations of attitudes toward the police and the law.

PATTERNS BASED ON VICTIMIZATION DATA

Victimization surveys have not been a common technique for studying juvenile delinquency for several reasons. For one thing, to differentiate between crime and delinquency, we need information on the *age of the*

offender. For such offenses as burglary, larceny, and auto theft, the characteristics of the offender are not likely to be known to the victim. Moreover, even for personal victimizations, the victim can usually only guess
at the offender's age: four out of five personal victimizations are by people
who are not known to the victim. A second limitation in applying victimization surveys to the study of delinquency is that such surveys deal
only with offenses that involve victims and, thus, exclude victimless
offenses. However, we can examine victimization data on offenses that
other statistics show to be committed most often by juveniles. We can
also consider surveys in which victims have estimated the ages of the
offenders. A few surveys have looked at juveniles as victims and at victimizations within schools.

Time

Since victimization survey data have been collected systematically on
a national scale only since 1972, such data are not available for those time
periods during which police data indicate sizable increases in crime in the
United States (see Chapter 3). However, in 1974 the Law Enforcement
Assistance Administration began publishing comparisons of victimization survey results over time. As of this writing, data are available regarding changes in victimization rates between 1973 and 1976 (Law Enforcement Assistance Administration, 1974, 1977).

LEAA's national crime survey data show declines in victimization
rates from 1973 to 1976 for rape (down 11.6 percent), robbery (down 4.2
percent), and motor vehicle theft (down 13.7 percent). Larceny (up from 6
to 16 percent), burglary of commercial establishments (up 6.7 percent),
and assault (up 1.6 percent) were the only offenses to increase in this time
period, and most of these increases occurred between 1973 and 1974.
From 1975 to 1976 the only significant change was a decline in motor
vehicle theft (down 15 percent). However, out of ten different types of
victimizations examined, the rates for eight were actually lower in 1976
than in 1975 (see Figure 4–1). The overall impression is one of stable or
declining victimization rates in the mid-1970s.

The picture that victimization survey data present of stable or declining crime rates in the mid-1970s is consistent with the statistics of the
Uniform Crime Reports, as is the observation that for the period from
1973 to 1976, most increases occurred between 1973 and 1974. However,
the two bodies of data do show one major disparity in patterns over time.
Specifically, while statistics of the *Uniform Crime Reports* show an
increase for rape (up 10 percent from 1973 to 1976), victimization data
show a decrease (down 12 percent). The LEAA victimization data indicate
no significant change or possible decline in the reporting of such victimizations; thus, this disparity does not appear to be a product of increased or
decreased citizen willingness to report rape. However, it may be that the

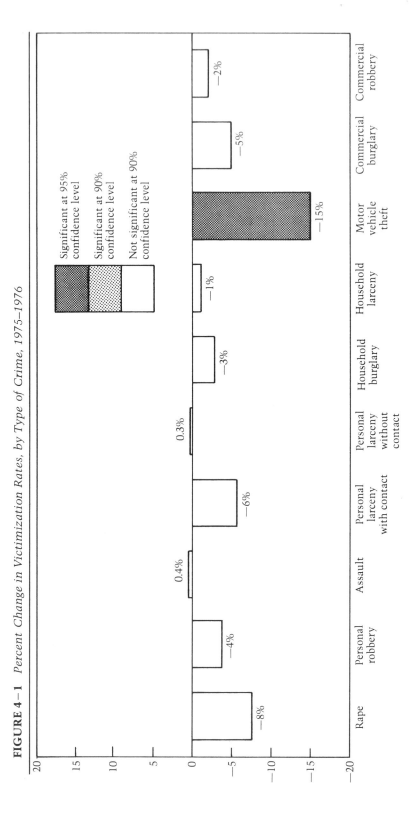

FIGURE 4–1 *Percent Change in Victimization Rates, by Type of Crime, 1975–1976*

Significant at 95% confidence level

Significant at 90% confidence level

Not significant at 90% confidence level

Rape −8%

Personal robbery −4%

Assault 0.4%

Personal larceny with contact −6%

Personal larceny without contact 0.3%

Household burglary −3%

Household larceny −1%

Motor vehicle theft −15%

Commercial burglary −5%

Commercial robbery −2%

Source: Law Enforcement Assistance Administration. *Criminal Victimization in the United States: A Comparison of 1975 and 1976 Findings,* p. 10. Washington, D.C.: U.S. Government Printing Office, 1977.

police have been responding more formally over time to reported rapes, which has led to increases in recorded rapes even though rape victimizations may have declined.

Space

Victimization survey data have been collected on a nationwide scale, and victimization rates have been computed for central-city, suburban, and nonmetropolitan residents. With regard to personal and household victimization, the risk has been found to be greatest for central-city residents, followed by suburbanites, with nonmetropolitan residents having the lowest risks of victimization. The variation in these data is consistent with statistics of the *Uniform Crime Reports.* This consistency extends to variations by type of offenses as well. The biggest differences in victimization rates between metropolitan and nonmetropolitan settings occur in the offense categories of robbery and motor vehicle theft, a finding that is also consistent with police statistics. However, in contrast to the trend suggested by police statistics, victimization data do not show a narrowing of the gap between nonmetropolitan and metropolitan victimization rates between 1973 and 1976.

The "safe school" study undertaken by the National Institute of Education (Boesel et al., 1978) gathered data from a variety of sources on offenses against teachers, students, and schools in a variety of settings. This study found that teachers in urban areas were most likely to indicate that they had been the victims of theft, robbery, or attack and that teachers in small cities and suburban areas were less likely and teachers in rural areas least likely to report such victimizations. The study reported that the chances that a teacher in an urban high school would be attacked within a month's time were 1 in 55, while the chances of a teacher in a rural high school were 1 in 500. Such findings about victimization of teachers by school location coincided with data gathered from students and with reports by principals of offenses against the school.

Perceived Gender, Age, and Race of Offenders

The national crime surveys of the Bureau of the Census have gathered data on perceived characteristics of the offender(s), but since such information depends on victims' perceptions, it is subject to greater error and distortion than other victimization survey findings. Such perceptions do, however, provide another source of data in constructing an image of crime and delinquency.

Consistent with police statistics and self-report survey data, victimization data show the vast majority of offenders in personal crimes of violence to be male. Moreover, as was also the case for police statistics and self-reports, victimization data indicate that the disparity between males

and females is greater for more serious offenses. An analysis of victimization data for eight cities (Hindelang, 1976:180) showed the perceived sex
of the offender to be female in 4 percent of all robbery victimizations and
in 8 percent of larcenies. Similarly, while offenders were identified as
female in 8 percent of instances of assault without theft, females
accounted for 4 percent of assaults with theft. Thus, the general conclusion concerning sex differences suggested by police and self-report data is
supported by victimization data.

Certain patterns by age suggested by victimization data are also comparable to those found in police statistics. For example, in his analysis of
victimization survey data, Hindelang (1976:167) found that the estimated
age of lone offenders (that is, only one offender involved) for larceny was
somewhat younger than the estimated ages for robbery. The estimated
ages for robbery were in turn lower than the estimated ages for assault.
When the assault also involved theft, the population of lone offenders
was younger than when no theft was involved. Thus, like police statistics, victimization data show that offenses involving theft and attacks on
property involve younger offenders than do crimes involving interpersonal conflict. Hindelang also found that in victimizations that involved
more than one offender, the offenders were perceived to be younger than
when the victimization involved only a lone offender. In other words,
group or gang delinquency and crime appear to involve younger offenders
than do offenses committed by lone offenders.

Victimization data on the perceived race of offenders show blacks to
be disproportionately identified as offenders (Hindelang, 1978). Although
in 1974 only 11 percent of the population was black, Hindelang's analysis
of NCS data for that year showed that in 39 percent of rape victimizations, 62 percent of robberies, 30 percent of aggravated assaults, and 29
percent of simple assaults, the offender was identified as black. Our own
calculations for these four types of victimizations show the rates for
perceived black offenders to be three times (for simple and aggravated
assault) to fourteen times (for robbery) greater than the rates for perceived
white offenders. In examining the statistics of the *Uniform Crime
Reports*, Hindelang found that blacks constituted a greater proportion of
arrests for rape and assault than was suggested by victims' perceptions of
the offenders. He attributed the disparity for rape to the likelihood that
more rapes involving black offenders are reported to the police than are
rapes committed by whites. Hindelang also suggested that blacks may
appear overrepresented in arrest statistics because of underreporting of
assault victimizations by blacks. Assault tends to involve people who
know one another and, as we noted earlier, victimizations involving
acquaintances are less likely to be reported than are victimizations
involving strangers. However, it is also possible that the overrepresentation of blacks in arrest statistics is more pronounced than in victimization survey data because of bias in the criminal justice system.

The victimization data on race and crime are generally consistent with police statistics and with the results of self-report surveys that take seriousness of offense into account. Hindelang's analysis focused on rape, robbery, and assault, none of which are common offenses among juveniles. Robbery does disproportionately involve juveniles, especially black male juveniles, but is nonetheless a rare offense in the total juvenile population. Many self-report surveys do not detail results for rape, robbery, and assaults in their research reports. Thus, measures of self-reported delinquency are heavily weighted with the most common juvenile offenses. When all offenses are lumped together, there is generally no significant difference between black and white juveniles in frequency of delinquent acts. However, as we noted in the section on self-reports, there is a tendency for blacks to differ from whites in their reports of the more serious delinquent offenses. In short, victimization data and self-report data are both consistent with the observation that the more serious the offense, the greater the disparity between blacks and whites.

WHO ARE THE VICTIMS?

In addition to providing another source of information on the distribution of crime and delinquency and a means of assessing the perceived characteristics of offenders, victimization data have been central to the growth of interest in *victimology,* that is, the study of victims. A considerable amount of descriptive detail is now available on the characteristics of victims. In fact, so much detailed information is available that it is not possible to summarize all of it in this text. The Law Enforcement Assistance Administration (1974) has drawn some conclusions based on victimization data:

> Victimization rates for personal crimes of violence were relatively higher for males, younger persons, blacks and other minorities, the poor, and for those separated and divorced. For personal crimes of theft, males, young persons, whites, and the more affluent were the more likely victims.

LEAA also reported that two-thirds of personal crimes of violence were committed by persons unknown to the victim. However, Hindelang's analysis revealed considerable variation in the relationship between victim and offender by offense: Offenses involving theft were more likely to involve strangers than were offenses in which theft was not involved. The offenses most likely to involve persons known to the victim were assault and rape.

While the "safe school" study by the National Institute of Education (Boesel et al., 1978) focused on some of the same issues as LEAA's national crime surveys, it concentrated on victimizations at school. This study found that most attacks and robberies at school involved offenders whom the victim had seen before and that in a large number of instances, the victim actually knew the offender by name (in 75 percent of the attacks and 47 percent of the robberies). In most cases the victim and offender were of the same sex. Males victimizing other males accounted for two-thirds of attacks and 72 percent of robberies. Older students were less likely to be attacked or robbed than were younger students. Although the study found no difference between black and white students for simple assault, it did find that blacks were more likely to be victimized in instances of more serious, aggravated assault. There were no differences in robbery victimization rates for black and white students. In their study of city life and delinquency, Savitz, Lalli, and Rosen (1977) found small differences between the victimization rates of black and white juveniles for robbery, assault, and extortion.

One issue examined by most victimization surveys is the relationship between the racial status of victims and the racial status of offenders. Hindelang's analysis showed that among minority groups, personal victimizations were "overwhelmingly" *intraracial*—that is, the victim and offender were of the same race (1976:197). For whites, however, only assault appeared to be an intraracial phenomenon in the majority of cases. For offenses involving theft, whites reported having been victimized by minority group members more often than by other whites.

The "safe school" study found that robberies were more likely than attacks to be *interracial* (victim and offender of a different race) and that this was the case especially when the victim was white (Boesel et al., 1978:106). One of the most interesting findings of the "safe school" study was the effect of membership in the school's dominant racial-ethnic group on the probability of victimization. In schools where they were in the minority, white students were more likely to be attacked or robbed than nonwhites. In schools where nonwhites were in the minority, the nonwhites had the greatest probability of being victimized.

SUMMARY

We began this chapter with Haney and Gold's statement that "the delinquent is a myth." When characteristics that *tend* to be associated with delinquency are abstracted and assigned to a "typical" delinquent *as if* they were the identifying properties of a distinct type of person, the depictions that result take on a mythical quality. Such attempts to summarize and generalize are oversimplifications of complex situations. Tentative generalizations about probable relationships are often transformed into "facts" about the definitive and unquestionable nature of delinquency in American society. In this chapter and Chapter 3, we have attempted to summarize very complex situations at the risk of some oversimplification. However, the images we have constructed are far less simplistic than those that abound in most proclamations about the "facts" of delinquency.

In this chapter we have tried to summarize a body of self-report survey research, as well as a body of research based on a more recently developed technique for studying crime—the victimization survey. Some conclusions suggested by the data produced by these two research methods conflict with patterns suggested by police and court statistics. However, there is also a surprising amount of consistency in some of the patterns of variation suggested by all three bodies of data. Below are several statements that are consistent with all three types of data. We deem these statements to be "consistent with the data" rather than "supported" or "demonstrated by the data" because they often go beyond the specific information available. For example, victimization survey data do not bear directly on statements about delinquency; this is often the case for national crime statistics as well. Thus, these statements are not statements of fact but, rather, tentative generalizations that appear at this time to be justified. The three types of data on crime and delinquency are consistent with the following observations:

1. Offense rates are higher among central-city youths than among youths in smaller communities and rural settings.
2. Offense rates are higher for males than females, with greater disparities occurring for more serious offenses.
3. Offense rates are higher for blacks than whites for offenses involving violence or major theft.
4. Young adults and juveniles account for a disproportionate amount of crime, but offenses involving theft tend to peak in younger age groups than offenses involving interpersonal violence (rape, assault, robbery).

While the above statements can be made using all three types of data on crime and delinquency, the following statements seem justified on the basis of self-report surveys and police statistics. Victimization data are not available on these issues.

1. Offense rates are higher in areas of cities experiencing racial succession than in more stable areas.
2. The disparity between male and female offense rates has been declining.
3. Asian Americans have the lowest offense rates, followed by whites and Chicanos, with blacks and Indian Americans exhibiting the highest rates.
4. Drug and alcohol offense rates have increased in both self-report and police data.

The alternative types of data produce several seemingly disparate findings. We specifically label the differences as "seemingly disparate" because the inconsistencies are often a matter of degree rather than of total contradiction. These findings include the following:

1. All three types of data show stable or declining offense rates in "recent" years, but the self-report data suggest such a pattern for an earlier time period than do victimization or police data.
2. The decline in rural-urban differences suggested by police statistics does not show up in self-report and victimization data, although self-report data suggest greater similarity over time between central-city and small-city youths.
3. The differences among racial categories in rates for serious offenses are greater in police statistics and victimization data than in self-report data, with self-reports showing little or no difference by race in the frequencies for all delinquent offenses combined.
4. Both self-reports and police data show social class to be weakly and inconsistently related to offense rates, but studies using police statistics are more likely to indicate such a relationship than studies using self-report data.

We present these statements with the warning that further research may negate or further qualify each and every one of them. Moreover, we feel it is equally important to realize that many of these statements are made on the basis of one or two studies or on the basis of studies conducted at different points in time and in different populations and settings. Although there have been literally thousands of studies of crime and delinquency, there has yet to be systematic research that can tell us to what degree variations in research findings are a product of the variable methods used or of other variations in research design and setting. As social scientists, we tend to believe that patterns or images consistently suggested in numerous studies using different methods are those that come closest to the "facts" of the matter.

REFERENCES

Akers, R. L. 1964. "Socioeconomic Status and Delinquent Behavior: A Retest." *Journal of Research in Crime and Delinquency* 1 (January):38–46.

Bidwell, C. E. 1975. "Commentary." In N. J. Demerath, III, et al., eds., *Social Policy and Sociology.* New York: Academic Press.

Block, R. L. 1970. "Police Action, Support for the Police and Support for Civil Liberties." Paper presented at American Sociological Association annual meeting. New Orleans.

Boesel, D., et al. 1978. *Violent Schools — Safe Schools: The Safe School Study Report to the Congress,* vol. 1. National Institute of Education. Washington, D.C.: U.S. Government Printing Office.

Chambliss, W. J., and R. H. Nagasawa, 1969. "On the Validity of Offical Statistics: A Comparative Study of White, Black, and Japanese High School Boys." *Journal of Research in Crime and Delinquency* 6 (January):71–77.

Clark, J. P., and E. P. Wenninger. 1962. "Socio-economic Class and Area Correlates of Illegal Behavior among Juveniles." *American Sociological Review* 27 (December):826–34.

Elliott, D. S., and H. L. Voss. 1974. *Delinquency and Dropout.* Lexington, Mass.: D. C. Heath.

Empey, L. T., and M. L. Erickson. 1966. "Hidden Delinquency and Social Status." *Social Forces* 44 (June):546–54.

Ennis, P. H. 1967. *Criminal Victimization in the United States: A Report of a National Survey.* Washington, D.C.: U.S. Government Printing Office.

Erickson, M. L., and L. T. Empey. 1963. "Court Records, Undetected Delinquency and Decision-Making." *Journal of Criminal Law, Criminology and Police Science* 54 (December):456–69.

Garofalo, J. 1977. *Local Victim Surveys: A Review of the Issues.* U.S. Department of Justice. Washington, D.C.: U.S. Government Printing Office.

Gold, M. 1970. *Delinquency Behavior in an American City.* Belmont, Calif.: Wadsworth.

Gold, M. and D. J. Reimer. 1974. "Changing Patterns of Delinquent Behavior among Americans 13 to 16 Years Old, 1967–1972." Report no. 1 of the National Survey of Youth, 1972. Institute for Social Research, University of Michigan.

Gould, L. C. 1969. "Who Defines Delinquency: A Comparison of Self-Reported and Officially-Reported Indices of Delinquency for Three Racial Groups." *Social Problems* 16 (Winter):325–36.

Haney, B., and M. Gold. 1973. "The Juvenile Delinquent Nobody Knows." *Psychology Today* (September):49–55.

Hawkins, R. O. 1973. "Who Called the Cops? Decisions to Report Criminal Victimization." *Law and Society Review* 7 (Spring):427–44.

Hindelang, M. J. 1971. "Age, Sex and the Versatility of Delinquent Involvements." *Social Problems* 18 (Spring):522–35.

———. 1976. *Criminal Victimization in Eight American Cities.* Cambridge, Mass.: Ballinger.

———. 1978. "Race and Involvement in Crimes." *American Sociological Review* 43 (February):93–109.

Hirschi, T. 1969. *Causes of Delinquency.* Berkeley: University of California Press.

Howard, M. K. 1975. "Police Reports and Victimization Survey Results: An Empirical Study." *Criminology* 12 (February):433–46.

Jensen, G. F., and M. L. Erickson. 1977. "Delinquency and Community: A Study of Juvenile Lawbreaking in Metropolitan and Small-Town Settings." Unpublished manuscript.

Jensen, G. F., and R. Eve. 1976. "Sex Differences in Delinquency: An Examination of Popular Sociological Explanations." *Criminology* 13 (February):427–48.

Jensen, G. F., J. H. Stauss, and V. W. Harris. 1977. "Crime, Delinquency, and the American Indian." *Human Organization* 36 (Fall):252–57.

Kapsis, R. E. 1978. "Residential Succession and Delinquency: A Test of Shaw and McKay's Theory of Cultural Transmission." *Criminology* 15 (February): 459–86.

Law Enforcement Assistance Administration. 1974. *Criminal Victimization in the United States.* Washington, D.C.: U.S. Government Printing Office.

————. 1977. *Criminal Victimization in the United States: A Comparison of 1975 and 1976 Findings.* Washington, D.C.: U.S. Government Printing Office.

Murphy, F. J., M. M. Shirley, and H. L. Witmer. 1946. "The Incidence of Hidden Delinquency." *American Journal of Orthopsychiatry* 16 (October):686–95.

Nagasawa, R. H. 1965. "Delinquency and Non-Delinquency: A Study of Status Problems and Perceived Opportunity." M.A. thesis. University of Washington.

Nye, F. I. 1958. *Family Relationships and Delinquent Behavior.* New York: John Wiley.

Nye, F. I., and J. F. Short, Jr. 1957. "Scaling Delinquent Behavior." *American Sociological Review* 22 (June):326–31.

Porterfield, A. L. 1946. *Youth in Trouble.* Fort Worth, Tex.: Leo Potishman Foundation.

Reiss, A. J. 1975. "Inappropriate Theories and Inadequate Methods as Policy Plagues: Self-Reported Delinquency and the Law." In N. J. Demerath, III, et al., eds., *Social Policy and Sociology.* New York: Academic Press.

Robison, S. M. 1936. *Can Delinquency Be Measured?* New York: Columbia University Press.

Savitz, L. D., M. Lalli, and L. Rosen. 1977. *City Life and Delinquency—Victimization, Fear of Crime and Gang Membership.* Washington, D.C.: Office of Juvenile Justice and Delinquency Prevention.

Schwartz, E. E. 1945. "A Community Experiment in the Measurement of Juvenile Delinquency." In *Yearbook, National Probation Association, 1945.* New York: National Probation Association.

Short, J. F., Jr., and F. I. Nye. 1958. "Extent of Unrecorded Juvenile Delinquency: Tentative Conclusions." *Journal of Criminal Law, Criminology and Police Science* 49 (November-December):246–302.

Skogan, W. G. 1974. "The Validity of Official Crime Statistics: An Empirical Investigation." *Social Science Quarterly* 55 (June):25–38.

————. 1976. "Citizen Reporting of Crime: Some National Panel Data." *Criminology* 13 (February):535–49.

Smith, P. E., and R. O. Hawkins. 1973. "Victimization, Types of Citizen-Police Contacts, and Attitudes towards the Police." *Law and Society Review* 8 (Fall):135–52.

Tittle, C. R., and W. J. Villemez. 1977. "Social Class and Criminality." *Social Forces* 56 (December):474–502.

Williams, J. R., and M. Gold. 1972. "From Delinquent Behavior to Official Delinquency." *Social Problems* 20 (Fall):209–29.

Wise, N. B. 1967. "Juvenile Delinquency among Middle-Class Girls." In E. W. Vaz, ed., *Middle Class Juvenile Delinquency.* New York: Harper & Row.

5.
EXPLANATIONS OF DELINQUENCY: BODY, MIND, AND LEARNING

At the sight of that skull, I seemed to see all of a sudden, lighted up as a vast plain under a flaming sky, the problem of the nature of the criminal—an atavistic being who reproduces in his person the ferocious instincts of primitive humanity and the inferior animals. Thus were explained anatomically the enormous jaws, high cheek bones, prominent superciliary arches, solitary lines in the palms, extreme size of the orbits, handle-shaped or sensile ears found in criminals, savages and apes, insensibility to pain, extremely acute sight, tattooing, excessive idleness, love of orgies, and the irresistible craving for evil for its own sake, the desire not only to extinguish life in the victim, but to mutilate the corpse, tear its flesh and drink its blood.
—Cesare Lombroso, *Crime, Its Causes and Remedies*

LOOKING FOR ANSWERS

The most common questions that people ask about delinquency are: "What makes kids do it?" "What's wrong?" "What can we do about it?" In this chapter and the next, we will examine several different ways of looking for answers to these questions. In the present chapter we will consider attempts to explain delinquency that focus on the biological and mental characteristics of individuals. We will also consider perspectives that focus on processes through which individuals learn delinquent behavior. We will concentrate primarily on theories that have been advanced as "scientific"—that is, anchored in fact and verifiable by means of observation.

However, to be able to evaluate theory and research on delinquency effectively, we must first consider varying points of view on how we should go about finding answers. Some people believe we can find answers by asking other people their opinions or by discussing the issues. Some believe we can find answers by asking the people who deal with delinquents every day. Others believe that such questions can only be answered through carefully conducted, objective, systematic research. Moreover, in seeking answers people have different expectations about what constitutes a satisfactory explanation, and understanding those expectations will help us to understand different ways of seeking answers.

Public Opinion

Most of us are familiar with public opinion polls that attempt to assess the beliefs, attitudes, and values of the American populace. One such poll by George Gallup asked a representative sample of American adults (twenty-one years of age and older): "What's behind the high crime rate in the United States?" The most commonly cited explanations focused on drugs, leniency of the law, lack of parental supervision, unemployment, poverty, and "permissiveness." In another Gallup poll, a similar sample was asked: "Which in your opinion is more to blame for crime and lawlessness in this country—the individual or society?" The majority of those polled (58 percent) felt that "society" was to blame, as compared to 35 percent who felt the individual was to blame and 7 percent who had no opinion.

In 1976 a youth council in a city in Arizona sponsored a panel discussion that included teenagers and representatives of labor unions, industry, and youth agencies. The participants were asked to develop a list of the top ten causes of juvenile delinquency. The subsequent newspaper headline read: "Ten Causes of Delinquency Identified." Foremost on the list was "lack of social education and intellectual freedom for students." After being combined with lists developed by other panels and submitted to a state planning agency, this list was to be presented to the federal Law Enforcement Assistance Administration.

Why then should we be concerned with uncovering the causes of delinquency? The people have spoken. Of course, the crucial question is whether or not the causes of delinquency can be decided by popular vote. If the majority vote that the world is flat, does that mean that the world is flat? Does the fact that a panel of citizens identifies "lack of social education and intellectual freedom" as a cause of delinquency mean that it is a cause? Moreover, if there is disagreement over causes, whose view is right? In the results of the Gallup poll that asked whether the "individual" or "society" is to blame for crime, differences of opinion among respondents reflected differences in occupation, age, education, party preference, region, and income. Those least likely to blame the individual were professionals and businessmen; the young (twenty-one to twenty-nine years of age); persons with higher levels of education; Democrats; persons not from the South; and persons with annual incomes of over $15,000. In short, people differ in their beliefs about the causes of crime, and such variation is linked with their social backgrounds.

Expert Testimony and Practical Experience

One response to the dilemma of trying to determine the causes of delinquency might be to ask an "authority." However, people accord legitimacy to different authorities. J. Edgar Hoover (who was director of the FBI for nearly half a century) was an authority on the causes of crime in the eyes of sizable segments of the American public, but not in the eyes of student protestors of the 1960s, such radical groups as the Black Panthers, most university criminologists, and many other American citizens. Our position in society and our attitudes toward various professions and institutions may decide which testimony we accept as "expert."

A common rationale for according legitimacy to certain people is the amount of "practical experience" those people have had in working with criminals and delinquents. This way of seeking answers can have its shortcomings. For example, one police inspector testified to the President's Commission on Obscenity and Pornography that "there has not been a sex murder in the history of our department in which the killer was not an avid reader of lewd magazines." In response to such testimony by police officers, Charles Keating, one of the Commissioners, stated: "In my opinion, their practical experience makes them experts which warrant special attention beyond that accorded the theoretician" (Keating, 1970).

The problem with "practical experience" is whether we can safely generalize from the experiences of an individual or even the experiences of a group. Suppose a group argues that pornography provides a safe alternative to overt sexual misconduct and—"in their experience"—has prevented thousands of sex crimes. Does "their experience" make it so? At one time or another, each of us has some "practical" experience with some aspect of crime—*but* our individual experience may be the "exception to the rule." To illustrate the dangers of generalization even further, consider the following statement by Edwin Schur: "Criminologists generally agree that *some* persons who suffer serious psychological disturbances commit crimes" (1969:62). However, as Schur goes on to note, criminologists also agree that some persons *without* such disturbances have committed crimes and that most persons, with or without a psychological disturbance, have knowingly broken the law at one time or another in their lives. If the personal experiences and testimonial cases used for generalizing about "causes" of crime were limited to only one of the categories of "some people," we might reach quite conflicting conclusions.

Individual and Probabilistic Causation

How, then, do we decide whether some condition is a "cause" of delinquency? If we focus on individual cases, we can find a wide range of statements about why particular individuals broke the law. In fact, our legal system is based on an ideology of *individual* motivational causes. An important factor in the search for suspects is the establishment of a motive, or reason, that a particular individual might have committed a crime, and the determination of guilt is supposed to be based on standards more definite than mere probabilities. In contrast, sociologists are interested in identifying factors or conditions that increase the *probability* of crime or delinquency in a population. Such factors or conditions may not *always* result in delinquency, and delinquency may not always follow from those factors or conditions. In short, as contemporary sociological criminologists, we do not presume to be searching for what are called "necessary and sufficient" causes. If we found some characteristic or circumstance that *always* resulted in delinquency and if we determined that delinquency never occurred unless that characteristic or circumstance was present, then we would have identified a necessary and sufficient cause. No one has done so yet, and it would be safe to predict that no one is likely to do so in the future. Rather, we are likely to find conditions that "tend" to generate delinquency—that is, that increase the probability of delinquency. It might be scientifically exciting to find necessary and sufficient causes, but we do not expect such a discovery.

REQUIREMENTS FOR ANSWERING CAUSAL QUESTIONS

If public opinion, expert testimony, and practical experience are not sufficient for identifying causes, then how do we decide between conflicting points of view? While there is considerable debate and controversy over the whole issue of causation, there does seem to be some agreement in sociology that certain minimum requirements must be met before any argument that some condition *causes* some other condition can be accepted as convincing (Hirschi and Selvin, 1967). These minimum requirements involve the determination of association, nonspuriousness, and causal order.

Association

The first requirement in trying to establish causality is that the conditions must be correlated, or *associated,* with one another in a probabilistic sense. For example, if "lack of parental supervision" is ever to qualify as a cause of delinquency, it had better be associated with a higher probability of delinquency than close parental supervision. It would not be enough merely to show that the parents of a large proportion of teenagers who come to the attention of the court rarely know where their children are, with whom they are, or what they are doing; many teenagers who *never* come to the attention of the court have parents who rarely know such things. The issue in demonstrating an association is whether the probability is "higher" in one circumstance than in the other.

Table 5–1 is taken from a study of high school students in and around Richmond, California, in the mid-1960s (Hirschi, 1969:89). This study measured parental supervision by asking students "Does your mother know where you are when you are away from home?" and "Does your mother know whom you are with when you are away from home?" Their answers were assigned scores and combined to yield a "score" in terms of "mother's supervision," which ranged from "low" to "high." Of those at the low end, 55 percent indicated in a questionnaire that they had committed two or more of a variety of delinquent acts, while only 12 percent

TABLE 5–1 *Self-Reported Delinquency, by Mother's Supervision (In Percent)*

Self-Reported Acts	Mother's Supervision				
	Low 0	1	2	3	High 4
None	0	28	45	59	63
One	45	31	26	21	26
Two or more	55	41	29	20	12
Totals	100	100	100	100	101
	(11)	(29)	(236)	(252)	(698)

Source: Travis Hirschi. *Causes of Delinquency,* p. 89. Berkeley: University of California Press, 1969.

of those at the high end indicated commission of two or more offenses. There is an association, but it is far from perfect; many highly supervised teenagers do report delinquent acts. The probabilities are, however, very different at the two ends of the continuum.

Many people mustering evidence to support their causal claims do not even bother to compare one condition with another to decide whether crime or delinquency is unusually high under the circumstances they are advocating as causal. For example, in his dissenting critique of the majority report by the President's Commission on Obscenity and Pornography, Charles Keating stated that he and his organization had found thirty-four cases "in which obscene material was related to an act of antisocial conduct." Keating noted that he did not have "the professional interest of social scientists in the academic aspect of whether or not obscenity is the direct cause of every anti-social act committed by a person 'addicted to' or the 'reader' of such materials. It is enough for me that a relationship has been found" (Keating, 1970).

But in what sense is "a relationship" demonstrated by Keating's thirty-four documented cases? What proportion of those *not* exposed to obscene material committed antisocial acts? What proportion of those who *were* exposed to such material did *not* commit antisocial acts because of their exposure? Keating's argument may be correct, but the data presented tell us nothing about a probabilistic connection between pornography and antisocial conduct. Furthermore, the issue is not an "academic" one. If the probability of antisocial conduct is lower for the nonreading population, as Keating's argument implies, then eliminating pornography might have its intended effect. If, however, there is no difference between non-readers and the rest of the population, eliminating pornography would make no difference. If pornography serves as an alternative to sexual deviance and the probability of antisocial conduct is thus higher among nonreaders, then eliminating pornography might increase antisocial conduct. A concern with demonstrating an association by comparing probabilities is good sense, *not* just an esoteric concern of academics.

Nonspuriousness

A second requirement in advancing a causal argument is to assess the possibility that two conditions are only *spuriously* related. Even when we can empirically demonstrate some measure of association between event A and event B, it is conceivable that the relationship is coincidental or misleading for one reason or another.

Some spurious relationships are totally due to chance coincidences, with no causal connection between the variables under consideration. For example, it might be possible to show some degree of association between the volume of smoke in German steel mills and the number of cloistered nuns in Australia. There really does not appear to be any connection between these two variables, but if by some coincidence there is, we may dismiss it as a random, spurious relationship.

Another type of spuriousness arises when two conditions are associated because of a connection with some third condition. Two variables, X and Y, may be related only because of some association with a third variable, Z. For example, the finding that adolescents *with* delinquent records watch more violent programs on television than adolescents *without* delinquent records does not demonstrate a causal connection. What an adolescent watches and what he or she does may coincide without being causally related. Both could reflect the operation of other influences, such as parental preferences and attitudes. Although it is difficult to anticipate all arguments of spuriousness, a careful thinker will anticipate as many as possible.

Once again, we should note that a concern for identifying spurious relationships is not an esoteric concern of "nit-picking" scientists. If two variables are only spuriously related, then changing one will not have any effect on the other. If other conditions are accounting for both, then it is those other conditions that will make a difference.

Causal Order

A theorist or researcher must also confront the issue of causal order. If two conditions, characteristics, or phenomena are associated and the relationship is nonspurious, then we will want to know which caused which—that is, the *causal order*, or the sequence of interrelations. For example, if incarcerated offenders were found to be anxious, fearful, and depressed, someone might argue that anxiety, fear, and depression "cause" or facilitate involvement in crime and delinquency. Someone else might argue that anxiety, fear, and depression are caused by the labeling or sanctioning experience itself. The mere fact that the two conditions are related does not automatically infer a causal ordering of events. Many instances involve processes of "reciprocal" causation, wherein both conditions feed upon each other. For example, failure in school may contribute to delinquency, and delinquency may be followed by reactions and experiences that further contribute to problems at school. Many theorists implicitly assume a certain causal order without considering alternatives or mustering any evidence that their assumption is correct.

Intervening Processes

While the minimum requirements outlined above are important for assessing claims about causation, another crucial question concerning causal relationships involves the processes that *intervene* and in essence explain how or why a connection between two conditions or characteristics comes to exist. Different theorists may agree that a causal characteristic or circumstance has been found but may disagree on the way it exerts causal influence. For example, we noted in chapters 3 and 4 that females are less likely to be delinquent than males. Some biologically oriented theorists have attempted to attribute this difference to chromosomes. In contrast, other theorists have attributed the difference to a greater risk of official labeling for boys than for girls. Still others have attributed such a difference to variation in parental supervision, variation in status problems, variation in cultural and subcultural values, or combinations of such conditions. Thus, even with a convincing demonstration of association, nonspuriousness, and causal order, the difference between a valid and an invalid theory may hinge on the successful identification of intervening or explanatory processes.

With these preliminary criteria for assessing claims about "causation" in mind, let us now consider biological and psychological perspectives on the causes of crime and delinquency.

BIOLOGICAL SCHOOLS OF THOUGHT

For much of the history of Western civilization, people have been viewed as occupying a special, unique niche in the universe by virtue of their possession of a soul, free will, and reason. Some of the earliest systematic thought about crime and criminal justice was based on such a premise. The "classical school" of criminology (prominent during the 1700s and represented by such philosophers as Montesquieu, Voltaire, Marat, Beccaria, and Bentham) believed that the law and criminal justice should be rational institutions. This school argued that human behavior is based on hedonism and that the pleasure-pain principle should serve as the guide for social control. Individuals choose actions that give pleasure and avoid those that give pain. Punishment should fit the crime and be certain, severe, and swift enough to be taken into account by rational human beings making decisions about their lives and actions.

By the mid-1800s, however, with the development of biology and theories of natural selection and evolution, the "uniqueness" of humankind was being called into question. If Charles Darwin's theories of evolution were correct, human beings could be viewed as one stage in the evolution of organic life and could be studied as such. The most famous criminological work along this line was carried out in Italy in the late 1800s and early 1900s and is referred to as "Italian positivism." Positivism got its name from its proponents' belief that their method, which purported to induce explanations of crime from observed, measurable "facts," was a "positive" approach to studying phenomena. The name most prominently associated with the positivistic school is that of Italian physician Cesare Lombroso. We will consider Lombroso's work, as well as that of a number of other scholars who, influenced by Lombroso, contributed to this approach.

Cesare Lombroso

Using data from government agencies, anthropological measurements, and tools of the medical sciences, Lombroso sought to discover the "causes" of crime. While Lombroso considered a wide range of social and societal forces that might contribute to crime (for example, population density, the price of bread, wealth, education, unemployment, newspapers, and so on), he is best known for his view of the "born" criminal, or "innate" criminal types. Lombroso argued that a large proportion of criminals (he estimated 40 percent) was "atavistic"—that is, genetic throwbacks. He reached this conclusion on the basis of observations of the physical and biological characteristics of criminals. Lombroso believed his observations revealed an unusual number of criminals to be more akin to lower forms of life and to primitive man than to "civilized" people.

Lombroso delineated several other types of criminals (criminals by passion, insane criminals, pseudocriminals, criminaloids, and habitual criminals). He also examined the social and environmental correlates of crime. Despite that examination, he continually advocated biological interpretations of differences that could be given sociological interpretations. Thus, when confronted with the fact that women had lower rates of crime than men, Lombroso argued as follows:

> That women less often are engaged in highway robbery, murder, homicide, and assault is due to the very nature of the feminine constitution. To conceive an assassination, to make ready for it, to put it into execution demands, in a great number of cases at least, not only physical force, but a certain energy and a certain combination of intellectual functions. In this sort of development women almost always fall short of men. It seems on the other hand that the crimes that are habitual to them are those which require a smaller degree of physical and intellectual force, and such especially are receipt of stolen goods, poisoning, abortion, and infanticide. (1911:184–85)

In this argument Lombroso appears not only to be bound to biological or "constitutional" explanations but to stereotypes of women as well. A logical outcome of his theory of biological inferiority and crime might be the argument that men are biologically inferior to women in that men are more primitive or animalistic. Instead, Lombroso depicted women as inferior to men, lacking the intellectual and constitutional ability to carry out the same acts as men. He typically proceeded by discovering a fact based on available statistics and then providing an interpretation that made the fact fit his theory. Since no predictions or hypotheses were ever presented before assessing the facts, Lombroso's theory could be bent to explain anything.

Lombroso's work can be criticized in terms of the criteria of causality that we established earlier in this chapter. For one thing, Lombroso did not establish an association between physical attributes ("biological inferiority," or "degeneracy") and the probability of criminal activity. The most he could say (and even that is debatable) is that he found some physical differences between incarcerated or dead Italian convicts and a sample of Italian soldiers. Moreover, once Lombroso had developed his working hypothesis that criminals tended to be atavistic ("throwbacks"), he selectively searched for and highlighted slight differences. He did not state in advance of his search any criteria for identifying atavism or biological inferiority but, rather, defined atavism in terms of whatever differences he found.

Even ignoring those shortcomings, some of the differences that Lombroso observed could have been spurious or acquired after involvement in crime. For example, Lombroso continually cited tattooing as indicative of "atavism." Yet, tattooing might have been disproportionately common among prisoners only because it was common within the occupations or social backgrounds from which most prisoners came. The same criticism is applicable to Lombroso's claims that the hair of criminals is "dark and thick" and that criminals are "taller and heavier" than noncriminals. Physical characteristics may be *coincidentally* connected with imprisonment if they are common in groups with a high risk of imprisonment.

Finally, even if Lombroso had established significant nonspurious associations between physical characteristics and crime, there would still be competing nonbiological interpretations. Such interpretations identify intervening social or cultural mechanisms that imbue physical characteristics with significance. For example, societies develop standards of beauty and conceptions of the ideal man and the ideal woman. Thus, variations in physical attributes may be a basis for differential treatment by others and may result in different *social* experiences. The color of one's skin and hair and characteristics such as height, weight, and sex may be whole or partially determined by one's genetic makeup, and there may be associations between some such characteristics and crime. However, that is not proof that "proclivities" toward crime are inherited or genetically determined. Such associations may mean nothing more than that certain physical characteristics have social significance and that such social significance comes to be reflected in behavior.

Despite all the serious errors in Lombroso's research, he is often referred to as "the father of scientific criminology." It may very well be that more has been written about Lombroso than about any other criminologist. He was a catalyzing force behind the movement to develop a science of criminology, stressing the need for a scientific method and admonishing the classical school that "the era of faith was over and the scientific age had begun" (Schafer, 1969:106).

Charles Goring

In *The English Convict,* published in 1913, Charles Goring, an English physician, delivered a devastating critique of Lombroso's work. Goring argued that Lombroso had not provided adequate statistical evidence of the differences claimed and that his theoretical biases had colored his interpretation of the data. Rather than merely criticize, however, Goring gathered data on 3,000 convicts and compared types of offenders within that sample. He then compared those findings to data available for the general population on ninety-six traits. Goring's statistical analysis, which used the latest techniques available, remains one of the most sophisticated in the history of criminology.

In his careful analysis, Goring could find no evidence of Lombroso's criminal types. However, he did find differences between convicts and norms for the English population in stature and measures of intelligence. Convicts were shorter, weighed less, and were classified as lower in intelligence than the general population. Other differences were found to exist only because of connections with stature and intelligence. After considering a wide range of characteristics, Goring found that these two were the only persistent, reliable differences.

Goring noted that although the differences he found could be given a number of interpretations, he was himself convinced that "the force of heredity plays some part in determining the fate of imprisonment" (1913:272). The differences between convicts and nonconvicts in stature and intelligence persisted when other factors were taken into account and were more prominent in his data than differences by family situation or social status. His findings led him to conclude that convicts were physically "inferior" to nonconvicts.

E. A. Hooton

Although Goring's work has been described as dealing a "crucial blow to Lombrosian theory" (Quinney, 1970:69), the controversy over Lombroso's work did not end there. In a work entitled *Crime and the Man*

(1939), E. A. Hooton attacked Goring on much the same grounds as Goring had attacked Lombroso. Hooton, a Harvard anthropologist, felt that Goring had been biased against Lombrosian theory and had interpreted his data in the manner least favorable to Lombrosian notions. After comparing data from over fifteen thousand prisoners, delinquents, and "insane" subjects to data from about two thousand "sane" subjects, Hooton concluded:

> One set of consistent contrasts rears itself in a solid, unbroken, and towering front. The putatively law-abiding citizen, however humble his social and economic status, is larger, superior in physique and in most anthropological characters, so far as judgments of quality can be made, to the White criminal of comparable ethnic and racial origin and drawn from approximately similar occupational levels. In metric and morphological features of the head and face the differences between criminals and civilians suggest more strongly lack of adaptability in the criminal organism than straightforward size diminution. On the whole, the biological superiority of the civilian to the delinquent is quite as certain as his sociological superiority. There are objectivity and substantiality in measured physical differences which are usually lacking to the appraisals of sociological phenomena. It is easier to measure a head than to estimate civic virtue, more simple to obtain lung capacity than capacity for civilization. (1939:376)

Despite Hooton's criticisms of Goring's work, his own findings were quite similar to the results published in *The English Convict*. Nowhere did Hooton present evidence of an atavistic criminal type, nor did he clearly separate biological from sociological differences. He noted that sociological and biological characteristics were interrelated but took the position that the organism creates the social environment and not the reverse. He did not demonstrate the validity of this position but instead stated it as a personal theoretical commitment.

Like Lombroso and Goring, Hooton based his comparisons primarily on convicts and an arbitrary sample of the "civilian" population. The noncriminal sample was drawn from such groups as visitors to a beach, students, firemen, and inpatients and outpatients at hospitals. Neither of Hooton's groups can be considered to be scientifically random or representative samples of the populations under consideration. In comparing his samples, Hooton reported significant differences for seven of thirty-three of his measurements. He found the criminal group to be younger, shorter, lighter, with smaller chest breadth, head circumference, upper face height, nose height, and ear length (1939:118). Figure 5–1 illustrates some of Hooton's measurements. Hooton reported many other differences as well, such as a higher proportion of "red-brown" hair, more eye folds, low and sloping foreheads, and thin lips. Hooton never did justify how these differences indicated biological "inferiority" or deficiency.

Hooton's research is subject to the same criticisms as the earlier studies. He did not clearly identify what characteristics should be used as a

FIGURE 5-1 *Hooton's Measurements*

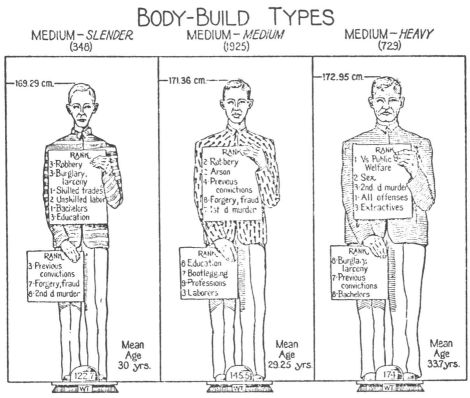

BODY-BUILD TYPES

| MEDIUM – *SLENDER* (348) | MEDIUM – *MEDIUM* (1925) | MEDIUM – *HEAVY* (729) |

— 169.29 cm. —

RANK
3-Robbery
3-Burglary,
 larceny
1-Skilled trades
2-Unskilled labor
1-Bachelors
3-Education

RANK
3-Previous
 convictions
7-Forgery, fraud
8-2nd. d. murder

Mean
Age
30 yrs.

122.7

— 171.36 cm. —

RANK
2-Robbery
2-Arson
4-Previous
 convictions
8-Forgery, fraud
1-1st d murder

RANK
8-Education
7-Bootlegging
9-Professions
3-Laborers

Mean
Age
29.25 yrs.

145.5

— 172.95 cm. —

RANK
1-Vs Public
 Welfare
2-Sex
3-2nd. d murder
1-All offenses
3-Extractives

RANK
8-Burglary,
 larceny
7-Previous
 convictions
8-Bachelors

Mean
Age
33.7 yrs.

17.1

Source: E. A. Hooton. *Crime and the Man.* Cambridge, Mass.: Harvard University Press, 1939. Copyright © 1939 by Harvard University Press. Reprinted by permission.

measure of biological or constitutional inferiority. He reached conclusions about biological causes of crime by comparing convicts and arbitrary samples of nonconvicts. He did not clearly untangle sociological and biological factors. He did not eliminate the possibility that the differences he observed were a product of selection into the convict population, nor did he address the social processes through which biological differences may have consequences for behavior.

William Sheldon

The most consistent difference between convicts and nonconvicts found in the works summarized above is stature. The convicts apparently were shorter and lighter than the comparison groups. Drawing on earlier work by Ernst Kretschmer, William Sheldon, a physician and professor of psychology, proposed a "constitutional psychology" in which the body is the starting point for understanding personality and behavior (*Varieties of Delinquent Youth,* 1949). Sheldon's focus was on body type, or "somatotype," which he defined as "a quantification of the primary components determining the morphological structure of the individual." A person's type was determined by the predominance of structures associated with digestion and assimilation of food ("endomorphy"), by the predominance of bone, muscle, and connective tissue ("mesomorphy"), or by the predominance of skin, appendages, and the nervous system ("ectomorphy").

Sheldon's hypothesis was that there would be differences between the somatotypes of delinquent boys and the somatotypes of the rest of the population, although he could not predict in advance what those differences might be. Bodies were somatotyped by measuring the intermixture of the three types of structures. Sheldon's data were based on 200 youths who were wards of a home for delinquent boys in Boston between 1939 and 1942. The measurements for the delinquent youths were compared with measurements for 4,000 college students drawn primarily from Harvard University, the University of Chicago, and Oberlin College. Compared to the college sample, the sample of delinquent youths tended to be mesomorphic. Sheldon concluded, "So far as the somatotype is concerned our sample of delinquents, far from being weaklings, are a little on the hefty and meaty side" (1949:730). In contrast to Hooton's criminal sample, Sheldon's delinquents were not shorter than the general population.

Although Sheldon showed, at best, a difference in body build between some delinquent youths and a college sample, he presumed that such data are relevant to understanding delinquent behavior in general. In fact, he claimed that further exploration of constitutional differences could "cure the lust for war and delinquency" and proposed a nationwide compilation of biological profiles in order to "find out who are the biological best" (1949:879). He did not examine the possibility that the differences between his two samples might have been related to differential selection by the institutions from which the samples were drawn. He also did not address the social meaning or cultural relativity of "inferiority," the social meaning of different body builds, and the differences in social experiences that might result from differences in physical appearance. Rather, he argued that different body types are reflected in different personality types and, ultimately, in behavior. Sheldon's data are inadequate for substantiating his more grandiose arguments and assumptions.

Sheldon Glueck and Eleanor Glueck

The last of the classic works dealing with bodily constitution and delinquency that we will review here is a study by Sheldon and Eleanor Glueck (*Unraveling Juvenile Delinquency,* 1950). This study involved 500 delinquent youths and 500 relatively "nondelinquent" youths in the

Boston area. The groups were matched as well as possible in terms of age, general intelligence, ethnicity, and residence in an underprivileged neighborhood. The study gathered data on a wide variety of social, psychological, and physical characteristics.

The Gluecks found no significant differences in health between their two samples but did report that a greater proportion of delinquent youths than of nondelinquent youths had been "restless" children. Delinquents actually had fewer "tics" and neurological handicaps than did nondelinquents. The Gluecks also reported that the delinquents were "superior" to nondelinquents in body size and conformity to a "masculine" physical type. As in William Sheldon's research, delinquent boys were found to be more mesomorphic than the control group of nondelinquents.

The Gluecks' work, together with Sheldon's, does suggest that boys who come to the attention of the court or end up in institutions are unusually likely to have mesomorphic body builds. Of course, whether mesomorphy is indicative of biological inferiority or superiority is a matter of social or cultural definition. Moreover, we still do not know how this preponderance is generated. It may be that boys with certain body builds are more likely to pursue aggressive activities of all sorts or to become members of groups in which such builds are an asset. Our own cultural definitions of masculinity may enhance the probability that persons with certain builds will behave in certain ways and will have certain social experiences as they grow up. Finally, we do not know if body type is correlated with *delinquent behavior*. Mesomorphic boys may be more likely to be processed officially when caught than endomorphic or ectomorphic boys because they appear tougher and more physically threatening.

Criminal Families

A common observation in the history of criminological research has been that the probability of a given person's having a criminal record is enhanced if another member of the family or a relative has a record. For example, Goring reported that parents who were "legally designated criminal" tended to have sons who acquired criminal records. In addition, the criminal record of one brother enhanced the probability that another brother would acquire a record. Goring also found a marital association— that is, there was a tendency for a spouse to have a criminal record if the other spouse had one. In sum, it appears that related persons tend to have related experiences.

The familial association can easily be given a sociological interpretation. However, the constitutional psychologists (including even Goring, who was so critical of Lombroso and whom Hooton attacked as biased against biological explanations) advocated explanations that emphasize the inheritance of dispositions toward crime. Since marital partners are not biologically related, the marital association would seem to be of questionable relevance to the inheritability of crime. However, Goring interpreted even that association as evidence of the inheritance of criminal tendencies. He argued that people who are predisposed to crime tend to marry others who are predisposed to crime.

The study of the Jukes family undertaken by Dugdale (1877) and Estabrook (1916) is one of the most famous in the literature on "criminal family trees." Of some 1,200 relatives, Dugdale and Estabrook found 140 (12 percent) who had been convicted of some crime. This finding was interpreted as support for the theory that criminal tendencies are inherited. However, there are many problems with such an interpretation. For one thing, whether 12 percent constitutes a "high" percentage can only be assessed by comparing it with the percentage occurring in a sample of unrelated persons. Moreover, any similarity in behavior could easily reflect a similarity in social circumstances for related persons. Thus, studies of so-called criminal families do not demonstrate the influence of genetic inheritance on crime or delinquency.

Another type of research that has been concerned with the inheritance of criminal tendencies has involved the study of twins. If dispositions toward crime are inherited, then identical twins who share identical genes should behave more similarly than fraternal twins whose genetic makeup varies. A review of such studies by Ashley Montague (1951) showed that when one identical twin had a criminal record, the other had a record in 67 percent of the cases studied, as compared to 33 percent for fraternal twins. In short, there is greater *concordance* for identical twins. According to Sutherland and Cressey (1970), sloppy methodology in some research has exaggerated the degree of concordance. For example, one study claimed concordance to be 3 times greater for identical twins than for fraternal twins when it was actually closer to 1.1 times. Similarly, Sutherland and Cressey noted that in three European studies the concordance was about 1.4 times greater for identical twins. Karl Christiansen (1973) reported 3 times greater concordance for males and about 5 times greater concordance for females. Christiansen's research also suggested variations resulting from other factors in that concordance was greatest for twins in rural settings and varied by offense.

Our criticism of the studies of criminal families applies to the studies of twins as well. We would expect that the more nearly alike two people are, the greater the probability that they will have similar learning experiences and grow up in a similar social environment. Even if separated at birth and raised apart, concordance in behavior between persons who look alike could reflect the social significance of physical variables in a given society. If the behavior of identical twins raised in radically different environments was found to be significantly more concordant than the behavior of fraternal twins raised in different environments, then twin studies would be far more convincing evidence of a genetic influence on crime.

A study directed toward explaining the concordant behavior of twins was carried out in Norway by Odd Dalgard and Einar Kringlen (1976). Like earlier researchers, Dalgard and Kringlen reported greater concordance in probabilities of having a criminal record among identical twins than among fraternal twins. However, they also considered the possibility that the identical twins may have behaved more similarly than the fraternal twins because of more nearly similar environmental experiences, rather than because of a common genetic inheritance. Comparing fraternal twins who had been exposed to nearly similar environmental circumstances with identical twins who also had experienced similar environments, they found that the greater concordance for identical twins disappeared. Their final conclusion was that such findings "support the view that *heredity factors are of no significant importance in the etiology of common crime"* (1976:232).

Chromosomal Abnormalities

There is considerable evidence that rates of crime and delinquency are higher for males than for females. Since a major difference between males and females is the Y-chromosome (males are XY and females XX), that chromosome has been suspect as a cause of aggression. Moreover, many people have reasoned that if one Y-chromosome can make such a difference, then two Y-chromosomes must lead to excessive aggression.

Reports of the discovery of inmates or notorious criminals with extra Y-chromosomes have been published in scientific journals and popularized by newspapers. *A Chicago Daily News* article in 1972 was headlined: "Government Psychologist Links Crime, Genes." The publicity that the issue has received gives the impression that scientists have demonstrated a link between chromosomal imbalance and crime. But have they? The research referred to in the newspaper article was based on examinations of "subnormal" or "mentally ill" male inmates in a maximum security hospital in Scotland (Jacobs et al., 1965). Dr. Patricia Jacobs and associates found that 9 of 315 of these inmates had an extra Y-chromosome. The estimated incidence for the general population was 0.15 percent. Hence, these inmates were unusually likely (3 percent as compared to 0.15 percent) to have this particular abnormality. However, it is also important to remember that even in this very unique population of inmates, 97 percent did not have an extra Y-chromosome.

Jacobs and her colleagues did not demonstrate that the Y-chromosome led to or was associated with violence. In another study that compared the nine XYY inmates with a random sample of XY males, Price and Whatmore (1967) found there was in fact evidence of *less* violence among the XYY cases than among the XY cases. Four of the nine XYY males had records of violent personal crimes, as compared to seventeen of eighteen in the XY group.

A more recent piece of research on the issue appeared in an article in the journal *Science* in 1976. In that article, Herman Witkin (a research psychologist with the Educational Testing Service) and his colleagues are critical of earlier research for a number of reasons:

> First, the search for XYY men has often been conducted in selected groups presumed to be likely to contain them, such as institutionalized men and tall men. Second, a number of reports now in the literature are based on observations of a single case or just a few cases. Third, many studies of XYY's have not included control XY's; and in those that did, comparisons were often made without knowledge of the genotype of the individuals being evaluated. The control groups used have varied in nature, and comparison of results from different studies has therefore been difficult. There has been a dearth of psychological, somatic, and social data obtained for the same individual XYY men. Finally, there do not yet exist adequate prevalence data for the XYY genotype in the general adult population with which the XYY yield of any particular study may be compared. (Witkin et al., 1976:548)

To avoid these problems, Witkin and his colleagues chose to gather data in Denmark by using social records that were available for a sample of the general population. They then compared normal males with males having different patterns of chromosomal abnormalities and attempted to identify the possible intervening factors that might account for any predominance of abnormalities among inmates or among men with criminal records. Out of a sample of 4,139 men, they found 12 XYY cases, 16 XXY cases, and 13 XY cases that had other chromosomal anomalies. Of the 12 XYY cases, 5 (42 percent) were found to have been convicted of one or more offenses, as compared to 3 of the 16 XXY cases (19 percent) and 9 of the 13 abnormal XY cases. There did appear to be an inordinately high probability that XYY men would have criminal records. However, there were 389 men with records and only 5 of them were XYY cases. The abnormality is so rare that it cannot account for very much criminal activity.

Further analysis by Witkin et al. yielded no evidence that XYY males are more prone to violent crimes than XY males. The elevated crime rate reflected property crimes, not aggressive acts against persons. The XYY males were found to have lower scores on intelligence tests and to be taller than XY males. However, even with these differences in intelligence and height taken into account, there was still a difference between XYY and XY cases. The researchers suggested that chromosomal anomalies may have pervasive developmental consequences but that there is no evidence that aggression against persons is one of them.

Biology and Delinquency: An Overview

The methodological problems characterizing most biological research make it impossible for us to reach any firm conclusions about biological variables and delinquent activity. However, this inadequacy is not sufficient grounds for rejecting biological notions about crime and delinquency altogether. One trend in the biologically oriented research that we have reviewed has been a shift away from the search for "born criminal types" to the study of the more subtle ways in which biological characteristics or processes may contribute to crime and delinquency. Goring's conclusion that there was no evidence of a born atavistic criminal type still stands. Similarly, there has been a shift away from the assumption that the "differences" found among offenders show them to be "inferior." Notions of inferiority are culturally and socially relative. Finally, there has also been a shift away from the view that biological factors automatically propel people into lives of crime to the view that biological factors may be just one among a variety of considerations relevant to understanding some proportion of involvement in crime and delinquency.

The Danish chromosomal research, the Norwegian study of twins, and the Gluecks' studies of physique and delinquency exemplify the trends we have just described. Certain body types and chromosomal patterns may show up disproportionately among persons who appear in police records and institutions. However, intervening processes accounting for any such tendencies have not been clearly identified. The Danish chromosomal research acknowledged the possibility of differential labeling of men of different stature and intelligence (two factors correlated with an XYY pattern). The Gluecks assumed real behavioral differences associated with body type but went on to argue that there are differences in strength, energy, and temperament associated with body type that may or may not *facilitate* delinquency, depending on the operation of extrabiological factors. The Norwegian twin study indicated that similar social experiences generate similarities in the behavior of twins.

Biological characteristics are so extensively infused with social meaning that we may never be able to clearly separate the impact of the organic from the social. For example, a study appearing in the sociological literature (Shoemaker, South, and Lowe, 1973) reported that when a sample of college students was presented photographs and asked to indicate which persons they believed to be most likely to have committed a crime, the choices were *not* random. Although the researchers could not identify the actual characteristics leading to student choices, their findings suggested that people do have images of what an offender looks like. The source of such images and their consequences for labeling and official processing have yet to be established. However, it is certainly possible that such images or conceptions do have consequences for labeling and processing; our institutions may be filled with people who *look* guilty or suspicious to us. From such a perspective, it is not a body type that causes delinquent behavior but the way in which society reacts to a certain body type.

Since Lombroso's early observations, biological interpretations of the variation in delinquency by gender have grown more sophisticated, recognizing the role of other factors and shying away from notions of inferiority. The following statement typifies this new trend:

> Notwithstanding the ethnographic curiosa reported by some anthropologists (Mead, 1935), there is abundant cross-cultural, and indeed cross-specific, evidence of gender differences in temperament. Males tend to be more dominant and aggressive and females more nurturant, not only in nearly all human societies but in most primate ones as well. Culture almost invariably elaborates on and reinforces these biological predispositions, but it very seldom succeeds in neutralizing or reversing them. Scarcely anyone would question the immense influence of culture in shaping the specific sex roles in a given society, but it would be equally foolish to deny sex-linked biological predispositions, which are probably regulated in good part through hormonal balances. (van den Berghe, 1973:281)

Such a position cannot be readily tested because biological sex and sex roles are so intimately interrelated in human society that it is difficult to untangle them. However, certain events could negate biological interpretations of gender differences. For example, if females came to exhibit crime rates comparable to males, it would then be difficult to argue that differences in the recent past were biologically produced. Similarly, if females experiencing the same patterns of socialization as males were found to have comparable rates, we could then argue that the gender difference is socially rather than biologically based. Some research (Jensen and Eve, 1976) has already shown that much of the sex difference in delinquency can be attributed to differences in parental supervision, school performance, and other measures of social experiences that differ between males and females. Of course, it can always be argued that the differences in social experience are biologically determined and, hence, that biological sex differences are the ultimate cause of differences in crime. At present, biological interpretations of gender difference are being questioned. They have not, however, been totally eliminated from the body of competing theories.

PSYCHOLOGICAL SCHOOLS OF THOUGHT

In our review of biological perspectives, we noted the gradual shift away from the assumption that lawbreakers are fundamentally different types of human beings. Beginning with the work of Sigmund Freud, a new perspective for understanding human behavior emerged. This perspective attributed troublesome behavior to psychological problems anyone could encounter in the course of human development. Leading further away from the notion of born criminal types, the new perspective emphasized experiences that *anyone* might have and learning processes that *anyone* might experience. We cannot deal here with all psychological perspectives but will instead concentrate on ideas that have been specifically advanced as relevant to understanding crime and delinquency: (1) the psychoanalytic approach to delinquency, (2) the concept of the psychopath, (3) the findings of personality research, and (4) learning theories of crime and delinquency. Finally, we will consider the relevance of social learning theories for the sociological perspectives on crime and delinquency that we will discuss in Chapter 6.

The Psychoanalytic Approach

The shift away from the assumption that people who break the law are biologically or constitutionally different from others is reflected in the work of Sigmund Freud and other psychoanalysts. Freud was not particularly concerned with explaining criminal behavior but, rather, with advancing his ideas on mental illness. However, the Freudian psychoanalytic approach opened a new dimension to the study of deviant behavior by proposing that problem behavior reflects problems in personality development.

Freud postulated that the human personality consists of three basic elements. At birth the only dimension of human personality that functions is the *id.* This id seeks immediate gratification and is concerned only with pleasure. As the child grows, an *ego* develops that is in close contact with social reality. The ego attempts to curb the drives and urges of the id and to direct behavior in a way that is consistent with physical and social reality. The *superego*, the last element of the personality to develop, is a type of conscience that attempts to restrain the id. Freud introduced the concept of the *unconscious* by describing the id and superego as basically unconscious elements of the personality and the ego as the conscious part.

From the Freudian perspective, the human personality is characterized by a struggle between the creative urges of the id and the constraining force of the superego. The "healthy" personality achieves a balance between these two forces. Personality disorders arise when one or the other force is too dominant. For example, domination of the id could be reflected in criminal activities, and an overdeveloped superego could result in anxiety neurosis. Normal socialization processes are conducive to healthy personality development, but if the socializing agents are punitive, inconsistent, or arbitrary, the child's personality may get out of balance. Thus, from the psychoanalytic view, delinquent behavior is symptomatic of deep emotional conflicts and unconscious motivations.

August Aichhorn, a Viennese psychoanalyst, was one of the first persons to approach the issue of delinquency from a Freudian perspective. In *Wayward Youth* (1936), Aichhorn argued that although there are "dissocial" types with inborn defects, individuals constitutionally predisposed to crime at birth are rare. He believed that such behavior as delinquency is a symptom of one of a variety of psychic problems or conflicts experienced by children as they are transformed from organisms dominated solely by instinctive needs to social beings. In Aichhorn's view, anyone could experience the problems that result in delinquency; social and dissocial persons differ merely in the degree to which they encounter problems in personality development.

From a psychoanalytic perspective, what are the problems that can result in delinquency? An almost endless list of specific problems could be compiled. There are, however, some basic categories of problems that psychoanalysts stress. One set of problems centers around the development of the superego. "Normal" personality development supposedly entails incorporation of ego ideals—that is, identification with the social and ethical standards of conduct of "significant others" in one's environment. If experiences or circumstances interfere with superego development, or if ego ideals are themselves criminal, then delinquency can result.

Another cause of delinquency from the psychoanalytic perspective is inadequate ego development. The infant is depicted as guided by the *pleasure principle* in seeking gratification of instinctive needs. However, normal personality development involves learning to take "reality" into account (the *reality principle*). To achieve normal development, the ego must learn to sacrifice immediate pleasures in order to achieve pleasure in the future. Thus, from the psychoanalytic perspective, the inability to defer gratification is indicative of disturbed ego development and is a potential source of delinquency.

The normal personality is characterized by harmony, or balance, between instinctive needs, reality, and the conscience. If the ego and superego are unable to control instinctive needs, the individual is likely to get into trouble with others in his or her environment. On the other hand, if such needs are denied or repressed by an overly rigid ego or superego, the individual may develop mental and behavioral problems that are a reflection of the inner tension or conflict. In Kate Friedlander's words (1947:185), "Generally speaking, delinquent behavior is the result of a disturbance in the relative strength of the three domains of the mind, the Id, the Ego and the Super-Ego."

Friedlander has outlined her view of the crucial steps in development that determine a child's potential for delinquency. She argues that the emotional link between mother and child is crucial to modification of instinctive urges. A boy's desire for his mother's attention and competition with his father for that attention (the *Oedipus complex*) may result in mental and behavioral problems, depending on the manner in which such conflicts are resolved. Friedlander depicts the formation of the conscience and cohesiveness of the family as other crucial factors in adaptation to social life.

The proof that psychoanalysts offer for such theories is very different from that demanded by sociologists. Psychoanalysts support their arguments with case histories of individuals who come to their attention. If a person is experiencing some sort of mental, emotional, or behavioral difficulty, analysts attempt to identify the source of the problem by encouraging the person to talk freely about past experiences that may have caused unconscious conflicts. Thus, causes are discovered "after the fact." Rather than identifying those conditions thought to generate delinquency, measuring them, and assessing whether or not such conditions increase the probability of delinquency, psychoanalysts point to cases that support their notions. It is unlikely that psychoanalytic theories will ever be tested in terms of the standards of causation that are central to the social sciences. In the psychoanalytic view, causes are unknown to the subject and can only be discovered with the help of experts who have special psychoanalytic training. Thus, there is no way for an outsider to prove or disprove the validity of psychoanalytic explanations. The "data" that support psychoanalytic theories are events and experiences that only the expert is qualified to interpret.

On the other hand, some basic psychoanalytic notions are quite compatible with the sociological explanations that we will consider in the next chapter. The assumption that the attempt to maximize pleasure can lead to conflict with the law if not checked by socialization is quite compatible with a brand of sociological theory known as social control theory. The emphasis in psychoanalytic theory on relationships with parents and identification with adult ego ideals is quite compatible with the emphasis of some sociological theories on the family in delinquency causation. However, sociological theorists are at odds with psychoanalytic explanations that attribute crime and delinquency to hidden mental conflicts. The focus in sociological explanations is on more observable and more readily measurable aspects of the external social environment and the groups to which an individual belongs. Moreover, although the psychoanalytic approach acknowledges that human social adaptation is a continuous, lifelong process, it focuses extensively on early childhood experiences and maternal relationships. Both may be important for understanding delinquency, but sociologists tend to focus more extensively on institutions that a child enters in later childhood and adolescence, such as the school and adolescent society. The sociological focus includes forces that are not likely to be recognized when the focus is on early childhood—for example, limited economic opportunity, legitimacy of the law, and social standing.

Sociologists also question the cultural biases that tend to be implicit in psychoanalytic notions. What is "normal" personality development? What is "criminal" behavior? The answers depend on the norms or standards of the system being studied. Psychoanalytic theory maintains that learning to defer gratification in the short run for the sake of gratification in the long run is a "normal," "healthy" stage in human social adaptation. But what if a child is born into an environment where the likelihood of gratification "in the long run" is extremely uncertain? Children in economically secure, predictable environments where parents and other agents insure future gratification have reason to follow such a pattern of adaptation. Under different circumstances, focusing on immediate gratification may be normal. Such sayings as "Live for today and let tomorrow take care of itself" were not invented and perpetuated by psychopaths.

The Concept of the Psychopath

Psychiatrists, psychologists, and some sociologists have used the concept of the psychopath in dealing with criminality. This concept grew out of the notion that some criminals are so depraved, so bad, or so "morally insane" that they stand out from the ordinary criminal population. The psychopath has been depicted as having a complex of character traits that supposedly makes him unique among criminals. Sociologists William and Joan McCord have described the psychopath as follows:

> The psychopath is asocial. His conduct often brings him into conflict with society. The psychopath is driven by primitive desires and an exaggerated craving for excitement. In his self-centered search for pleasure, he ignores restrictions of his culture. The psychopath is highly impulsive. He is a man for whom the moment is a segment of time detached from all others. His actions are unplanned and guided by his whims. The psychopath is aggressive. He has learned few socialized ways of coping with frustration. The psychopath feels little, if any, guilt. He can commit the most appalling acts, yet view them without remorse. The psychopath has a warped capacity for love. His emotional relationships, when they exist, are meager, fleeting, and designed to satisfy his own desires. These last two traits, guiltlessness and lovelessness, conspicuously mark the psychopath as different from other men. (1964:16)

An "underdeveloped conscience" and "inability to identify with others" are cited as especially crucial defining characteristics, but it is the entire pattern of traits that supposedly defines the psychopath.

Labeling certain criminals "psychopaths" cannot take us very far in explaining criminal or delinquent behavior. In fact, attempts to use the concept to explain the behavior of the psychopath can easily result in a circular argument. To argue that a person commits an antisocial, aggressive, and impulsive act because he or she is antisocial, aggressive, and impulsive is hardly a satisfactory explanation. Since the concept is defined in terms of both the deviant behavior and social-psychological characteristics, it cannot be used to explain the behavior itself. People with the characteristics listed are defined as psychopaths. The notion itself does not explain the behavior included in the definition.

As we will see in Chapter 6, there is evidence that persons who are unable to identify with others and who do not define lawbreaking as wrong are more likely to break the law. However, to say that people with those two characteristics are psychopaths adds nothing to the explanation of criminal and delinquent behavior. Moreover, the term psychopath is used to refer to a type of person with certain specific characteristics when in reality people vary considerably in terms of those characteristics—that is, in the degree to which they are socially bound to others, in the degree of their acceptance of the standards embodied in the law, in their tendency to defer gratification, in aggression, and in all of the other characteristics cited as symptoms of the psychopath. The point at which variation in these characteristics justifies application of the label has never been specified.

In fact, the concept of the psychopath is so vague (even as defined by the McCords) that the label can be readily applied to any person or group whose behavior is frowned on by other persons and groups. The McCords argue that "from the ranks of the psychopaths come political demagogues, the most violent criminals, the riot leaders, sexual misfits, and drug addicts" (1964:2). None of the theorists using the notion so broadly has ever bothered to demonstrate the degree to which "psychopathic" persons or groups exhibit "psychopathic" characteristics. The only evidence presented has come from studies of carefully selected, extreme cases.

Personality Research

Some psychological researchers have attempted to provide empirical support for the notion that certain personality types are unusually prone to delinquency. Research aimed at providing support for such an argument has often involved the use of the Minnesota Multiphasic Personality Inventory (MMPI), a self-administered inventory of 550 items designed to assist in the identification of personality problems. In fact, reviews of personality research have concluded that the MMPI is the only test that has consistently differentiated delinquents from nondelinquents. For example, Waldo and Dinitz (1967) reported that of ninety-four studies using the MMPI between 1950 and 1965, 81 percent found a difference between the norms for delinquents and the norms for the general population of "nondelinquents." However, the test as a whole has not yielded consistent results; its most consistent findings have been produced with a subscale known as the psychopathic deviate scale (Pd scale). A review of this type of research through 1975 (Tennenbaum, 1977) yielded similar observations regarding the consistency of MMPI findings.

But what does the difference indicated by such personality research mean? Can we conclude that delinquents differ from nondelinquents in psychopathic personality traits? A partial answer to this question can be found by considering the items in the MMPI and Pd scale. At least fourteen items in the MMPI inventory actually measure self-reported delinquency, and one item in the Pd scale calls for a response to the statement "I have never been in trouble with the law." We have already seen that the concept of psychopath does not get us very far in explaining delinquency since the definition of psychopath includes reference to the very behaviors that the concept is meant to explain. Similarly, the Pd scale itself includes measures of the very behavior that the scale is introduced to explain. In other words, the scale may show nothing more than that adolescents who have been in trouble with the law are more likely than those who have not been in trouble with the law to indicate they have been in trouble with the law! We have to conclude that such tests do not tell us much about the causes of delinquency.

Even if we ignore the questionable relevance of the MMPI research to conclusions about personality and delinquency, we must recognize that virtually all personality-delinquency research has focused on adolescents who have acquired delinquent records of some sort. People who get caught and labeled may have certain characteristics that differ from those who are not caught and labeled, even though their actual offense behavior may be the same. Moreover, if the personality assessment is done *after* the labeling, any differences found could be the result of the labeling experience itself.

There is also a serious question of "spuriousness" in personality research. Personality inventories measure behavior on the basis of responses to statements. Responses that indicate "deviant" performance may be correlated with "deviant" performance in relation to the law, but both may be a product of other characteristics of a person's social environment. In fact, one study (Volkman, 1958) that used the MMPI found that when age, race, intelligence, and father's occupation were taken into account, the delinquent category did not differ significantly from other categories. Although the study had too few subjects to be conclusive, it did suggest the very real possibility that the relationship between personality test scores and delinquency may be spurious.

Personality assessments conducted by persons who are aware of the current circumstances of the subject are also suspect. Knowledge that an individual has come to the attention of the police or the courts can easily influence the interpretation of that individual's "personality." Each of our lives and the sum of our experiences are sufficiently complex that there is bound to be something in our backgrounds that would justify applying certain psychiatric or psychological labels. Thus, although our initial response to a surprising crime may be "He seemed perfectly normal!" in retrospect we can usually find something abnormal that makes the offender's background seem consistent with this new event.

One means of circumventing problems of sampling bias and spuriousness is to compare self-report data on delinquency with the results of personality tests. Michael Hindelang administered the Pd scale from the MMPI and several similar scales from the California Personality Inventory to high school students in California. He also gathered data on self-reports of delinquency. Hindelang found that scores on the personality scales were related to the self-reports of delinquency and that this relationship was not spurious. In other words, it was not due to links with gender, age, or social status. Hindelang concluded:

> The findings of the present study indicate that those engaging in a wide range of delinquent activities, relative to those not engaging in those delinquent activities, are more stubborn, undependable, and deceitful in dealing with others . . . the former are immature, moody, and undercontrolled . . . more impulsive, shrewd, uninhibited, aggressive, and pleasure-seeking, and show an absence of deep emotional response, an inability to profit from experience, and a disregard of social mores. (1972:81)

Hindelang did not address problems of circularity involved in the use of personality inventories nor did he adequately justify the vague labels applied on the basis of scale scores. As noted above, personality scales sometimes include behavioral reports of deviance. Such reports obviously should correlate with similar behavioral self-reports: people who disregard social mores certainly *do* disregard social mores. However, what do such statements contribute to the explanation of delinquency? To say people do impulsive, shrewd, uninhibited things because (relative to those who do not) they are impulsive, shrewd, and uninhibited does not provide a satisfactory understanding of such behavior. Moreover, lumped together under all those vague terms and spread throughout such personality inventories are measures of social relationships, which, in fact, *are* important for understanding delinquency. However, these relationships are slighted by the emphasis on personality traits.

Learning Theories

As we have seen, psychological perspectives have been characterized by the view that the individual's problems reflect developmental experiences rather than inborn defects. In that sense, then, there is a tendency to view delinquency as a product of learning. Several different types of learning theories have been applied to the study of delinquency.

Most college students have heard of Russian physiologist Ivan Pavlov and of "Pavlov's dogs." Pavlov conducted experiments in which he sounded a buzzer before giving a dog a piece of meat. Pavlov found that after he had repeated this procedure thirty or forty times, the dog began to salivate at the sound of the buzzer even when it was not given meat. The dog's salivation was a *conditioned response* to a stimulus (the buzzer) that had come to signal, or cue, the presentation of food. Over time, if the buzzer was not followed by food, the response gradually faded (*extinction*), although it could reappear (*spontaneous recovery*). Pavlov also found that such learned associations or conditioned responses could be transferred to new but similar situations and stimuli (*generalization*).

Building on the work of psychologist Hans Eysenck, Gordon Trasler applied some of Pavlov's classic principles of learning to the explanation of criminality. Trasler (1962) argued that learning experiences when we are very young affect the probability of delinquency and crime later in life. For example, when parents respond negatively to a child's breaking rules at home, the child will experience anxiety, an involuntary reaction like the salivation of Pavlov's dogs. Such anxiety can become a conditioned response to a variety of similar situations. Since anxiety is viewed as a state that people like to avoid, people supposedly avoid or escape situations that give rise to it. Thus, Trasler's theory is that conformity is escape-avoidance behavior and that the inhibition of criminality is a learned, conditioned response that is strongly resistant to extinction because it functions to reduce anxiety. Trasler did introduce personality notions into his theory in that he argued that some people are more resistant to such conditioning than others—specifically, that people who are outgoing and crave excitement (extroverts) are resistant to escape-avoidance conditioning, while people who are quiet, self-controlled, and introspective (introverts) are readily subject to such conditioning. The most central principle in Trasler's theory, however, is the idea that cues in learning situations come to be coupled with reactions of the involuntary nervous and glandular system and that these conditioned reactions come to act as a barrier to crime.

Fundamental to Trasler's theory is the idea that through a training procedure, the individual learns *not* to become a criminal. Trasler illustrated his concept of "passive avoidance conditioning" with experiments in which rats were given an unpleasant stimulus when they touched a lever that normally released food pellets. Even after the negative reinforcement was removed, the rat still would not touch the lever. The "anxiety" that the rat had acquired in anticipation of punishment continued, even though the punishment no longer existed. Similarly, if an individual is conditioned to experience punishment for wrongdoing during early years of socialization and thereby acquires anxiety, the individual will experience anxiety in contemplating delinquent behavior, even when the actual probability of punishment is remote. In this fashion, deviant behavior is avoided.

Operant theory is another brand of learning theory that has been applied to the study of crime and delinquency. Operant theory draws on the theoretical formulations of B. F. Skinner, a well-known Harvard psychologist. Rather than focusing on ill-defined concepts of personality or on involuntary conditioned reactions, operant theorists focus on behaviors that are considered to be voluntary and controlled by the central nervous system. For example, when a child touches a candle flame, the behavior results in pain. The withdrawal of the child's hand may be a reflex action, but the future inhibition of the behavior (touching flames) can be viewed in operant terms. *Operant behavior* is behavior that has consequences that in turn affect the future probability of the behavior. Stimuli that increase or strengthen the behavior are called *reinforcers,* and stimuli that decrease or weaken the behavior are known as *punishers.* Stimuli that become learned cues associated with reinforcement or punishment are called *discriminative* stimuli.

The emphasis in operant theory is on *behavior* and the explanation of behavior in terms of observable aspects of the individual's environment. Radical behaviorists feel that such concepts as personality are unobservable artifacts that contribute nothing to the explanation of behavior but, rather, hinder scientific progress. B. F. Skinner (1971) has been particularly adamant in attacking theories that assume the existence of autonomous human beings who act of their own free will. Skinner believes that a science of behavior will be achieved only if such notions as free will and personality are abandoned. Of course, proponents of other psychological schools of thought do not agree. This disagreement is reflected in divergent definitions of psychology as the science of the "mind" and as the science of "behavior."

We noted in Chapter 1 that as early as 1896 American sociologists had postulated that criminal or delinquent behavior is learned behavior. A formal statement of this position—known as the *differential association theory* of criminal behavior—was first presented by Edwin Sutherland in 1939. Sutherland modified his statement in 1947 (*Principles of Criminology*). He named the perspective differential association theory because delinquency was attributed to the balance of associations with people who defined lawbreaking in favorable and unfavorable terms. The differential association theory consists of nine propositions. The most important propositions concerning the learning process are: (1) "criminal behavior is learned in interaction with other persons in a process of communication" and (2) "the principal part of the learning occurs within intimate personal groups." Burgess and Akers have modified and restated these principles in "operant" terms:

> Criminal behavior is learned both in nonsocial situations that are reinforcing or discriminative and through that social interaction in which the behavior of other persons is reinforcing or discriminative for criminal behavior. . . .
>
> The principal part of the learning of criminal behavior occurs in those groups which comprise or control the individual's major sources of reinforcement. (1966:137, 140)

Sutherland's other propositions have also been reformulated, but for present purposes these two give the essential flavor of an operant approach.

Fundamental to differential association theory is the view that deviant behavior is learned in much the same way as conforming behavior.

Sutherland stated that "criminal behavior as human behavior, has much in common with noncriminal behavior, and must be explained within the same general framework used to explain other human behavior" (Sutherland and Cressey, 1970:73). Although many criticisms have been leveled at the difficulty, if not impossibility, of empirically testing the theory of differential association, Sutherland's concepts greatly contributed to the demise of the view of crime and delinquency as some form of pathology and shifted attention to the issue of differential social values.

Sociology and Social Learning

The social learning theories that we have just described deal with the processes through which criminal and conformist behavior are established and sustained. By themselves, those theories tell us little about the conditions or circumstances under which such learning processes are most or least likely to occur. It may be true that criminal and delinquent behavior is ultimately a product of "differential reinforcement of such behavior over conforming behavior," but such statements do not identify the conditions that weight reinforcement in the direction of criminal and delinquent behavior.

Burgess and Akers and Trasler have suggested some possibilities for identifying the social reinforcers of criminal and delinquent behaviors. They have noted that minority group members who live in slum conditions are likely to have been deprived of many social reinforcers for conforming behavior and that such conditions increase the probability that reinforcement will become contingent on behaviors defined as criminal. Furthermore, Trasler has observed that passive avoidance conditioning is more characteristic of middle-class parents than of lower-class parents.

Explicitly or implicitly, the sociological perspectives that we will consider in the following chapter make assumptions about the conditions affecting the differential reinforcement of criminal and conforming behavior. For example, "social disorganization" perspectives attribute variation in crime to variation in the vitality of certain institutions that have traditionally smiled on conformity and frowned on crime (such as the family, the neighborhood, the church, and the school). If these social institutions are "disorganized" because of such factors as population change, urbanization, and industrialization, the probability that crime will be punished and conformity rewarded may be quite low. Similarly, the "strain" theorists whom we will discuss in the next chapter argue that when people find that the legitimate opportunity to obtain certain goals or rewards is limited, they are likely to explore or invent illegitimate alternatives. If specific social groups come to approve illegitimate avenues for achieving success, or if new standards of conduct and order emerge where conventional institutions have failed, crime and delinquency may then become subculturally acceptable ways of behaving.

Thus, variable crime rates may reflect normative conflict, which is the central tenet of the "cultural conflict" theories we will consider.

Social learning theories are quite compatible with sociological perspectives. These theories postulate that other people play a major role in the process through which individuals learn delinquent behavior. They also attempt to delineate the nature of learning processes, which sociologists have taken for granted. On the other hand, sociologists have been more concerned than psychologists and learning theorists with identifying the social conditions that structure the distribution of differential learning processes. As Akers has noted:

> The general culture and structure of society and the particular groups, subcultures, and social situations in which the individual participates provide learning environments in which the norms define what is approved and disapproved and the reactions of others (for example, in applying social sanctions) attach different reinforcing or punishing consequences to his behavior. In a sense, then, social structure is an arrangement of sets and schedules of reinforcement contingencies. (1977:64)

We turn to such perspectives in the next chapter where we consider theory and research that attribute delinquency to the structural, cultural, and group characteristics that shape learning processes.

SUMMARY

We began this chapter by outlining the different sources people rely on in seeking answers to questions about the causes of delinquency—public opinion and expert testimony and experience. As an alternative to these sources, social scientists have attempted to gather and analyze data on crime and criminals and on delinquency and delinquents, with the aim of identifying characteristics of people or their environments that increase the probability of crime and delinquency. In the course of these efforts, scientists have developed a set of standards for assessing claims that some characteristic or condition is a cause of crime or delinquency. Such standards require that causal claims be backed up with evidence that (1) shows an *association*, (2) eliminates possibilities of *spuriousness*, and (3) establishes a *causal order*. Causal claims should also be preceded by a concerted effort to acquire data representative of the populations under study and to create valid, reliable measures of variables. Even when these standards have been taken into account, there may be divergent views concerning the mechanisms or processes through which the causal relationship is established. Different theorists may identify different intervening variables. It is important to have a rudimentary understanding of these issues because most criticisms of research focus on failures to take one or more of them into account.

In terms of those standards for assessing causal claims, assessments of biological research on the causes of crime and delinquency generally result in such conclusions as "biological explanations of crime have repeatedly failed to withstand critical examination" and "most criminologists today believe that in light of the available evidence, such explanations are of little use in understanding criminal behavior" (Sykes, 1978:231). The biological research we reviewed was often characterized by sampling bias, ill-defined or undefined concepts, possibilities of spuriousness, alternative causal orders, and failure to consider nonbiological interpretations. The shortcomings of these studies mean that we cannot accept their results as conclusive.

However, neither can we rule out the possibility of genetically, physiologically, or biologically determined differences in behavior. More than one study has found differences in body build between delinquent and nondelinquent youth, and more than one study has found higher than expected proportions of property offenders among men with chromosomal abnormalities. In addition, more than one study has reported that identical twins are more similar in their criminal behavior than are fraternal twins. These findings do not demonstrate that tendencies toward crime are inherited or generated by our bodies, but neither do methodological shortcomings allow us to reject such possibilities.

Biological characteristics are so infused with social meaning that we may never be able to separate the impact of the organic from the social. Moreover, in terms of their contribution to explaining crime or delinquency, many of the sociological variables we will examine in subsequent chapters do a much better job of differentiating between delinquents and nondelinquents than do genetic or biological distinctions. Characteristics such as an extra Y-chromosome cannot explain very much because they are too rare. Delinquency is quite a common activity among adolescents, and sociologists are inclined to search for the explanation in experiences and characteristics that are common as well.

The development of psychoanalytic and psychological schools of thought represented a shift away from the assumption that criminals and delinquents are basically different types of organisms to the view that they are simply people who have encountered problems while in the process of developing into social beings. The standards of proof for such theories are very different from those expected in the social sciences. We cannot judge whether psychoanalytic perspectives are correct or incorrect explanations of delinquency since they have not been tested in terms of the standards of causation that are central to the social sciences.

The concept of the psychopath and attempts to measure the dimensions of the psychopathic personality have not advanced our understanding of crime and delinquency. Definitions of the concept, as well as scales that are presumed to measure it, actually include reference to the very phenomenon to be explained. We certainly do not doubt that people's feelings, attitudes, and beliefs are correlated with their behavior, but we do question whether the search for personality differences has in any way provided scientifically adequate or consistent evidence about such correlations.

One issue on which sociological and psychological theories are likely to agree is that delinquent behavior is primarily learned behavior. Psychologists and social psychologists vary in the learning processes that they emphasize and in the degree to which they incorporate notions of personality into their theories. Some focus on principles of classic conditioning and involuntary anxiety reactions, while others focus on operant conditioning that involves voluntary behavior and on the interplay between behavior and its consequences. Sociologists have actually used principles of operant conditioning to restate sociological theory. Such efforts show lines of convergence between sociological and pyschological perspectives, with the latter identifying learning processes and the former identifying characteristics of society, culture, or groups that structure distribution of those learning processes.

REFERENCES

Aichhorn, A. 1936. *Wayward Youth.* New York: Viking Press.

Akers, R. L. 1977. *Deviant Behavior.* Belmont, Calif.: Wadsworth.

Burgess, R. L., and R. L. Akers. 1966. "A Differential Association-Reinforcement Theory of Criminal Behavior." *Social Problems* 14 (Fall):128–47. Copyright 1966 by the Society for the Study of Social Problems. Reprinted by permission.

Christiansen, K. O. 1973. "Mobility and Crime among Twins." *International Journal of Criminology and Penology* 1 (February):31–45.

Dalgard, O. S., and E. Kringlen. 1976. "A Norwegian Twin Study of Criminality." *British Journal of Criminology* 16 (July):213–32.

Dugdale, R. L. 1877. "The Jukes: A Study in Crime." In *Pauperism, Disease, and Heredity,* 4th ed. New York: Putnam.

Estabrook, A. H. 1916. *The Jukes in 1915.* Washington, D.C.: Carnegie Institute.

Friedlander, K. 1947. *The Psycho-Analytic Approach to Juvenile Delinquency.* New York: International Universities Press.

Glueck, S., and E. Glueck. 1950. *Unraveling Juvenile Delinquency.* New York: Commonwealth Fund.

Goring, C. 1913. *The English Convict.* London: His Majesty's Stationery Office.

Hindelang, M. J. 1972. "The Relationship of Self-Reported Delinquency to Scales of the CPI and MMPI." *Journal of Criminal Law, Criminology and Police Science* 63 (1):75–81.

Hirschi, T. 1969. *Causes of Delinquency.* Berkeley: University of California Press.

Hirschi, T., and H. C. Selvin. 1967. *Delinquency Research: An Appraisal of Analytic Methods.* New York: Free Press.

Hooton, E. A. 1939. *Crime and the Man.* Cambridge, Mass.: Harvard University Press. Copyright © 1939 by Harvard University Press. Reprinted by permission.

Jacobs, P. A., et al. 1965. "Aggressive Behavior, Mental Subnormality, and the XYY Male." *Nature* 208 (December):1351.

Jensen, G. F., and R. Eve. 1976. "Sex Differences in Delinquency." *Criminology* 13 (February):427–46.

Keating, C. 1970. "Memorandum re Statistical Study of Relationship of Obscenity to Crime and Other Antisocial Behavior." In President's Commission on Obscenity and Pornography, *The Report of the President's Commission on Obscenity and Pornography,* Exhibit C. New York: Bantam Books.

Lombroso, C. 1911. *Crime, Its Causes and Remedies.* Boston: Little, Brown.

McCord, W., and J. McCord. 1964. *The Psychopath: An Essay on the Criminal Mind.* Princeton, N.J.: Van Nostrand. Copyright 1964 by Litton Educational Publishing, Inc. Reprinted by permission of Van Nostrand Reinhold Company.

Montague, A. 1951. "The Biologist Looks at Crime." *Annals of the American Academy of Political and Social Science* 217 (September):53.

Price, W. H., and P. B. Whatmore. 1967. "Behavior Disorders and Patterns of Crime among XYY Males Identified at a Maximum Security Hospital." *British Medical Journal* 1:533–37.

Quinney, R. 1970. *The Problem of Crime.* New York: Dodd, Mead.

Schafer, S. 1969. *Theories in Criminology.* New York: Random House.

Schur, E. M. 1969. *Our Criminal Society.* Englewood Cliffs, N.J.: Prentice-Hall.

Sheldon, W. H. 1949. *The Varieties of Delinquent Youth.* New York: Harper.

Shoemaker, D. J., D. R. South, and J. Lowe. 1973. "Facial Stereotypes of Deviants and Judgments of Guilt or Innocence." *Social Forces* 51 (June):427–33.

Skinner, B. F. 1971. *Beyond Freedom and Dignity.* New York: Alfred A. Knopf.

Sutherland, E. H. 1939. *Principles of Criminology,* 3rd ed. Philadelphia: J. B. Lippincott.

———. 1947. *Principles of Criminology,* 4th ed. Philadelphia: J. B. Lippincott.

Sutherland, E. H., and D. Cressey. 1970. *Criminology,* 8th ed. Philadelphia: J. B. Lippincott.

Sykes, G. M. 1978. *Criminology.* New York: Harcourt Brace Jovanovich.

Tennenbaum, D. J. 1977. "Research Studies of Personality and Criminality: A Summary and Implications of the Literature." *Journal of Criminal Justice* 5 (3):1–19.

Trasler, G. 1962. *The Explanation of Criminality.* London: Routledge & Kegan Paul.

van den Berghe, P. 1973. "Sex and Age: The Tyranny of Older Men." In *Society Today,* 2nd ed. Del Mar, Calif.: CRM Books. Copyright © 1973 by Random House.

Volkman, A. P. 1958. "A Matched Group Personality Comparison of Delinquents and Non-Delinquents." *Social Problems* 6 (Winter):238–45.

Waldo, G. P., and S. Dinitz. 1967. "Personality Attributes of the Criminal: An Analysis of Research Studies, 1950–1965." *Journal of Research in Crime and Delinquency* 4 (July):185–202.

Witkin, H., et al. 1976. "Criminality in XYY and XXY Men." *Science* 193 (August):547–55. Copyright © 1976 by the American Association for the Advancement of Science.

6.
EXPLANATIONS OF DELINQUENCY: STRUCTURE, CULTURE, AND INTERACTION

The way men behave is largely determined by their relations with each other and by their membership in groups. *Social relations are at the foundation of both motivation and control. The goals and aspirations that set people into motion are greatly influenced by their social relations. Social relations are also instruments of control, for they limit action and restrain impulses that might threaten the orderly arrangement of independent lives.*
—L. Broom and P. Selznick, *Sociology*

SOCIOLOGICAL CONCEPTS OF DELINQUENCY

In their pursuit of a sociological explanation of crime and delinquency, sociologists have devoted considerable attention to the study of individual offenders and nonoffenders. However, as we observed in Chapter 1, sociologists have also been interested in delinquency as a "group" or "subcultural" phenomenon. In fact, many of the early sociologists specifically excluded the explanation of individual lawbreaking from their theories. For example, Clifford Shaw and Henry McKay (1942) developed a theory of delinquency during the 1920s and 1930s that they intended to apply "primarily to those delinquent activities which become embodied in groups and social organization." Thus, although they have often concentrated on explaining the behavior of individuals, sociologists have also attempted to explain the emergence, distribution, and persistence of delinquent groups, organizations, and traditions.

Today, there are at least four different concepts of delinquency in sociological literature. Such diversity makes it difficult to summarize sociological explanations, if for no other reason than that a theory developed to explain delinquency conceived of in one sense may not be relevant to explaining another conception. First, there is the concept of delinquency as a type of behavior involving a type of group—the delinquent *gang.* Second, delinquency is often conceived of in terms of a set of values, norms, beliefs, and techniques that is passed on from one generation of adolescents to another—a delinquent *subculture* or *contraculture.* Third, sociologists have dealt with delinquency as an *individual* phenomenon, focusing on the differentiation of *delinquents* from *nondelinquents.* Fourth, most current sociological theory and research has shifted to a concept of delinquency as *behavior in violation of the law,* regardless of whether it is the behavior of individuals, groups, or subcultures.

The shift to a behavioral focus has occurred both as a product of self-report methodology, which focuses on individual admissions, and as a result of criticisms of other concepts of delinquency. Some sociologists have criticized the focus on gangs because it limits the study of delinquency to groups which account for only a small amount of the total volume of delinquency in America (Hirschi, 1969:52–53). Similarly, critics have questioned the assumption that there are "delinquent subcultures" or "contracultures" to be explained (Matza, 1964; Sykes and Matza, 1957). Several theorists have also questioned whether such concepts as subculture are necessary for understanding delinquent behavior.

On the other hand, a recent study for the Law Enforcement Assistance Administration of the Department of Justice, conducted by Harvard anthropologist Walter Miller, concluded that teenaged gangs are currently a major dimension of the crime problem and have been mistakenly ignored in recent years (see Display 6–1). This point of view does not fit the image suggested by self-report studies. Martin Gold has summarized his impressions and reasons for denying that "gang boys are responsible for most delinquency":

> The "gang" image seldom fit the teen-age groups involved in delinquent behavior. That is, the groups did not regularly and frequently commit delinquent acts together; their members did not characterize themselves as especially delinquent compared with other teen-agers; and their behavior together was not usually delinquent. Rather, the groups of teen-agers who committed delinquent acts consisted usually of two or three youngsters who often hung around together, doing all sorts of things that teenagers do together, and from time to time engaging in delinquent behavior. From the point of view of even the most delinquent boys, their companions in crime were drawn from the ranks of the many fellows they knew and spent time with; seldom were any particular boys ever consistent fellow offenders. More important than the particular company was the presence of an opportunity for delinquency at a time when everyone's mood was ripe for the action.
>
> Perhaps gang delinquency, not much a part of the Flint [Michigan] scene, is more characteristic of the hearts of great cities where teen-agers may stick closer together with fewer friends than they do in Flint, and where the delinquent opportunity and the daring-defiant mood are more often coincident. Yet observers of delinquency in the inner-city slums of London and New York report that the gang image is much overblown even there.
>
> Delinquent behavior, as our data describe it, is more casual, spontaneous, and loosely organized than the gang myth would lead us to believe. We have suggested that delinquent activity more closely resembles the pickup games of ball we used to get into at the park or on the street, when someone showed up with a bat and ball, the environment provided an adequate setting, and we had the spirit for the game.[*]

*From *Delinquent Behavior in an American City*, pp. 118–19, by M. Gold. Copyright © 1970 by Wadsworth, Inc. Reprinted by permission of the publisher, Brooks/Cole Publishing Company, Monterey, California.

In their study of youths in Philadelphia, Savitz, Lalli, and Rosen (1977:49) found that police records of gang membership were not adequate for assessing the extent of gang delinquency. Thus, they chose to gather information on delinquent gangs through interviews. They defined the gangs in two different senses. Drawing on William Arnold's work, they classified youths as either *structural* gang members or as *functional* gang members. A structural gang member belonged to a group with "acknowledged leadership, common gang meeting place, and a territory or 'turf' within which the group feels safe and where entry by others can provoke the group to violence." Such gangs were defined solely on the basis of their structural characteristics and not according to whether they actually engaged in aggressive behavior. A functional gang member was one who belonged to a group that did get into fights with other groups and that expected fighting of its members.

Among males with delinquent records, structural gang membership was quite rare. Of blacks with delinquent records, 16 percent were classified as structural gang members, as were 22 percent of whites. While few youths belonged to structural gangs, a greater proportion indicated that their group of friends fought with other groups and that they were expected to join in the fighting. This type of functional gang membership was true of 44 percent of the blacks with records and 68 percent of the whites. In short, the territorially based gang with acknowledged leadership was relatively rare, even among youths with records. It was even rarer among Philadelphia youths who did not have official records (11 percent of blacks and 14 percent of whites).

The Philadelphia data are essentially consistent with the arguments of Lewis Yablonsky that gangs are misconceived as having a measurable number of members, clearly defined membership, specific roles for different members to play, a set of norms that are mutually agreed upon, and a definite leadership structure. Yablonsky (1959:108) argued that a more accurate image is that of a "near group." Such a group is characterized by (1) diffuse role definitions, (2) limited cohesion, (3) impermanence, (4) minimal consensus of norms, (5) shifting membership, (6) disturbed leadership, and (7) limited definition of membership expectations. From this perspective, even identifiable gangs in large cities would be viewed as falling somewhere between the structural gang and the casual pickup groups described by Gold.

Acknowledging that the structural gang is rare and accounts for a small share of the delinquency problem, we nonetheless have to recognize that delinquency is behavior that tends to occur in the company of peers. Thus, while the type of groups traditionally conceived of as "gangs" may not account for much of the total volume of delinquency in the United States, delinquent behavior has been and remains a form of *group* behavior. Table 6–1 summarizes the proportion of delinquent offenses in which the offender indicated that he or she was with someone else at the time

TABLE 6-1 *Delinquent Acts Reported as Committed in the Company of Peers (Group Violation Rates)*

	% of Utah Males (No. = 150)	% of Utah Males (No. = 336)	% of Arizona Small-Town Males	% of Arizona Urban Males
Vandalism	91	75	72	81
Burglary	84	67	81	74
Drinking	78	82	86	86
Grand theft	78	64	68	69
Narcotics	77	—	78	82
Petty theft	72	60	45	60
Auto theft	72	61	52	67
Armed robbery	69	—	58	52
Truancy	60	55	65	63
Fights	55	58	14	23
Runaway	50	45	44	38
Defying parents	17	27	16	23

Source: Maynard L. Erickson and Gary F. Jensen. "Delinquency Is Still Group Behavior!: Toward Revitalizing the Group Premise in the Sociology of Deviance," *Journal of Criminal Law and Criminology* 68 (2):262–73.

the offense was committed. This summary of several different studies shows not only that delinquency tends to be group behavior, but also that such a view holds true over time and across a number of different subgroups in the United States (Erickson and Jensen, 1977).

Sociologists continue to debate over the "best," "most sociological," and "most comprehensive" concepts of delinquency. For purposes of this text, we are merely concerned that the reader recognize the distinctions between different concepts and the possibility that a theory applicable to explaining delinquent behavior does not necessarily explain the phenomenon of delinquent gangs. Moreover, a theory relevant to delinquent behavior *in general* may not incorporate exactly the same explanatory variables as a theory focusing on group delinquency. On the other hand, most theories have been applied explicitly or implicitly to the concept of delinquency as a gang phenomenon and to the concept of delinquency as behavior that is in violation of the law. Similarly, most theories have been applied to explaining how individuals come to be involved in delinquency, as well as to explaining variations in delinquency rates among different groups or settings.

One concept over which sociological theories differ considerably is that of the delinquent subculture. Many theorists take it for granted that subcultures do exist and have developed theories to explain their development, content, or form. However, the specific meaning of the word *subculture* when dealing with delinquency is vague. If we accept the *cultural* referent of the concept, then we are assuming the existence of values, norms, beliefs, and techniques (supposedly held by identifiable groups)

DISPLAY 6-1   *Urban Gang Violence in the 1970s*

Hundreds of gangs and thousands of gang members frequent the streets, buildings, and public facilities of major cities; whole communities are terrorized by the intensity and ubiquity of gang violence; many urban schools are in effect in a state of occupation by gangs, with teachers and students exploited and intimidated; violent crime by gang members is in some cities equivalent to as much as one-third of all violent crime by juveniles; efforts by local communities to cope with gang crime have, by and large, failed conspicuously; many urban communities are gripped with a sense of hopelessness that *anything* can be done to curb the unremitting menace of the gangs.

Examination of the character of gang member violence indicates that gang members engage in combat with one another in a wide variety of ways. The classic "rumble" still occurs, but forays by small bands, armed and often motorized, appear to have become the dominant form of inter-gang violence. Prevalent notions that non-gang members have become the major victims of gang violence are not supported by available data; however, there does appear to be a definite trend toward increasing victimization of adults and children, particularly in the largest cities. Gang-member violence appears as well to be increasingly motivated by desire for material gain and a related desire to exert "control" over public facilities and resources.

Probably the single most significant development affecting gang-member violence during the present period is an extraordinary increase in the availability and use of firearms to effect violent crimes. This development is in all likelihood the major reason behind the increasingly lethal nature of gang violence. It is likely that violence perpetrated by members of youth gangs in major cities is at present more lethal than at any time in history.

The present period is also unique in the degree to which gang activities are conducted within the public schools. Gangs are active at all three levels—elementary, junior, and senior high schools. In some city schools gangs claim control over the school itself or over various rooms and facilities, with such control involving the right to set disciplinary policy, the right to collect fees from fellow students for such privileges as attending school, traversing the corridors, and not being subject to gang beatings, and the right to forbid teachers and other school staff from reporting illegal activities to authorities. Largely as a consequence of such gang activities, many city schools have been forced to adopt security measures of unprecedented scope, and to abandon a traditional policy of handling student discipline as an internal problem.

Comparing earlier with later periods of the past decade in the six gang-problem cities shows significant increases in levels of gang violence in New York, Los Angeles, Philadelphia, Detroit, and San Francisco, justifying the notion of a "new wave" of gang violence in major United States cities. In Chicago such violence has remained high throughout the decade. Data relative to future trends suggest conditionally that gang problems during the next few years will worsen in Los Angeles, Detroit, and San Francisco, improve in Philadelphia, and remain fairly stable in New York and Chicago. Moreover, the notion of a coming decline in the size of the youth population which serves as a "recruitment pool" for gangs and other criminally-active youth does not appear to be supported by current demographic projections, which indicate increases rather than decreases in these youth populations during the next five to ten years.

The basic question — "How serious are problems posed by youth gangs and youth groups today, and what priority should be granted gang problems among a multitude of current crime problems?" — must be approached with considerable cau-

tion, owing to a persisting tendency to exaggerate the seriousness of gang activity, and to represent the "gang of today" as more violent than at any time in the past. Exercising such caution, the materials presented in this report appear amply to support the conclusion that youth gang violence is more lethal today than ever before, that the security of a wider sector of the citizenry is threatened by gangs to a greater degree than ever before, and that violence and other illegal activities by members of youth gangs and groups in the United States of the mid-1970's represents a crime problem of the first magnitude which shows little prospect of early abatement.

Source: Walter B. Miller. *Violence by Youth Gangs and Youth Groups as a Crime Problem in Major American Cities.* National Institute for Juvenile Justice and Delinquency Prevention, U.S. Department of Justice. Washington, D.C.: U.S. Government Printing Office. 1975.

---

that call for or facilitate delinquency. While there is consensus that gangs and groups that engage in delinquent behavior do exist, there is little consensus that these groups are the embodiment of such a distinct culture. In fact, contemporary sociological explanations of delinquency are at odds over whether there are group-linked systems of values, norms, beliefs, and techniques that can explain gang delinquency, let alone delinquent behavior.

SOCIOLOGICAL SCHOOLS OF THOUGHT

There are several different ways to summarize the body of theory in a field. We could present the field in historical sequence—in terms of specific contributions of specific theorists or in terms of schools of thought. At the risk of oversimplification, we will take the latter approach and attempt to summarize three systems of ideas that have dominated sociological theory and research on juvenile delinquency. Our choice is based on the reasoning that no one theorist necessarily addresses all the issues or assumptions characteristic of a particular perspective, but certain similarities in fundamental assumptions tend to locate theorists in one or another school of thought. Moreover, theorists may draw on more than one system of ideas to explain delinquency. By approaching sociological perspectives on delinquency as schools of thought, we will discover areas where the theories are in marked conflict, as well as areas where they are in agreement.

Since the views that we will consider are all "sociological," they do tend to share certain basic sociological assumptions. One basic assumption (shared by several psychological perspectives) is that delinquency can be best understood if it is approached as *learned*, rather than biologically determined, behavior. This assumption is closely linked to a second assumption, which is that as learned behavior, delinquency is *not* totally random or unpredictable but is instead more common in some circumstances than in others. What those exact circumstances are varies from one sociological theory to another, but all such theories share the view that it is dimensions of the *social environment* that explain the distribution of delinquency and the probability that individuals will learn delinquent behavior. Important aspects of the social environment are its values, norms, beliefs, and techniques. These cultural patterns are variably learned depending on the nature and operations of such *socializing forces* as the family, school, church, community, and adolescent society. Learning also depends on the *structure of opportunities* for engaging in delinquent and nondelinquent activities.

Thus, the basic sources of delinquency are viewed as *originally external* to the individual. People are not born delinquent but are born into circumstances or subsequently experience circumstances that are *conducive* to delinquency. Individual values, beliefs, and conceptions of right and wrong become part of the individual's personal makeup, or self, through processes of social learning and socialization. This argument does not mean that genetic or biological factors are totally irrelevant to explaining delinquency. Instead it reflects a belief that we can more adequately predict and explain delinquency by considering the influence of relationships with other people and institutions, as well as the values, norms, beliefs, and techniques learned as a product of such relationships. The research summarized in this and the following chapter provides considerable support for such a position.

We will consider three sociological schools of thought. The first incorporates theories of social disorganization and social control; the second is based on social disorganization-strain theory; and the third conceptualizes delinquency in terms of cultural conflict. Our discussion of each school will be organized around the following topics: (1) basic causal processes operating to explain rates of delinquency and probabilities of individual involvement; (2) the motivation for delinquency; (3) the role of values, norms, and beliefs in the causation of delinquency; and (4) the "image" of the delinquent suggested by each theory.

Social Disorganization—Social Control Theory

The concept of *social disorganization* was widely used in early American sociology and criminology to refer to unsettled conditions of urban life generated by growth and change. It is not surprising that the notion came into use among sociologists at the University of Chicago in the early 1900s since Chicago was a booming, industrial city increasingly populated by recent immigrants of diverse racial and ethnic backgrounds. In their study (*The Polish Peasant*, 1918), W. I. Thomas and Florian Znaniecki described social disorganization in terms of the failure of existing "social rules" to control behavior. Robert Park argued that city life is characterized by a breakdown in the "traditional" schemes of control that have always depended on intimate personal relationships, such as occur in "the home, neighborhood and other communal institutions" (1952:58).

Clifford Shaw (1929) and Edwin Sutherland (1939), both Chicago sociologists, used the concept of social disorganization and social control to develop theories of delinquency. Shaw argued:

> Under the pressure of the disintegrative forces which act when business and industry invade a community, the community thus invaded ceases to function effectively as a means of social control. Traditional norms and standards of the conventional community weaken and disappear. Resistance on the part of the community to delinquent and criminal behavior is low, and such behavior is tolerated and may even become accepted and approved. (1929:204–05)

Thus, the expansion of business and industry, coupled with immigration, growth, mobility, and cultural diversity, was seen to weaken or inhibit certain traditional forms of control, which, in turn, facilitated high rates of delinquency.

Sutherland's view of social disorganization was very similar to Shaw's in that he believed the disorganization of institutions that have traditionally reinforced the law facilitates the development and persistence of "systematic" crime and delinquency. He also believed that such disorganization fosters cultural traditions that support such activity. Sutherland wrote that "if the society is organized with reference to the values expressed in the law, the crime is eliminated; if it is not organized, crime persists and develops" (1939:8).

The value of the concept of social disorganization for explaining crime and delinquency has been challenged on grounds of circularity: crime and delinquency have often been cited as *indexes* of social disorganization, as well as phenomenon to be explained by social disorganization. Moreover, since there is generally *some* order to social life even under the most dire circumstances and even when it is organized around illegal activities, the concept of social disorganization can be misleading. Although the concept itself may be vague and difficult to use in a noncircular fashion, it does tie together a variety of explanations of crime and delinquency that focus on the social conditions that affect conventional social institutions, as well as the bonds between people and those institutions.

In fact, social-psychological versions of social disorganization theory are currently the most popular explanations of delinquent behavior. Such contemporary versions of the social disorganization perspective are referred to as *social control, containment, commitment,* or *social bond* theories. Like social disorganization theory, social control theory focuses our attention on the strength of the individual's bonds to conventional institutions, persons, goals, and values. The focus is on barriers to delinquent behavior rather than the causes that propel an individual into delinquent activities.

Social control theory, like social disorganization theory, has been criticized for circularity. In one of the first systematic presentations of a social control theory of delinquency, A. J. Reiss, Jr., wrote:

> Delinquency may be defined as the behavior consequent to the failure
> of personal and social controls to produce behavior in conformity with the
> norms of the social system to which legal penalties are attached. Personal
> control may be defined as the ability of the individual to refrain from
> meeting needs in ways which conflict with the norms and rules of the
> community. Social control may be defined as the ability of social groups or
> institutions to make norms or rules effective. (1951:196)

The difficulty with such statements is that delinquency is *by definition* behavior that does not conform with certain norms. Thus, the statement is circular: "Failure to abide by norms occurs when people fail to abide by norms." However, when we consider the specific conditions cited or measured in the development of social control theories, we find that they are not necessarily circular. For example, the author of the above statement went on to identify the failure of such "primary groups" as the family to provide reinforcement for nondelinquent roles and values as a crucial variable in the explanation of delinquency. Such conditions can be defined and measured in different terms than the delinquent behavior they supposedly explain.

Another term sometimes used to refer to social control theory is *drift theory,* which derives from David Matza's work *Delinquency and Drift.* Matza saw the delinquent as an "actor neither compelled nor committed to deeds nor freely choosing them; neither different in any simple or fundamental sense from the law abiding, nor the same; conforming to certain traditions in American life while partially unreceptive to other more conventional traditions" (1964:28). The word *drift* does convey some of the distinctive characteristics of social control theory. It is essentially an "amotivational" perspective—that is, rather than seeking an answer to the question "What *motivates* adolescents to commit delinquent acts?" it seeks to answer "What *prevents* an adolescent from committing such acts?" If an adolescent has few stakes in conformity, then he or she is *freer* to break rules than the adolescent who has high stakes in conformity.

Social control theorists use several different tactics in dealing with the issue of motivation. Some control theorists argue that because delinquent acts commonly have some kind of motivation, motives do not tell us much about who will and will not commit criminal and delinquent acts (Briar and Piliavin, 1965). Moreover, rather than being generated by one or a few dominant forces, the motives for delinquency are quite diverse, ranging from instrumental needs (for example, stealing when one is poor and hungry) to emotional rage, frustration, and sheer thrill and excitement. Other control theorists merely acknowledge that human beings are active, flexible organisms who will engage in a wide range of activities unless the range is limited by processes of socialization and social learning. Thus, although several control theorists address the issue of motivation, social control theory views the search for mechanisms that prevent or deter crime and delinquency as far more fruitful than the search for motivation.

We noted in Chapter 1 that different sociological theories take quite different stands on the role that values and norms play in the explanation of crime and delinquency. Social disorganization-social control theorists have taken a variety of positions on the issue. According to Hirschi (1969), there is a general consensus in American society that criminal and delinquent activities involving personal harm and loss or damage to property are improper or immoral. By "consensus," Hirschi did not mean that everyone feels equally strongly about the impropriety of lawbreaking. Some people accept the law as more morally binding than other people do and are therefore less likely to break it. Rather, Hirschi argued against the notion that any sizable racial, ethnic, or status groups in America have subcultural systems of values and norms that require criminal or delinquent behavior.

David Matza and Gresham Sykes (1961) have observed that although "official" proclamations and conventional institutions stress the importance of obeying the law, "subterranean" traditions are conducive to crime. Supposedly law-abiding citizens accord respect and admiration to the person who "pulls off the big con," who takes risks and successfully engages in exciting, dangerous activities, whether legal or illegal. Movies about this type of risk taker are popular among all groups and classes of people, which reflects a widespread ambivalence toward the law. Sykes and Matza (1957) have also pointed out that although conventional institutions prevail upon us not to break the law, other social norms and values tell us that breaking the law is not so bad under certain circumstances: when the victim "had it coming" (denial of an innocent victim); when those supporting the law are not morally pure themselves (condemnation of the condemners); when the offender "had no choice" (denial of responsibility); when "no one was hurt" (denial of injury); or when the offense was motivated by social purposes more important than the law (appeal to higher loyalties). Such beliefs, or "techniques of neutralization," can be learned in quite conventional contexts. They are reflected in legal codes as "extenuating circumstances" and in the public's reaction to certain types of crime. In this view, then, delinquency is not a response to different, "subcultural" values but to rationalizations that reduce the impact of the traditional forces of social control.

Thus, some social control theorists view delinquency as a reflection of rather pervasive beliefs that encourage illegal and immoral activities. For them, delinquency reflects an ambivalence about lawbreaking or the lack of a consistent moral stance against lawbreaking. Other social control theorists merely emphasize the *lack* of commitment to the law: the person who is not morally bound to the law is freer to violate the law.

In sum, social disorganization-social control theorists generally believe that social conditions that attenuate or inhibit bonds to conventional institutions are the cause of individual and gang delinquency. To paraphrase Jackson Toby (1957), "the uncommitted adolescent is a candidate for gang socialization." Harold Finestone (1976:10) has characterized this view of the delinquent as a "disaffiliated" drifter. This image of the individual delinquent is consistent with the social control perspective on the nature of delinquent gangs; uncommitted or disaffiliated adolescents are seen as drifting together to form tenuous, unstable aggregates, which Yablonsky (1959) has labeled "near groups." Gangs, or "near groups," are held together by lack of alternatives and conflict with authority. In contrast to other sociological schools of thought, the social control perspective views the gang delinquent as "committed to neither delinquent nor conventional enterprise" (Matza, 1964:1).

Social Disorganization-Strain Theory

A second major perspective on delinquency emerged in the late 1930s and grew in popularity through the mid-1960s. We refer to it as *social disorganization-strain* theory because it relates crime and delinquency to a particular type of stressful disorganization. This disorganization results from a combination of the American cultural emphasis on "success" with a social structure in which the realistic possibilities of attaining success are limited. Four sociologists have been especially prominent in the development of this perspective: Robert Merton, Albert Cohen, Richard Cloward, and Lloyd Ohlin.

According to the French sociologist Emile Durkheim, "No living being can be happy or even exist unless his needs are sufficiently proportioned to his means" (1951:246). Writing in the late 1800s and early 1900s, Durkheim argued that when a society becomes complex and highly differentiated, a sense of social "deregulation" may result. Durkheim referred to this state of normlessness as *anomie.* Robert Merton extended Durkheim's concept of anomie into a social and cultural explanation of deviant behavior.

Merton (1957) believed that deviance of various kinds could be attributed to the disparity between the cultural emphasis on success and the actual opportunity to achieve success. This disparity, coupled with a weakening of norms that define acceptable means of achieving success, causes people to turn to illicit means of obtaining their goals. In short, Merton viewed crime and delinquency as "innovative" behavior that is most characteristic of lower-class persons because of their relative lack of economic success. People who are strongly bound to norms precluding criminal or delinquent behavior can respond to disparities between valued goals and limited opportunity by giving up their aspirations and conforming in a "ritualistic" fashion. Merton viewed ritualism as a common lower-middle-class adaptation to problems that generate crime and delinquency in the lower classes. He also argued that some people give up the pursuit of success and reject conventional norms. Their behavior is characterized by drug use, alcoholism, and vagrancy. Merton referred to this type of adaptation as "retreatism." Other people may adopt new goals and norms and rebel against the existing system.

The disparity between success and opportunity can have consequences for people of every social standing. However, in Merton's view, criminal and delinquent behavior is a lower-class response to this type of social disorganization because the lower-class youth is more thoroughly socialized to aspire toward success than to abide by legal norms. Under such circumstances, the norms are likely to be ignored.

In his classic work *Delinquent Boys* (1955), Albert Cohen's explanation of delinquency is strongly influenced by Merton's version of strain theory. Cohen concluded that delinquent behavior represents a collective effort by juveniles to resolve adjustment problems caused by their loss of social status in American society. The lower-class child is constantly measured by the "middle-class measuring rod," which is discriminatory because socialization experiences differ according to class. Lower-class youth are not adequately socialized to fulfill the status requirements of middle-class society. Differential socialization experiences result in what Cohen referred to as "status frustration." Status frustration is supposedly most common among boys from lower- or working-class families since the middle-class measuring rod stresses characteristics that working-class socialization does not (for example, thrift, neatness, the ability to defer gratification, and good manners).

When status problems are experienced collectively—that is, by a number of adolescents who interact with one another—one outcome may be the creation of an alternative set of criteria for determining status. According to Cohen, delinquents create a new set of standards *contrary* to those emphasized in middle-class institutions. Thus, Cohen viewed delinquent gangs as a *contracultural* phenomenon. The concept of contraculture refers to a system of values that are in opposition to dominant standards and that are the result of problems experienced with those standards. From Cohen's perspective, the criteria that delinquent gangs use to allocate status are the opposite of middle-class criteria. The delinquents' criteria develop in response to status problems experienced by working-class boys who cannot get ahead in terms of middle-class standards. Delinquent activities are supposedly marked by a wholesale repudiation of middle-class standards and the adoption of nonutilitarian, malicious, rebellious attitudes. Although Cohen refers to a delinquent "subculture," the term *contraculture* conveys the sense of his explanation much better (Yinger, 1960).

A more recent elaboration of social disorganization-strain theory is found in Richard Cloward and Lloyd Ohlin's *Delinquency and Opportunity* (1960). Cloward and Ohlin argued that the motivation to deviate is provided when one accepts culturally prescribed goals of success and finds that legitimate avenues for achieving such goals are limited. Cloward and Ohlin attempted to merge Merton's use of anomie with approaches that emphasize illegal opportunity and criminal traditions. They analyzed the outcome of Merton's discussion regarding the discrepancy between culturally valued goals and socially available means in terms of the availability of the *illegitimate opportunities* in a given setting. If status problems are experienced in a setting in which criminal activities are well organized, then involvement in a criminal subculture is a likely resolution to such problems. If no such well-organized illegitimate activities are available, then gang life centered around conflict, fighting, or violence may be the collective resolution to status problems. Finally, boys who are ill-equipped for well-organized criminal activity or for gang life oriented toward conflict can solve their status problems through "retreat" (for example, drug use).

Although the social disorganization-strain theorists whom we have reviewed are at odds on a number of points (for example, whether delinquent behavior is irrational and malicious or rational and utilitarian), they all emphasize a particular type of motivation in their explanations of crime and delinquency: status problems induced by discrepancies between conventional culture and limits set by our social structure. Strain theorists point out that rates of crime and delinquency are highest in those categories of the population in which such discrepancies are most likely to occur. Delinquency is viewed as a form of social behavior that functions to solve the status problems induced by these discrepancies. Thus, strain theorists introduce a special motivation to explain delinquency: structurally induced status frustration.

Strain theorists also share the view that persons born into our society at least initially want to conform to the conventional standards that are reflected in the law. According to Cohen, delinquent boys try to live up to the standards of middle-class adults but are unable to do so. Alternatives are explored *after* status problems are experienced. In fact, strain theorists believe that people are always trying to be moral, whether by adhering to conventional norms and values or by elaborating new norms that define delinquency and crime as good and acceptable.

In describing the delinquent as a "frustrated social climber," Harold Finestone (1976:12) summed up the strain theorists' image of delinquent youth. Delinquency, especially gang delinquency, is viewed as a solution to status problems. The gang delinquent is a "problem solver" who is involved in a problem-solving contracultural or subcultural system. The delinquent's problem is generated by the social system, and strain theory sees the delinquent as responding in a quite moral, social fashion to a social predicament. As Cohen (1955) expressed it, "The same value system, impinging upon children differentially equipped to meet it, is instrumental in generating both delinquency and respectability." The strain theorists' image of the delinquent, then, is that of an essentially moral, striving human being who has been forced by circumstances beyond his or her control to explore new ways of attaining respect and self-esteem.

Cultural Conflict Theory

Thus far we have considered theories that view delinquency as a product of (1) freedom from or inconsistencies in conventional expectations and (2) status problems generated by disparities between cultural aspirations and social reality. A third perspective advances the argument that in certain social contexts delinquency and crime are approved, required, or expected behavior. Some advocates of this last position have specifically repudiated the basic assumptions of strain theory. For example, Walter Miller (1958) has argued that the strain theorists' image of a "delinquent subculture" is erroneous. Miller does not believe that the value systems of lower-class gangs are "contracultural" (that is, a rejection of dominant middle-class values). Rather, Miller has argued, the values, or "focal concerns," of gang members are a product of "the lower class community itself—a long established, distinctively patterned tradition with an integrity of its own" (1958:5–6). According to Miller, the gang boy conforms to the values or standards of a larger subculture that is generally linked to regional, racial, or social status. Thus, delinquency is supposedly a reflection of the values, norms, and beliefs of large, but distinct, segments of the population.

Along similar lines, Ralph England (1960) suggested that middle-class teenagers derive many of their delinquent motivations from the adult world. The youth subculture seizes upon many legitimate adult activities that become slightly distorted, "caricatured fragments from the adult culture" (1960:539). Because the youth subculture is a product of immature and inexperienced persons, the translation of adult values into adolescent values inadvertently encourages the creation of delinquent behavior. Neither England nor Miller saw any need for viewing delinquent behavior as a social pathology resulting from what Cohen referred to as a process of "social degradation."

From the cultural conflict perspective, the basic source of variation in delinquency rates is cultural diversity in standards of right and wrong. When a region of the nation, particular sections of a city, or particular groups or categories of people have high crime rates, cultural conflict theorists posit that the values, norms, and beliefs of those particular segments of the population differ from the standards embodied in the law. Contrary to the strain and control theorists, cultural conflict theorists view society as characterized by quite diverse standards of right and wrong, with some standards more likely than others to be expressed in the law. Groups or segments of the population whose cultures are in conflict with the law are more likely to come into actual conflict with the law. Sutherland and Cressey have noted that the "principle of normative conflict . . . makes sense out of variations in crime rates by observing that modern societies are organized for crime as well as against it, and then observing further that crime rates are unequally distributed because of differences in the degree to which various categories of persons participate in this normative conflict" (1974:89). This concept of normative conflict differs from the concept of "subterranean" values in that it attributes the values that are conducive to delinquency to disadvantaged groups whose cultures are in conflict with the dominant middle class. In contrast, the type of inconsistency or conflict that Matza and Sykes have described as "subterranean" characterizes the value systems of the dominant groups in society.

Once such cultural conflict, or diversity in standards of right and wrong, is assumed, then the process of learning delinquency becomes one of "differential association" with different standards. Hence, the basic principle of Sutherland and Cressey's differential association theory is that "a person becomes delinquent because of an excess of definitions favorable to violation of law over definitions unfavorable to violation of law" (1974:75–77). The emphasis is on the learning of normative or cultural standards, some of which define lawbreaking in favorable terms while others define it in unfavorable terms.

From a cultural conflict perspective, delinquency is explained by the same processes as is lawfulness. The motivation for delinquency, like the motivation for lawfulness, is quite natural—the human tendency to live up to the expectations of significant others. Children ultimately become involved in delinquency because the cultural standards they learn are in conflict with the standards reflected in the law. As John DeLamater (1968:447) has noted, cultural deviance (in this case delinquency) "occurs through the normal process of social learning." Thus, cultural conflict theorists view deviance as a product of successful subcultural socialization; strain theorists view it as a product of "resocialization" through the collective development of contracultural standards; and control theorists view it as a product of failures or inconsistencies in conventional socialization. Because they see delinquent behavior as conforming behavior that is only deviant from some other group's perspective, cultural conflict theorists need posit no special motivation for deviance.

Since this school of thought defines delinquency as conforming behavior that is shaped by normative standards and the expectations of others, its image of the delinquent differs from the images of the other two perspectives that we have reviewed. Delinquents tend to be depicted as among the most able, persevering, and gregarious members of their particular communities. For example, Walter Miller (1958) has argued that to become a gang member, a boy must be able to subordinate individual preference to group interest and that lower-class gang members "possess to an unusually high degree both the *capacity* and *motivation* to conform to perceived cultural norms." From such a perspective, it is the best products of a "lower-class culture," rather than the worst, who are likely to become delinquent. Those most sensitive to the opinions and expectations of members of their subculture are those most likely to become involved in delinquency. To borrow Hirschi's (1969) term, the image of the delinquent is one of "hypermorality." The delinquent is a conformist in a subculture whose standards are in conflict with the law.

Sociological Theories and Delinquency: An Overview

Several sociologists have summarized different perspectives on deviance, crime, and delinquency, and we can get a good overview of the three approaches outlined above by drawing on their works. Table 6–2 describes these three approaches in terms of the causal and socialization processes emphasized by each, their images of the delinquent and of the law and moral standards, and their views of culture and motivation.

Referring to Table 6–2, we see that the three causal perspectives on delinquent behavior envision a causal process that operates on a macro, or societal, level, as well as a causal process that operates on a micro, or individual, level. On the societal level, control theory postulates the emergence of social disorganization, or the breakdown in the restraining impact of traditional institutions of social control. Strain theory relies on the notion of the social structure exerting pressure on members of society, some of whom cannot meet society's demands. Cultural conflict theory assumes the presence of multiple cultures or subcultures within a particular society that inadvertently produces a clash among the cultural prescriptions of these varying groups. Moving down to the individual

TABLE 6-2 *Causal Theories*

	Control	*Strain*	*Cultural Conflict*
Societal causal process:	Social disorganization	Structural strain	Normative conflict
Individual causal process:	Stakes in conformity	Status frustration	Differential association
Socialization process:	Failures or inconsistencies in socialization	Resocialization	Successful subcultural socialization
Image of the delinquent:	Drifter	Problem solver	Conformist
Image of the law and moral standards:	Consensus and existence of subterranean values	Consensus and creation of a contraculture	Subcultural conflict
View of culture:	Infraculture	Contraculture	Subculture
View of motivation:	Situational, common, diverse, natural	Special, structurally induced status problems	Cultural, social, natural

unit of analysis, control theory argues for the existence of barriers to delinquency that take the form of an investment, or stake, in conformity. Strain theory translates social strain into the emergence of status frustration, which occurs when individuals cannot attain socially prescribed goals. Finally, cultural conflict theory introduces the concept of differential association to explain how members of differing subcultures acquire and maintain attitudes and behaviors that nonmembers of the subcultural groups see as deviant.

John DeLamater (1968) has delineated three perspectives on the deviant "socialization" process. Becoming deviant may reflect: (1) inadequate socialization into conventional norms, (2) initial socialization into deviant subcultural norms, or (3) problem-solving resocialization. Each of these perspectives is associated with one or another of the three theories of delinquency. Control theorists tend to emphasize failures or inconsistencies of socialization, cultural conflict theorists focus on successful subcultural socialization, and strain theorists focus on processes of deviant resocialization. The last process is referred to as "resocialization" because it is assumed that the individual initially learns conventional standards and tries to abide by them. If such attempts lead to frustration, then the individual may turn to delinquent activity and the collective creation of alternative standards.

Travis Hirschi (1969) and Harold Finestone (1976) have dealt with the general image of the delinquent suggested by different theories. In the social control perspective, the delinquent is "disaffiliated" (Finestone) or "amoral" (Hirschi). By "amoral," Hirschi meant that the delinquent is less bound to conventional moral standards and can therefore deviate more freely, with fewer moral complications and less guilt. According to this view, delinquent youth are also "uncommitted" (Matza, 1964). From a cultural conflict perspective, delinquent youth are actually "hyper-moral" (Hirschi) in the sense that they make the greatest effort to live up to expectations in their subcultural environment. They are conformers. Finally, from the perspective of strain theory, delinquent youth are "moral" (Hirschi) in that they initially do their best to get ahead by adhering to conventional standards and seeking moral solutions to status problems. Finestone has depicted this image as one of "frustrated social climber."

Each theoretical approach is also characterized by a particular image of the law and moral standards. Cultural conflict theorists stress normative conflict in society and a view of the law as representative of the standards of certain powerful segments of society. In this view, society is character-ized by dissension and conflict between the standards of some sizable subcultures and the standards that are reflected in the law. In contrast, both control and strain theorists view society as characterized by consen-sus regarding the impropriety of most types of crime and delinquency. Hirschi has noted that control theory assumes "a common value system within the society whose norms are being violated" and that "deviance is not a question of one group imposing its rules on the members of another group" (1969:23). Control theory does not deny that traces of deviant values are buried or embedded within our culture. These "subterranean" values occasionally serve as convenient rationalizations for delinquent behavior. Strain theorists also assume that there is a common value sys-tem, as well as basic agreement on the impropriety of criminal and delin-quent activity, but that those who experience frustration may construct an alternative moral order (contraculture) to cope with such problems.

Cultural concepts are used differently in each of these theories as well. For example, Yinger (1960) has noted that the concept of the delinquent subculture characteristic of Cohen's strain theory is really that of a contraculture—a system of values, norms, and beliefs that specifically develops in reaction to problems in coping with the dominant system. In contrast, the cultural conflict theorists use the concept of subculture in a more conventional way. Their focus is on a system of values, norms, and beliefs that is in conflict with standards reflected in the law but that exists as an enduring set of traditions characteristic not merely of delinquent gangs or youth but of whole subpopulations, communities, or neighborhoods as well. Finally, for control theorists like Hirschi, such concepts as contraculture or subculture are not necessary for understanding delinquency since an overall cultural consensus regarding moral standards is assumed and delinquency is seen as resulting from freedom from moral constraints.

Empey (1967) has noted that control theorists have advanced a third concept of American culture—that of an *infraculture,* the system of "subterranean" values, norms, and beliefs that we discussed earlier. According to this concept, certain values, norms, and beliefs are conducive to delinquency but are part and parcel of the dominant system rather than the standards of specific subgroups. Such infracultural aspects of American culture are not viewed as *requiring* crime but as tending to *neutralize* abstract moral commitments to the law. However, this concept has not been incorporated specifically into any explanatory theory. To be relevant to explaining variation in delinquent activity, subterranean beliefs would have to be viewed as "variably" learned aspects of American culture and some effort made to identify the circumstances associated with such learning. On the other hand, to the degree that subterranean beliefs are viewed as "neutralizing" the moral constraints of the dominant system and "freeing" the individual to deviate, the concept seems to fit better with control theory than with strain or cultural conflict theory. Both strain theory and cultural conflict theory point to norms among gangs or minority populations that require delinquency.

Finally, the three perspectives differ in their approaches to the motivational issue. Cultural conflict theory and control theory focus on quite "natural" motives, while strain theory is characterized by a "special motivation" (Hirschi, 1969). Cultural conflict theory focuses on the natural tendency of people to abide by the cultural expectations and normative standards prominent in their own social environments. (In other words, delinquents learn the delinquent standards of their particular subcultural environments.) For control theorists, motives are natural in a very different sense. Hirschi did not feel that control theory need pay *any* attention to the motivational issue (1969:33), while control theorists who *have* focused on motivation have merely outlined short-term, situationally induced desires experienced by all boys. The motives for delinquency are diverse, situational, and so common that they have little explanatory power. In contrast, the strain theorist identifies a very special, structurally induced type of motive: status frustration. People have to be *forced* to deviate by circumstances largely beyond their control. The introduction of a special force is necessary in neither cultural conflict theory nor in control theory.

THEORY-RELATED RESEARCH

Each of the three sociological schools of thought that we have reviewed developed in an attempt to "make sense" out of presumed "facts" about delinquency and crime. Arrest rates were highest in the areas surrounding the central business district of cities and decreased in zones outside of the city centers. Why did rates vary in such a fashion? Social disorganization-control theorists attributed such variation to the deleterious effect of growth and change on conventional institutions. Social disorganization-strain theorists argued that people living in areas with the highest arrest rates are those most likely to experience a disparity between aspirations and reality. Cultural conflict theorists argued that such areas are characterized by cultural traditions that define lawbreaking in favorable terms. In short, all these perspectives explain commonly believed "facts" about delinquency.

Although each of these theoretical perspectives offers different explanations, we should recognize that all three may contribute to our understanding of delinquency. Some people do get involved in delinquency because of status problems. Some groups do define lawbreaking as acceptable, approved behavior. Some people do drift into delinquency because they have little to lose. However, the focus in sociology is on whether such patterns are *regularities*. Are people who experience discrepancies between aspirations and reality more likely to form delinquent gangs, develop delinquent subcultures, or commit delinquent acts than those who do not experience such disparities? Are there large status or racial categories with distinct value systems that automatically lead to delinquency? Do adolescents with few bonds to such institutions as the family and school have higher rates of delinquency than those who are strongly bound to such institutions? In assessing theory, we are interested in the search for theoretically predicted regularities. In the remainder of this chapter, we will attempt to summarize research relevant to each of the major theories.

Research Findings and Strain Theory

Research has provided less support for strain theory than it has for the other two major theoretical explanations of crime and delinquency. As we have noted, strain theorists attribute the nature and distribution of delinquent gangs to the existence of delinquent subcultures that have distinctive values, norms, and beliefs. Thus, Cohen claimed to be explaining the "content" of a delinquent gang subculture, or contraculture. However, actual research on the values of gang delinquents has not supported the notion of a delinquent contraculture. Several studies

(Gordon et al., 1963; Lerman, 1968; Gold, 1963) have found that gang boys evaluate deviant and conventional behaviors in terms of their "goodness" much the same as do nondelinquents. For example, Short and Strodtbeck (1965) compared gang boys in Chicago with lower-class and middle-class nongang boys in terms of their evaluations of conventional images (for example, "someone who works for good grades at school," "someone who saves his money") and deviant images (for example, "someone who is a good fighter with a tough reputation," "someone who knows where to sell what he steals"). They found that all of their samples evaluated middle-class, conventional images in equally high terms. Moreover, each sample ranked conventional images more highly than any of the unconventional images. Gang boys did tend to "tolerate" deviant lifestyles or images more than nongang boys, but there was no evidence of a reversal in evaluations of different lifestyles. Thus, contrary to Cloward and Ohlin's theory, gang boys do not appear to deny the legitimacy of middle-class norms. Hyman Rodman (1963) has suggested the notion of the "lower-class value stretch," which is an adaptive mechanism that enables lower-class persons to share the general values of society but stretch them to fit their particular circumstances. Similarly, Lee Rainwater (1970) has argued that certain groups may develop a "set of survival techniques for functioning in the world of the disinherited." However, Rainwater's argument does not infer the negation of conventional norms.

Another basic argument of the strain theorists has been that the disparity between aspirations and opportunity provides the motivation for delinquency. Much of the evidence on this point is inconsistent with the predictions of strain theory. According to the strain theorists, the highest rate of delinquency should be among youths who have high aspirations but low expectations of achieving success. Similarly, since it is the *disparity* between aspirations and realistic expectations that is presumed to generate status frustration, youths with low aspirations *and* low expectations should have a *lower* probability of delinquency than the youths with high aspirations and low expectations. Contrary to this prediction, the highest delinquency rates have been found among boys who have low aspirations and low expectations (Hirschi, 1969; Short, Rivera, and Tennyson, 1965). A more recent test of the strain theorists' arguments has concluded that status frustration as measured by anticipated failure to achieve culturally prescribed goals of success *is not related* to rates of self-reported delinquency (Elliott and Voss, 1974).

Another prediction derived from strain theory is that delinquent youths with delinquent companions should be higher in feelings of self-esteem than delinquent youths with no delinquent friends. If delinquent activity or participation in delinquent gangs *does* solve status problems, then delinquent gang members should exhibit no more status problems than their nondelinquent peers. Although there has been only one study relevant to that issue, its findings are contrary to the prediction. In a study of a random sample of black and white youth in California, Jensen (1971) found that the more delinquent friends a delinquent youth had, the lower the delinquent's feelings of self-esteem. In addition, delinquents with delinquent friends were lower in self-esteem than nondelinquents. In short, there is no evidence thus far that delinquency regularly functions to solve status problems.

Research Findings and Cultural Conflict Theory

Cultural conflict theory assumes that society is characterized by socially differentiated groups who have conflicting definitions of right and wrong and that delinquency is the product of differential learning of conflicting definitions. Paul Lerman has captured the essense of cultural conflict theory, noting that "in a traditional conflict of conduct codes, it appears that one of the codes prescribes explicitly illegal behavior while the other proscribes it" (1968:235). Research, however, has failed to reveal the types of class-linked definitions that cultural conflict theorists posit.

In his study of white youths in California, Hirschi (1969) compared the sons of fathers in lower-class occupations with the sons of semiskilled, white-collar, and professional fathers. He found no significant differences among these groups in attitudes that supposedly characterize lower-class youths (for example, an expedient attitude toward the law, admiration of "sharp" operators, or sensitivity to adult criticism). He did find that the sons of professionals were less likely to feel "fatalistic" (that is, that "there is no sense looking ahead since no one knows what the future will be like") than sons of fathers in other occupations. However, when Hirschi took measures of academic success or failure into account, he also found that the academically incompetent middle-class child was much more likely than the academically competent lower-class child to exhibit fatalistic attitudes. Thus, Hirschi suggested that fatalistic attitudes, rather than being an enduring aspect of a class culture, are anchored in *experiences* that may be more common in the lower than in the middle classes. In short, even the minimal differences in attitudes that Hirschi observed may be produced and reproduced through socially structured experiences rather than through cultural transmission.

Another set of research findings tends to contradict the argument that the "focal concerns" of a lower-class culture automatically lead to law-breaking. Studies of attachment to or identification with parents have consistently shown that children attached to their parents are less likely to be delinquent in a variety of different samples and settings (Glueck and Glueck, 1950; Hindelang, 1973; Elliott and Voss, 1974) and regardless of social class (Hirschi, 1969). If lower-class focal concerns *are* conducive to delinquency, then adolescents who are most sensitive to the opinions of lower-class adults should be *most likely* to violate the law. Research has yet to support this argument.

The finding most often cited as support for the differential association theory of cultural conflict has been the observed relationship between delinquent peers and involvement in delinquency. Adolescents with delinquent friends are themselves more likely to get into trouble with the law or report involvement in delinquency than are adolescents without delinquent friends (Glueck and Glueck, 1950; Short, 1957; Voss, 1964; Erickson and Empey, 1965; Hirschi, 1969). The relationship is one of the strongest and most persistent in delinquency research. However, this finding can be used to support other criminological theories and is therefore not evidence of the unique validity of cultural conflict theory.

In fact, there is some evidence that the causal order of delinquent relationships may be opposite to that proposed by cultural conflict theorists. In their study of a cohort of ninth graders whom they followed through to high school graduation, Elliott and Voss (1974) found that the "perception of official delinquency among one's friends is largely an effect of prior delinquency rather than a cause of future delinquent behavior." Elliott and Voss also reported that a subject's perception of delinquency in the community appears to be a product of involvement in delinquency rather than a cause of such involvement.

The image of the gang delinquent as one of the most able, persevering, and gregarious members of the community has also been challenged. Several researchers have argued that internal sources of gang solidarity or cohesiveness are weak and that it is conflict with authority that holds delinquent gangs together. Lewis Yablonsky has depicted gang members and gang life as far from gregarious:

> A prime function of the gang is to provide a channel to act out hostility and aggression to satisfy the continuing and momentary emotional needs of its members. The gang is a convenient and malleable structure quickly adaptable to the needs of emotionally disturbed youths, who are unable to fulfill the responsibility and demands required for participation in constructive groups. A boy belongs to the gang because he lacks the social ability to relate to others and to assume responsibility for the relationship, not because the gang gives him a "feeling of belonging."
>
> Because of the gang youth's limited "social ability," he constructs a social organization which enables him to relate and to function at his limited level of performance. In this structure norms are adjusted so that the gang youth can function and achieve despite his limited ability to relate to others. (1959:116)

Yablonsky's description is consistent with Short and Strodtbeck's findings that gang boys are less "self-assertive," less gregarious, and "slightly more neurotic and anxious" than nongang boys (1965:230). It is also consistent with Hirschi's (1969) study of high school students in California and with several other studies (see Rothstein, 1962; Bandura and Walters, 1959).

A final issue in cultural conflict theory involves its emphasis on "definitions" as *the* most crucial variables in the explanation of delinquency. Cultural conflict theorists tend to present what one critic has called an "oversocialized" conception of human beings (Wrong, 1961). From such a perspective, when people break the law, it *must be* because they have learned a set of moral standards that require lawbreaking or because they have learned an "excess of definitions favorable to the violation of the law." Definitions control behavior to such a degree that what appears to be deviant behavior is really conforming behavior. People are always doing what they believe to be morally correct.

While there is a definite correlation between what people do and what they believe to be right and wrong (between "definitions" and behavior), the correlation is far from perfect. Many adolescents report involvement in delinquency even though they define such activity as wrong (Jensen, 1972). Moreover, factors commonly found to be correlated with delinquency, such as delinquent companionships and attachment to parents and school, are persistently related to delinquency *regardless* of cultural definitions favorable or unfavorable to the violation of the law. Cultural conflict theory stresses definitions and internalization of "cultural" standards (values, norms, and beliefs) to such an extent that other processes that may shape human behavior (such as sensitivity to the actual and potential reactions of others) tend to be slighted.

Research Findings and Social Control Theory

While the cultural conflict theorist attributes the motivation for lawbreaking to subcultural socialization and the strain theorist attributes it to structurally induced status problems, the social control theorist makes few claims about motivation. The important variables for the control theorist are those that act as barriers to crime and delinquency. Hence, research relevant to control theory has focused on attitudes toward the law and its agents, commitments to conventional goals, involvement in conventional activities, or relationships with parents, the school, and the church. Much of this research is summarized in Chapter 7 where we consider several key sources of adolescent socialization. However, we will outline here research relevant to some of the crucial issues that differentiate control theory from cultural conflict and strain theory.

One argument for which control theory has received considerable support has been that studying the strength of barriers will provide us with a better explanation of delinquency than will studying motivations. We have already noted that structural strain, which is the most commonly cited motivation for delinquency, has not been found to explain delinquency when such strain is measured in terms of the discrepancy between aspirations and perceived reality. Neither does delinquency appear to be required by class or subcultural traditions. Arguing in favor of control theory's perspective on motivation, Briar and Piliavin have written:

> Because delinquent behavior is typically episodic, purposive, and confined to certain situations, we assume that the motives for such behavior are frequently episodic, oriented to short-term ends, and confined to certain situations. That is, rather than considering delinquent acts as solely the product of long-term motives deriving from conflicts or frustrations whose genesis is far removed from the arenas in which the illegal behavior occurs, we assume these acts are prompted by short-term situationally induced desires experienced by all boys to obtain valued goods, to portray courage in the presence of, or be loyal to peers, to strike out at someone who is disliked, or simply to "get kicks." (1965:36)

The support for the social control view of motivation has been rather indirect. For one thing, the *lack* of research to support arguments that emphasize structurally and culturally induced motives has been interpreted as an indication that the motives must be much more diverse and difficult to predict than motivational theories suggest. Second, the fact that delinquency *itself* is episodic and sporadic, occupying very little time (even among gang delinquents), has been cited as support for the idea that the motives are similarly sporadic and episodic. Finally, the fact that delinquent activity is so common has suggested that the motives are quite commonly experienced and not concentrated in any one social class or social setting.

Martin Gold's research into the degree of premeditation involved in delinquent behavior, as well as the intensity of delinquent participation, led him to compare delinquency to a "pickup game" of basketball or football (1970). Such games are casual, unplanned, and short-term. Some youngsters are strongly committed to the game, but many are indifferent or unwilling to play. With the proper "ingredients" of time and place, a game can be organized, but in many instances sufficient catalyzing forces do not emerge. If and when the stage is set and the game begins, performance becomes an important aspect. The fact that a group of friends is present is not so important as the notion of the performance. In other words, Gold sees delinquency as a spontaneous, unplanned event with certain members of the group performing as players and others being more passive and performing as the audience. Gold believes that the image of delinquency as an impromptu performance is closer to the truth than the image of the delinquent as chronic offender or disturbed adolescent. Thus, Gold's findings support social control theory's downplaying of motivational factors and strong emphasis on the situational nature of delinquent behavior.

Research studies have persistently supported the argument that focusing on barriers is more fruitful than focusing on motivations. Such studies have shown significant relationships between involvement in delinquency and attachment to conventional others, values, and institutions.

Youths who identify with their parents, care what their teachers think about them, aspire toward high occupational or educational status, and respect the law and its agents are significantly less likely to commit delinquent acts than are youths with fewer "stakes in conformity" (Hirschi, 1969; Hindelang, 1973; Jensen, 1972; Hepburn, 1976).

Control theory is at odds with strain theory over the relationship between conventional aspirations and delinquency. As noted above, strain theorists argue that high aspirations, coupled with limited opportunity, generate status problems and that such problems are concentrated in the lower or working classes. On the other hand, control theorists believe that conventional aspirations constitute a "stake" in conformity and therefore act as a barrier to delinquency. The data tend to support the control theorists' position in that high aspirations for conventional behavior have been found to act as a barrier to delinquency regardless of realistic expectations and race (Hirschi, 1969). However, there has been some evidence supporting the argument of strain theory that disparities between aspirations and expectations are associated with involvement in delinquency—but among middle-class, rather than lower-class, youths (Stinchcombe, 1964; Hirschi, 1969). Both Hirschi and Stinchcombe have presented data that suggest that aspirations or pressures to succeed may not act as barriers to delinquency under all circumstances or in all groups. Overall, however, most research on the issue indicates that aspirations are more likely to operate as barriers to delinquency than as causes and that the circumstances under which aspirations might act as causes are not those generally emphasized in strain theory.

The scope of factors that control theory presents as barriers to delinquency is quite broad. For example, Briar and Piliavin (1965) have cited the following barriers: (1) fear of material deprivations and punishments, (2) protection of self-image, (3) maintenance of valued relationships, and (4) preservation of future status and activities. Hirschi has differentiated four dimensions of the "social bond" between youths and conventional society that act as a barrier to delinquency: (1) attachment or identification (for example, with parents), (2) commitment to conventional goals (such as high occupational status), (3) belief in the legitimacy of conventional norms, and (4) involvement in conventional activities.

Several studies of involvement in conventional activities have failed to support the predictions of control theory. Hirschi found that participation in work, sports, recreation, and hobbies were unrelated to delinquency (1969:189–90). Robin reported that involvement in antipoverty job corps or neighborhood youth corps programs had no significant impact on delinquent behavior during or after participation in the programs (1969:323–31). Schaefer found no significant relationship between participation in interscholastic athletics and delinquency when controlling for grade point average and social class (1969:40–47). Even amount of time under direct parental control or surveillance has been found to be only weakly related to delinquency. On the other hand, involvement in school-related activities has been shown to be negatively related to delinquency (Hirschi, 1969:191–92; Hindelang, 1973:481–83). In short, although control theory predicts that participation in conventional activity should deter delinquency, many forms of participation do not. There is little overall support for the folk belief that "idle hands are the devil's workshop." Those forms of participation that *are* related to delinquency (for example, time spent on homework) are those that are likely to reflect real commitment and valued relationships. Control theorists have not been able to predict what forms of participation are important barriers to delinquency.

Research has also failed to support some control theorists' claims that attachment to others is a barrier to delinquency even if those others are involved in delinquency. One of the most prominent control theorists has argued that "we honor those we admire not by imitation, but by adherence to conventional standards" (Hirschi, 1969:152). This argument represents an extreme version of control theory in which it does not matter to whom a person is attached. The actual support for that argument is very weak, and there are several studies whose findings are to the contrary. Hirschi reported a weak negative correlation between "wanting to be like one's friends" and delinquency, even for youths with several delinquent friends. However, further analysis of the same body of data (Jensen and Erickson, 1977) showed no significant association between peer commitment and delinquency among black youths. Moreover, at least four studies have reported positive associations—that is, the greater the attachment to peers, the greater the delinquency (Empey and Lubeck, 1971; Hindelang, 1973; Erickson and Empey, 1965; Elliott and Voss, 1974). One study (Elliott and Voss, 1974) concluded that commitment to delinquent peers is positively correlated with delinquency. Another (Linden and Hackler, 1973:41) reported that boys with weak ties to conventional associates but with moderate or strong ties to deviant peers are more involved in delinquency than are boys who are not tied to their delinquent peers. In short, the bulk of the research at present suggests that there are weak but positive associations between attachment to peers and delinquency and that boys who are "tied," "committed," or "attached" to their delinquent peers are more likely to be involved in delinquency than those who are not so committed. However, contrary findings have yet to be explained and will no doubt be the subject of further research.

RECENT THEORETICAL DEVELOPMENTS

As we noted earlier, Cloward and Ohlin attempted to combine notions of strain theory with some aspects of cultural conflict theory. Similarly, other theorists have attempted to combine notions derived from cultural conflict and social control theory. To do so obviously requires "toning down" or modifying some of the claims of each theory.

Linden and Hackler (1973) have developed an *affective ties* theory that focuses on ties to delinquent peers as a source of delinquent activity and on ties to conventional persons in one's environment (parents, teachers, and some peers) as barriers to delinquency. This theory combines many of the basic elements of control theory with differential association theory. However, in contrast to cultural conflict theorists, Linden and Hackler do not assume that all factors that might influence delinquency do so through their influence on cultural "definitions." Such definitions are viewed as relevant to explaining delinquency but not as mediating the impact of all other influences. According to this theory, ties to conventional and unconventional persons are relevant to explaining delinquency, *regardless* of what an adolescent feels to be right or wrong.

The social learning theories of Rand Conger (1976) and Ronald Akers (1977) are similar to Linden and Hackler's theory in that they view delinquent peers as a source of reinforcement for delinquent action and bonds to conventional institutions as barriers to delinquency. In addition, social learning theorists believe that although "definitions" play a role in the learning of conventional and unconventional behavior, such definitions do not mediate all other influences. Finally, social learning theorists believe that the activity of delinquency is reinforcing (for example, obtaining food by stealing when hungry; getting "kicks" when bored) and is "motivated" or learned in the context of rewards or punishments. Social learning theory goes beyond social control theory by arguing that the notion of a bond entails reinforcing stimuli that maintain a particular mode of behavior.

Research has supported the theoretical integration evident in the affective ties and social learning theories. It has been demonstrated that delinquency is associated with delinquent peers, ties to conventional others, and cultural definitions and that each of these three factors is associated with delinquency independently of the other two. The one issue, however, still subject to debate is that of causal direction. Elliott and Voss's (1974) longitudinal study suggested that delinquent friendships are more likely to be a consequence of delinquency than a cause. On the other hand, Elliott and Voss did note a weak relationship in the direction predicted by cultural conflict theories (that is, that exposure to delinquent friendships is predictive of eventual delinquent behavior). Their findings have raised problems for all theories that view delinquent peers as a major source of delinquency.

Although the disparity between long-term goals and prospects for realizing those goals does not seem to explain delinquent activity, several authors have suggested that more immediate pressures and goals, coupled with limited ability or opportunity, might be relevant to such an explanation. We have already noted that there is some support for this argument (Stinchcombe, 1964; Hirschi, 1969). Another study by Quicker (1974) concluded that "long range goal discrepancy is untenable as a cause of delinquency," but that more immediate short-range discrepancy *is* strongly related to delinquency. Quicker observed that the frustrations leading to delinquency are generated by more immediate circumstances than Merton or Cloward and Ohlin recognized. However, even if we modify the role of frustration, we still have to realize that such motivating circumstances are only one among a variety of motivating forces for delinquency.

Social control theory is currently also being extended to encompass new variables thought to act as barriers to delinquency, such as adolescent perceptions of the risk of legal sanctioning (Jensen, 1969; Waldo and Chiricos, 1972; Jensen, Erickson, and Gibbs, 1978). Furthermore, there is a growing concern about identifying the circumstances or factors that determine the strength of barriers to delinquency. It may be true that attachments to parents and school act as barriers to delinquency, but we do not know what determines the strength of such attachments.

Another goal for future theory and research is the identification of social control mechanisms that may be unique to specific social groups. For example, delinquent activity may vary according to religious involvement for some denominations but not others (Jensen and Erickson, 1979). Similarly, it is commonly argued that weak attachment to the family may be more predictive of female delinquency than of male delinquency (Rodman and Grams, 1967). Control theorists, who have tended to concentrate on general processes of social control, have yet to pay much attention to specifying how these processes vary in importance over time and social space.

Strain theory is the only one of the three major sociological schools of thought that has addressed different "types" of delinquent or criminal offenses. Both control theory and cultural conflict theory have been advanced as general theories, and when they have been tested in empirical research, the focus has been on indexes consisting of a variety of delinquent acts. Numerous theorists (Gibbons, 1968; Clinard and Quinney, 1967; Ferdinand, 1966) have argued that different offenses may be affected by different processes, but there is very little research relevant to the issue.

Several studies (Burkett and White, 1974; Higgins and Albrecht, 1977; Albrecht, Chadwick, and Alcorn, 1977), which we will review in Chapter 8, have suggested that religious involvement is more closely associated with various forms of drug use than with delinquent offenses against persons or property. Thus, some types of conventional involvement that have generally been dismissed as barriers to delinquency may be relevant to understanding certain types of delinquent behavior. The concept of juvenile delinquent may mask more information than it clarifies. Since delinquent behavior is episodic, transitory, and diverse, the causal processes involved may be diverse as well.

In sum, progress in understanding delinquency is most likely to result from efforts to combine and integrate theories and to identify those settings, circumstances, groups, and offenses to which certain barriers or motivating forces may be particularly crucial. We seem to be at a dead end in our ability to explain delinquency using traditional, general, or "grand" theories. However, we are beginning to elaborate on such theories in new and exciting ways.

SUMMARY

Sociology has provided us with several different concepts of delinquency. Delinquency has been viewed in terms of the behavior of gangs; as a subcultural system of values, norms, and beliefs; as the behavior of a type of individual; and, finally, as behavior or acts in violation of the law. Sociological perspectives are distinct from psychological and biological theory and research in their emphasis on delinquency as a form of group behavior. Most juvenile offenses are, in fact, committed in the company of other persons. However, sociologists also study delinquency as individual behavior and concern themselves with differentiating between delinquents and nondelinquents as well.

When focusing on delinquency in any of these senses, sociological perspectives share the assumption that delinquency is learned and more common in some social environments than in others. Important aspects of that social environment are its cultural patterns, social institutions and groups, and structure of opportunities. Different sociological theories are characterized by different ideas about the exact nature and relative importance of different environmental circumstances in the learning of delinquency. Three prominent theories that differ sufficiently to be considered unique schools of thought are (1) social disorganization-social control theory, (2) social disorganization-strain theory, and (3) cultural conflict theory.

Social disorganization-social control perspectives emphasize the failure of the social system or of agencies of conventional socialization to give juveniles stakes in conformity. As a result, a sizable proportion, having little or nothing to lose, is free to drift into delinquent involvements. *Social disorganization-strain* perspectives emphasize the difficulties experienced by some segments of society in achieving learned goals. Under such circumstances, juveniles experience status problems. And if enough similarly situated juveniles interact with one another, one outcome can be the development of an oppositional culture, or a "contraculture." *Cultural conflict* perspectives assume that there are certain segments of society or social settings characterized by values, norms, and beliefs that require, encourage, or tolerate delinquency. Differential exposure to such subcultural values is thought to explain delinquency rates as well as variable individual involvement in delinquency.

Research relevant to strain theory has failed to substantiate a number of assumptions crucial to the perspective. There has been no evidence that gang boys or delinquent youth are characterized by a contracultural value system. High conventional aspirations appear to act as a barrier to delinquency even in groups or among youths whose probability of failure is high. Involvement in delinquency tends to be associated with lower self-esteem than does involvement in conventional activities, even for boys with delinquent friends. In fact, among males reporting delinquent offenses, the greater the number of delinquent friends, the lower their self-esteem.

The variations in subcultural definitions of lawbreaking that cultural conflict theory posits have not been substantiated in actual research. Studies of public evaluations of the seriousness of criminal and delinquent activities, of public disapproval of such activity, and of adolescent attitudes toward lawbreaking have not supported the notion of a class subculture requiring, encouraging, or tolerating crime and delinquency. Researchers have presented evidence that questions the causal order of the relationship between delinquent companions and delinquent behavior and that challenges the assumption that delinquent youths are among the most able, persevering, and gregarious members in their particular social settings. The stress on "definitions," or cultural phenomena, as the key factor determining the influence of other social forces has been found to be in error as well.

Research has been consistent with social disorganization-social control theory in a number of key areas but inconsistent in others. In support of control theory, research has shown that the greater the attachment to conventional persons and institutions and the greater the commitment to conventional goals, the less the involvement in delinquency. Research has also shown that control theory's focus on barriers is of greater utility in predicting or explaining variable involvement in delinquency than is the search for motivations. On the other hand, control theorists have not been able to predict what forms of involvement in conventional activities are important as barriers, although they posit that such involvement should decrease delinquency. Moreover, the view of one of the most prominent contemporary control theorists that attachment to peers (whether they are conventional or delinquent) acts as a barrier to delinquency has not been substantiated in research.

A considerable amount of research in the 1970s was oriented around either testing and extending control theory or integrating it with other theories. Further progress in the explanation of delinquency may require that sociologists pay more attention to several issues that have been raised repeatedly over the decades but that have rarely been investigated in any systematic fashion. Specifically, we need to learn far more about the relevance of different control mechanisms for specific social groups or settings, for different types of delinquent offenses, and for group delinquency, as opposed to individual delinquent activities.

REFERENCES

Akers, R. L. 1977. *Deviant Behavior: A Social Learning Approach,* 2nd ed. Belmont, Calif.: Wadsworth.

Albrecht, S. L., B. A. Chadwick, and D. S. Alcorn. 1977. "Religiosity and Deviance: Application of an Attitude-Behavior Contingent Consistency Model." *Journal for the Scientific Study of Religion* 16 (September):263–74.

Bandura, A., and R. H. Walters. 1959. *Adolescent Aggression.* New York: Ronald Press.

Briar, S., and I. Piliavin. 1965. "Delinquency, Situational Inducements, and Commitments to Conformity." *Social Problems* 13 (1):35–45. Copyright 1965 by the Society for the Study of Social Problems. Reprinted by permission.

Broom, L., and P. Selznick. 1968. *Sociology.* New York: Harper & Row.

Burkett, S. R., and M. White. 1974. "Hellfire and Delinquency: Another Look." *Journal for the Scientific Study of Religion* 13 (December):455–62.

Clinard, M., and R. Quinney. 1967. *Criminal Behavior Systems: A Typology.* New York: Holt, Rinehart and Winston.

Cloward, R. A., and L. E. Ohlin. 1960. *Delinquency and Opportunity.* New York: Free Press.

Cohen, A. K. 1955. *Delinquent Boys.* New York: Free Press.

Conger, R. D. 1976. "Social Control and Social Learning Models of Delinquent Behavior: A Synthesis." *Criminology* 14 (May):17–40.

DeLamater, J. 1968. "On the Nature of Deviance." *Social Forces* 46 (June):445–55.

Durkheim, E. 1951. *Suicide.* Translated by J. A. Spaulding and G. Simpson. New York: Free Press.

Elliott, D. S., and H. L. Voss. 1974. *Delinquency and Dropout.* Lexington, Mass.: Lexington Books.

Empey, L. T. 1967. "Delinquency Theory and Recent Research." *Journal of Research in Crime and Delinquency* 4 (January):32–42.

Empey, L. T., and S. G. Lubeck. 1971. *Explaining Delinquency.* Lexington, Mass.: Lexington Books.

England, R. W. 1960. "A Theory of Middle-Class Juvenile Delinquency." *Journal of Criminal Law and Criminology* 50 (April):535–40.

Erickson, M. L., and L. T. Empey. 1965. "Class Position, Peers and Delinquency." *Sociology and Social Research* 49 (April):268–82.

Erickson, M. L., and G. F. Jensen. 1977. "Delinquency Is Still Group Behavior!: Toward Revitalizing the Group Premise in the Sociology of Deviance." *Journal of Criminal Law and Criminology* 68 (2):262–73.

Ferdinand, T. N. 1966. *Typologies of Delinquency.* New York: Random House.

Finestone, H. 1976. *Victims of Change: Juvenile Delinquents in American Society.* Westport, Conn.: Greenwood Press.

Gibbons, D. 1968. *Society, Crime and Criminal Careers.* Englewood Cliffs, N.J.: Prentice-Hall.

Glueck, S., and E. Glueck. 1950. *Unraveling Juvenile Delinquency.* Cambridge, Mass.: Harvard University Press.

Gold, M. 1963. *Status Forces in Delinquent Boys.* Ann Arbor, Mich.: Institute for Social Research, University of Michigan.

———. 1970. *Delinquent Behavior in an American City.* Monterey, Calif.: Brooks/Cole.

Gordon, R. A., et al. 1963. "Values and Gang Delinquency." *American Journal of Sociology* 69 (Summer):109–28.

Hepburn, J. R. 1976. "Casting Alternative Models of Delinquency Causation." *Journal of Criminal Law and Criminology* 67 (December):450–60.

Higgins, P. C., and G. L. Albrecht. 1977. "Hellfire and Delinquency Revisited." *Social Forces* 55 (June):952–58.

Hindelang, M. J. 1973. "Causes of Delinquency: A Partial Replication and Extension." *Social Problems* 21 (Spring):471–87.

Hirschi, T. 1969. *Causes of Delinquency.* Berkeley: University of California Press.

Jensen, G. F. 1969. "Crime Doesn't Pay: Correlates of a Shared Misunderstanding." *Social Problems* 17 (Fall):189–201.

———. 1971. *Delinquency and Adolescent Self-Conceptions: A Study of the Personal Relevance of Infraction.* Ph.D. dissertation. University of Washington.

———. 1972. "Parents, Peers and Delinquent Action: A Test of the Differential Association Hypothesis." *American Journal of Sociology* 78 (November): 562–75.

Jensen, G. F., and M. L. Erickson. 1977. "Peer Commitment and Delinquency: New Tests of Old Hypotheses." Unpublished manuscript.

———. 1979. "The Religious Factor and Delinquency." In Robert Wuthnow, ed., *The Religious Dimension: New Directions in Quantitative Research.* New York: Academic Press.

Jensen, G. F., M. L. Erickson, and J. P. Gibbs. 1978. "Perceived Risk of Punishment and Self-reported Delinquency." *Social Forces* 57, no. 1 (September): 57–78.

Lerman, P. 1968. "Individual Values, Peer Values and Subcultural Delinquency." *American Sociological Review* 33 (April):219–35.

Linden, E., and J. C. Hackler. 1973. "Affective Ties and Delinquency." *Pacific Sociological Review* 16 (January):27–46.

Matza, D. 1964. *Delinquency and Drift.* New York: John Wiley.

Matza, D., and G. M. Sykes. 1961. "Juvenile Delinquency and Subterranean Values." *American Sociological Review* 26 (October):712–17.

Merton, R. K. 1957. *Social Theory and Social Structure.* New York: Free Press.

Miller, W. 1958. "Lower Class Culture as a Generating Milieu of Gang Delinquency." *Journal of Social Issues* 14:5–19.

———. 1975. *Violence by Youth Gangs and Youth Groups as a Crime Problem in Major American Cities.* National Institute for Juvenile Justice and Delinquency Prevention, U.S. Department of Justice. Washington, D.C.: U.S. Government Printing Office.

Park, R. E. 1952. "Community Organization and Juvenile Delinquency." In Everett C. Hughes et al., eds., *Human Communities: The City and Human Ecology.* Glencoe, Ill.: Free Press.

Quicker, J. C. 1974. "The Effect of Goal Discrepancy on Delinquency." *Social Problems* 22 (October):76–86.

Rainwater, L. 1970. "The Problem of Lower Class Culture." *Journal of Social Issues* 26 (Winter):133–48.

Reiss, A. J., Jr. 1951. "Delinquency as the Failure of Personal and Social Controls." *American Sociological Review* 16:196–207.

Robin, G. D. 1969. "Anti-poverty Programs and Delinquency." *Journal of Criminal Law, Criminology and Police Science* 60 (Fall):323–31.

Rodman, H. 1963. "The Lower Class Value Stretch." *Social Forces* 42 (December): 205–15.

Rodman, H., and P. Grams. 1967. "Juvenile Delinquency and the Family: A Review and Discussion." In President's Commission on Law Enforcement and Administration of Justice, *Task Force Report: Juvenile Delinquency and Youth Crime,* Appendix L. Washington, D.C.: U.S. Government Printing Office.

Rothstein, E. 1962. "Attributes Related to High Social Status: A Comparison of the Perceptions of Delinquent and Non-delinquent Boys." *Social Problems* 10:75–83.

Savitz, L. D., M. Lalli, and L. Rosen. 1977. *City Life and Delinquency — Victimization, Fear of Crime and Gang Membership.* Washington, D.C.: Law Enforcement Assistance Administration.

Schaefer, W. E. 1969. "Participation in Interscholastic Athletics and Delinquency: A Preliminary Study." *Social Problems* 17 (Summer):40–47.

Shaw, C. 1929. *Delinquency Areas.* Chicago: University of Chicago Press. Copyright 1929 by the University of Chicago Press.

Shaw, C., and H. McKay. 1942. *Juvenile Delinquency and Urban Areas.* Chicago: University of Chicago Press.

Short, J. F. 1957. "Differential Association and Delinquency." *Social Problems* 4:233–39.

Short, J. F., and F. L. Strodtbeck. 1965. *Group Process and Gang Delinquency.* Chicago: University of Chicago Press.

Short, J. F., R. Rivera, and R. A. Tennyson. 1965. "Perceived Opportunities, Gang Membership and Delinquency." *American Sociological Review* 30 (February):56–67.

Stinchcombe, A. L. 1964. *Rebellion in a High School.* Chicago: Quadrangle Books.

Sutherland, E. H. 1939. *Principles of Criminology.* Philadelphia: J. B. Lippincott.

Sutherland, E. H., and D. R. Cressey. 1974. *Criminology,* 9th ed. Philadelphia: J. B. Lippincott.

Sykes, G. M., and D. Matza. 1957. "Techniques of Neutralization: A Theory of Delinquency." *American Journal of Sociology* 22 (December):664–70.

Thomas, W. I., and F. Znaniecki. 1918. *The Polish Peasant in Europe and America.* New York: Alfred A. Knopf.

Toby, J. 1957. "Social Disorganization and Stake in Conformity: Complementary Factors in the Predatory Behavior of Hoodlums." *Journal of Criminal Law, Criminology and Police Science* 48:12–17.

Voss, H. L. 1964. "Differential Association and Delinquent Behavior: A Replication." *Social Problems* 12:78–85.

Waldo, G. P., and T. G. Chiricos. 1972. "Perceived Penal Sanctions and Self-Reported Criminality: A Neglected Approach to Deterrence Research." *Social Problems* 19 (Spring):522–40.

Wrong, D. 1961. "The Oversocialized Conception of Man in Modern Sociology." *American Sociological Review* 26 (April):183–93.

Yablonsky, L. 1959. "The Delinquent Gang as a Near Group." *Social Problems* 7 (Fall):108–17. Copyright 1959 by the Society for the Study of Social Problems. Reprinted by permission.

Yinger, M. 1960. "Contraculture and Subculture." *American Sociological Review* 25 (October):625–35.

7.
CONTEXTS FOR ADOLESCENT SOCIALIZATION: FAMILY, SCHOOL, AND ADOLESCENT SOCIETY

"The teachers would always pick me out for not doing work or eat me out for something. I mean, if I attended regularly they would find fault with my haircut or something else. Sometimes I felt like strangling them—so I would just cut.

My father's the one who always gives me a bad time. I like him, but I wish he would leave me alone. You can't talk to him—he jumps all over you. My grandfather was the only one I could talk to. He would keep me cool. But when he died that was it.

. . . My mother! Well, she's all right but she keeps comparing me to my kid sister. And, you know, she's real good in school—and I get tired of hearing how she's so good and I'm so bad."

—Statement by "Duke," Manhattan gang leader,
in Lewis Yablonsky, *The Violent Gang*

MAJOR SOCIALIZING FORCES

In Chapter 6 we outlined the similarities and differences among sociological theories of the causes of delinquency. One of the common themes characterizing those theories is that most human behavior, including delinquent behavior, is learned and that the major source of human learning involves interaction with other people. People become human beings through processes of social interaction and social learning that are referred to as "socialization." Socialization takes place in a variety of settings. For the child growing up in the United States, the settings of family, school, and peer group are generally viewed as particularly crucial to socialization. Although there is disagreement over their relative importance, parents, teachers, and peers are considered the most significant or consequential people in the child's environment. These three contexts have received the bulk of attention in sociological theory and research, and we will summarize the relevant literature in the following sections as we deal with family, school, and adolescent society. In Chapter 8 we will consider the state of research on how religion, mass media, and communal bonds affect delinquency.

THE FAMILY

The family has typically been viewed as the most crucial institution in our society for shaping the child's personality, attitudes, and behavior. At the same time, however, many social commentators have noted a decline in the range of functions performed by the family. Over forty years ago, William Ogburn (1938) observed that of seven functions served by the family throughout history (economic production, status allocation, education, religious training, recreation, protection, and provision of affection), only its role in providing affection was not declining. Although the family may have been a *more* important institution at earlier points in history, most scholars are willing to accept that it remains a major setting for socialization in American society.

The centrality of the family to delinquency theory and research has varied over the years, and the theme receives more attention in some theoretical traditions than others. Karen Wilkinson (1974) has classified the ebb and flow of attention to the family into three periods: 1900–1932, 1933–1950, and 1950–1972. The first period was one of acceptance of the theme in that sociologists and criminologists of that time tended to view the family as "the most important of human institutions" (Ellwood, 1919:91). Social reformers and "child savers" emphasized the importance of stable family life in the prevention of delinquency. In fact, as noted in Chapter 2, the invention of the juvenile court was coupled with a correctional ideology that emphasized the home and family as targets of treatment.

Wilkinson characterized the second period as one of rejection of the importance of the family setting. During this time, the decline of family functions and the role of other institutions in the socialization and control of children was emphasized. The popular sociological theories of the time focused on social class standing and the learning of delinquent behavior in interaction with peers. Thus, the emphasis had shifted from social disorganization and the breakdown of traditional institutions to "differential social organization"—that is, development of new patterns of cooperative relationships among neighbors, relatives, and peers that were viewed as more suitable to urban living. Delinquent behavior was considered either a normal response to limited opportunity or a product of normal learning in stable, but subcultural, environments.

Wilkinson argued that beginning in the 1950s interest in the family revived. Along with a concern for the broken home, there emerged a renewed interest in the effect of family relationships on delinquency. Rather than concentrating on the *structure* of the home, researchers began considering the nature of interaction between parents and children, styles of parental discipline and supervision, and such variables as "family integration" and "cohesion." This trend in research is exemplified in the work of Reiss, 1951; Glueck and Glueck, 1950; Nye, 1958; Hirschi, 1969; and Larson and Myerhoff, 1967.

The ebb and flow of concern about the family is associated with the popularity of the various theories of delinquency that we summarized in Chapter 6. For example, strain theory emphasizes such variables as aspirations, limited opportunities for success, status frustration, and delinquent subcultures. The family plays a role in the strain theory of delinquency insofar as it determines a youth's social standing, his or her chances of getting ahead by legitimate means, and, hence, the probability of status problems. In Merton's version of strain theory (1957), the family is also important in that working-class children are depicted as more thoroughly socialized to aspire toward culturally prescribed goals of success than to accept norms limiting the means to do so. In short, the family is important as the determinant of social-class position.

The role of the family in cultural conflict perspectives varies from one theorist to another. Sutherland and Cressey (1974) have argued that the family is important to the degree that it affects the chances of exposure to definitions favorable and unfavorable to lawbreaking. In cultural conflict theory, such definitions are always intervening to explain the effects of various institutions on delinquency. Walter Miller's emphasis on lower-class "focal concerns" suggests that the lower-class family *facilitates* delinquency insofar as the values conveyed by adults lead to trouble with the law (1958). However, like Sutherland and Cressey, Miller contended that it is the "one-sex peer unit" and not the two-parent family unit that is *most* relevant to understanding the behavior of members of the lower-class community. Miller argued that such peer units are especially salient for understanding adolescent males who come from female-based households since it is within peer groups that they solve problems of sex-role identification and learn the "male" role.

Of the three major theories, social control theory accords the most central role to family variables in the explanation of delinquency. Social control theorists argue that delinquent acts result when an individual's bond to society is weak or broken. Attachment to parents becomes a central variable in control theory because this bond symbolizes the bridge to parental values, ideals, expectations, and aspirations. The family becomes a key socialization agent; the stronger the tie between parent and child, the less the involvement in delinquency.

An emerging theory of delinquency causation that accords considerable importance to the family is social learning theory. The central hypothesis of social learning theory is that models of human behavior that are rewarding are more likely to be emulated than nonrewarding models. Social learning theory predicts that if the reward for delinquent behavior is greater than the reward for nondelinquent behavior, the delinquent behavior will be maintained. The family is initially a primary source of learning and reinforcement. The child seeks approval and esteem from his or her parents by acting in ways that the parents will approve and admire and avoiding those behaviors that elicit disapproval or negative reinforcement. The social learning school accords parents a role as a key reference group. Thus, both social control theory and social learning theory have emphasized the importance of the family in juvenile delinquency research.

RESEARCH ON THE FAMILY AND DELINQUENCY

There are literally hundreds of studies dealing with various aspects of family life and delinquency. We will organize our presentation around certain aspects of the family that have been the subject of considerable research. First, we will consider certain *structural* characteristics of the family and a child's place in the family. In this regard, we will focus on the broken home, ordinal position, family size, and maternal deprivation. Then we will turn to research concerning actual *relationships* among family members (that is, affective relationships between parents and between parent and child, methods of parental control, and parental supervision).

The Broken Home

A very common observation about juvenile delinquency is that it is the product of a "broken" home, and numerous studies have suggested that a broken home does indeed seriously disrupt the life of a child and severely hamper the socialization of children. In fact, the belief in the deleterious effect of a broken home on children is so firmly entrenched in many quarters of the juvenile court system that it would be surprising not to find the system producing "facts" to support this assertion. The conviction that family disruption is a cause of delinquent conduct can act as a self-fulfilling prophecy: a juvenile from a broken home who is trouble may have a greater chance of juvenile court intervention than a similar case from an intact home.

Table 7–1, from a study by Chilton and Markle (1972), compares the family situations of children in the general population with those of children referred to the juvenile and county courts of Florida. The table suggests that juveniles living in something other than an intact family situation are disproportionally represented in status and delinquent offense categories. For instance, although only 17 percent of juveniles were from broken families, they accounted for 40 percent of the delinquent referrals to the juvenile court. Similarly, the state of California (California Youth Authority, 1971) has pointed out that 57 percent of male and 66 percent of female delinquents had parents who were not living together at the time the child was committed to the California Youth Authority. Moreover, an examination of selected juvenile court annual reports indicates that in excess of 50 percent of juveniles referred to the juvenile justice system are from broken families. Thus, the concentration of juveniles from broken homes is pronounced in official statistics. However, Chilton and Markle found that when they classified families on the basis of income, the economic position of families appeared to

TABLE 7-1 *Distribution of Family Situations of Children Aged 10–17*

	% of Children in the General Population	% of Children Charged with Offenses	
		Offenses Applicable to Juveniles Only	Offenses that Would Be Crimes for Adults
Family Situation			
Husband/wife family	83.0	60.3	60.0
Mother only	11.7	25.0	27.5
Father only	1.6	4.1	3.1
Neither parent	3.7	10.6	9.4
Total	100.0	100.0	100.0

Source: Roland J. Chilton and Gerald E. Markle. "Family Disruption, Delinquent Conduct and the Effect of Subclassification." *American Sociological Review* 37 (February 1972):93–99.

have more to do with referral to the juvenile justice system than did family living arrangements.

Studies using self-report techniques (discussed in Chapter 4) have yielded results that are inconsistent with the common view of broken homes and delinquency. For example, Nye (1958) and Dentler and Monroe (1961) found no significant relationship between delinquency and family composition, and both Hirschi (1969) and Gold (1970) found the greatest delinquency in families with stepfathers. Hirschi found that nearly the same proportion of blacks from intact homes (46 percent) as blacks from homes with no father present (47 percent) reported delinquent acts, but that a somewhat greater proportion of blacks with stepfathers (55 percent) reported such acts. The pattern was similar for whites. Gold found that being raised by a natural mother and stepfather was conducive to more delinquent behavior than being raised by a mother alone. This pattern held true for both boys and girls.

In 1965 the Department of Labor's Office of Policy Planning and Research published *The Negro Family* (Moynihan, 1965). Better known as the "Moynihan Report," this study advanced the thesis that the black family had evolved a structure that was contributing to problem behavior and a "tangle of pathology." Of particular concern were the predominance of the "matrifocal" (mother-centered), matriarchical (mother-dominated), female-headed family and the consequences of such a family structure for black male youths. Dominance of the black family by the female and absence of a father from the home have been viewed as sources of a "compulsive masculinity" that is ultimately reflected in a high rate of conflict with the law (Clark, 1965; Hannerz, 1969). Talcott Parsons (1947) had earlier advanced a similar hypothesis regarding adolescent males in general. Parsons felt that boys in female-headed households have a real problem in establishing a "masculine" identity and react by becoming compulsively masculine. Because such patterns of family life are more common among blacks, the problem has been viewed as especially pertinent to black delinquency.

However, research findings on the broken home and delinquency do not provide a great deal of support for the argument that compulsive masculinity is a cause of delinquency. For example, L. Rosen (1969) considered the relationship between delinquency and a variety of measures of matriarchy (father absence, sex of main wage earner, main decision maker, most influential adult) for a sample of black male youths between the ages of thirteen and fifteen. Rosen reported a "small association." Alan Berger and William Simon (1974), who examined data on youths aged fourteen to eighteen in Illinois, could find no support for the argument that delinquency among black males grows out of the female-based household. In fact, Berger and Simon argued that coming from a broken home in social environments where it is an infrequent experience may be more conducive to delinquency than in environments where broken homes are more common. Furthermore, their overall findings led them to conclude that "in general, the data simply do not support the conclusions generally imputed to Moynihan's work—namely, that the black family is drastically different from the white family in the way it treats its children and in the results it produces" (1974:160).

On the other hand, Silverman and Dinitz (1974) have provided evidence that black delinquents and delinquents from broken homes rank higher on self-ratings of "manliness," "toughness," and "compulsive masculinity" than white delinquents and delinquents from other types of households. However, since there were no nondelinquents in Silverman and Dinitz's study, there is no basis for attributing delinquency to either compulsive masculinity or the female-centered household. Their findings merely tell us that some types of delinquents exhibit more signs of hypermasculinity than do others. Given the general pattern of findings by Hirschi, Gold, Rosen, and Berger and Simon, the safest conclusion is that matriarchy makes little or no difference for involvement in delinquency.

Ordinal Position

There has been periodic interest in ordinal position, or birth order, in relation to juvenile delinquency. For example, a study in England by Lees and Newson (1954) found that intermediate children who had older and younger siblings (that is, brothers and/or sisters) tended to be overrepresented among delinquents. The explanation posited for this finding is that the firstborn sibling lives the first years as an only child and receives the undivided attention and affection of his or her parents. The child born last enters into a complex family arrangement: the parents are experienced in raising children and there are older siblings who function as role models. The intermediate sibling may get "squeezed out" of affection and may gravitate into delinquent gangs to compensate.

Lees and Newson's findings are not unique. At least three other studies (Nye, 1958; McCord, McCord, and Zola, 1959; Glueck and Glueck, 1950) have reported similar findings. In Hirschi's self-report study, middle children reported the greatest proportion of delinquency (49 percent), first-born children and last born had nearly identical proportions (41 percent and 42 percent), and only children had the smallest proportion (33 percent). However, since middle children obviously come from families of at least three children, their high rate could reflect family size rather than ordinal position. Hirschi explored this possibility and found it to be the most plausible explanation. In any case, the relationship of ordinal position to delinquency is far from impressive.

Family Size

Family size has often been cited as an important factor in delinquency causation. The rationale for this hypothesis has been that familial control, discipline, resources, and socialization may be spread too thinly in large families. Research findings have in fact demonstrated a relationship between family size and delinquency. For example, using self-reports, Hirschi found that children from families of seven or more children reported about twice as many instances of two or more delinquent acts as did only children (29 percent as compared to 14 percent).

However, the impact of family size has yet to be fully explained. Hirschi (1969) found that the relationship between family size and delinquency persisted regardless of academic achievement. Further analysis of Hirschi's data (Joachim, 1978) has indicated that the effects of family size persist for different offenses, among blacks and whites, and among juveniles whose fathers fall in the same educational category. It has been argued that the relationship between family size and delinquency is spurious because both factors are related to social class or social status. However, there has been very little research on the issue either to support such an argument or to establish the causal role of family size.

Maternal Deprivation

During the blitzkrieg of London in World War II, British officials built large nurseries in the rural countryside where infants and young children could be safely cared for by "nannies" and child care personnel, while their parents continued the war effort in the urban areas. Despite the professional care that was ministered to these children, many of them appeared to have developmental difficulties. Listlessness, emotional outbursts, and mental aberrations seemed to be the result of maternal deprivation. Elaborating on this observation, Bowlby (1951) attempted to determine the importance of the maternal relationship for juvenile delinquency. Studying a group of juvenile delinquents drawn from patients at a child guidance center, Bowlby found a relationship between the absence of the mother and delinquent behavior. He concluded that "on the basis of this varied evidence it appears that there is a very strong case indeed for believing that prolonged separation of a child from his mother (or mother-substitute) during the first five years of life stands foremost among the causes of delinquent character development and persistent misbehavior" (1951:11).

Bowlby's findings have been severely criticized, and no supporting evidence has been provided to substantiate his theory of maternal deprivation. Research has suggested that it is not the absence of a parent per se that results in delinquency, but the quality of the relationship that exists between the child and the remaining parent. Moreover, Robert Andry (1962) has criticized Bowlby for his emphasis on maternal deprivation and total disregard for paternal deprivation. Andry argued that it is the quality of the parent-child interaction, rather than the sheer quantity of time spent with the child, that matters. Naess (1959) revealed another weakness of Bowlby's theory by demonstrating that the separation of a mother from her children does not result in "affectionless" children, as Bowlby suggested. Furthermore, Naess found that many delinquents who may have been maternally deprived had nondelinquent siblings. Finally, Hakeem (1958) dismissed Bowlby's study because of its poor methodology and the probability of sampling bias. Bowlby's sample was of juvenile thieves who were suffering from an inability to enter into affectionate relationships.

However, research has definitely established that children who feel unwanted by their mothers are more likely to report involvement in delinquency (Hirschi, 1969; Hindelang, 1973). This finding holds true whether the children are black or white (Austin, 1978). In further refinement of this finding, McCord, McCord, and Zola (1959) and Nye (1958) have shown that children whose homes were broken before the children had reached age five do not differ in delinquency from children whose homes were broken at later points in time. Similarly, Hirschi (1969) could find no difference between children who had been living with both parents before age five and those separated from one or both parents before that age. The most common argument in recent times is that the presence or absence of parents is less relevant to an understanding of delinquency than the quality of the parent-child relationship.

Family Relationships

A considerable volume of research suggests that actual relationships within the family are more relevant to understanding delinquency than are the structural variables just discussed. Researchers and commentators have argued that quarrelsome and negligent homes are more conducive to delinquent behavior than are broken homes (McCord, McCord, and Zola, 1959).

Many intact families are in fact "broken" in terms of the actual relationships among family members. David Abramsen (1960) has argued that family tensions greatly contribute to delinquent behavior. Long-term tension supposedly reduces family cohesiveness and impairs the parents' ability to provide an atmosphere conducive to meaningful adolescent growth and development. If the family environment is disruptive and unstable and parents display constant hostility toward one another, it is doubtful whether they will be able to exert a positive influence on their children.

Some research has focused on the parental relationship in terms of its impact on delinquency rates. Nye (1958) found a strong association between the reported marital happiness of parents and delinquent behavior: 46 percent of the boys and 49 percent of the girls from "unhappy" homes were in the highest delinquent category, compared to 23 percent of the boys and 22 percent of the girls from "completely happy homes." Similarly, the Gluecks (1950) found more delinquents than nondelinquents coming from homes with poor marital relationships. Jaffe (1963) found that families characterized by a high level of disagreement within the family had concomitantly high scores on a delinquency-proneness scale.

Hirschi (1969) has argued that an affective tie between parent and child is one of the strongest convention-inducing variables in delinquency research. The weaker the bond between parent and child, the greater the probability of delinquent behavior. Hirschi found definite relationships between self-reported delinquency and various measures of attachment to and communication with parents. Of those adolescents reporting little intimate communication with their fathers, 43 percent had committed two or more delinquent acts, while among those with high levels of communication with their fathers, only 5 percent reported two or more delinquent acts.

There is also some evidence that parental methods of control or discipline can help to explain the relationship between the family and delinquency. Nye (1958) found evidence that the type of discipline employed can have a pronounced effect on adolescent behavior. Extremely strict discipline appeared to affect adolescents in their relationships with peer groups by hindering normal interaction. Permissiveness and lax discipline were associated with a high probability of delinquency as well. Nye reported that 49 percent of delinquents who felt their mothers failed to carry out threats of punishment were in the highest delinquent category, compared to 30 percent of the boys and 22 percent of the girls who reported consistent follow-up of threatened punishment. Similarly, the McCords and Zola (1959) found a relationship between lax or erratic discipline and delinquency. Nye also found that discipline that could be categorized as "fair" or "equitable" tended to be associated with low involvement in delinquent behavior. In summary, discipline and the way it is administered appear to be important variables in understanding the relevance of the family environment to delinquency.

Social learning theorists also accord the family and parent-child relationships a central role in understanding juvenile delinquency. Utilizing a social learning perspective, Rand Conger argued that "willingness to respond positively to one's children will raise the reinforcement value of the home and increase the rate of interaction from juvenile to parents as well as increase the probability that a juvenile will emulate conventional parental patterns of behavior" (1976:31). Conger found that communication between parent and child acts as a barrier to delinquency only if the interaction is positive. Thus, communication in an excessively punitive home does not act as a barrier to delinquency. Conger reported similar results for "identification" with parents in that such identification appears to decrease the probability of delinquency only when parents tend to respond positively to a child's efforts to communicate and are not excessively punitive. In short, it appears that certain qualities of interaction, rather than the amount of interaction taking place, are important for understanding the impact of the family on delinquency.

This finding is further substantiated by Hirschi's observation that the amount of time spent under the direct supervision and control of parents is only weakly related to delinquency (1969:88). Hirschi argued that since delinquent activities require little time, only the most extreme amount of "direct" control could make much difference. From his perspective, the important variable is the "psychological" presence of the parent in tempting situations. It is the *anticipated* parental reaction that is most crucial in determining delinquent behavior. Conger's research has pointed to the conditions under which such indirect control mechanisms are likely to operate.

THE SCHOOL

While the range of functions served by the family has been declining, the importance of the school as a context for socialization has been growing. What was viewed as a luxury for the affluent during the seventeenth and eighteenth centuries has grown to encompass a greater and greater proportion of the population. School has become a central and growing force in the lives of Americans. As depicted in Table 7–2, the dropout rate in 1924 was so high that in the tenth grade less than 50 percent of students were still in school and only 30 percent of the 1924 cohort graduated from high school. By 1962 we find a dramatic increase in school retention rates, with over 90 percent entering the tenth grade and over 75 percent of that cohort graduating from high school. In fact, 45 percent of the 1962

TABLE 7-2 *School Retention Rates, 1924–1970*

School Year Pupils Entered 5th Grade	Retention Rates per 100 Pupils Who Entered 5th Grade								
	5th Grade	6th Grade	7th Grade	8th Grade	9th Grade	10th Grade	11th Grade	12th Grade	High School Graduation
1924	100.0	91.1	79.8	74.1	61.2	47.0	38.4	34.4	30.2
1934	100.0	95.3	89.2	84.2	80.3	71.1	60.0	51.2	46.7
1944	100.0	95.2	92.9	85.8	84.5	74.8	65.0	54.9	52.2
1954	100.0	98.0	97.9	94.8	91.5	85.5	75.9	68.4	64.2
1962	100.0	99.0	98.3	97.6	96.3	93.1	86.3	79.3	75.2

Source: Office of Education. *Digest of Educational Studies.* Washington, D.C.: National Center for Educational Statistics, 1972.

Funky Winkerbean by Tom Batiuk. © Field Enterprises, Inc. 1974. Courtesy of Field Newspaper Syndicate.

cohort entered college and 22 percent earned a college degree in 1975. The upward tendency in education rates has been accompanied by the inclusion of kindergarten in the public education system. Moreover, before entering kindergarten, more and more children are attending preschool and day-care facilities.

Since so much of the average American's life is encompassed by school, it is hardly surprising that the schools are viewed as central to an understanding of delinquency. According to some brands of strain theory (see Chapter 6), adolescents are *driven* to delinquency as a way of rebelling against school authority (Stinchcombe, 1964) or as a way of solving status problems generated by school experiences. The school is also central in social control theory, which generally views the school as an institution designed to encourage conventional attitudes and behavior. As Hirschi has expressed this point of view:

> Between the conventional family and the conventional world of work and marriage lies the school, an eminently conventional institution. Insofar as this institution is able to command his attachment, involvement and commitment, the adolescent is presumably able to move from childhood to adulthood with a minimum of delinquent acts. (1969:110)

While the strain theorist views school experiences as a source of frustration and rebellion, the control theorist views school experiences as important to the degree that they affect bonds to that institution. The person who is not attached, involved, or committed to school or concerned about the teachers' opinions is "freer" to drift into delinquency.

RESEARCH ON THE SCHOOL AND DELINQUENCY

A special task force report to the President's Commission on Law Enforcement and Administration of Justice pointed out several years ago (1967) that schools can facilitate delinquency in several different ways.

The authors of the report, Walter Schaefer and Kenneth Polk, listed the following as "defects in the schools that heighten educational failure and deterioration, and hence delinquency": (1) belief in the limited potential of disadvantaged pupils, (2) irrelevant instruction, (3) inappropriate teaching methods, (4) testing, grouping, and "tracking," (5) inadequate compensatory and remedial education, (6) inferior teachers and facilities in low-income schools, (7) school-community distance, and (8) racial and economic segregation (President's Commission on Law Enforcement and Administration of Justice, 1967:236–46). While plausible arguments concerning the contributory influence of each condition have been advanced, there is not a large body of research relevant to the specific conditions. Some studies have, however, dealt with delinquency in specific relation to school achievement, attachment to teachers and school, dropout, tracking, and intelligence tests. In addition to reviewing those studies, we will consider some research on the association between characteristics of schools, victimization rates, and violence against schools.

Achievement

One of the most persistent findings concerning the school and delinquency is that students who are not doing well in school have higher rates of delinquency than those who are faring better. For example, in his study of high school students in Oregon, Frease (1973) reported that no student with a grade-point average of 3.00 (B) or better had a police record, but that the percentage of delinquents was as high as 75 percent among boys with the lowest grades. Several self-report studies have shown a similar pattern (Hirschi, 1969; Gold, 1970; Polk, 1969).

Using data gathered by Wolfgang, Figlio, and Sellin (1972) on achievement level (based on school tests), Jensen (1976) found that achievement level is significantly related to delinquent status and that the relationship persists regardless of socioeconomic status and racial classification. The nature of the relationship is depicted in Figure 7–1. For both whites and nonwhites, the higher the achievement, the lower the odds that a youth will acquire a delinquent record before his eighteenth birthday. The findings also suggested that differences in delinquency status occur only when we move beyond the lowest levels of achievement. The most impressive changes in delinquency rates occur in the middle of the continuum of achievement levels. In sum, research thus far is consistent with the notion that academic success and achievement at school act as a barrier to delinquency.

Attachment to Teachers and School

As we noted earlier, control theory emphasizes the strength of the bond between students and their school and teachers as an important barrier to involvement in delinquency. And there is, in fact, persistent

FIGURE 7–1   *Odds of Acquiring a Delinquency Record, by Achievement Level and Race*

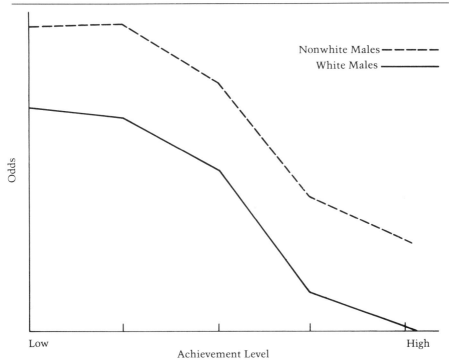

Nonwhite Males — — — — —
White Males ————————

Odds

Low   High

Achievement Level

Source: Gary F. Jensen. "Race, Achievement and Delinquency: A Further Look at Delinquency in a Birth Cohort." *American Journal of Sociology* 82 (September 1976):379–87. Copyright 1976 by the University of Chicago Press. Reprinted with permission.

evidence that students who do not like school or who do not like their teachers are more likely to report delinquency than those who are more strongly attached to their teachers and school (Jensen, Erickson, and Gibbs, 1978; Hirschi, 1969; Hindelang, 1973). Of course, such findings can be interpreted from more than one theoretical perspective. A strain theorist would argue that status frustration generated by school failure leads to adolescent rebellion and delinquency. In this view, delinquency is a mode of adjustment to frustration. In contrast, Travis Hirschi (1969), a control theorist, has argued that it is not acute discontent or intense frustration with school that produces delinquent behavior but *indifference.* Hirschi sees a lack of interest in school as an attenuation of a crucial social bond. That attenuation "frees" the student from the moral power of the educational system. Hirschi's data tend to support his argument in that measures of school-generated frustration (for example, feeling "picked on" by teachers; feeling "nervous and tense" at school) were not significant correlates of delinquency, while measures of "ties" to school and teachers did make a significant difference for delinquency.

Dropout

Research by Elliott (1966) and Elliott and Voss (1974) has specifically addressed the issue of school dropout and delinquency. Following several cohorts of boys over several years, Elliott kept track of the delinquency referral rates of boys who eventually graduated from high school and of those who dropped out. Data on the dropouts included delinquency rates while in school and afterward. Elliott found that lower-status youths who eventually dropped out had a higher rate of delinquent referrals than lower-status youths who eventually graduated. Lower-status dropouts *who were still in school* had the highest delinquency referral rate of all groups studied. However, *after* dropping out, the referral rate for lower-status dropouts was actually the *lowest* of all the groups studied. This finding is contrary to the expectation that school dropouts will continue or perhaps escalate delinquent activities once they are out of school. On the other hand, boys of both lower and higher status who graduated had comparable referral rates, and the rates of higher-status youths who graduated were comparable to the rates of the higher-status dropouts. Elaborating on these findings, Elliott and Voss (1974) found that over the time that future dropouts were in school, there was a progressive escalation of their delinquency rates: before they dropped out, their police contact rate was anywhere from four to nine times greater than the rate of those who graduated. However, after dropping out, their referral rates fell off dramatically.

Elliott and Voss interpreted this pattern as support for a strain-frustration-delinquency argument. They suggested that students who eventually drop out of school grow increasingly frustrated the longer they are in school and that their increasing referral rate reflects their increasing frustration. Dropping out alleviates their school-generated frustrations, and (so the argument goes) their involvement in delinquency falls off. Of course, there are other possible interpretations that do not require that the potential dropout be viewed as frustrated. We could argue that the school experiences that attenuate the student's bond to the school and lead to dropping out progressively "free" the student to violate the law. After dropping out, new bonds (for example, marriage, a job) are formed, and the delinquency rate therefore drops. However, whether delinquency and school dropout are viewed as results of frustration or progressive detachment, Elliott and Voss's findings support the argument that school experiences are important in explaining involvement in delinquency.

Tracking

One educational technique that has received a significant amount of attention as a potential contributor to delinquency is the use of educational "tracks" for students of varying abilities. In general, tracking refers to a method of course assignment that places students in a college track or noncollege track, according to scores on intelligence tests and level of academic achievement. The criticism of such an educational process is that students assigned to the lower track are accorded "second-class" status. It may also be the case that students who are not placed in college tracks are denied opportunities for achievement and success and that "slow bloomers" are not given the opportunity of being transferred to the upper track.

Schaefer, Olexa, and Polk (1972) gathered data on the impact of track placement on academic achievement and delinquency. They found that students in the college track achieved far better grades than those in the noncollege track. While 37 percent of the students in the college track fell in the top quarter of their class and only 11 percent in the bottom quarter, students in the noncollege track achieved significantly lower grades: 2 percent in the top quarter and 52 percent in the bottom quarter. If students who are not in college tracks are simply less intelligent than those who are, the results of this study are not particularly surprising.

However, Schaefer, Olexa, and Polk analyzed their data, controlling or holding constant father's occupation, IQ scores, and grade-point average for the last semester of junior high school. They found that significant differences still persisted between the two tracks. Of the students in the college track, 30 percent fell in the top quarter and only 12 percent in the bottom quarter, whereas 4 percent of students in the noncollege track fell in the top quarter and 35 percent in the bottom quarter. The researchers concluded that assignment to the noncollege track has a pronounced negative effect on grades.

Schaefer, Olexa, and Polk found that track assignment was also associated with dropout, lack of participation in school activities, and delinquency. Students in the noncollege track tended to be less involved in extracurricular activities during high school than students in the college track, and far more of them dropped out of high school. Finally, track position appeared to be a powerful explanatory variable in predicting deviant behavior. Schaefer, Olexa, and Polk found that although students in the noncollege track comprised 29 percent of their sample, they accounted for 53 percent of all students disciplined once, 70 percent disciplined three or more times, and 51 percent of those who were suspended from school. Similarly, they were more than twice as likely as students in the college track to have a juvenile court record. The researchers argued that the alienation, frustration, and stigma caused by this second-class citizenship may have been partly to blame for the marginality of this group.

Other research on tracking has supported the notion that school status is a far more important determinant of delinquent behavior than the traditional variable of parental social class. David Hargreaves (1968) studied an English secondary school and found that boys in the lowest "stream" tended to be social isolates and were more involved in delinquent activities than were those in higher "streams." Kelly and Balch (1971) put forth a "school status" theory of delinquency, arguing that one's location in the reward structure of the school is an important predictor of delinquent involvement. In further analysis, Kelly (1974) found that track position, compared to gender and social class, emerged as the strongest predictor of some twenty-five different forms of delinquent activity.

Such findings have been interpreted as the results of a "self-fulfilling prophecy." According to this interpretation, students in noncollege tracks do not do as well in school as they should because school personnel "expect" them to do poorly. In one of the several experiments that have explored "self-fulfilling prophecies," Rosenthal and Jacobson (1968) gave three kinds of IQ tests to 650 elementary school students. They told the teachers that these tests would predict which children were about to "bloom" or "spurt" intellectually. After administering the tests, the researchers merely selected at random a certain proportion of students as "intellectual bloomers" *regardless* of their IQ scores. The teachers assigned to these students were told to expect them to make marked intellectual gains. The remaining children constituted a control group, with no purported intellectual superiority. At the end of the first year, the IQ gains of the "specially gifted" students greatly exceeded the gains of the control group; the same results occurred at the end of the second year. Rosenthal and Jacobson concluded that teacher expectations had a definite effect on the performance of students. Their research, however, has to be viewed as inconclusive since it had some very real methodological problems (see Snow, 1969; Thorndike, 1968). Moreover, considerable subsequent research has failed to replicate Rosenthal and Jacobson's findings. The argument appeals to many people, but the data at this time do not clearly support or refute the role of the self-fulfilling prophecy.

Intelligence Tests

Another issue involving socialization in the schools is the use of standardized tests as a means of categorizing students. This issue is closely related to the controversy over "tracking." The task force report that we mentioned earlier argued that intelligence test performance is heavily influenced by certain types of learning opportunities and by familiarity with certain kinds of tests and motivation and that the use of intelligence tests results in underestimates of the actual potential of lower-income and minority children. The members of the president's task force and numerous others have described such tests as culturally biased, questionable measures of actual ability, and even more questionable if interpreted as measures of inborn or innate ability. We have to recognize, however, that such views have been countered by researchers (most notably Arthur Jensen) who have argued that some dimensions of intelligence or ability measured by these tests cannot be learned and are "culture-free" indicators of innate ability. Arthur Jensen (1969) and William Shockley (1971) have both generated considerable and heated controversy by arguing that blacks score lower on culture-free tests, as well as on culturally biased tests, because they are genetically different from Caucasians. On the other hand, it can be argued that the difference in test scores is a product of differences in sociocultural backgrounds. Research has not yet adequately explored these factors. As it stands now, the controversy over using standardized tests to categorize students has not been and may never be fully resolved.

No matter what our interpretation of IQ tests, we might expect a relationship between IQ test performance and delinquency. Yet, as Hirschi and Hindelang (1977) have noted, sociological texts on delinquency generally either ignore IQ or question its relevance to delinquency. Arguments that low intelligence is associated with delinquency and crime are linked to theoretical and political emphases that sociologists tend to reject. Nonetheless, it is quite reasonable from a sociological perspective to expect that all sorts of measures of ability, achievement, and intelligence may be related to delinquency. Students who do not fare well in terms of the criteria that a particular institution uses to evaluate people are likely to be less sensitive to the emphases and concerns of that institution. The reason that they do not do well in terms of those criteria can be debated. However, it would be surprising to find anything other than lower test scores among delinquents since school experiences are important in the explanation of delinquency. And, as Hirschi and Hindelang concluded in their review of the literature, the relationship between IQ test performance and measures of official delinquency is at least as strong as relationships found for social class and race. Furthermore, the relationship between IQ test performance and *self-reported* delinquency is actually stronger than relationships involving race and class. Hirschi and Hindelang have also suggested that the effect of IQ on delinquency is mediated by school variables. Their research, as well as two other studies (Wolfgang, Figlio, and Sellin, 1972; West, 1973), has indicated that IQ affects delinquency through its association with school performance—that is, as compared to students who score well on IQ tests, students who do not score well tend not to score well in terms of grades and academic achievement and, hence, have a higher probability of involvement in delinquency.

School Characteristics

Although there is a growing body of research demonstrating the impact of school experiences on delinquency, we still know very little about the actual characteristics of schools that may contribute to or deter delinquency. The research on tracking might lead people to conclude that tracking should be eliminated. However, all we really know is that those in certain stigmatized tracks are more likely to get into trouble than are those in more prestigious tracks. For all we know, schools with tracking systems may have lower rates of delinquency than those without tracking. Tracking may increase the delinquency rate for those tracked and yet decrease the overall delinquency rate for a school. In short, we cannot say whether tracking as an *organizational characteristic* is associated with delinquency.

One of the primary concerns of the "safe school" study undertaken by the National Institute of Education (Boesel et al., 1978) was the identification of school characteristics that are associated with low levels of school crime. Using data from mail surveys, in-person interviews, and intensive case studies, the study identified ten characteristics that appear to be associated with low levels of violence and twelve that are associated with relatively low property loss. These factors, which are shown in Display 7–1, were identified by means of an analysis of those aspects of a school, its students, and its setting that were associated with low levels of school crime at the time of the study. The researchers were careful to point out that a low level of school crime may allow for the development of some of these school characteristics, rather than the characteristics themselves accounting for the lower level of crime.

Many people may be surprised that minority composition of schools is not included in the characteristics listed by the "safe school" study. The researchers did, in fact, explore the relationship between minority composition and school crime and found that victimization of teachers and students tended to be higher in minority schools than in predominantly white schools. However, when they took the level of crime in the surrounding community into account, they found "essentially no relationship between the racial composition of schools and the amount of violence or property loss experienced in the schools" (Boesel et al., 1978:131). Minority schools were more hazardous because of other characteristics that relate to school crime. Racial composition of the school itself did not appear to be the determining factor.

One interesting pattern of findings in this study was that some of the conditions associated with low levels of violence were associated with high levels of property loss. Emphasis of students on high grades was associated with low levels of violence against teachers and students but with high levels of attacks against school property. The researchers suggested that an emphasis on good grades, coupled with a limited supply of good grades, generates frustration, which is then vented against school property since the school is the perceived source of the problem. In contrast, higher levels of personal violence were associated with *lack of concern* for grades. These results highlight the importance of further research on the relevance of school variables to different types of offenses.

DISPLAY 7−1 *Characteristics of Schools with Low Rates of Violence and Property Loss*

Student violence is lower in:

1. Schools whose attendance areas have low crime rates and few or no fighting gangs.
2. Schools that have a smaller percentage of male students.
3. Schools that are composed of higher grades.
4. Small schools.
5. Schools where students rate classrooms as well disciplined, where rules are strictly enforced, and where the principal is considered strict.
6. Schools where students consider school discipline to be fairly administered.
7. Schools where there are fewer students in each class and where teachers teach fewer different students each week.
8. Schools where students say that classes teach them what they want to learn.
9. Schools whose students consider grades important and plan to go on to college.
10. Schools whose students believe they can influence what happens in their lives by their efforts, rather than feeling that things happen to them that they cannot control.

Property loss is lower in:

1. Schools whose attendance areas have low crime rates.
2. Schools where fewer students live close to the school.
3. Schools that do not have many nonstudents on the campus during the day.
4. Schools where families support school disciplinary policies.
5. Small schools.
6. Schools whose students say that classrooms are well controlled, rules are strictly enforced, and where teachers say they spend more time in non-classroom supervision.
7. Schools where teachers say that the principal works cooperatively with them and is fair and informal in dealing with staff.
8. Schools in which teachers do not express hostile and authoritarian attitudes toward students.
9. Schools whose students value their teachers' opinions of them.
10. Schools where teachers do not lower students' grades for disciplinary reasons.
11. Schools whose students do not consider grades important and do not plan to go on to college.
12. Schools whose students do not consider being school leaders important personal goals.

Source: D. Boesel et al. *Violent Schools—Safe Schools,* Tables 5−1 and 5−2. National Institute of Education, U.S. Department of Health, Education, and Welfare. Washington, D.C.: U.S. Government Printing Office, 1978.

PEERS AND ADOLESCENT SOCIETY

It is generally accepted that peer group relationships (that is, relations with persons of similar age status) play a major role in the socialization of adolescents and that such relationships are crucial for understanding adolescent involvement in delinquent conduct. In fact, cultural conflict theorists consider peer group phenomena in adolescent socialization to be the most important factor in the explanation of delinquency. For instance, Sutherland and Cressey have stated that "children of the same age and sex probably are more important than parents in presenting patterns of behavior, whether the patterns presented are delinquent or antidelinquent" (1970:212). Sutherland and Cressey's claim leaves open the possibility of both delinquent and antidelinquent patterns. In contrast, some theorists dealing with the world of adolescent peer groups present an image of adolescent society as essentially unconventional and in conflict with the norms and laws of parents.

In one of the best-known works on adolescent society, James Coleman wrote:

> Our adolescents today are cut off, probably more than ever before, from the adult society. They are still oriented toward fulfilling their parents' desires, but they look very much to their peers for approval as well. Consequently, our society has within its midst a set of small teen-age societies which focus teen-age interests and attitudes on things far removed from adult responsibilities, and which may develop standards that lead away from these goals established by the larger society. (1961:9)

The fact that teenage societies have emerged does not necessarily mean that involvement in those societies is conducive to delinquency, but the imagery of pursuing goals "different from" those of the larger society suggests such a possibility.

Ernest Smith has argued that there is a distinct "youth culture" characterized by norms that conflict with adult norms. According to Smith, "Cliques and gangs are characteristic of the adolescent age" (1962:67). Smith defined gangs as lower-class peer groups consisting largely of school dropouts and cliques as peer groups developing among middle-class students. He viewed both as naturally evolving, intimate, primary groups that are characterized by "withdrawal, secrecy, and conflict with authorities" (1962:83).

A similar image of adolescent society is conveyed in the writings of Talcott Parsons (1964), Urie Bronfenbrenner (1968), and Ralph England (1960). England specifically attributed much of the increase in delinquency to the rise in "youth culture." According to England, youth culture is characterized by irresponsibility, the search for a "good time," and a strong emphasis on athletics, dating, and alcohol consumption. Bronfenbrenner describes adolescent peer groups as a source and setting for unconventional behavior, whereas Parsons tended to view youth culture as a setting for rebellion.

The emphasis on the unconventional aspects of youth culture has not gone unchallenged. For example, in an article entitled "The Myth of Adolescent Culture" (1955), Frederick Elkin and William A. Westley argued that the "distinctiveness" of youth culture has been exaggerated.

They suggested that adolescents are far more conventional than the "youth culture" stereotype allows. Other scholars have attacked the emphasis on the distinctiveness of youth culture by arguing that the adult world is not as prudish and square as it is commonly depicted. Bennett Berger (1963) pointed out that many adults share the values and interests of adolescents regarding cars, sports, and romance, as well as their emphasis on status, popularity, and antiintellectualism. S. N. Eisenstadt has described youth culture in the lower classes:

> In many ways the pattern of behavior prevalent in these groups— emphasis on drinking, some gambling, various types of unorganized recreation, unplanned spending of money, earlier sexual experience and sometimes perhaps some extent of promiscuity, great extent of aggressiveness, etc.—is to some extent a continuation of the pattern of adult life within these sectors; or at least there is a stronger emphasis on some of the patterns of behavior accepted in the adult group, and not a distinctive opposition to it. (1965:96–97)

The values and interests that some people have posited as characteristic of youth culture have been posited by others as characteristic of delinquent peer groups (for example, the restless search for excitement, disdain for traditional occupational goals and work, a readiness for action). We noted in Chapter 6 Matza and Sykes's conclusions regarding juvenile delinquency and subterranean values (1964); their claims are relevant to the issue of youth culture as well. Matza and Sykes's argument is that the values of delinquent youths reflect aspects of the *dominant* value system. The values attributed to them are the values of a "leisure class" and are shared to some extent by all adolescents. Matza and Sykes's perspective suggests that it is not just lower-class youths or delinquents who share these values but, rather, adolescents at all class levels. Moreover, these "leisure-class values," which are reflections or caricatures of powerful subterranean values, are shared by the adult world, too.

RESEARCH ON ADOLESCENT SOCIETY AND DELINQUENCY

Compared to the amount of attention that adolescent society has received, there is actually very little data bearing on the accuracy of the different images of adolescent society that have been presented. Little of James Coleman's considerable data on adolescents relates to the distinctiveness of youth culture. However, one interesting study has indicated that there may be elements of truth to both sides of the argument over youth culture. Analyzing questionnaire data gathered from eleventh and twelfth graders at a North Carolina high school and from a random sample of teachers at the same school, Raymond Eve (1975) found that the level of approval was higher among students than teachers when both groups were asked about cheating, disruptive mischief, physical confrontations, partying, and drinking. Students and their teachers were only slightly different in attitudes toward the buying and selling of drugs and the importance of automobiles. There were no differences in the evaluation of the importance of athletics. However, even where there were differences, the majority of both groups tended to disapprove of "anti-adult" activities (with the exception of mischief directed against the school). Eve noted that if we focus on "absolutes" (asking for either approval or disapproval), adolescents appear very conventional, but if we focus on "degrees" of approval, there are significant differences between students and teachers for some evaluations. He concluded that "taken as a whole, this study has provided evidence that although students do maintain a statistically distinct value system, this system is primarily conventional in its orientation and differs only to a relatively small degree from the value system of the adult world" (1975:165).

Alan Wilson, Travis Hirschi, and Glen Elder's study (1965) of junior and senior high school students in Richmond, California, suggests a similar conclusion. In that study the majority of four groups (black and nonblack males and females) rejected such statements as "It is all right to get around the law if you can get away with it," indicating a basic acceptance of the law as morally binding. The degree of rejection ranged from 54 percent for black males to 82 percent for nonblack females. The pattern was similar for measures of respect for the police and other measures of attitudes toward the law. Moreover, the majority rejected such statements as "The only reason to have a job is for money," although they agreed they were worried about what they were going to do after high school. The subjects were also asked what one thing (work, family, friends, hobbies, house, church) would give them the most satisfaction in life. The most frequent response was future family, followed by work. The proportions who answered friends, church, and hobbies were about even. On the other hand, the majority of all groups agreed that they "don't like being criticized by adults" and that "having a car is important." The students were quite involved in adolescent activities, such as going to drive-in restaurants, riding around in cars, and spending more of their free time with peers than with adults.

The importance of peers in the lives of adolescents and the existence of a youth *culture* are two quite distinct issues. At present, there is little support for the argument that adolescents in general share values, norms, or beliefs that conflict with or cut them off from the adult world. Nonetheless, there are ways in which participation in peer group activities characteristic of the adolescent world can facilitate delinquency. For one thing, although the majority of adolescents may express quite conventional values and beliefs, their structural position in modern America gives them considerable leisure time and freedom from many types of conventional social bonds. They are not children, but they are not readily incorporated into the work force either. Such marginality, coupled with the age-grading of schools, sets the stage for the development of a high level of peer group interaction and considerable free time. Those adolescents who spend that time dating and riding around in cars and who feel cars are important in their lives are, in fact, more likely to report involvement in delinquent activities (Hirschi, 1969:168–69). There is also evidence that boredom is quite common among adolescents and that those who are most bored are most likely to commit delinquent acts. Wilson, Hirschi, and Elder (1965) reported that between one-quarter and one-third of their black and nonblack male and female subjects often felt that "there's nothing to do" and another half felt that way at least sometimes. Moreover, Hirschi reported that 51 percent of those who often felt bored had committed one or more delinquent acts, as compared to 38 percent of those who never felt bored (1969:193).

Another set of studies relevant to the impact of adolescent society and peer groups on delinquency deals with the relationship between delinquent behavior and *commitment* to peers. We summarized that literature in the last chapter in relation to cultural conflict theory but will consider it again here because of its relevance to our discussion of adolescent society. As we noted, most studies have found a positive relationship between attachment to peers and involvement in delinquency—that is, the greater the attachment, the greater the delinquency (Hindelang, 1973; Elliott and Voss, 1974; Empey and Lubeck, 1971; Erickson and Empey, 1965). In contrast, one study reported that attachment to peers was a barrier to involvement in delinquency (Hirschi, 1969), even among adolescents with several delinquent friends. In a more recent study, Jensen and Erickson (1978) found attachment to peers to be *unrelated* to delinquency.

Why such a disparity? Part of the answer seems to have to do with the way in which "commitment to peers" is measured. Elliott and Voss (1974:164) first asked students to list their friends and then used answers to the following question to assess degree of peer commitment: "If you found that this group of friends was leading you into trouble, would you still run around with them?" In contrast, Hirschi's question was: "Would you like to be the kind of person your best friends are?" Erickson and Empey (1965) and Empey and Lubeck (1971) asked students whether they would go along with peers in situations of conflict with the law or to choose between that activity and alternative conventional activities. When researchers have specifically introduced a degree of conflict into the measure of commitment to peers, the results have suggested that peer commitment increases the chances of delinquency. However, the questions posed in these measurements measure much more than commitment to peers. Responses involve attitudes toward the proposed activity and the alternatives, as well as attitudes toward peers. The mystery of the divergent findings resulting from these various questions regarding peer commitment might be solved by the following observation: *Youths who say they would go along with peers in situations involving lawbreaking are likely to actually do so in real situations or to say they have done so.* When commitment to peers is measured without introducing such conflicts and choices (that is, Hirschi's type of measure), there is no consistent relationship of any kind and the relationships found are uniformly weak.

Jensen and Erickson (1978) have attempted to assess the impact of incorporating elements of conflict into questions about peers. Students were asked whether they would "go along with their friends" or join their families if their families were planning on going to a show. There was no significant relationship between a student's choice of answers to this question and self-reported delinquency (although a slightly greater proportion of those who indicated they would go along with friends did report delinquent activities). On the other hand, when an element of conflict was introduced by asking them whether they would go riding around with friends after school if their parents had told them *never* to do that, there was a sizable relationship: students who indicated they would disregard parental authority reported significantly more delinquency. Similarly, students who indicated they would go along with peers in situations of conflict with the law reported significantly more delinquency than did those who indicated they would not go along. In short, questions with conflictual content involve attitudes toward authority, *as well as* attitudes toward peers. The findings of this study suggest that adolescents who would go along with peers *despite conflict with conventional authorities* are more likely to report delinquent activities than those who would not go along.

In considering socialization within the context of adolescent society, it is important to ask the following questions: Just how common are experiences of conflict between peer commitment and conventional authority? What are the general tendencies of the adolescent population in making such choices? Although we cannot answer the former question, we can look at some findings concerning the latter question. In advocating an image of a distinct adolescent culture, James Coleman argued that his data show that "adolescents as a whole are *not* delinquent, and their activities although quite different from adult activities and sometimes irresponsible, are not in general antisocial or delinquent" (1961:15). Data gathered from high school students in southern Arizona have shown that the tendency of the adolescent to go along with peers is highly variable and depends on the choice of situations involved (Jensen and Erickson, 1978). Between 37 and 41 percent of the students in three urban high schools indicated they would go along with peers in a situation in which family plans were to go to a show. Between 42 and 46 percent indicated they would go along with friends rather than do homework. In contrast, only between 18 and 25 percent indicated they would go along to paint up windows at school; 9 to 17 percent would go along with friends to steal something at a store; and between 5 and 11 percent would go along to break into a place to steal something. Between 71 and 73 percent indicated they would go along with peers rather than stay home to view an educational program on television that their teachers had recommended they watch. In sum, adolescents choose to go along with their friends most often when the degree of conflict with conventional authority is minimal. And, as we indicated above, the type of choice adolescents would make in situations of minimal conflict is not as relevant to delinquency as the type of choice they would make in situations of conflict with the law. Most adolescents indicate they would not go along with peers in the more serious conflictual situations, but those who would do so are those most likely to become involved in delinquency.

Overall, we doubt very much that adolescent society is characterized by values, norms and beliefs that clearly cut them off from the adult world or that facilitate delinquency. However, as a leisure class or as a large segment of the population with time to bide, adolescents have considerable freedom to commit delinquent acts. Moreover, those most involved in the activities that, in the eyes of adults, characterize adolescent society are those most likely to become involved in delinquency. When adolescents choose to please their peers despite the possibility of conflict with authority, the probability of their involvement in delinquency is very high.

MUTUAL INTERDEPENDENCE

Although we have dealt with family, school, and peers individually, it is important to recognize that social reality involves an interrelated web or matrix of influences. At several points in the discussion, we commented on the difficulty of isolating the impact of one *specific* characteristic of a situation that intertwines many other characteristics. Experiences and relationships in one setting are shaped and influenced by experiences and relationships in other settings. The complexity of these interrelationships is what makes it so difficult to differentiate causal relationships from spurious relationships.

Consider, for example, the relationship between conditions of family life and experiences at school. The stronger the bond between parents and child, the stronger the bond between the child and teachers. Of course, there are numerous exceptions to that observation, but there is definitely an association between the two variables. Similarly, the stronger the bond between a youth and school, or between a youth and parents, the weaker the chances that he or she will acquire delinquent friends or choose to go along with peers in situations of conflict with authority.

In attempting to understand delinquency in terms of adolescent social-ization, we are dealing with an interdependent set of influences. How-ever, there is some evidence of *independence* as well. By independence, we mean that school experiences appear to be relevant to understanding delinquency, regardless of conditions of family life. In turn, certain aspects of family life are relevant to understanding delinquency, indepen-dent of experiences at school. Hirschi's analysis showed that participa-tion in certain stereotypical "youth-culture" activities is related to delin-quency, "regardless of commitment to education and involvement in school-related activities" (1969:196).

Although it has been shown that relationships in each context are interrelated and independently important, we know very little about the relative significance of parents, school, and peers for involvement in delinquency among *different* categories of youths. For example, it is com-monly argued that female delinquency is more likely than male delin-quency to reflect problems at home (Morris, 1964). Jackson Toby (1957) has suggested that since parents have usually supervised girls more closely than boys, family disorganization may be more consequential for girls' involvement in delinquency. In terms of actual research, some studies have indicated that the argument that female delinquency is related to family disorganization may be true only among whites (Austin, 1978) and only for certain types of offenses (Datesman and Scarpitti, 1975). In his study of youths in Flint, Michigan, Martin Gold concluded that family conditions appear to be more important among girls than boys but that "further research must measure parent-child relations among girls and boys in order to measure more thoroughly their associa-tion with delinquent behavior" (1970:128). At present, we cannot say whether female delinquency is more sensitive than male delinquency to variations in family life.

One area in which gender differences in delinquency have recently received attention is the influence of peers. Delinquency has commonly been conceived of as a male problem; this conception is even more common when the subject is delinquent gangs. In comparison to male gangs, female gangs are, in fact, quite rare. Walter Miller (1975) estimated that in the six cities with gang problems that he studied, male gang members outnumbered female gang members ten to one. Other research (Thompson and Lozes, 1976) has suggested that female gangs are informal organizations or cliques akin to the loosely structured groups with changing membership that Yablonsky (1962) referred to as "near groups."

Although distinct gangs appear rare among females, there is substan-tial evidence that delinquent offenses, whether committed by males or females, tend to occur in the company of others. Erickson and Jensen (1977) reported that the proportion of delinquent offenses committed while with a companion was just as high, if not higher, for females as for males. Gold (1970) reported similar findings in his study of youths in Flint, Michigan. Thus, it appears that female juveniles commit fewer offenses on the average, but when they do commit them, they do so in the company of others. To view delinquency as the activity of loners is just as inappropriate in regard to females as it is in regard to males.

An interesting finding concerning female delinquency is the influence of males on female drug use. Research by Lee Bowker has suggested that girls' use of alcohol and marijuana is influenced more by their boyfriends than by their girlfriends (1978:63). For boys, peer influences appear to be "homosocial" (that is, boy influencing boy), whereas for girls, peer influences appear to be "heterosocial" (boy influencing girl). It appears that drug use spreads more from males to females than from females to other females. There is a good deal of evidence that males provide illicit drugs and receive sexual favors in return. Bowker has summarized the situation as follows:

> The combination of biological and social pressures may lead to ambivalence about sex among females. For males the pressures are all toward engaging in sexual behavior. As a result, males try to get their girlfriends to agree to participate in sexual intercourse. Females are socialized to please males (on dates and everywhere else), yet expected to avoid pleasing them so much that they ruin their reputations. A reasonable solution to this double-bind dilemma is for females to join their boyfriends in recreational drug use and use it as an excuse for participation in initial and subsequent drug seductions ("I'm not that kind of girl, but I was just so drunk . . .").*

In sum, peer influences are important for understanding both male and female delinquency, but specific details concerning such influence vary.

There is evidence that delinquency may also vary according to the relationship between racial status and family structure. Several studies have suggested that the significance of a "broken home" varies depending on how unusual it is in a particular environment. For example, Datesman and Scarpitti (1975) have argued that the absence of an ever present father has been a sufficiently common experience for blacks that black families have adapted to the situation. Roy Austin (1978) has advanced a similar argument. Austin's data showed that black girls with no father present actually felt closer to their mothers than black girls whose homes were intact. White girls whose fathers were present felt closer to their mothers. For both the black and the white girls, the bond to the mother inhibited delinquency, but those bonds were related to the absence of a father in quite different ways. As with gender differences, we cannot say whether delinquency among blacks is any more or less sensitive to variations in family life than white delinquency. There is, however, some indication that family structure may have different consequences in different groups and settings.

---

*Reprinted by permission of the publisher, from Lee H. Bowker, *Women, Crime, and the Criminal Justice System*, p. 90 (Lexington, Mass.: Lexington Books, D. C. Heath and Company, Copyright 1978, D. C. Heath and Company).

SUMMARY

Sociologists have regarded the influences of family, school, and peer group on adolescent society as particularly crucial to understanding delinquency. However, sociological theories vary in the amount of influence they attribute to each setting and in the specific nature of such influence. There is a growing concern with identifying the variable relevance of family, school, and peers for adolescent socialization among different groups and within different settings.

Studies of family structure and interaction in relation to delinquency support a number of observations:

1. Children from broken homes are disproportionately likely to appear in police, court, and institutional statistics, *but* absence of the father does not appear to be significantly related to indexes of self-reported delinquency. Self-reported delinquency appears higher among children with a stepfather than among children with no father or with the original father present.

2. There is no consistent relationship between delinquency and matriarchy or mother-dominance of a family, although one study has reported a "small association."

3. Middle children tend to have higher probabilities of involvement in delinquency, *but* there is some indication this tendency may be a product of family size.

4. The greater the number of children in a family, the greater the probability of involvement in delinquency.

5. The nature of relationships between children and parents is more relevant to explaining delinquency than is the broken or intact nature of the home.

6. The greater the reciprocal communication and mutual bonds between parent and child, the lesser the involvement in delinquency.

7. The extremes of permissiveness and overly strict discipline are more often associated with higher rates of delinquency than is a mild emphasis on discipline administered according to standards that appear fair and equitable to children.

8. The amount of time spent under the direct surveillance or control of parents makes little difference for involvement in delinquency, whereas perceived parental concern for the activities of a child makes a sizable difference.

There has been far more speculation than actual research on the specific aspects of school that are relevant to an understanding of delinquency. Since the results of the "safe school" study are fairly complex and are summarized in Display 7–1, we will not reiterate them here. The following observations seem justified in view of the research to date:

1. The higher a student's academic achievement or performance, the lower the involvement in delinquency.
2. The stronger the bond between students and teachers and the more favorable the attitudes of students toward school, the weaker the involvement in delinquency.
3. Persons who eventually drop out of school appear to have higher delinquency rates while in school than after dropping out.
4. Students in remedial or noncollege "tracks" have higher probabilities of delinquent involvement than students in college "tracks," regardless of IQ scores, father's occupation, or grade-point average before tracking.
5. The lower the performance on IQ tests, the poorer a student's school performance, and the poorer the school performance, the greater the probability of delinquent involvement.

We have noted that there is some controversy over the nature of the relationship between delinquent peers and a youth's involvement in delinquency. Some research findings suggest that delinquent involvement affects the acquisition of delinquent companions who may in turn reinforce involvement in delinquency. However, the view that teenagers have interests and attitudes that set them apart from the adult world and the view that a general orientation toward peers is conducive to delinquency are both subject to debate. The following observations are consistent with research findings:

1. The attitudes of teenagers toward the law, delinquent activities, and goals are primarily conventional, occasionally differing according to degrees of approval and disapproval from adults.
2. Teenagers do appear concerned about maintaining autonomy and resisting adult control, and those most involved in activities that facilitate such freedom have higher probabilities of involvement in delinquency.
3. Teenagers who indicate a willingness to go along with peers despite conflicts with parents, school, and the law have a higher probability of involvement in delinquency than those who indicate they would not do so. *However,* such peer commitments are greatly affected by the degree of conflict involved, and the majority of teenagers are unwilling to go along when severe conflict with the law is involved.

All these observations are presented with the same warnings that we have reiterated throughout our analysis. Each may be challenged, and each is subject to qualification and specification. There is a growing concern with the variable effects of family, school, and peer relationships on people in different groups and settings, as well as on different types of delinquent behavior. Although there is a huge volume of research on the correlates of delinquency, there is very little research that addresses these more precise issues.

REFERENCES

Abramsen, D. 1960. *The Psychology of Crime.* New York: Columbia University Press.

Andry, R. 1962. "Parental Affection and Delinquency." In Wolfgang et al., eds., *The Sociology of Crime and Delinquency.* New York: John Wiley.

Austin, R. L. 1978. "Race, Father-Absence, and Female Delinquency." *Criminology* 15 (February):487–504.

Berger, A. S., and W. Simon. 1974. "Black Families and the Moynihan Report: A Research Evaluation." *Social Problems* 22 (December):145–61.

Berger, B. M. 1963. "Adolescence and Beyond." *Social Problems* 10 (Spring): 394–408.

Boesel, D., et al. 1978. *Violent Schools —Safe Schools.* National Institute of Education, U.S. Department of Health, Education, and Welfare. Washington, D.C.: U.S. Government Printing Office.

Bowker, L. H. 1978. *Women, Crime, and the Criminal Justice System.* Lexington, Mass.: D. C. Heath.

Bowlby, J. 1951. *Maternal Care and Mental Health.* Geneva: World Health Organization.

Bronfenbrenner, U. 1968. "Standards of Social Behavior among School Children in Four Cultures." *International Journal of Psychology* 3:31–41.

California Youth Authority. 1971. *Statistical Report.* Sacramento: California Department of Youth Authority.

Chilton, R. J., and G. E. Markle. 1972. "Family Disruption, Delinquent Conduct and the Effect of Subclassification." *American Sociological Review* 37 (February):93–99.

Clark, K. 1965. *Dark Ghetto: Dilemmas of Social Power.* New York: Harper & Row.

Coleman, J. S. 1961. *The Adolescent Society.* New York: Free Press of Glencoe. Copyright 1961. Reprinted by permission of Macmillan Publishing Company.

Conger, R. D. 1976. "Social Control and Social Learning Models of Delinquent Behavior." *Criminology* 14 (May):17–40.

Datesman, S. K., and F. R. Scarpitti. 1975. "Female Delinquency and Broken Homes: A Reassessment." *Criminology* 13 (May):33–55.

Dentler, R. A., and L. J. Monroe. 1961. "Social Correlates of Early Adolescent Theft." *American Sociological Review* 26 (October):733–43.

Eisenstadt, S. N. 1956. *From Generation to Generation.* New York: Free Press. Copyright 1956. Reprinted by permission of Macmillan Publishing Company.

Elkin, F., and W. Westley. 1955. "The Myth of Adolescent Culture." *American Sociological Review* 20 (December):680–86.

Elliott, D. S. 1966. "Delinquency, School Attendance and Dropout." *Social Problems* 13 (Winter):306–18.

Elliott, D. S., and H. L. Voss. 1974. *Delinquency and Dropout.* Lexington, Mass.: Lexington Books.

Ellwood, C. A. 1919. *Sociology and Modern Social Problems*. New York: American Book.

Empey, L. T., and S. G. Lubeck. 1971. *Explaining Delinquency*. Lexington, Mass.: D. C. Heath.

England, R. 1960. "A Theory of Middle Class Juvenile Delinquency." *Journal of Criminal Law, Criminology, and Police Science* 50:535–40.

Erickson, M. L., and L. T. Empey. 1965. "Class Position, Peers and Delinquency." *Sociology and Social Research* 49 (April):268–82.

Erickson, M. L., and G. F. Jensen. 1977. "Delinquency Is Still Group Behavior!: Toward Revitalizing the Group Premise in the Sociology of Deviance." *Journal of Criminal Law and Criminology* 68 (2):262–73.

Eve, R. 1975. "'Adolescent Culture,' Convenient Myth or Reality? A Comparison of Students and Their Teachers." *Sociology of Education* 48 (Spring):152–67.

Frease, D. E. 1973. "Delinquency, Social Class, and the Schools." *Sociology and Social Research* 57 (July):443–59.

Glueck, S., and E. Glueck. 1950. *Unraveling Juvenile Delinquency*. Cambridge, Mass.: Harvard University Press.

Gold, M. 1970. *Delinquent Behavior in an American City*. Monterey, Calif.: Brooks/Cole.

Hakeem, M. 1958. "A Critique of the Psychiatric Approach." In Joseph S. Roucek, ed., *Juvenile Delinquency*. New York: Philosophical Library.

Hannerz, A. 1969. "Roots of Black Manhood." *Trans-Action* 6 (October):112–21.

Hargreaves, D. 1968. *Social Relations in a Secondary School*. New York: Humanities Press.

Hindelang, M. J. 1973. "Causes of Delinquency: A Partial Replication." *Social Problems* 21 (Spring):471–87.

Hirschi, T. 1969. *Causes of Delinquency*. Berkeley: University of California Press.

Hirschi, T., and M. J. Hindelang. 1977. "Intelligence and Delinquency: A Revisionist Review." *American Sociological Review* 42 (August):571–87.

Jaffe, L. W. 1963. "Delinquency Proneness and Family Anomie." *Journal of Criminal Law, Criminology and Police Science* 54:146–54.

Jensen, A. 1969. "How Much Can We Boost I.Q. and Scholastic Achievement?" *Harvard Educational Review* 39:273–74.

Jensen, G. F. 1976. "Race, Achievement and Delinquency: A Further Look at Delinquency in a Birth Cohort." *American Journal of Sociology* 82 (September):379–87.

Jensen, G. F., and M. L. Erickson. 1978. "Peer Commitment and Delinquent Conduct." Unpublished manuscript.

Jensen, G. F., M. L. Erickson, and J. P. Gibbs. 1978. "Perceived Risk of Punishment and Self-Reported Delinquency." *Social Forces* 57 (September):57–78.

Joachim, T. 1978. "Family Size, Social Class, and Delinquency." Unpublished manuscript.

Kelly, D. H. 1974. "Track Position and Delinquent Involvement: A Preliminary Analysis." *Sociology and Social Research* 58 (July):380–86.

Kelly, D. H., and R. W. Balch. 1971. "Social Origins and School Failure." *Pacific Sociological Review* 14 (October):413–30.

Larson, W. R., and B. G. Meyerhoff. 1967. "Family Integration and Police Contact." In M. Kelin, ed., *Juvenile Gangs in Context: Theory, Research, and Action*. Englewood Cliffs, N.J.: Prentice-Hall.

Lees, J. P., and L. J. Newson. 1954. "Family or Sibship Position and Some Aspects of Juvenile Delinquency." *British Journal of Delinquency* 5:46–65.

Matza, D., and G. M. Sykes. 1964. "Juvenile Delinquency and Subterranean Values." *American Sociological Review* 26 (October):712–17.

McCord, W., J. McCord, and I. Zola. 1959. *Origins of Crime.* New York: Columbia University Press.

Merton, R. K. 1957. *Social Theory and Social Structure,* rev. ed. New York: Free Press of Glencoe.

Miller, W. G. 1958. "Lower Class Culture as a Generating Milieu of Gang Delinquency." *Journal of Social Issues* 14:5–19.

_____ . 1975. *Violence by Youth Gangs and Youth Groups as a Crime Problem in Major American Cities.* Washington, D.C.: U.S. Government Printing Office.

Morris, R. 1964. "Female Delinquency and Relational Problems." *Social Forces* 43 (October):82–89.

Moynihan, D. P. 1965. *The Negro Family: The Case for National Action.* Washington, D.C.: Office of Policy Planning and Research, U.S. Department of Labor.

Naess, S. 1959. "Mother-Child Separation and Delinquency." *British Journal of Delinquency* 10:22–35.

Nye, F. I. 1958. *Family Relationships and Delinquent Behavior.* New York: John Wiley.

Office of Education. 1972. *Digest of Educational Statistics.* Washington, D.C.: National Center for Educational Statistics.

Ogburn, W. F. 1938. "The Changing Family." *Family* 19 (July):139–43.

Parsons, T. 1947. "Certain Primary Sources and Patterns of Aggression in the Social Structure of the Western World." *Psychiatry* 10 (May):167–81.

_____ . 1964. "Youth in the Context of American Society." In T. Parsons, ed., *Social Structure and Personality.* Glencoe, Ill.: Free Press of Glencoe.

Polk, K. 1969. "Class, Strain and Rebellion among Adolescents." *Social Problems* 17 (Fall):214–24.

President's Commission on Law Enforcement and Administration of Justice. 1967. *Juvenile Delinquency and Youth Crime.* Washington, D.C.: U.S. Government Printing Office.

Reiss, A. J., Jr. 1951. "Delinquency as the Failure of Personal and Social Controls." *American Sociological Review* 16 (April):196–207.

Rosen, L. 1969. "Matriarchy and Lower-Class Negro Male Delinquency." *Social Problems* 17 (Fall):175–89.

Rosenthal, R., and L. Jacobson. 1968. *Pygmalion in the Classroom.* New York: Holt, Rinehart and Winston.

Schaefer, W. E., C. Olexa, and K. Polk. 1972. "Programmed for Social Class Tracking in High School." In K. Polk and W. E. Schaefer, eds., *Schools and Delinquency.* Englewood Cliffs, N.J.: Prentice-Hall.

Shockley, W. 1971. "Negro I.Q. Deficit: Failure of a 'Malicious Coincidence' Model Warrants New Research Proposals." *Review of Educational Research* 41 (June):227–28.

Silverman, I. J., and S. Dinitz. 1974. "Compulsive Masculinity and Delinquency: An Empirical Investigation." *Criminology* 11 (February):498–515.

Smith, E. A. 1962. *American Youth Culture: Group Life in Teenage Society.* New York: Free Press.

Snow, R. 1969. "Unfinished Pygmalion." *Contemporary Psychology* 14:197–99.

Stinchcombe, A. 1964. *Rebellion in a High School.* Chicago: Quadrangle Books.

Sutherland, E. H., and D. R. Cressey. 1970. *Criminology,* 8th ed. Philadelphia: J. B. Lippincott.

———. 1974. *Criminology,* 9th ed. Philadelphia: J. B. Lippincott.

Thompson, R. J., and J. Lozes. 1976. "Female Gang Delinquency." *Corrective and Social Psychiatry and Journal of Behavior Technology Methods and Therapy* 22 (3):1–5.

Thorndike, R. L. 1968. "Review of R. Rosenthal and L. Jacobson, 'Pygmalion in the Classroom.'" *American Educational Research Journal* 5:708–11.

Toby, J. 1957. "The Differential Impact of Family Disorganization." *American Sociological Review* 22 (October):505–12.

West, D. J. 1973. *Who Becomes Delinquent?* London: Heinemann.

Wilkinson, K. 1974. "The Broken Family and Juvenile Delinquency: Scientific Explanation or Ideology." *Social Problems* 21 (June):726–39.

Wilson, A. B., T. Hirschi, and G. Elder. 1965. "Technical Report No. 1: Secondary School Curves." Berkeley, Calif.: Survey Research Center. Mimeographed.

Wolfgang, M., R. M. Figlio, and T. Sellin. 1972. *Delinquency in a Birth Cohort.* Chicago: University of Chicago Press.

Yablonsky, L. 1962. "The Delinquent Gang as a Near Group." *Social Problems* 7 (Fall):108–17.

———. 1966. *The Violent Gang.* Baltimore: Penguin Books.

8.
CONTEXTS FOR ADOLESCENT SOCIALIZATION: RELIGION, MEDIA, AND COMMUNITY

The failure of present-day religion to penetrate in any real and vital way the experience of the gang boy may be cited as a ... negative factor which makes possible the free life of the gang. The lack in this case is the failure to provide controls of the boy's behavior and interesting activities for his leisure time to supplement those of the home, the school, and the playground.
—F. M. Thrasher, *The Gang*

OTHER SOCIALIZING FORCES

The family, school, and peer group, together with the basic background characteristics of age, gender, race, and social class, have dominated the sociological literature on causes of delinquency. However, at one time or another, a number of other forces have been viewed as relevant to understanding delinquency and have often dominated popular discourse and public debate about the causes of delinquency. We will examine arguments and research relevant to three such forces in this chapter— religion, mass media, and communal bonds. The literature concerning each of these forces is less adequate for stating any generalizations than is the case for the family, school, and peers. Since religion and the mass media have not been incorporated into major sociological theories of delinquency, they have not received the amount of conceptual or empirical attention that other institutions have. Moreover, while community and neighborhood characteristics have been studied in relation to crime and delinquency, the focus has been on characteristics that can be measured through available government or census data. Other characteristics, such as "neighborliness" or a "sense of community," that often underlie explanations of communal differences have not been measured directly. Such research would be quite expensive and has not been undertaken in the study of delinquency.

RELIGION

The most prominent general theorists in the historical development of sociology were all concerned with the nature and consequences of religion. Emile Durkheim viewed religion as a basic integrative mechanism in human society and felt that social order could be maintained only if

228

people had common beliefs in something greater than themselves. He saw the basic problem in the Western civilization of his time to be a trend toward "individualism" and the demise of shared values, norms, and beliefs that are vital to social order. Karl Marx accorded religion a role in the prevention of crime, unrest, and revolution. For Marx, religion was the "opium of the masses" in that it directed their attention away from repressive, alienating economic systems. Religion was a force maintaining a status quo that Marx believed inevitably had to be brought down by a revolution of alienated human beings. Finally, a third "grand master" of sociology — Max Weber — felt that religious institutions were intertwined with other institutions and with the economic development of society. Weber stimulated considerable sociological research on the role that Protestantism, Catholicism, and other religious beliefs play in facilitating or inhibiting economic development and achievement.

The "sociology of religion" has been and remains a major specialty in sociology. However, those specializing in the sociology of religion pay little attention to its relationship to crime or delinquency. Similarly, while every delinquency text discusses the relevance of the family, school, and peers for understanding delinquency, it is quite rare to find a text that gives any consideration to religion. In fact, a search of the subject index of three recent delinquency texts (Empey, 1978; Haskell and Yablonsky, 1978; Sanders, 1976) reveals no reference to religion. Moreover, none of the major sociological theories incorporates religious variables as important to the understanding of delinquency. It is not that it would be particularly difficult to do so (for example, as a dimension of the social bond) but, rather, that theorists have just not felt it necessary to do so. Given the amount of attention paid to variables that have a small or negligible relevance to delinquent behavior (such as a broken home, social class, peer commitment), it would be understandable for a student to guess that religious variables have been shown to be totally irrelevant to delinquency.

Despite sociology's neglect of religion as a variable in delinquent behavior, popular belief has frequently assumed such a relationship. However, the relationship is far from clear-cut. Several summaries of the literature on religion and crime have noted the complexities surrounding the issue. For example, in his review of the literature on religion and delinquency for the President's Commission on Law Enforcement and Administration of Justice, Father Joseph Fitzpatrick (1967) summed up the situation by labeling the relationship as "very obscure." He concluded that there is evidence that religion may be (1) irrelevant to deviant behavior, (2) a cause of deviant behavior, or (3) a barrier to deviant behavior. In *Our Criminal Society* (1969), Edwin Schur took a similar stand. Schur noted that religious beliefs may lead people to violate the laws of the state and may contribute to the amount of labeled crime through the proliferation of religiously based laws that regulate private morality. He concluded that "in any area of human outlooks and behavior we might choose to consider, the role of religion turns out to be far from clear-cut and one-directional" (1969:83). In yet another review of religion and crime, Donald Cressey concluded that "there is no specific evidence regarding the effect of religion, considered as something different from anti-criminal values, on crime" (Sutherland and Cressey, 1978:234).

RESEARCH ON RELIGION AND DELINQUENCY

An examination of references to religion in studies of labeled delinquents reveals a hodgepodge of results: (1) delinquents are more religious than nondelinquents (Middleton and Fay, 1941); (2) delinquents do not differ from nondelinquents in their attitudes toward religion (Kvaraceus, 1944; Mursell, 1930; Hightower, 1930; Hartshorne and May, 1930); and (3) non-delinquents are more religious than delinquents (Healy and Bronner, 1936; Glueck and Glueck, 1950; Miller, 1965). Moreover, no matter which of the three patterns researchers have found, the actual differences they have reported are small.

Self-report research has also yielded seemingly divergent findings. Rhodes and Reiss (1970) and Nye (1958) concluded that church attendance is associated with lower rates of delinquency, while Hirschi and Stark (1969) reported no significant relationships. We will consider Hirschi and Stark's research here in some detail for two reasons. First, their study reinforced the common sociological opinion of the 1960s that organized religion is irrelevant to understanding delinquency. Second, their research stimulated a whole new line of inquiry, as evidenced by the flourish of research on religion and delinquency that began in the mid-1970s.

Using data gathered from junior and senior high school students in Richmond, California, Hirschi and Stark investigated the relationship between church attendance and attitudes toward the law, the police, people in general, and supernatural beliefs (that is, a life after death and the existence of the devil). They found no significant relationship between church attendance and attitudes toward people and some weak, but significant, relationships between church attendance and positive attitudes toward the police and the law. The strongest relationship was between church attendance and belief in supernatural sanctions. In turn, Hirschi and Stark found that positive attitudes toward people, the law, and the police were associated with low involvement in delinquency, while belief in the supernatural was unrelated to delinquency. In short, those attitudes that were *unrelated* or weakly related to church attendance were the most relevant for delinquency, and those beliefs that *were related* to church attendance were not related to delinquent behavior. In view of these findings, it is not surprising that Hirschi and Stark found no relationship between church attendance and delinquency. The results of this study appeared to further substantiate Glock and Stark's earlier observation in *Religion and Society in Tension*: "Looking at American society as a whole . . . organized religion at present is neither a prominent witness to its own value system nor a major focal point around which ultimate commitments to norms, values, and beliefs are formed" (1965:184).

Five years after the publication of Hirschi and Stark's study, Burkett and White's study "Hellfire and Delinquency: Another Look" appeared (1974). Burkett and White argued that when secular values do not clearly define certain criminal or delinquent activities as wrong, then religious participation or beliefs may be relevant to understanding delinquent behavior. They suggested that for offenses about which there is moral ambiguity in everyday life and for offenses that run counter to religious traditions of self-control and self-denial, involvement in delinquency may be sensitive to religious variables. Thus, they hypothesized that activities such as alcohol use and marijuana use should be less common among the religiously active than among the inactive and among those who believe in the supernatural than among those who do not. Their findings were in large part consistent with their expectations. After analyzing questionnaire data from high school students in a city of about 170,500 in the Pacific Northwest, Burkett and White concluded that belief in the supernatural is only "slightly" related to the use of alcohol and marijuana, but that "a very definite relationship" exists between religious participation and the use of those substances. In comparison to Hirschi and Stark, Burkett and White reported stronger associations between religious participation and attitudes toward worldly authority and endorsement of conventional moral positions.

It should also be noted that before Burkett and White's study, Bruce Johnson (1972) had concluded that among college students, religious participation is one of four variables (the others being sex, political liberalism, and cigarette smoking) that are good predictors of marijuana use. In Johnson's study, 77 percent of regular church attenders reported never having used marijuana, while only 26 percent of nonattenders were complete abstainers. Church attenders were also less likely to be "regular" users.

Since the Burkett and White study, additional studies dealing with the relevance of religiosity to delinquency have appeared. Using self-report data from tenth graders in Atlanta, Georgia, Paul Higgins and Stan Albrecht (1977) found a "moderate" relationship between church attendance and a wide variety of delinquent activities. They suggested that "church attendance in Altanta might indicate a stronger commitment to general ethical and moral values than does church attendance in California." Stan Albrecht, Bruce Chadwick, and David Alcorn (1977) collected data from Mormon teenagers in three western states and found that religious variables were more strongly related to victimless deviance (for example, drug use) than to deviance involving victims and that a good prediction of deviance was possible when religious variables were combined with measures of peer and family relationships. In yet another study, Rick Linden and Raymond Currie (1978) reported that among their sample of youths aged fifteen to twenty-four in Calgary, Canada, the greater the ties to the church, the lower the probability of drug use.

Gary Jensen and Maynard Erickson (1979) attempted a reconciliation of divergent findings by analyzing aspects of Hirschi and Stark's data, as well as data gathered from high school students in southern Arizona. The analysis of Hirschi and Stark's data on students in Richmond, California, showed that church attendance is significantly related to smoking, drinking, and truancy (the only victimless offenses on which data were available from the Richmond youths). This finding is consistent with the findings of the other five studies summarized above and was replicated in the analysis of the southern Arizona data.

While all recent studies indicate that religious participation is relevant to some types of delinquency, there is no comparably consistent observation concerning religious affiliation and delinquency. Some studies have indicated lower delinquency rates for Jews than for Protestants and higher rates for Catholics than for Protestants (Goldscheider and Simpson, 1967; Rhodes and Reiss, 1970). In an analysis of arrest statistics, Roy Austin (1977) found that Jews had significantly lower rates than Catholics and that this difference could not be explained solely by the social-class composition of the samples. Austin found no significant differences between Catholics and Protestants. In comparing Catholics, Protestants, and all "other" denominations, Burkett and White found no significant differences in self-reported delinquency. Similarly, Hirschi and Stark reported no significant differences by denomination.

Rather than considering denomination and church attendance as totally separate variables, Jensen and Erickson (1979) proposed that the "meaning," or relevance, of religious involvement for behavior should be *variable* by denomination. Higgins and Albrecht (1977) suggested a similar possibility when they argued that religious variables appear more relevant to understanding delinquency in the South because of regional variation in the meaning of religion. Jensen and Erickson hypothesized that the denominational composition, rather than the regional composition, of the samples studied may have accounted for some of the variation in research findings.

Jensen and Erickson's findings were consistent with their hypothesis. In analyzing Hirschi and Stark's data, they found that church attendance was more relevant to delinquency in "fundamentalistic" or highly "ascetic" denominations (such as Church of Christ, Church of God, Disciples of Christ, and so on). Among Baptists, the overall relationships turned out to be quite comparable to those reported in Higgins and Albrecht's study of Atlanta youth. Further evidence of the intertwining relevance for delinquency of denomination and church attendance was found in Jensen and Erickson's analysis of southern Arizona data. Catholic, Protestant, and Mormon differences in delinquency were most prominent among regular church attenders. Attendance made the greatest difference among Mormons, particularly with regard to those activities strongly and distinctively prohibited by the Mormon church (smoking, drinking, and drug use). In sum, it appears that there is considerable similarity in research results when analyzed in terms of similar offenses for similar groups and settings. Given the research available, the most plausible explanation of divergent findings and complicated inconsistencies may rest with the variable and complicated nature of our society.

At the beginning of this section, we mentioned the position taken by some critics and scholars that religion can *cause* crime and delinquency. A behavioral interpretation of such an argument—that is, that the most religious are the most likely to commit criminal and delinquent acts—is not supported by the bulk of research. However, there are interesting findings concerning the effects of strong norms of prohibition on those who do engage in the prohibited activity. Ephraim Mizruchi and Robert Perrucci (1968) have argued that when groups are characterized by norms of abstinence, there are no "directives" to regulate or limit the prohibited activity when it does occur. This argument is supported by two studies of drinking among college students (Straus and Bacon, 1954; Snyder, 1958). Both studies found the intoxication rate much higher for ascetic Protestant and Mormon groups than for nonascetic Jewish students. In Jensen and Erickson's study (1977), a similar pattern was noted among Mormon high school students. Mormon students who did not attend church had higher rates of smoking, drunkenness, and marijuana use than Catholics or Protestants, while regularly attending Mormon youth ranked well below Protestants and Catholics for every drug-related offense studied. When a faith is characterized by a "hard line" on certain forms of behavior, those on the fringes may have a higher incidence of those behaviors than those on the fringes of more liberal denominations, possibly as a result of rebellion, stigmatization, or the lack of norms regulating prohibited behavior when it does occur.

THE MEDIA

In his study of adolescent society almost twenty years ago, James Coleman reported that nearly one-half of the students he studied spent two hours or more per day watching television (1961:18–23). Over one-half went to movies at least twice a month. Over 20 percent spent three hours or more per day watching television and over 25 percent went to movies once a week. In Wilson, Hirschi, and Elder's study four years later (1965), in a different part of the country over half of the black youths and nearly a quarter of the nonblacks reported spending four or more hours per day watching television. About one-half of all the youths included in the study reported going to movies at least twice per month. Over one-half of the black youths and over one-quarter of the nonblacks spent some time each day reading comic books or romance, movie, or teenage magazines. Obviously, in addition to the family, school, peers, and religion, the media constitute another force with potential to shape adolescent socialization in America.

The idea that exposure to the media contributes directly to crime and delinquency has been advanced with considerable emotional fervor for many decades. Referring to the impact of newspaper publicity of crime, Lombroso leaves us with little doubt about where he stood on the issue early in the century:

> This morbid stimulation is increased a hundred-fold by the prodigious increase of really criminal newspapers, which spread abroad the virus of the most loathsome social plagues, simply for sordid gain, and excite the morbid appetite and still more morbid curiosity of the lower social classes. They may be likened to those maggots which, sprung from putrefaction, increase it by their presence. (1911:211)

In recent years several civil law suits based on the same premise—that publicity may elicit crime through imitation and overstimulation—have been filed against the media.

Despite the alleged influence of the media, the major theories of delinquency do not accord that influence a major role. There are, however, ways in which the media could be specifically incorporated into these theories. For example, control theorists could argue that media content fosters values, norms, and beliefs that "free" a youth to commit delinquent acts, or that the media convey the "subterranean" aspects of American culture that facilitate delinquency. From a strain perspective, the media emphasis on advertising could be seen as facilitating strain by raising wishes and aspirations that cannot be met. Cultural conflict theorists might argue that the media present "definitions favorable to lawbreaking." However, as they do with religion, sociologists tend to relegate the media to the category of "questionable crime theories" (Schur, 1969:73–82).

RESEARCH ON THE MEDIA AND DELINQUENCY

The particular targets of concern regarding the effects of the media on crime and delinquency have varied over the years. For example, a major concern in the late 1940s and early 1950s was the impact of comic books on the young. Frederic Werthman (1954) argued that comic books were seducing the innocent and contributing to crime and delinquency by exposing the young to violence, sex, and sadism. As a psychiatrist, he supported this point of view with his own clinical experience. However, the idea that reading comic books may be associated with certain attitudes or behaviors has also been supported by more systematic research. In a study of 374 schoolboys in grades six through eight, S. H. Lovibond (1967) reported that the more a youth read comic books, watched television, or attended movies, the more likely he was "to endorse an ideology which makes the use of force in the interest of egocentric needs the essential content of human relationships." Whereas Lovibond could only suggest that such media exposure may be associated with delinquency, Thomas Hoult (1949) and Travis Hirschi (1969) did, in fact, report such an association. Hirschi noted that "the more time a boy spends watching television, reading romance magazines and comic books, or playing games, the *more* likely he is to have committed delinquent acts" (1969:190). However, Hirschi added that such relationships are "*very* weak."

We should also note that showing an association is only one step in reaching conclusions about the causal impact of exposure to media. Lovibond did suggest that the relationship between media exposure and children's attitudes might be *spurious*—that is, that children's preferences in reading and viewing material and their attitudes could both be products of other personal and social characteristics. Moreover, it is difficult to untangle the *causal ordering* of this relationship: children who commit delinquent acts or share attitudes favorable to violence may, *as a result* of those behaviors and attitudes, be media-oriented or choose certain forms of programming. It is also very difficult to isolate the impact of one set of experiences from a host of others. Consider, for example, "going to the movies." For many, if not most, teenagers, this activity combines "exposure to movies" with interaction with peers, freedom from adult surveillance, and a range of interests (cars, drive-in restaurants) common in the adolescent social world. Thus, a study showing that going to the movies is correlated with delinquency may tell us nothing about the impact of the media.

Much of the scholarly debate over "television violence" centers around the issues of causation outlined in Chapter 5. For example, in a 1972 issue of the *American Psychologist*, L. D. Eron and his colleagues claimed to have "demonstrated that there is a probable causative influence of watching violent television programs in early formative years on later aggression" (Eron et al. 1972:263). This claim immediately (and quite legitimately) drew criticism. Kay Herbert argued that the relationship described by Eron et al. was spurious and that the important factor in shaping both viewing preferences and aggressive behavior is parental response to aggression in a child's early years (1972:970–73). Dennis Howitt presented a similar argument, positing that media exposure is part of a subculture and that participating in such a subculture accounts for relationships between media preferences and behavior (1972:969–70).

A methodological critique by Gary Becker suggested not only that the relationship could be spurious but also that (given possibilities too complex to be discussed here) the study by Eron et al. could actually support conclusions directly contrary to its authors' claims (1972:967–68).

Similar debates can also be found in popular magazines. For example, in 1975 a special issue of *TV Guide* was headlined "Does TV Violence Affect Our Society?" (See Figure 8–1). Answering "Yes," Neil Hickey, (1975) cited reviews that focus on findings similar to those reported by Eron et al. Answering "No," Edith Efron (1975) pointed to the criticisms of such research and argued that those who watch the most TV and select the most violent content "have always been the chief reservoir of violent crime, and it was so well *before* the invention of TV." Science fiction writer Isaac Asimov also contributed to the debate with the opinion that from a historical perspective violence is as "human as the thumb" and is not a product of modern television.

Efron and Hickey both made reference to a three-year, $1 million research project by the Surgeon General's Scientific Advisory Committee on Television and Social Behavior (1971). The conclusion of that research was that violence on television can induce mimicking in children shortly after exposure and that *under certain circumstances* television violence can lead to an increase in aggressive acts. The committee acknowledged that it had been unable to determine either the size of the population of susceptible children or the exact reason why some children imitate media content and others do not. The committee did suggest that those most responsive to television violence are those who are prone to aggression to begin with, or those who respond with pleasure to violent content.

The Surgeon General's Scientific Advisory Committee paid considerable attention to experimental work since it avoids many of the criticisms that have been directed at survey studies. By manipulating exposure and content, measuring the subsequent outcome, and randomly assigning subjects to different conditions or experiences, experimental researchers can avoid problems of spuriousness and causal order. However, such research has *not* consistently demonstrated a relationship between media exposure to violence and subsequent aggression. For example, Stein and Friedrich (1971) observed a group of preschoolers who had been exposed to "aggressive" programming, "neutral" programming, and "prosocial" programming and found no significant differences overall. On the other hand, a study by Liebert and Baron (1971) found that children who viewed aggressive episodes on television were more willing to engage in interpersonal aggression than a control group. One review has summed up the complex situation as follows:

> Robert D. Singer and I recently have completed a comprehensive review of the television and aggression literature. We have found that the majority of the experimental studies showed that witnessing violence can instigate "aggressive" behavior. These experiments, however, most frequently

FIGURE 8–1 *Debate over Television Violence and Crime and Delinquency*

Source: Edith Efron and Neil Hickey. "Does TV Violence Affect Our Society?" Reprinted with permission from *TV Guide* ® Magazine. Copyright © 1975 by Triangle Publications, Inc. Radnor, Pennsylvania.

gained their effectiveness through the intentional arousal of subjects and the use of dependent measures that removed ordinary sanctions against aggression. Instigation effects were rarely found in studies or experimental conditions in which the subjects were not aroused intentionally. When the measure of aggression has been some naturally occurring behavior, it has been shown that television violence either has no effect . . . or only affects children who were initially highly aggressive. . . . Thus we would argue that the link between televised violence and aggression has not been established clearly. (Kaplan, 1972:969)

A study by Hartnagel, Teevan, and McIntyre (1975) is one of the better examples of survey research on the relationship between television violence and violent behavior. The study was based on questionnaires administered to junior and senior high school students in one county in Maryland. Students were asked to specify their favorite television shows, total amount of time they spent watching television, and their perceptions of violent content in their favorite shows. Other questions asked about the students' involvement in violence (fights and assaults) and their background characteristics. Hartnagel, Teevan, and McIntyre found that television violence had no significant relationship to violent behavior for the entire sample or for any subcategories of students in the sample. Their final interpretation of the results was consistent with the reservations expressed by Kaplan (1972). They noted that because laboratory studies use stimuli that elicit aggression, create situations where the opportunity for aggression is specifically provided, and assess immediate effects, the possibility of generalizing from these studies is limited. They also noted that laboratory studies use young children, whereas their own study focused on junior and senior high school students. Moreover, their study dealt with violent offense behavior rather than with the types of aggression studied in a laboratory setting. Although the researchers found no significant relationship between individual exposure, preference for violent programming, and self-reports of violence, they did not rule out the possibility that television violence might have subtle and indirect effects on attitudes toward violence in our society as a whole. However, any such effects are merely speculative and have not been established through research.

Another heated debate involving the media and delinquency centers on the effects of erotica or pornography. This topic was the subject of considerable review and research by the President's Commission on Obscenity and Pornography (1970). Like the Surgeon General's report, the report of this commission generated considerable controversy, yet failed to resolve the issue that it addressed. For example, in response to the commission's final report, one of the commissioners, Charles Keating, took the position that the public has "enough common sense to know that one who wallows in filth is going to get dirty. This is intuitive knowledge. Those who spend millions of dollars to tell us otherwise must be malicious or misguided, or both" (President's Commission on Obscenity and Pornography, 1970:ix). Others called the report a "Magna Carta for the pornographers."

Some of the conclusions that generated such a reaction concern the relationship between pornography and criminal or delinquent behavior. One of the commission's conclusions was that there was "no evidence to date that exposure to explicit sexual materials plays a significant role in the causation of delinquent or criminal behavior among youths or adults" (1970:32). Support for this observation came from (1) studies comparing delinquent and nondelinquent youth, (2) statistical studies of the relationship between availability of erotic materials and rates of sex crimes in both Denmark and the United States, and (3) comparisons of sex offenders with other adults.

A more recent study by Harold S. Kant and Michael Goldstein (1976:61–64) arrived at similar conclusions. After comparing sixty molestation cases, fifty-two cases of "users of pornography," and sixty-three supposedly normal males, Kant and Goldstein concluded that sexual deviates have little exposure to erotica during adolescence. In fact, these researchers suggested that such adolescent exposure is associated with "adult patterns of acceptable heterosexual interest and practice." They noted that exposure to erotica appeared to be a quite common aspect of adolescence and that there was no evidence in their study that such exposure was associated with sex crimes. Their findings seemed to suggest the opposite—that is, that such exposure may be associated with acceptable sexual patterns.

Most of the research summarized above focused on either the *immediate impact* of various media and media content or differences *among individuals* who have been variably exposed. Thus, the research findings are largely irrelevant to some of the larger issues concerning the impact of mass media "in the long run" or on society as a whole. The Danish experience with pornography indicated that increased availability of sexual materials was accompanied by a decrease in sex offenses (President's Commission on Obscenity and Pornography, 1970:31). In the United States during a period characterized by a marked increase in pornography, the juvenile arrest rate for sex crimes decreased, while the rate for nonsexual crimes increased. Furthermore, juveniles are not disproportionately represented in murder and rape statistics, yet are disproportionately involved with the media. John Conklin observed that although there was a 50 percent increase in robbery incidents between 1967 and 1969, the amount of television violence remained constant during that time (1972:46–48). The age groups supposedly most susceptible to violence in the media actually account for very few robberies. Conklin's conclusion was that available data do not show a connection between violence in the media and increased robbery rates in the 1960s.

It is highly unlikely that there will ever be research providing clear-cut evidence on the subtle or long-term influences of the media. Current emphases and popular theory focus on negative consequences, which have not been clearly demonstrated. The various government investigations into the media have focused on such negative consequences because they are of concern to many people and organizations. However, the content and messages conveyed in the media are very complex, and negative outcomes may be balanced by positive outcomes. For example, the President's Commission on Obscenity and Pornography developed a list of "presumed consequences of exposure to erotica" (see Display 8–1).

DISPLAY 8-1 *Presumed Consequences of Exposure to Erotica*

	Sexual	Nonsexual
Criminal or Generally Regarded as Harmful:	1. Sexually aggressive acts of a criminal nature. 2. Unlawful sexual practice. 3. Nonconsensual sex acts. 4. Incest. 5. Sexually perverse behavior. 6. Adultery. 7. Illegal sexual activities. 8. Socially disapproved sexual behavior. 9. Sexual practices harmful to self. 10. Deadly serious pursuit of sexual satisfaction. 11. Dehumanized sexual acts. 12. Preoccupation (obsession) with sex. 13. Change in direction of sexual development from natural pathway. 14. Blocking psychosexual maturation. 15. Misinformation about sex. 16. Moral breakdown.	17. Homicide. 18. Suicide. 19. Delinquency. 20. Criminal acts. 21. Indecent personal habits. 22. Unhealthy habits. 23. Unhealthy thoughts. 24. Rejection of reality. 25. Ennui. 26. Submission to authoritarianism.
Neutral	27. Sex attitudes. 28. Sex values. 29. Sex information. 30. Sex habits.	
Beneficial/ Helpful:	31. Draining off of illegitimate sexual drives. 32. Outlet for otherwise frustrated sex drives. 33. Release of strong sexual urges without harming others. 34. Pleasure. 35. Discharge of "antisocial" sexual appetites. 36. Consumation of legitimate sexual responsibilities.	

Source: President's Commission on Obscenity and Pornography. *The Report of the Commission on Obscenity and Pornography.* New York: Bantam Books, 1970.

The list of consequences, some of which are regarded as "beneficial," was compiled on the basis of all the arguments presented by various theorists and parties to the pornography issue.

Similarly, although numerous television programs have violent content, the actual meaning of that content can be complex, and arguments can be advanced listing beneficial consequences as well (for example, television's "bad guys" tend to lose in the end). We have to note that some of the presumed "negative" consequences of violence in the media are actually traits that are accorded considerable admiration in the United States. There are probably as many parents concerned that their children are not sufficiently aggressive and "do not stand up for themselves" as there are parents concerned about violence and aggression among the young.

Crime has been a theme of the American entertainment industry since its beginning and is a common feature of tourist attractions around the United States. A city in Kansas stages an annual "Jesse James festival." Tombstone, Arizona, publicizes itself as "The Town Too Tough to Die!" and celebrates "Helldorado Days." Visitors to Disneyland's "Pirates of the Caribbean" sail through the sacking of a harbor town, complete with shooting, hanging, and the pursuit and sale of female victims. It is all in the spirit of "good clean fun," but it is not fundamentally different from violent television programs or movies. It endures because it is popular, entertaining, and profitable. The presentation of crime for fun and profit *may* reinforce crime and delinquency, but it is extremely difficult to isolate those enterprises that merely reflect preferences and those that shape them. Thus, the relationship between the media and crime and delinquency will no doubt continue as a source of debate and controversy.

COMMUNITY AND DELINQUENCY

A common lament about American society has been focused on the demise of a "sense of community" or common bonds among people living in a certain territory. In his introduction to Shaw and McKay's classic work on juvenile delinquency in urban areas (1942:xi), Ernest Burgess wrote that "the common element" explaining the distribution of delinquency was "social disorganization or the lack of organized community effort to deal with these conditions." Shaw and McKay's solution to the delinquency problem rested with establishing neighborhood organizations.

In *A Nation of Strangers*, Vance Packard (1972) argued along similar lines. He wrote that "great numbers" of Americans "feel unconnected" to people or places as a result of mobility. Moreover, Packard continued, not only are the "rootless' viewed as prime candidates for mental problems, aggression, alcoholism, and crime, but in addition the turnover of people in a community "demoralizes" those who remain behind. Packard felt we needed more stability in neighborhoods, limits on population growth and density, and "settings small enough in scale to meet people's needs for social interaction and a sense of significant citizenship" (1972:302). He listed the following as the characteristics of communities that would reduce fragmentation and reestablish a sense of community:

1. The natural human community is one that is small enough to be in scale to man.

2. It provides a natural way for people to come together if they wish to do so.

3. It offers a natural setting for individuals to achieve personal recognition, to share experience, to find assurance of emotional and other support, and to develop some enduring friendships.

4. Its stability and diversity provide a sense of wholeness and coherence to a participant's life, a sense that what is happening today is part of an ongoing process.

5. It provides people with a sense that they have some control over events about to happen that can affect their lives.

6. And it offers people a special group and a special place that they can think of as their own. They have a living environment they can seek to improve and one in which they can come to feel a proprietary pride. (1972:334–35)

The emphasis on community and neighborhood controls is reiterated in James Q. Wilson's *Thinking About Crime* (1975). Wilson argued that the population of the central city consists disproportionately of childless, affluent whites, the elderly, the poor, and the transient, who either have no interest in maintaining a sense of community or lack the ability to work actively to maintain one. The failure to develop communal bonds is viewed as facilitating crime and delinquency, which in turn contribute to further suspicion, isolation, and withdrawal. Wilson describes the process as a vicious cycle, with community disorganization contributing to crime and delinquency, which lead to further disorganization.

RESEARCH ON COMMUNAL BONDS AND DELINQUENCY

Most of the research relevant to arguments about communal bonds and delinquency is only indirectly related to the issue. For example, Karl Schuessler and Gerald Slatin (1964) examined the characteristics of major American cities and found substantial intercorrelations among offense rates, divorce rates, and suicide rates. They concluded that their findings were "suggestive of a social process which leads to demoralization in the person and consequent abandonment or denial of generally recognized social obligations" (1964:147). This observation is consistent with earlier research by Shaw and McKay (1931) that showed delinquency rates of urban neighborhoods to be related to population change, poor housing, tuberculosis, mental disorders, and adult crime. The general underlying condition that Shaw and McKay identified was "neighborhood disorganization," which was facilitated by population change and economic deprivation. Other studies have yielded similar results, indicating that the delinquency rate in areas of cities is related to overcrowding, transiency, poor housing, and a variety of economic indicators. However, as Roland Chilton has noted in his research (1964:83), the relationship of these conditions to delinquency rates does not directly demonstrate that neighborhood disorganization or lack of communal bonds generates high rates; such an interpretation is one possible explanation of the findings. Gresham Sykes reached a similar conclusion about city size and crime rates, noting that variations *may* reflect anonymity, depersonalization, and social disorganization but that a good deal more research is needed before such arguments can be viewed as something more than interpretation (1978:153).

In his comparison of crime and delinquency in Swiss, American, Scandinavian, and German societies, Marshall Clinard (1978) suggested that the very low offense rates in Swiss society may be due (among other things) to the importance of "cantons" and political "communes" in that society. While Switzerland is an affluent, urban country with a heterogeneous population, its government power is decentralized into twenty-five federated states, or cantons, with each of these divided into smaller political communes. Clinard noted that the Swiss maintain "both a physical and a social psychological tie to the cantons and communes from which they come." Since there are several characteristics of Swiss society that might account for its low crime rate, Clinard could not be certain which specific feature is responsible. He did feel that his findings support recommendations to limit city size, to develop small governmental units operating on a neighborhood or "commune" level, and to encourage more direct citizen participation at such a level.

Some studies of individuals have attempted to test the argument that mobility inhibits the development of communal bonds, which in turn facilitates delinquency. Sheldon and Eleanor Glueck posited that "frequent moving about means relative anonymity and the likelihood of failure to develop a feeling of loyalty and responsibility to neighborhoods; it tends rather to develop a sense of instability" (1950:155). They contrasted the instability of neighborhoods in recent times to earlier times when "people were born, reared, and lived their lives in one small community, and everyone was known to his neighbors." In comparing 500 delinquent youths and 500 nondelinquent youths, the Gluecks found no significant difference between these groups in length of residence in a neighborhood. However, they did find that the delinquent boys had moved from one house to another significantly more often than the nondelinquent boys. They concluded that "whatever the effect of greater mobility may be upon the tendency to disregard neighborhood opinion as a guide to behavior, it must have operated more excessively upon the delinquents than the nondelinquents" (1950:156). However, as in the studies of cities and urban areas, lack of neighborhood bonds is only one possible interpretation of the relationship. It may be that family circumstances associated with frequency of moves are also associated with delinquency. In short, the relationship could easily be spurious.

Studies of mobility and its consequences for children have not shown mobility to be particularly detrimental. For example, one study found that length of time spent in a particular school did not appear to affect a student's degree of acceptability into peer groups (Miller, 1952). Other studies have indicated that school moves do not affect students' reading achievement (Bollenbacher, 1962) or their performance on IQ tests (Downie, 1953; Evans, 1966). In a study of the effect of student mobility on academic achievement, John Evans concluded that "if moving must be considered a 'handicap' as we have traditionally thought it is, then this study shows definite ability on the part of the mobile students to adjust" (1966:22).

In a more recent study, Butler, McAllister, and Kaiser (1973) found that moving had "little effect" upon informal social relations, alienation, unhappiness, and mental disturbance. Yet another study found that children who had moved did not differ from a sample of their peers who had not moved in terms of mothers' perceptions of disability, aggression, or measures of inhibition (Barrett and Noble, 1973).

In sum, the overall body of research suggests that school changes, frequency of moves, and long-distance moves do not make much difference for a variety of factors that are typically associated with delinquency. On the other hand, the Gluecks' study, which dealt directly with delinquency, suggested that frequency of moves and delinquency are related. Since there are numerous interpretations of that relationship, we cannot reach any one conclusion concerning the interrelationships among mobility, communal ties, and delinquency.

Arguments based on the idea that transiency inhibits the development of community or neighborhood bonds and facilitates delinquency can be presented at several different levels. For instance, Packard argued that transiency demoralizes those left behind *as well as* those who move and thus fosters crime and delinquency even among long-term residents. If that is so, then we would expect no significant differences in crime and delinquency between movers and nonmovers. Rather, the greater the transiency of an *area,* the greater the crime rate should be for that area. In other words, it is at the neighborhood or communal level that transiency should facilitate delinquency since transiency supposedly affects the bonds among people whether they are long-time residents or frequent movers. Population growth does appear to have an effect on crime and delinquency rates, but the thesis that this is due to communal demoralization or lack of communal bonds has not been demonstrated.

Our inability to state any definite conclusions about neighborhood or communal bonds and delinquency is reflected in the Law Enforcement Assistance Administration's solicitation of research proposals to study "safe and secure neighborhoods" (1979). The LEAA noted that there are "neighborhoods which appear to be conspicuously successful in terms of providing safe and secure living environments" and urged the development of research aimed at identifying characteristics that inhibit crime. Among the processes that the LEAA urged researchers to explore are the "communication processes," which act informally to socialize and control behavior at the neighborhood level; the "cognitive processes which operate in an individual's identification of the area to which he belongs"; and the "affect-based processes," which involve emotional bonds to neighborhoods. The LEAA's review of the research led to the conclusion that the operation of such processes in safe and secure neighborhoods "is still poorly understood."

The term used by Oscar Newman (1972) to refer to the characteristics of neighborhoods or residential environments that make them safe and secure is *defensible space.* By defensible space, Newman did not mean armed camps or vigilante defense of areas but, rather, architectural arrangements that reinforce a sense of "territoriality" and a "sense of community." In a comparison of two housing projects, Newman found that the crime rate was lowest in the project that was divided into small, manageable zones where residents could maintain surveillance over commonly shared space (see Figure 8–2). Vandalism was lower than in less

FIGURE 8– 3 *Brownsville Houses from Street.* The buildings' dispositions at Brownsville create triangular buffer areas that are used for play, sitting, and parking. These areas are easily observed from the street and from apartment windows. Entry to buildings is typically from the street through these buffer zones. Residents regard these areas as an extension of their own buildings and maintain active surveillance over them.

Source: Used with permission of Macmillan Publishing Co., Inc. From *Defensible Space* by Oscar Newman. Copyright © 1972 by Oscar Newman.

defensible arrangements, as was the rate of persons vacating the projects. Newman has warned us not to take this comparison as proof that architectural arrangements that create defensible space reduce crime; however, the analysis is basically consistent with the recommendations outlined by Packard. Whether defensible space reduces vandalism among inhabitants by reinforcing communal bonds or merely keeps outsiders under control is not known.

SUMMARY

Religion, the media, and communal or neighborhood bonds have not been central to major sociological perspectives or to research on delinquency during the last several decades. Although the grand masters of sociology in the late 1800s and early 1900s accorded a significant role to religion in the maintenance of social order, contemporary criminologists and specialists in the sociology of religion rarely address the relationship between religious variables and delinquency or crime. Since the mid-1970s, however, there has been a revival of interest in this relationship, and a tentative set of generalizations has been *suggested* by pertinent studies:

1. Church participation is more likely to be related to illegal drug use than to other delinquent offenses.
2. Church participation is most relevant to drug use in denominations that prohibit such activity and is more relevant to delinquent offenses in general among ascetic or fundamentalistic denominations than among liberal denominations.
3. When religious groups are characterized by norms of abstinence, peripheral or fringe members appear to violate those norms to a greater degree than fringe members of other religious groups.

We are reluctant to state any other tentative conclusions because, typically, new issues and possible reconciliations of divergent findings have been explored in single pieces of research. There are promising indications that further research on the relationship between dimensions of religiosity and delinquency will find relevance for this relationship in some social contexts but not in others.

A considerable body of research can be cited as somehow relevant to the impact of the media on delinquency and crime. However, most of it has been criticized on some grounds or other as either irrelevant or inadequate for assessing such relationships. The following observations reflect the current state of research and the qualifications that the criticisms demand:

1. Experimental studies have shown that exposure to televised content intended to arouse aggressive behavior increases the probabil-

ity of interpersonal aggression in controlled situations where the opportunity for aggression is provided following exposure. However, these findings cannot be automatically generalized to the relationship between delinquent behavior and exposure to television outside the laboratory setting.

2. The more time a person spends watching television, reading comic books, or romance magazines, the greater the probability of involvement in delinquency, *but* arguments concerning the causal order and spuriousness of this relationship have not been eliminated. Moreover, a study specifically examining preferences for violent programming in relation to self-reports of violence found no significant relationship.

3. The conclusion of the President's Commission on Obscenity and Pornography still stands: There is no evidence that exposure to erotica increases the probability of sex crimes or delinquent behavior.

Once again we will state that we are focusing on regularities. There are undoubtedly people who are incited to commit a crime by something they have seen or read, but there are also people who may refrain from crimes as a result of such stimuli. *On balance,* there is no basis for concluding that television violence or erotic literature enhances the probability of delinquency.

One of the oldest sociological notions about crime and delinquency attributes such problems to urbanization and mobility. Urbanization and mobility are seen as inhibiting the development of bonds among people in communities or neighborhoods. This idea has been popularized in recent years by Vance Packard and is at the root of proposals to design living environments that encourage a sense of community. Our review of the literature on the topic justifies the following observations:

1. No research studies have directly focused on the impact of communal or neighborhood bonds on delinquency. Rather, the concept of communal bonds has been introduced into various studies to make sense out of the relationships between community size, population change, and crime rates, as well as the relationships between a variety of characteristics of areas of cities and rates of crime and delinquency.

2. Several studies have shown physical mobility among students to be unrelated to school achievement and social relationships. One study did show that the number of residential changes for delinquents was greater than the number for nondelinquents, but there are several possible interpretations for that finding.

Since physical and architectural characteristics of neighborhoods or communities can be planned and controlled (to some degree), there is growing interest in identifying those characteristics of neighborhoods that affect rates of crime and delinquency, as well as the processes through which such characteristics have an impact. Thus, research on crime and delinquency is likely to return to some of the same issues that dominated criminology earlier in this century—the variable degrees and types of organization or disorganization that inhibit or facilitate crime and delinquency among people inhabiting a common territory.

REFERENCES

Albrecht, S. L., B. A. Chadwick, and D. S. Alcorn. 1977. "Religiosity and Deviance: Application of an Attitude-Behavior Contingent Consistency Model." *Journal for the Scientific Study of Religion* 16 (3):263–74.

Austin, R. 1977. "Religion and Crime Control." Paper presented at American Society of Criminologists convention. Atlanta, Ga.

Barrett, C. L., and H. Noble. 1973. "Mother's Anxieties versus the Effects of Long Distance Moves on Children." *Journal of Marriage and the Family* 35 (May):181–88.

Becker, G. 1972. "Causal Analysis in R-R Studies: Television and Aggression." *American Psychologist* 27:967–68.

Bollenbacher, J. 1962. "A Study of the Effect of Mobility on Reading Achievement." *Reading Teacher* 15 (March):356–60.

Burkett, S. R., and M. White. 1974. "Hellfire and Delinquency: Another Look." *Journal for the Scientific Study of Religion* 13 (December):455–62.

Butler, E. W., R. J. McAllister, and E. J. Kaiser. 1973. "The Effects of Voluntary and Involuntary Residential Mobility of Females and Males." *Journal of Marriage and the Family* 35 (May):219–27.

Chilton, R. J. 1964. "Continuity in Delinquency Area Research: A Comparison of Studies for Baltimore, Detroit, and Indianapolis." *American Sociological Review* 29 (February):71–83.

Clinard, M. B. 1978. *Cities with Little Crime: The Case of Switzerland.* Cambridge: Cambridge University Press.

Coleman, J. S. 1961. *The Adolescent Society.* New York: Free Press of Glencoe.

Conklin, J. 1972. *Robbery and the Criminal Justice System.* Philadelphia: J. B. Lippincott.

Downie, N. M. 1953. "A Comparison between Children Who Have Moved from School to School with Those Who Have Been in Continuous Residence on Various Factors of Adjustment." *Journal of Educational Psychology* 44 (January):50–53.

Efron, E. 1975. "Does TV Violence Affect Our Society? No." *TV Guide,* June 14:22.

Empey, L. T. 1978. *American Delinquency.* Homewood, Ill.: Dorsey Press.

Eron, L. D., et al. 1972. "Does Television Violence Cause Aggression?" *American Psychologist* 27:253–63.

Evans, J. W., Jr. 1966. "The Effect of Pupil Mobility upon Academic Achievement." *National Elementary Principal* 45 (April):18–22.

Fitzpatrick, J. P. 1967. "The Role of Religion in Programs for the Prevention and Correction of Crime and Delinquency." In President's Commission on Law

Enforcement and Administration of Justice. *Juvenile Delinquency and Youth Crime.* Washington, D.C.: U.S. Government Printing Office.

Glock, C. Y., and R. Stark. 1965. *Religion and Society in Tension.* Chicago: Rand McNally.

Glueck, S., and E. Glueck. 1950. *Unraveling Juvenile Delinquency.* Cambridge, Mass.: Harvard University Press.

Goldscheider, C., and J. E. Simpson. 1967. "Religious Affiliation and Juvenile Delinquency." *Sociological Inquiry* 37 (Spring):297–310.

Hartnagel, T. F., J. J. Teevan, and J. J. McIntyre. 1975. "Television Violence and Violent Behavior." *Social Forces* 54 (December):341–51.

Hartshorne, H., and M. A. May. 1930. *Studies in Deceit,* vol. 1. New York: Macmillan.

Haskell, M. R., and L. Yablonsky. 1978. *Juvenile Delinquency.* Chicago: Rand McNally.

Healy, W., and A. J. Bronner. 1936. *New Light on Delinquency and Its Treatment.* New Haven, Conn.: Yale University Press.

Herbert, K. 1972. "Weaknesses in the Television Causes Aggression Analysis by Eron et al." *American Psychologist* 27 (October):970–73.

Hickey, N. 1975. "Does TV Violence Affect Our Society? Yes." *TV Guide,* June 14:8.

Higgins, P. C., and G. L. Albrecht. 1977. "Hellfire and Delinquency Revisited." *Social Forces* 55 (June):952–58.

Hightower, P. R. 1930. "Biblical Information in Relation to Character and Conduct." *University of Iowa Studies in Character* 3:33–34.

Hirschi, T. 1969. *Causes of Delinquency.* Berkeley: University of California Press.

Hirschi, T., and R. Stark. 1969. "Hellfire and Delinquency." *Social Problems* 17 (Fall):202–13.

Hoult, T. F. 1949. "Comic Books and Juvenile Delinquency." *Sociology and Social Research* 33:279–84.

Howitt, D. 1972. "Television and Aggression: A Counter Argument." *American Psychologist* 27 (October):969–70.

Jensen, G. F., and M. L. Erickson. 1977. "Delinquency and Damnation." Paper presented at Pacific Sociological Association convention. San Francisco.

———. 1979. "The Religion Factor and Delinquency: Another Look at the Hellfire Hypothesis." In R. Wuthnow, ed., *The Religious Dimension: New Directions in Quantitative Research.* New York: Academic Press.

Johnson, B. 1972. *Social Determinants of the Use of Dangerous Drugs by College Students.* New York: John Wiley.

Kant, H. S., and M. J. Goldstein. 1976. "Pornography." *Psychology Today* 4 (7):61–64.

Kaplan, R. M. 1972. "On Television as a Cause of Aggression." *American Psychologist* 27:968–69.

Kvaraceus, W. 1944. "Delinquent Behavior and Church Attendance." *Sociology and Social Research* 28:284–89.

Law Enforcement Assistance Administration. 1979. *Safe and Secure Neighborhoods.* Washington, D.C.: Criminal Justice Research Solicitation, Law Enforcement Assistance Administration.

Liebert, R. M., and R. A. Baron. 1971. "Short-Term Effects of Televised Aggression on Children's Aggressive Behavior." In J. P. Murray, E. A. Rubenstein, and G. A.

Comstock, eds., *Television and Social Behavior.* Washington, D.C.: U.S. Government Printing Office.

Linden, R., and R. Currie. 1978. "Religiosity and Drug Use: A Test of Social Control Theory." *Canadian Review of Anthropology and Sociology* 15:346–55.

Lombroso, C. 1911. *Crime, Its Causes and Remedies.* Boston: Little, Brown.

Lovibond, S. H. 1967. "The Effect of Media Stressing Crime and Violence upon Children's Attitudes." *Social Problems* 15 (Summer):91–100.

Middleton, W., and P. Fay. 1941. "Attitudes of Delinquent and Non-Delinquent Girls toward Sunday Observance, the Bible and War." *Journal of Educational Psychology* 32:555–58.

Miller, L. R. 1952. "Identifying the Outsider." *National Elementary Principal* 32 (September):156–61.

Miller, M. 1965. "The Place of Religion in the Lives of Juvenile Offenders." *Federal Probation* 29:50–54.

Mizruchi, E., and R. Perrucci. 1968. "Prescription, Proscription and Permissiveness: Aspects of Norms and Deviant Drinking Behavior." In M. Lefton, J. K. Skipper, Jr., and C. H. McCaghy, eds., *Approaches to Deviance.* New York: Appleton-Century-Crofts.

Mursell, G. R. 1930. "A Study of Religious Training as a Psychological Factor in Delinquency." Ph.D. dissertation. Ohio State University.

Newman, O. 1972. *Defensible Space.* New York: Macmillan.

Nye, F. I. 1958. *Family Relationships and Delinquent Behavior.* New York: John Wiley.

Packard, V. 1972. *A Nation of Strangers.* New York: David McKay.

President's Commission on Obscenity and Pornography. 1970. *The Report of the Commission on Obscenity and Pornography.* New York: Bantam Books.

Rhodes, A., and A. Reiss, Jr. 1970. "The Religious Factor and Delinquent Behavior." *Journal of Research in Crime and Delinquency* 7:83–98.

Sanders, W. B. 1976. *Juvenile Delinquency.* New York: Praeger.

Schuessler, K., and G. Slatin. 1964. "Sources of Variation in U.S. City Crime, 1950 and 1960." *Journal of Research in Crime and Delinquency* 1 (July):127–48.

Schur, E. M. 1969. *Our Criminal Society.* Englewood Cliffs, N.J.: Prentice-Hall.

Shaw, C. R., and H. D. McKay. 1931. *Social Factors in Juvenile Delinquency,* vol. 2. Report no. 13 of the National Commission on Law Observance and Enforcement. Washington, D.C.: U.S. Government Printing Office.

———. 1942. *Juvenile Delinquency and Urban Areas.* Chicago: University of Chicago Press.

Snyder, C. R. 1958. *Alcohol and the Jews.* Glencoe, Ill.: Free Press.

Stein, A. H., and L. K. Friedrich. 1971. "Television Content and Young Children's Behavior." In J. P. Murray, E. A. Rubinstein, and G. A. Comstock, eds., *Television and Social Behavior.* Washington, D.C.: U.S. Government Printing Office.

Straus, R., and S. D. Bacon. 1954. *Drinking in College.* New Haven, Conn.: Yale University Press.

Surgeon General's Scientific Advisory Committee on Television and Social Behavior. 1971. *Television and Growing Up: The Impact of Televised Violence.* Washington, D.C.: National Institute of Mental Health.

Sutherland, E. H., and D. R. Cressey. 1978. *Criminology,* 10th ed. Philadelphia: J. B. Lippincott.

Sykes, G. M. 1978. *Criminology.* New York: Harcourt Brace Jovanovich.

Thrasher. F. M. 1927. *The Gang.* Chicago: University of Chicago Press.

Werthman, F. 1954. *Seduction of the Innocent.* New York: Holt, Rinehart and Winston.

Wilson, A. B., T. Hirschi, and G. Elder. 1965. "Technical Report No. 1: Secondary School Survey." Berkeley, Calif.: Survey Research Center. Mimeographed.

Wilson, J. Q. 1975. *Thinking about Crime.* New York: Vintage Books.

9.
DETERRENCE AND LABELING

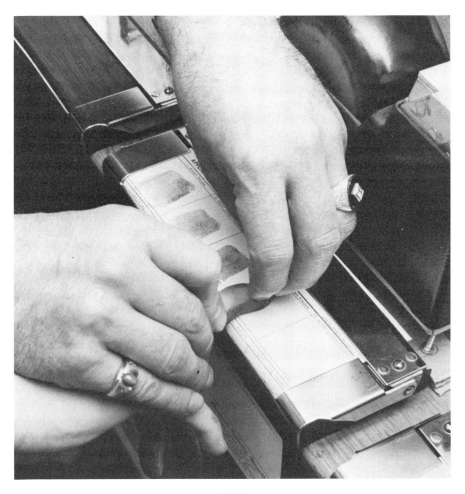

If society is to be protected from the violent young, respect for punishment must be restored. Youngsters should know just what to expect if they commit a particular crime. An adult crime—like armed robbery, rape or murder—deserves adult treatment. Yet in many states, a juvenile cannot be tried in adult court for any offense. Says Harlem Detective Wilson: "There are no ifs, ands or buts about it, the laws have to be changed. The idea was to protect kids who had minor skirmishes with the law from getting a record. This kind of treatment was not made for 14- and 15-year-old kids who are killers."
—*Time*, July 11, 1977

REACTIONS TO DELINQUENCY

The assumptions of the theory and research summarized in the last several chapters are that juveniles who commit delinquent acts differ in measurable ways from those who do not and that variable degrees of involvement in delinquency can be explained by considering characteristics of the juvenile and his or her environment. These assumptions are *not* shared by all sociologists who study delinquency. Consider, for example, the following statement by Edwin Schur: "So-called delinquents . . . are not significantly different from non-delinquents—*except* that they have been processed by the juvenile justice system. . . . We must repudiate the prevailing assumption that the delinquent is basically different" (1973:153–54). Schur and others argue that rather than focusing on causes of delinquent behavior, we should be studying "reaction agencies" and the unanticipated consequences of reactions to deviance. In other words, we should be cognizant of the social audience that observes and responds to certain behavioral acts. Agencies of social control, such as the police, the courts, and correctional institutions, only react to specific types of acts, and we should be aware of the consequences of their reactions. This school of thought argues that more insight can be gained from the study of social reactions to deviant acts than from the study of individual deviants. Such points of view are at the heart of a popular perspective in the sociology of deviance. That perspective is referred to as *labeling theory*.

The plausibility of Schur's statements about differences between delinquents and nondelinquents hinges on the meaning of the words *significantly* and *basically different*. There are numerous "statistically significant" differences among juveniles variably involved in delinquency. Whether delinquents are "basically" different is another matter. Delinquency is encouraged or inhibited by natural learning processes and by social circumstances that touch most of us *but to variable degrees.* There are differences, but the differences do *not* set one segment of humanity apart from another. If that is the rationale for rejecting the assumption that delinquents are basically different, then most sociologists would agree. On the other hand, arguments to the effect that there are *no differences* are wrong.

Labeling theory was first introduced in the 1930s by Frank Tannenbaum, who argued that the proper focus for the study of deviance is not the behavior itself but the reaction to deviant persons. In the 1950s Edwin Lemert added a number of new concepts to the basic principles set forth by Tannenbaum. During the 1960s such theorists as Edwin Schur, Howard Becker, and Thomas Scheff applied the basic tenets of labeling theory to a wide range of deviant behavior. The most distinct contribution of the labeling theorists is the challenge they present to traditional notions that "the law" or legislation solves problems and that law enforcement deters people from lawbreaking. Labeling theorists ask us to consider the possibility that legislation, rather than solving social problems, can cause or magnify them. Labeling theorists also challenge us to consider the possibility that law enforcement, rather than deterring crime, can reinforce involvement in delinquency and facilitate criminal careers.

The concepts of labeling theory run counter to those of *deterrence.* In the latter view, stiffer sentences are required to "set things right" (*retribution*); to "get criminals off the street" (*incapacitation*); to deter young criminals from further crime (*specific deterrence*); or to deter would-be criminals (*general deterrence*). The opposition to emphasis on these aims of punishment is based on the belief not only that such aims are unattainable but also that the justice system "grinds up" young people and generates worse problems than it solves. In this chapter we will address both sets of ideas about reactions to delinquency—those of deterrence and those of labeling theory.

DETERRENCE THEORY AND JUVENILE JUSTICE

The idea that a primary aim of legal sanctioning or punishment is to deter offenders, as well as the general public, from future transgressions developed in the eighteenth century. It is associated with a perspective on crime called the "classical school of criminology." The classical view was rational and utilitarian, emphasizing that a punishment is "just" only if it contributes to the greatest happiness for the greatest number. The major justification for legal sanctioning was its presumed inhibiting effect on the extent of crime. For a punishment to serve such a purpose and contribute to the social good, there had to be (so it was argued) a measure of equality between the crime and the punishment. Thus, Cesare Beccaria, an Italian classical theorist, maintained that "for a punishment to attain its end, the evil which it inflicts has only to exceed the advantage derivable from the crime" (1767). Criminal activities were viewed as a product of free choices made by rational beings on the basis of a consideration of profit and cost. Consistent with this view, the function of criminal law and criminal justice was to design punishments that would *deter*, but that would do so without inflicting more pain than was necessary. Classical theorists attacked arbitrary and cruel practices of the criminal justice system in many European countries. Their strong emphasis on human reason and the perfectibility of social institutions had a lasting impact on the treatment of criminal offenders.

Although the classical school's principles of deterrence became part of the philosophical foundation for our criminal justice system, they were attacked while the juvenile justice system was developing. The optimism of the classical school of criminology during the eighteenth century gave way to the reformatory movement of the nineteenth century, which sought to save the child from the perils of contemporary society. The function of the juvenile court, according to the nineteenth century reformers, was not to punish, nor was it to design and implement penalties that would deter. Rather, the court was to find appropriate techniques for "treating" or "helping" troubled youths. However, most evaluations of the system as it has actually developed claim that such distinctions have not been realized:

> In theory the juvenile court was to be helpful and rehabilitative rather than punitive. In fact the distinction often disappears, not only because of the absence of facilities and personnel but also because of the limits of knowledge and technique. In theory the court's action was to affix no stigmatizing label. In fact a delinquent is generally viewed by employers, schools, the armed services—by society generally—as a criminal. In theory the court was to treat children guilty of criminal acts in noncriminal ways. In fact it labels truants and runaways as junior criminals.
>
> In theory the court's operations could justifiably be informal, its findings and decisions made without observing ordinary procedural safeguards, because it would act only in the best interest of the child. In fact it frequently does nothing more nor less than deprive a child of liberty without due process of law—knowing not what else to do and needing, whether admittedly or not, to act in the community's interest even more imperatively than the child's. In theory it was to exercise its protective powers to bring an errant child back into the fold. In fact there is increasing reason to believe that its intervention reinforces the juvenile's unlawful impulses. In theory it was to concentrate on each case the best of current social science learning. In fact it has often become a vested interest in its turn, loathe to cooperate with innovated programs or avail itself of forward-looking methods. (President's Commission on Law Enforcement and Administration of Justice, 1967:9)

Thus, despite the efforts of the nineteenth century reformers to influence the philosophical underpinnings of the juvenile justice system, it appears that the issue of deterrence—whether it develops out of a fear of "punishment" or a fear of "treatment"—is potentially relevant to juveniles.

DETERRENCE THEORY AND EXPLANATIONS OF DELINQUENCY

Deterrence was not only rejected as part of the underlying philosophy of the juvenile court but was also viewed by most social scientists as irrelevant to explaining or understanding either crime or delinquency. For instance, in his influential *Principles of Criminology*, Edwin Sutherland wrote that "control . . . lies in the group pressure, the recognition and response secured by lawful conduct rather than fear of punishment. Not the fear of legal penalties but the fear of loss of status in the group is the effective deterrent" (1924:374). Sutherland argued that the whole psychology underlying the classical school, with its emphasis on free will and the calculations of pleasures and pains, was questionable.

Of the three dominant sociological theories of delinquency examined in Chapter 6, none specifically includes deterrence in its explanation of delinquency. The most popular sociological theories have been motivational theories, which focus on the social, cultural, and interactional forces that push and pull people into lawbreaking. The emphasis has been on people as social and moral beings who make decisions on the basis of values, norms, and beliefs, rather than on the basis of rational calculations of losses and gains. Although social control theory, as an amotivational theory, could readily encompass legal sanctions as a potential barrier to crime and delinquency, most formulations have ignored this potentiality. Social control theorists have instead focused on what are referred to as "informal" control mechanisms and "positive" social bonds (such as attachment, commitment, involvement, and acceptance of conventional beliefs).

Although it has generally been ignored in major theories and has been questioned repeatedly by prominent criminologists, the study of deterrence emerged as a major research topic in the late 1960s and continued to grow in prominence in the 1970s. This growth in interest appears to have been stimulated by the development of the labeling perspective, which focuses on the role that laws, law enforcement, and sanctioning can play in magnifying, rather than reducing, social problems. From a labeling perspective, not only is deterrence questionable, but criminalization, stigmatization, and legal sanctioning are also potential *sources* of the very problems they are supposed to solve. Labeling theory sees reactions to deviance as a process that escalates the problem of deviance by attaching labels to people. Deterrence theory argues that by reacting to deviance with the imposition of sanctions, we can deter individuals from deviance. The two perspectives are polar opposites for the most part. However, the development of the labeling perspective had the effect of shifting the emphasis from deviant behavior to *reactions* to deviance and, especially, the *consequences* of reactions to deviance. Thus, although labeling theorists attacked deterrence, the very fact that they did so (coupled with the surge of interest in reactions to deviance) helped to generate new interest in deterrence.

CONCEPTS OF DETERRENCE

Before we can examine the research literature on deterrence, we must deal with several conceptual matters. First, some deterrence theorists insist that a distinction be made between "deterrence" and the "general preventive effects of punishment." Jack Gibbs, one of the most prominent deterrence theorists, has defined deterrence as "the omission of an act as a response to the perceived risk and fear of punishment for *contrary* behavior" (1975:2). From Gibbs's perspective, certain ways of preventing or inhibiting lawbreaking do *not* involve fear of punishment and therefore should be viewed as "preventive consequences of legal punishment" rather than deterrence. For example, locking people up may prevent certain forms of crime (such as auto theft) while those people are locked away, but this preventive consequence is called *incapacitation* rather than deterrence. In addition, people may refrain from lawbreaking because they know and respect the law. If that knowledge and respect were influenced by punishment, it would be called an *enculturation* or *socialization* consequence of punishment. In this case, punishment would prevent crime through socialization rather than fear of punishment. Gibbs listed a total of ten preventive effects of punishment other than deterrence, but the important point here is that some theorists restrict the term *deterrence* specifically to the inhibiting effects of *fear of punishment.* On the other hand, Gibbs himself noted that we may never be able to isolate the effect of fear of punishment from other preventive effects of punishment. Thus, the research we will summarize in the next section deals with the preventive effects of punishment but is generally phrased in terms of the study of deterrence.

Another very important conceptual matter in examining the research literature on deterrence (or "preventive effects") is the distinction between *specific deterrence* and *general deterrence*. Specific deterrence refers to the omission of *further* criminal or delinquent acts *by the individual who was punished.* For instance, if a juvenile refrains from shoplifting because he or she was caught and fears being caught again, such an occurrence would be an instance of specific deterrence. In contrast, general deterrence refers to the omission of criminal or delinquent acts as a result of *anticipated or feared punishment* among those who have not been punished. If a juvenile refrains from shoplifting out of fear of punishment even though he or she has never been punished, that occurrence would be an instance of general deterrence. The two types of deterrence are distinct, and in this chapter we will focus most extensively on the general deterrence literature. Studies of the impact of different reactions to delinquency on delinquents will be considered in the next two chapters.

Another distinction of some importance for understanding the research literature on deterrence is the difference between two types of general deterrence: *absolute deterrence* and *restrictive deterrence.* Jack Gibbs has defined the two as follows:

> The term "absolute deterrence" denotes instances where an individual has refrained throughout life from a particular type of criminal act because in whole or in part he or she perceived some risk of someone suffering a punishment as a response to the crime.
>
> Defined explicitly, "restrictive deterrence" is the curtailment of a certain type of criminal activity by an individual during some period because in whole or in part the curtailment is perceived by the individual as reducing the risk that someone will be punished as a response to the activity, even though no one has suffered a punishment as a consequence of that individual's criminal activity. (1975:32–33)

In short, if people never break the law as a result of fear of punishment, the deterrence process would be "absolute." If people merely restrain themselves to some degree, then the process would be "restrictive."

These conceptual distinctions are important for assessing the arguments for and against deterrence because parties to the debate may be referring to quite different issues. For example, someone might advance the following argument: "Sending people to prison does not deter crime but, instead, increases it. Look at the high recidivism rate among convicts. Obviously, the prisons are not deterring." This particular argument focuses on *specific* deterrence. It has no bearing on whether the threat of imprisonment deters the *general* public. It would be possible for imprisonment to increase crime among those imprisoned and yet decrease crime among potential offenders. The net effect of an increase in the use of imprisonment might be a decrease in the crime rate (via general deterrence), even given an increase in recidivism (that is, a failure of specific deterrence). The main point is that we should at least make certain that we are talking about the same phenomenon when debating the issue of deterrence.

Another possible critique of deterrence might take the following form: "Most Americans drank during Prohibition. Most adolescents have tried marijuana. Virtually all people break the law sometime during their lives. Obviously people are not deterred by the law." This type of statement focuses on *absolute* deterrence. It has no necessary bearing on whether people *restrict* their involvement in crime or delinquency as a result of threat or fear of punishment. If *everyone* in a population violates a law sometime, then absolute deterrence does not exist. However, even then, the threat of punishment might restrict people's involvement to one or two transgressions on the average, rather than ten or twelve.

RESEARCH ON GENERAL DETERRENCE

Most of the research on deterrence does not deal directly with juveniles since it is based on crime rates for the general population and focuses on punishments that are more commonly meted out to adults than to juveniles. For example, many studies have attempted to measure the deterrent effect of capital punishment by analyzing homicide rates for states or for the total United States population. Homicide is actually quite rare among juveniles, as is the probability of being executed or sentenced to death. The median age of prisoners under sentence of death in 1975 was twenty-six, and only 9 percent of those prisoners were under the age of twenty. However, we will include the research on capital punishment in our discussion for two reasons. First, attacks on the deterrence doctrine in general quite commonly draw on research on capital punishment. Second, there is still dissension over whether juveniles should be treated differently than adults. It is conceivable that punishments that have been primarily limited to adults could be more commonly extended to juveniles in the future.

Capital Punishment

Several types of evidence have been brought to bear on the general deterrent effects of capital punishment. One type of evidence has been based on comparisons of capital crime rates for states with and without the statutory possibility of capital punishment. Such comparisons have shown that states without the death penalty do not have higher capital crime rates than states with the death penalty. Similarly, rates in single states before and after abolishment of the death penalty, as well as comparisons of those before and after statistics with data for states retaining capital punishment, have failed to show a deterrent effect. These findings hold true even in comparisons of similar or contiguous states (Bowers, 1974; Schuessler, 1952; Sellin, 1967).

Such research has been criticized, however, in that the statutory possibility of the death penalty does not mean that it is actually used or that those so sentenced are executed. Actually, the number of people executed has declined steadily during the period for which national statistics are available (see Table 9–1). The peak year for actual executions was 1938 when 190 prisoners were executed. By the 1950s the number had declined to less than 100 per year, and by 1960 there were 56. From 1968 to 1976 there were none.

TABLE 9‑1 *Prisoners Executed under Civil Authority in the United States, by Race and Offense, 1930–1976*

Year	All Races				White			
	All Offenses	Murder	Rape	Other Offenses[1]	All Offenses	Murder	Rape	Other Offenses[1]
All Years	3,859	3,334	455	70	1,751	1,664	48	39
1976	0	0	0	0	0	0	0	0
1975	0	0	0	0	0	0	0	0
1974	0	0	0	0	0	0	0	0
1973	0	0	0	0	0	0	0	0
1972	0	0	0	0	0	0	0	0
1971	0	0	0	0	0	0	0	0
1970	0	0	0	0	0	0	0	0
1969	0	0	0	0	0	0	0	0
1968	0	0	0	0	0	0	0	0
1967	2	2	0	0	1	1	0	0
1966	1	1	0	0	1	1	0	0
1965	7	7	0	0	6	6	0	0
1964	15	9	6	0	8	5	3	0
1963	21	18	2	1	13	12	0	1
1962	47	41	4	2	28	26	2	0
1961	42	33	8	1	20	18	1	1
1960	56	44	8	4	21	18	0	3
1959	49	41	8	0	16	15	1	0
1958	49	41	7	1	20	20	0	0
1957	65	54	10	1	34	32	2	0
1956	65	52	12	1	21	20	0	1
1955	76	65	7	4	44	41	1	2
1954	81	71	9	1	38	37	1	0
1953	62	51	7	4	30	25	1	4
1952	83	71	12	0	36	35	1	0
1951	105	87	17	1	57	55	2	0
1950	82	68	13	1	40	36	4	0
1949	119	107	10	2	50	49	0	1
1948	119	95	22	2	35	32	1	2
1947	153	129	23	1	42	40	2	0
1946	131	107	22	2	46	45	0	1
1945	117	90	26	1	41	37	4	0
1944	120	96	24	0	47	45	2	0
1943	131	118	13	0	54	54	0	0
1942	147	115	25	7	67	57	4	6
1941	123	102	20	1	59	55	4	0
1940	124	105	15	4	49	44	2	3
1939	160	145	12	3	80	79	0	1
1938	190	154	25	11	96	89	1	6
1937	147	133	13	1	69	67	2	0
1936	195	181	10	4	92	86	2	4
1935	199	184	13	2	119	115	2	2
1934	168	154	14	0	65	64	1	0
1933	160	151	7	2	77	75	1	1
1932	140	128	10	2	62	62	0	0
1931	153	137	15	1	77	76	1	0
1930	155	147	6	2	90	90	0	0

[1]Includes 25 executed for armed robbery, 20 for kidnapping, 11 for burglary, 6 for sabotage, 6 for aggravated assault, and 2 for espionage.

TABLE 9-1   *(Continued)*

Black				Other			
All Offenses	Murder	Rape	Other Offenses[1]	All Offenses	Murder	Rape	Other Offenses[1]
2,066	1,630	405	31	42	40	2	0
0	0	0	0	0	0	0	0
0	0	0	0	0	0	0	0
0	0	0	0	0	0	0	0
0	0	0	0	0	0	0	0
0	0	0	0	0	0	0	0
0	0	0	0	0	0	0	0
0	0	0	0	0	0	0	0
0	0	0	0	0	0	0	0
0	0	0	0	0	0	0	0
1	1	0	0	0	0	0	0
0	0	0	0	0	0	0	0
1	1	0	0	0	0	0	0
7	4	3	0	0	0	0	0
8	6	2	0	0	0	0	0
19	15	2	2	0	0	0	0
22	15	7	0	0	0	0	0
35	26	8	1	0	0	0	0
33	26	7	0	0	0	0	0
28	20	7	1	1	1	0	0
31	22	8	1	0	0	0	0
43	31	12	0	1	1	0	0
32	24	6	2	0	0	0	0
42	33	8	1	1	1	0	0
31	25	6	0	1	1	0	0
47	36	11	0	0	0	0	0
47	31	15	1	1	1	0	0
42	32	9	1	0	0	0	0
67	56	10	1	2	2	0	0
82	61	21	0	2	2	0	0
111	89	21	1	0	0	0	0
84	61	22	1	1	1	0	0
75	52	22	1	1	1	0	0
70	48	22	0	3	3	0	0
74	63	11	0	3	1	2	0
80	58	21	1	0	0	0	0
63	46	16	1	1	1	0	0
75	61	13	1	0	0	0	0
77	63	12	2	3	3	0	0
92	63	24	5	2	2	0	0
74	62	11	1	4	4	0	0
101	93	8	0	2	2	0	0
77	66	11	0	3	3	0	0
102	89	13	0	1	1	0	0
81	74	6	1	2	2	0	0
75	63	10	2	3	3	0	0
72	57	14	1	4	4	0	0
65	57	6	2	0	0	0	0

Source: Law Enforcement Assistance Administration, National Criminal Justice Information and Statistics Services. *Capital Punishment.* Washington, D.C.: U.S. Government Printing Office, 1977.

Does the actual occurrence of executions reduce capital crime rates? The safest answer to that question is that there is no consistent evidence of a deterrent effect. For example, Leonard Savitz (1958) examined the frequency of felony murders in Philadelphia (that is, murders committed in the act of committing another crime) several weeks before and after well-publicized executions and found no evidence of a deterrent effect. In contrast, a more recent piece of research on the issue by an economist, Isaac Ehrlich (1975), claimed to show a deterrent effect of executions on homicide rates. After analyzing homicide rates and executions from 1933 to 1969, Ehrlich concluded that each additional execution per year may have prevented seven or eight murders. The reason we indicate that he "claimed" to show a deterrent effect is because subsequent evaluations and replications of Ehrlich's analysis have seriously challenged his conclusions. One of the problems is that after 1962 the homicide rate climbed rapidly, while the number of executions continued to decline (as it had been doing for several decades). These factors accounted for most of the association that Ehrlich observed. Moreover, further analysis of data from the 1960s (Forst, 1976) led to the same old conclusion: There is at present no scientifically acceptable support for the view that capital punishment is any more of a deterrent to capital crime than imprisonment (Zeisel, 1976).

Certainty and Severity of Punishment

The issue of capital punishment was central to research on deterrence from the 1930s through the 1960s. Beginning in the late 1960s, attention shifted to the issue of whether variations in the certainty and severity of arrest and imprisonment had a deterrent effect on crime rates. Since its inauguration in a study by Jack Gibbs (1968), a common procedure in United States research has been to create measures of the certainty of punishment (for example, the number of admissions to prison for a certain offense relative to the number of such offenses known) and the severity of punishment (for example, the number of months served in prison for a certain type of offense) within the different states. If deterrence notions are to be supported, then states that have a higher degree of certainty and severity of punishment for a certain offense should have a lower incidence of that offense than states in which the punishment is less certain and less severe. In general, the data have supported that hypothesis (although, as always, with some controversy). Research has also indicated some variations in deterrence by type of offense.

Atunes and Hunt (1973) noted that research results have been consistent with the conclusion that certainty of punishment "has a mild deterrent impact," but that severity of punishment appears to be relevant only to homicide. Their own analysis led them to similar conclusions. They found that the greater a state's certainty of punishment, the lower that state's crime rates, but that severity of punishment only made a difference for crime rates when certainty of punishment was high. If the chances of being punished are quite low, then it appears that the severity of the punishment does not matter.

There are several major problems with deterrence research that uses official statistics. Two of them are the same problems we have dealt with throughout this text: causal order and spuriousness. It is conceivable that states with high crime rates have low rates of certainty of punishment because of the "overload" on the criminal justice system. Hence, a relationship between low certainty and high crime rates could reflect the overload rather than deterrence, (that is, fear of punishment). Moreover, any such relationship could be due to other factors, such as the moral climate or degree of social condemnation regarding particular types of offenses. When the populace is relatively intolerant of a certain crime, that crime may have both a high certainty of punishment and a low crime rate because of moral and social condemnation rather than because of deterrence (Erickson, Gibbs, and Jensen, 1977). Finally, a third major problem confronting such research is separating *incapacitation* effects from *deterrence* effects. If a state has a high rate of certainty of imprisonment, then the crime rate for that state may be low because heavy contributors to the crime rate are locked away. This would be an incapacitation effect, rather than an effect of fear of punishment.

A study by Michael Geerken and Walter Gove (1977) attempted to assess which of several possible interpretations of the relationship between certainty of punishment and crime rates was most plausible— deterrence, overload, or incapacitation. Through an analysis of data for all cities with a population of 500,000 or more they concluded that predictions derived from deterrence theory receive more support than do those derived from interpretations of the relationship as the result of overload or incapacitation. To reach this conclusion, Geerken and Gove tested the argument advanced by numerous deterrence theorists (for example, Chambliss, 1967; Andenaes, 1971; Zimring and Hawkins, 1973) that rational, "instrumental" crimes (such as stealing) are more readily deterred than emotional, "expressive" sorts of crimes (such as most murders). They posited that the deterrence model, being a rational model, should be most applicable to rational, property-oriented offenses directed at profit and least applicable to emotional crimes of interpersonal violence, such as murder and assault. Their findings (as well as some earlier research) were consistent with this hypothesis. They found that certainty of arrest had a strong effect on property crimes, a moderate association with rape, and little or no relationship to homicide or assault.

EXPERIMENTAL RESEARCH ON DETERRENCE

The ideal procedure for dealing with problems of causal order and spuriousness is an experimental model. By manipulating the certainty and severity of punishment and measuring the subsequent effects, the problem of causal order is solved, and by controlling other conditions, problems of spuriousness can be minimized. However, controlled experiments relevant to many deterrence issues are ethically impossible. To illustrate these problems, Hans Zeisel outlined some possible experiments with the death penalty:

> How morally and legally impossible such an experiment is can easily be seen if its details are sketched out. In one conceivable version a state would have to decree that citizens convicted of a capital crime and born on odd-numbered days of the month would be subject to the death penalty; citizens born on even-numbered days would face life in prison. A significantly lower number of capital crimes committed by persons born on uneven days would confirm the deterrent effect. The date of birth here is a device of randomly dividing the population into halves by a criterion that we will assume cannot be manipulated.
>
> The equally impossible experiment that would test the effect of differential frequencies of execution would require at least three randomly selected groups. In the first group everybody convicted of a capital crime would be executed. In the second, only every other such convict (again selected by lot) would be executed. In the third, nobody would be executed. (1976)

The deterrence experiments that have been done have been limited to such activities as classroom cheating and paying taxes. For instance, Charles Tittle and Allan Rowe (1973) carried out an experiment in which college students were allowed to grade their own exams. Students were initially reminded of their moral obligation to grade their exams honestly. Such an appeal had no effect. Later the students were told that spot checks of their accuracy in grading would be made and offenders punished. The threat of sanction did reduce cheating. It was less effective for males than for females and less effective for those experiencing disparity between earned grades and expected grades. Those who were dissatisfied with their grades were less likely to be deterred than those who were content with their grades.

With the cooperation of the Internal Revenue Service, Richard Schwartz and Sonja Orleans (1967) designed a field experiment in which sets of people were randomly assigned (1) to be interviewed and made aware of the penalties for income tax evasion, (2) to be interviewed and reminded of their moral obligation to pay taxes, (3) to be interviewed with neither of these messages, and (4) not to be interviewed at all. Subjects in both the moral-appeal and sanction-threat groups paid more taxes than either of the other two groups, with the moral appeal apparently making the biggest difference.

Although experimental studies can avoid the problems confronting statistical studies, experimental research has its own problems. Classroom cheating is not a crime, and the way people behave in regard to tax payments may not be generalizable to other types of behavior. Moreover, in the real world people may not perceive the threat of sanctions, whereas in experimental research the threat can be directly communicated.

SURVEY RESEARCH ON DETERRENCE

Several deterrence theorists have noted that deterrence theory is a psychological theory in that it makes certain assumptions about the *perception* of risk of apprehension or punishment (Jensen, 1969; Waldo and Chiricos, 1972; Erickson, Gibbs, and Jensen, 1977). As a "perceptual" theory, deterrence theory presumes some public knowledge and awareness of legal sanctions. In fact, Jensen, Erickson, and Gibbs have argued that the central assertion of the deterrence doctrine is that "the more members of a population perceive the punishment for a type of offense as being certain, severe and celeritous (swift), the lower the rate for that population" (1978:58). Thus, subjective or perceptual estimates of risk of punishment are viewed as more directly relevant to testing deterrence hypotheses than the probabilities reflected in official statistics. Moreover, by focusing on perceptions of the nonincarcerated public, the problem of incapacitation effects is solved.

Although most of the research on perceptions of risk has been consistent with the deterrence doctrine, such research has not yielded a perfectly consistent set of conclusions. For example, in interviews with a sample of youths thirteen to sixteen years old, Martin Gold (1970) asked: "Out of every ten kids who commit an offense, how many get caught?" Gold found very little difference between delinquents and nondelinquents in such perceptions and concluded that his findings cast considerable doubt on deterrence theory.

A study of college students by Bailey and Lott (1976) also failed to support deterrence notions. Bailey and Lott gathered data from 268 college students enrolled in sociology courses and found no significant relationships between number of reported criminal offenses and perceived certainty of punishment (likelihood of arrest and conviction) or between number of reported criminal offenses and perceived severity of punishment.

In contrast to these two studies, eight others have reported some degree of support for the deterrence theory of certainty of punishment (Jensen, 1969; Waldo and Chiricos, 1972; Grasmick and Milligan, 1976; Kraut, 1976; Minor, 1976, Silberman, 1976; Tittle, 1977; Jensen, Erickson, and Gibbs, 1978). Like objective deterrence research, survey research is more likely to support arguments regarding certainty of punishment than it is to support those regarding severity of punishment. Two of the most recent survey studies suggested that the more socially intolerable property-oriented offenses may be the most deterrable.

Table 9–2, which is from a perceptual study by Jensen, Erickson, and Gibbs (1978), suggests that the three variables—degree of social condemnation of delinquent acts, number of delinquent friends, and perceived

TABLE 9–2 *Delinquent Offenses, by Perceived Personal Risk, Social Condemnation, and Delinquent Friends*

Number of Delinquent Friends	Number of Self-Reported Offenses	High Social Condemnation			Low Social Condemnation		
		Low Perceived Risk	Medium Perceived Risk	High Perceived Risk	Low Perceived Risk	Medium Perceived Risk	High Perceived Risk
No delinquent friends	0	42%	52%	68%	23%	31%	48%
	1–2	38%	37%	27%	35%	49%	32%
	3+	20%	11%	5%	42%	20%	19%
One or two delinquent friends	0	30%	38%	41%	12%	33%	22%
	1–2	29%	41%	43%	38%	42%	61%
	3+	41%	21%	16%	50%	26%	17%
Three or more delinquent friends	0	11%	22%	29%	6%	15%	38%
	1–2	25%	42%	48%	27%	32%	38%
	3+	63%	36%	22%	68%	52%	23%

Source: G. Jensen, M. L. Erickson, and J. P. Gibbs. "Perceived Risk of Punishment and Self-Reported Delinquency." *Social Forces* 57 (September 1978):57–78.

risk of getting caught—are all related to delinquency. Comparing the extremes, we find that only 5 percent (third row of percentages, third column) of the high school students in this study who had no delinquent friends and who were high in condemnation of delinquent acts and in perceived risk of getting caught had committed three or more delinquent acts. At the other end of the continuum, we find that 68 percent (bottom row of percentages, fourth column) of students with several delinquent friends, low condemnation, and low perceived risk of getting caught had committed three or more delinquent acts. Jensen, Erickson, and Gibbs found perceptions of risk to be associated with delinquency no matter what additional variables were taken into account. Thus it appears that the relationship between perceived risk of punishment and delinquency is not spurious.

The one key issue confronting perceptual research on deterrence is causal order. It has not been demonstrated that the perceived threat or fear of punishment *precedes* involvement in delinquency. Those who perceive low risk may be those who have violated the law already and have not been caught. Beliefs about punishment and delinquent behavior may be interrelated. Environmental responses to behavior may shape perceptions or beliefs about risk, and those beliefs in turn may affect the probability of future delinquency. Perceptual studies have only shown an association between perception of risk and delinquent behavior; the relationship has not been fully untangled.

Although each type of deterrence research has its shortcomings, the shortcomings vary from one type to another. Thus, perceptual research has not demonstrated causal order, but it has suggested an association between perceived risk and criminal or delinquent behavior in many different samples of the population. Experimental work solves the problem of causal order, but it has been limited to a narrow range of lawbreaking activities and its findings may not be generalizable to everyday situations. Deterrence research has been confronted with issues of spuriousness, incapacitation, overload, and all the problems stemming from the use of official statistics. At present, the whole body of research supports the *tentative* conclusion that stiffer law enforcement could reduce the extent of several forms of crime and delinquency. Although this hypothesis has not been proven conclusively, there appears to be more compatible than contrary evidence.

LABELING THEORY AND GENERAL LABELING EFFECTS

Our criminal and juvenile justice systems are based on the assumption that laws that accord the state the right to regulate certain types of conduct are necessary for the prevention and control of undesirable or injurious behavior. Moreover, the enforcement of those laws is presumed to be necessary if they are to have their intended effects. Such assumptions, at one time taken for granted, have been challenged for several decades now by labeling theorists, who advocate examining the unanticipated, hidden, and negative consequences of law and law enforcement.

In considering the deviance of individuals, labeling theorists emphasize the role that organizational processing plays in "engulfment" in deviant careers. In considering deviance on a societal level, they focus on the "secondary expansion" of social problems as a result of the legal reaction to them. Arguments that processing children as delinquent has the self-fulfilling consequence of encouraging further delinquency reflect the approach of labeling theorists to individual deviance, while arguments concerning the consequences of "overcriminalization" or "overlegislation" reflect their societal concern. In both instances, the emphasis is on the role that law and law enforcement can play in compounding the problems that they are intended to solve.

Although not specifically identified as a labeling theorist, the late Arnold Rose (1968) outlined several ways in which he felt "law innovators" and law enforcers create new problems in trying to cope with present problems. In Rose's words, "the law helps to cause social problems" in the following ways:

> (1) A social value was enacted into statute, or it entered the common law, at an earlier period, and is inappropriate to current expectations for behavior. (2) There exists a certain conflict of social values, and the law supports one set, thereby driving the other set underground and defining behavior in conformity with this second set of social values as criminal or against public policy. (3) The law socially defines some manifestations of common "everyday" behavior as criminal or deviant, both to the individual who is apprehended in the behavior and to the community at large, and hence makes this behavior seem serious and inescapable, whereas without the law or the apprehension, the deviant behavior would appear trivial and transitory. (4) The law inhibits therapy for certain kinds of illnesses or addictions. (5) It makes certain kinds of illegitimate businesses highly lucrative and hence perpetuates them. (6) It rewards certain deviant forms of behavior, making it difficult for the deviator to return to normal behavior. (7) It drives certain kinds of compulsive deviants to larceny in order to maintain their compulsions. (8) It creates certain avoidable dangers to health, such as abortions practiced under careless conditions. (9) It encourages certain collusions and perjuries to "get around the law," which are themselves illegal and encourage disrespect for law. (10) It "cements" or stabilizes certain social problems that would otherwise wither away and disappear. (11) It expands and "systematizes" certain minor and limited social problems into major and comprehensive ones. (1968:42–43)

In developing this list, Rose drew upon the work of Edwin Schur. A chapter in Schur's book *Our Criminal Society* (1969a) is entitled "Unnecessary Crimes: The Perils of Overlegislation." Among the behaviors that

Schur felt were unnecessarily labeled as crimes are abortion, homosexuality, drug addiction, prostitution, and gambling. In Schur's view, laws that make such behaviors crimes are "blatantly ineffective and unenforceable" since the behaviors involve consensual transactions and lack complaining victims. According to Schur, enforcement of legislation in these areas is not only ineffective but has negative consequences as well. Drug legislation that makes drug use a criminal act is cited as necessitating questionable law enforcement practices (for example, entrapment and paid informers), supporting a black market and organized crime, forcing people to engage in other forms of crime (such as theft and prostitution), and reinforcing the development and expansion of a drug subculture. In sum, rather than deterring consensual crimes, Schur's belief is that the labeling of such activities as criminal generates new and (in ways) more serious problems.

Drug Legislation

As we have noted, labeling theorists believe that legislation can create new problems and that labeling certain acts as criminal can actually increase the very activity that the labeling was intended to deter. With regard to drug laws, Erich Goode has written that "ironically and tragically, it is the law and its enforcement that is principally responsible for the size of the addict population, for the recent increase in addiction, and for a majority of the most harmful features of drug use and the drug scene" (1972:181). However, in supporting such labeling arguments the emphasis tends to be on the way the law and law enforcement transform the "drug problem" *in general*, rather than on the way they affect the specifically targeted behavior. For example, Goode summarized data that suggested that the number of heroin addicts decreased but that addiction in general was transformed, following the passage of the Harrison Act in 1914 and the establishment of the Bureau of Narcotics in 1930. With the passage of the Harrison Act, over-the-counter sale of narcotic preparations was outlawed. A deterrence theorist could legitimately argue that that legislation had a general deterrent effect on heroin addiction. However, in attacking deterrence arguments, Goode shifted the focus to addiction in general. After noting the apparent deterrent impact of the outlawing of heroin, Goode argued:

> Clearly, then, what happened as a result of the Harrison Act was not a
> diminution of a once large addict population but the appearance of a
> totally different population altogether. Far from reducing a problem, leg-
> islation and enforcement practices on drugs appear to have *created a*
> *problem* out of whole cloth. The federal laws outlawing the sale of nar-
> cotics seem to have created three distinct groups from the existing

addict population. The first of these groups represents the majority of the middle class addicts, mostly women; when the supply of opium and morphine was discontinued for the nervous, distressed housewife, she eventually turned to the use of barbiturates, under the care of her physician. What the law did for this segment of the population of addicts was to take the over-the-counter narcotics away and replace them with sedatives, by prescription. *Exactly the same types of people who used narcotics in 1900 are now using barbiturates* —middle-aged, middle-class white women with various quasi-medical, largely emotional problems that (they feel) can be solved by taking a drug. The laws did absolutely nothing to terminate this class of addicts, who certainly were in the majority in 1900—they simply changed the drug to which people were addicted.

The second group created by the narcotic laws consists of those addicts who discontinued use altogether. But it is likely that this segment comprised the least addicted of the turn-of-the-century addict population. Thus the legislation probably "helped" only those who were most capable of being helped, and who constituted the least troublesome problem anyway. The third segment of the addict population constitutes the present group of "street" addicts. A certain proportion of the earlier addicts refused to discontinue the use of narcotics, and since they did not, or could not, obtain legally available drugs, they became dependent on an illegal supply and thus automatically joined the ranks of the criminal underworld.

It is obvious then, that the first half of the 1920s witnessed the dramatic emergence of a criminal class of addicts—*a criminal class that had not existed previously.* The link between addiction and crime—the view that the addict was by definition a criminal—was forged. The law itself created a new class of criminals. (1972:193–94)

In sum, the evidence mustered is not directly contrary to deterrence arguments. No data indicate that the outlawing of heroin led to an overall increase in the extent of heroin addiction. The arguments and evidence presented are more relevant to the *shaping* or *transformation* of the drug problem than to the inability of the legislation to deter the prohibited activity.

Even arguments concerning some of the secondary problems generated by the outlawing of heroin have been challenged. For instance, both Schur and Goode believed that drug legislation and law enforcement contributed to the creation of an addict subculture. Goode argued that before the passage of the Harrison Act there was "no addict subculture of any significance" and that "it was the criminalization of addiction that created addicts as a special and distinctive group" (1972:195). On the other hand, William McAuliffe argued that "there can be no doubt that there was . . . a substantial subculture of drug users" before the outlawing of heroin (1975:225). In analyzing research published in 1928, McAuliffe found what he considered to be all the major features of a "criminal-addict subculture" *before punitive laws came into effect.* According to McAuliffe, the legislation did not cause the problem; rather, the problem developed because of the absence of controls. Thus, punitive drug laws were a response to an already existing problem. Moreover, following the passage of the Harrison Act, the prevalence of heroin addiction in some settings declined (O'Donnell, 1967).

The argument that addicts are driven to commit other "secondary" forms of crime as a result of the law has been criticized as well. McAuliffe claimed that "almost all heroin addicts are deviant prior to drug dependence and are not mere victims of an innocently acquired habit and unreasonable laws" (1975:228). James Q. Wilson argued along similar lines (1975:153–55). He noted that we really do not know the extent to which other crimes would be affected if heroin were legalized because as many as three-fourths of known addicts have been found to have records for delinquent acts before their drug dependence. However, Wilson also noted that "heroin addiction does necessitate some degree of involvement in crime beyond that which would occur without addiction." In contrast, Greenberg and Adler (1974) have argued that criminal activity in general would be about the same regardless of addiction.

In a recent study of narcotic addicts admitted to the California Civil Addict Program, McGlothlin, Anglin, and Wilson (1978) found that addicts had a higher rate of property crime (both in terms of arrests and self-reports) during periods of addiction than at times when they were not using narcotics daily. In short, criminal activity does seem to be reinforced by addiction even though many addicts would have been involved in criminal activity despite their addiction. McGlothlin and his colleagues concluded that although policies that *limit* daily use of narcotics may not lead to total abstinence, they show promise of minimizing the social costs of addiction.

Criminalization of Homosexuality

Another area where there is considerable difference of opinion over the impact of the criminalization of behavior involves consensual homosexuality among adults. Proponents of criminal sanctions for homosexual activity argue that such sanctions are necessary to deter people from homosexuality, to communicate moral disapproval of the activity, and to prevent other crimes, such as child molestation and sadistic crimes of violence (Davis, 1973). On the other side, advocates of the decriminalization of homosexuality argue that criminal sanctions are inappropriate for the control of consensual sexual behavior, that they facilitate exploitation and blackmail of homosexuals, and that such legislation is not backed by any evidence that homosexuals are prone to other forms of crime (Schur, 1965).

Gilbert Geis and several colleagues (1976) have approached the issue of the decriminalization of homosexuality by gathering questionnaire data from police, prosecuting attorneys, and organizations for homosexuals in states that had decriminalized such activity for consenting adults at the time of their survey (Colorado, Delaware, Oregon, Hawaii, Ohio, Illinois, and Connecticut). They found that only a small minority of police and prosecuting attorneys perceived that decriminalization had had any negative impact. According to persons in law enforcement, as well as homosexuals, the change did not have the dire consequences predicted by opponents of decriminalization. Moreover, although 44 percent of the police had approved of the decriminalization of homosexuality initially, 57 percent approved of it in the postdecision survey.

Juvenile Law

The earliest statement of a labeling argument specifically relating to juvenile delinquency appeared in Frank Tannenbaum's *Crime and the Community* (1938). Tannenbaum argued that the tagging and processing of the young delinquent was a "dramatization of evil" that had self-fulfilling consequences:

> The process of making the criminal, therefore, is a process of tagging, defining, identifying, segregating, describing, emphasizing, making conscious and self-conscious; it becomes a way of stimulating, suggesting, emphasizing, and evoking the very traits that are complained of. If the theory of relation of response to stimulus has any meaning the entire process of dealing with the young delinquent is mischievous in so far as it identifies him to himself or to the environment as a delinquent person.
>
> The person becomes the thing he is described as being. Nor does it seem to matter whether the valuation is made by those who would punish or by those who would reform. In either case the emphasis is upon the conduct that is disapproved of. The parents or the policeman, the older brother or the court, the probation officer or the juvenile institution, in so far as they rest upon the thing complained of, rest upon a false ground. Their very enthusiasm defeats their aim. The harder they work to reform the evil, the greater the evil grows under their hands. The presistent suggestion, with whatever good intentions, works mischief, because it leads to bringing out the bad behavior that it would suppress. The way out is through a refusal to dramatize the evil. The less said about it the better. The more said about something else, still better. (1938:19–20)

This line of argument has been extended to deviance in general (see Lemert, 1967) and to a variety of specific types of deviance (for example, mental illness). However, the basic logic is the same in each instance: Official processing results in the application of labels to which others react in such a manner that they propel those so labeled into careers of crime and delinquency.

Since the juvenile court does not adjudicate criminal matters, discussions of criminal labeling do not technically concern juvenile delinquents. Nonetheless, it has been the labeling theorists who have mounted the most vociferous criticisms of juvenile justice in the United States. Although the juvenile court was initially conceived as an experiment in the decriminalization of juvenile lawbreaking, labeling theorists tend to view the actual changes that the court has wrought as minimal. Schur has argued that despite the terminology employed in juvenile justice, the "adjudicated delinquent is in fact stigmatized, punished, and potentially criminalized" (1973:87). The focus in this statement, however, is on how the experience of being processed through the juvenile justice system affects the individual juvenile. This specific focus is in contrast to the labeling theorists' concern over the more general effects of drug legislation and consensual crimes. The labeling theorists' major criticism of the juvenile court has been the alleged impact of adjudication on those processed through the system, or what we might call specific labeling (in contrast to specific deterrence).

Ideas about the general labeling effects of juvenile law and its enforcement are only hinted at in the literature. For example, the broad scope of juvenile delinquency statutes might promote a view among adolescents in general that laws are totally arbitrary and deserving of little respect. This possibility is suggested by Schur's argument that increased clarity, precision, and limits on the legal compass of juvenile law and juvenile court jurisdiction "would probably generate among young people greater respect for the legal system" (1973:169). An implicit assumption underlying such a statement is that juvenile law and its enforcement may have consequences for the attitudes of the juvenile population in general and not just for those who directly experience the system.

RESEARCH ON THE SPECIFIC EFFECTS OF LABELING

As we have just noted, the labeling theorists' major criticism of juvenile justice has been the possible deleterious consequences of official processing and adjudication for those juveniles who are netted by the system. In this view, the intervention of the juvenile justice system does not deter further delinquency through fear of further apprehension and processing, nor does it prevent additional delinquency through rehabilitation of the offender. Rather, the labeling critique has emphasized the role that intervention by the juvenile justice system may play in facilitating further delinquent or criminal behavior.

In this section we will consider research that has focused on the consequences of official processing by the juvenile justice system for future behavior and adolescent self-images. The latter topic is of most significance to the labeling theorists since they are interested in deviant behavior that represents or reflects a person's identity or self-image. A behaviorist would be most interested in the consequences of official processing for future *behavior* and would not feel it necessary to consider the effects of labeling on identity or self-image (see Chapter 5). These topics would be viewed by the behaviorist as hypothetical mental constructs that contribute little or nothing to understanding actual behavior. Most labeling theorists would find the focus on the consequences of official processing for subsequent rates of crime and delinquency as *relevant* to labeling theory but not necessarily *crucial*. From a labeling perspective, Edwin Schur has argued that sociologists have been challenged to study the self-concept of the deviating individual as a crucial dependent variable "to which we should pay more attention than to the deviating behavior itself" (1969b:311). Of course, the value of such a point of view depends on the theoretical inclinations of different publics, and certainly a behaviorist would not find such an emphasis crucial. Recognizing that there are divergent points of view, we will consider research on attitudes and self-conceptions, as well as future behavior. First, however, we will consider research that has attempted to determine whether official processing of juveniles has a specific deterrent or a specific labeling effect.

Specific Deterrence vs. Specific Labeling

How can we tell if official processing by the juvenile justice system increases involvement in crime and delinquency? One answer might be to determine the relationship between adult crime and juvenile delinquency. Why not just look at the proportion of juveniles who acquire a record who go on to acquire a record as adults? For instance, in a study of males and females born in 1949, Shannon (1976) reported the following progression of contacts with the police: Of 677 white males, about 61 percent (414) acquired a record between the ages of six and eighteen. Of those 414, 326 acquired a record after age eighteen. In sum, of those white males labeled as juveniles, around 78 percent acquired a subsequent record. In contrast, of the white males who did not acquire a record from ages six through seventeen, about 50 percent acquired a record as an adult. Thus, those labeled as delinquent as youths were more likely than those not so labeled to acquire records when they were older (78 percent as compared to 50 percent). *One* possible conclusion based on such a difference is that labeling when young increases the chances that further delinquent or crimnal acts will be committed in the future.

However, there are other possible explanations. We have already encountered a number of social characteristics, experiences, and attitudes that are correlated with juvenile delinquency. These characteristics may account for involvement in lawbreaking activity over a period of time. Thus, a high-risk youth at age thirteen may remain a high-risk person at eighteen, twenty-one, and beyond, whether caught and labeled or not. In short, such a finding does not tell us whether the *labeling experience* increases the probability of future crime.

The scientifically ideal methodological procedure for assessing whether official processing of juveniles increases involvement in crime or delinquency would be an experiment in which youths were ignored or processed on a random basis. Under the right circumstances, the groups would be nearly the same on every conceivable characteristic *except* the one under experimental control (that is, being processed or labeled). Since such experiments are legitimately challenged on ethical grounds, the alternative is to examine the relationship between labeling and future delinquency among youths who are as similar as possible in terms of other characteristics. This procedure involves comparing "matched pairs" and was the basis for Martin Gold and Jay Williams's study of "the aftermath of apprehension" (1969). Gold and Williams's data included self-reports of delinquent activity, as well as police and court records. On this basis, they were able to compare youths involved in delinquency who had been caught with youths who had not been caught. Out of 847 cases, 74 youths had been apprehended. Gold and Williams were able to match 35 of these cases with boys who had committed similar offenses and who had other similar characteristics, but who had not been apprehended. Labeling effects would be suggested if those apprehended subsequently committed *more* offenses than those not apprehended. Specific deterrence or rehabilitative effects would be suggested if the apprehended youths subsequently committed *fewer* offenses than those who got away. Of the 35 pairs, 20 comparisons supported labeling notions in that the apprehended youth had higher subsequent delinquent involvement than the nonapprehended youth. On the other hand, in 10 comparisons the youth who had been apprehended reported *less* involvement than the nonapprehended youth, and 5 pairs exhibited comparable involvement. Overall, 20 pairs supported labeling theory with regard to subsequent delinquency, while 15 pairs did not. The data are contrary to the view that apprehension reduces the chances of further delinquency and suggest that the opposite may be a more likely occurrence. However, the findings can also be interpreted as support for the view that apprehension may have *both* deterrent and labeling effects or that it may simply be *inconsequential.*

In contrast to Gold and Williams's study in which one set of cases had experienced a legal reaction and the other had experienced absolutely none, most of the research cited as relevant to labeling effects on future crime or delinquency focuses on the effects of *different reactions* to crime. For example, comparisons have been made between juveniles who received a court hearing and those who were released short of any formal procedure (Meade, 1974). Other studies have compared youths who became wards of the court with youths who did not (McEachern, 1968). Thornberry (1971) analyzed the subsequent offense records of youths in terms of the degree of severity of the dispositions they originally had received. In the study of deterrence, these comparisons would be viewed as relevant to establishing the "marginal deterrent efficacy" of a reaction to delinquency (Gibbs, 1975:33) since the comparison is between or among *different possible reactions*. When assessing marginal deterrent effects, the question is what "margin" of delinquency is deterred by a particular reaction beyond that which would occur given an alternative reaction. Similarly, studies of different reactions cited as relevant to labeling theory are really dealing with "marginal labeling effects" (in that these studies attempt to determine the extent to which a more severe reaction leads to a higher subsequent rate of delinquency). Actually, the topics dealt with in the next two chapters (alternative reactions, imprisonment, and diversion) are all potentially relevant to issues of labeling effects and specific deterrence. In the remainder of this section, we will deal with research that has been cited or presented as relevant to labeling theory or that has been couched in labeling terms.

Labeling and Future Behavior

The three studies of marginal labeling effects mentioned above (Meade, McEachern, and Thornberry) have generated findings that are both consistent and inconsistent with labeling arguments. For example, in a study of over two thousand youths in eight California counties, McEachern (1968) reported that those who were made wards of the court showed *less* subsequent involvement in delinquency than those dealt with less severely, but that those probationers who had the most contact with their probation officers had the highest rates of subsequently detected offenses. The latter finding could mean that the risk of *detection* increases as contact with probation officers increases. Thus, the finding may not be evidence of a labeling effect. Thornberry's study (1971) of the delinquent careers of all boys born in Philadelphia in 1945 yielded similar equivocal results. He found that youths who had been institutionalized had a lower subsequent volume of delinquency and lesser involvement in terms of seriousness of the offenses committed than youths who had not been institutionalized. On the other hand, other measures of the severity of disposition were associated with a *higher* volume of delinquency for *some* offenders. It was among the white youths and the less serious offenders that severity of reaction was associated with higher subsequent delinquency. Finally, Meade's research (1974) indicated that youths who faced a court hearing had higher subsequent rates of detected delinquency than those dealt with less formally.

These results are so variable that we cannot reach a firm conclusion about the effects of labeling. Moreover, the findings are not clearly relevant to labeling theory to begin with, since they focus on alternative reactions *after* initial apprehension and labeling. In addition, studies that

focus on subsequent delinquent activity *that is detected* (that is, "recidivism" rates derived from police data) do not have a clear bearing on the
effects of labeling on actual subsequent behavior. As we will discover in
Chapter 10, some experimental programs appear to have low recidivism
rates as compared to the recidivism rates of available alternatives. The
lower rates may reflect the unwillingness of more tolerant probation
officers to officially recognize a subsequent offense for youths in an
experimental program. Recidivism rates may therefore not be accurate
reflections of actual delinquent behavior. Thus, the results of recidivism
research can be given a number of alternative interpretations that have
little to do with either labeling or deterrence effects.

Labeling and Adolescent Attitudes and Self-Images

Another line of research relevant to labeling and delinquency has
focused on the consequences of labeling in a youth's social environment
or the potential impact of labeling on values, commitments, or self-
images. The results of this type of research have been both consistent and
inconsistent with labeling notions. For example, Foster, Dinitz, and
Reckless (1972) interviewed boys in trouble with the law and found that
very few perceived that their predicaments had generated any difficulties
with family or friends. Sethard Fisher (1972) examined the school grade-
point averages of probationers before and after being processed and found
no demonstrable effect of that experience on school grades. Probationers
were found to have lower grades on the average than other students both
before and after acquiring that legal status.

David Matza (1964) has argued that violation of the commonly held
expectations of adjudication gives rise to a "sense of injustice" and that
that sense of injustice in turn weakens "the bind of the law." In Matza's
view, the actual operation of the juvenile court regularly violates "norms
of fairness" or "due process," which confirms the delinquent's "conception of irresponsibility and feeds his sense of injustice."

Peggy Giordano (1976) has attempted to test such arguments in a study
of juvenile reactions to the justice system. She interviewed youths who
had (1) been reprimanded by the police and released, (2) proceeded as far as
an intake hearing, (3) been placed on probation, (4) been placed on probation at least twice, or (5) had not been processed by the justice system at
all. She found no significant difference in attitudes or behavior between
the group with no contact and the contact groups. Among youths who
had had some contact, the extent of system contact made no difference
for attitudes toward police but was associated with positive attitudes
toward probation officers and judges. Youths with more extensive contact
did judge police, probation officers, and judges as less "effective" than did
those with less contact. However, there was no evidence that contact or
adjudication generated a sense of injustice.

Jensen (1972) examined the differences in self-images of youths with police records and those without and found that the relationship was quite variable in different categories of junior and senior high school students. Table 9–3 shows that among black males who had police records for one offense or two or more offenses, about 47 percent at least sometimes thought of themselves as delinquent, as compared to 56 percent of the white males with a record for one offense and 72 percent of the white males with a record for two or more offenses. Among both blacks and whites, about one-third of those without records at least sometimes thought of themselves as delinquent. Thus, in both groups, those with a record were more likely to think of themselves in terms of the label. However, the biggest differences between the labeled and nonlabeled occurred among whites. Jensen also found that labeling differentiated the most among youths who held fairly positive attitudes toward the law. His analysis was consistent with an earlier study by Leroy Gould (1969) in which it was argued that if the label *delinquent* or *troublemaker* is commonly applied to a particular group, then the labeling process may have little personal relevance.

Ageton and Elliott (1974) improved upon Jensen's study by examining changes in attitudes over time and by limiting their analysis to subjects who had had no contacts with the police or court at the beginning of the study. They found that respondents with subsequent police contacts demonstrated "substantial" gains in measures of delinquent orientations as compared to respondents who had no such subsequent contacts. Moreover, neither controls for self-reported delinquency nor controls for delinquent friends altered this finding. However, further analysis revealed that police contact was related to increased delinquent orientations only for white youth. Thus, two separate studies based on large random samples or populations have yielded quite similar observations. Labeling may be more consequential for whites than for blacks.

TABLE 9–3 *Percentage Thinking of Themselves as Delinquent (Never, Sometimes, Often), by Number of Offenses and Race*

Delinquent Self-Image	Blacks			Whites		
	No Offenses	One Offense	Two or More Offenses	No Offenses	One Offense	Two or More Offenses
Never	65	53	53	62	44	28
Sometimes	27	32	34	34	47	58
Often	7	15	14	3	9	15

Source: Gary F. Jensen. "Delinquency and Adolescent Self-Conceptions: A Study of the Personal Relevance of Infraction." *Social Problems* 20 (Summer 1972):84–103. Copyright 1972 by the Society for the Study of Social Problems. Reprinted by permission.

John Hepburn (1977) gathered data from two samples: (1) 105 white males (aged fourteen to seventeen) with no record of police contact who were randomly selected from school enrollments, and (2) 96 white males (aged fourteen to seventeen) who had had formal contact with the municipal police. Hepburn found that official intervention was not significantly related to self-concept variables when other variables, such as self-reported delinquency, were taken into account. On the other hand, some measures of official intervention did have an impact on respondents' predictions of future delinquency, measures of "commitment to delinquent others," and attitudes toward the police. Hepburn suggested that the relationships between official intervention and measures of "self-satisfaction" or "delinquent identification" are spurious. He argued that the greater the involvement in delinquency, the greater the chances of being labeled and of developing a delinquent identity. However, according to Hepburn, official labeling or intervention itself has no impact on delinquent identity.

Once again, we are confronted with some consistent and some divergent findings. Data from Hepburn's study, as well as from Ageton and Elliott's, suggest that labeling affects the development of delinquent value orientations. The studies by Jensen, Ageton and Elliott, and Thornberry (1971) suggest that labeling effects are more prominent for whites than for blacks. However, Hepburn found a spurious relationship between official intervention and measures of delinquent identity, whereas Jensen implied that official intervention did have effects on the degree to which an adolescent thought in terms of the label.

The inconsistency may reflect differences in the samples studied by different researchers. Jensen (forthcoming) found that youths who acquired a record were more likely to express delinquent self-evaluations than those without police records, even when the variable of delinquent behavior was controlled. Hepburn found that official intervention had no impact when self-reported delinquency was taken into account. However, Hepburn's sample was purposely designed to overrepresent delinquents with records. Jensen's sample included only those officially recorded delinquents who happened to be included in a representative sample of the junior and senior high school populations in the area studied. In short, Hepburn's sample included more labeled delinquents than Jensen's, and possibly more heavily involved delinquents as well. If labeling has different consequences depending on the extent to which the sample is involved in delinquency, then the apparently disparate findings of these two studies could be reconciled. In a further analysis of the issue, Jensen (forthcoming) found that the differences in delinquent self-evaluations between the labeled and unlabeled are very slight among youths who report having committed several delinquent acts. However, among adolescents who are less involved in delinquency, differences between the labeled and unlabeled are more prominent. In view of this finding and the others outlined above, it appears that the effects of official intervention, processing, or labeling may be quite variable from one group or setting to another.

THE SOCIAL MEANING OF SANCTIONS

The observation that labeling and sanctions may reinforce, deter, or make no difference for subsequent behavior or self-images has stimulated theoretical attempts to specify the conditions under which sanctions or labels may have different consequences. For instance, Bernard Thorsell and Lloyd Klemke (1972) argued that the labeling process may be both a reinforcement and a deterrent. Its positive and negative consequences for future behavior depend upon several conditions that have yet to be studied. In addition to the stage in a person's deviant career when labels are applied, these conditions include: (1) whether or not the label is confidential; (2) whether the person labeled cares about or acknowledges the legitimacy or authority of the labeler; (3) whether the label can be easily removed; and (4) whether official labels generate a negative social response.

Other theorists (for example, Charles Tittle, 1975) have attempted to develop comparable lists of factors that might improve our knowledge of the conditions under which sanctions have different effects. However, very little research has been done in this area. We have seen evidence that perceived threat of punishment may deter some types of offenses more than it does others, but that observation is the only specification suggested thus far in research literature. The fact of the matter is that we know very little about such seemingly simple (but, in reality, complex) issues as the actual meaning of the labeling process or the threat of labeling to juveniles.

In research carried out among high school students in southern Arizona (Jensen and Erickson, 1978), students were asked to imagine that they had been caught and taken to juvenile court. They were then asked how much each of the following would worry them (to which response categories were "definitely yes," "probably yes," "uncertain," "probably not," and "definitely not"): (1) the police might hurt you; (2) the judge might send you to a reformatory; (3) the judge might put you on probation; (4) how your parents might react; (5) a delinquent record might keep you out of college; (6) a record might keep you from getting a good job; (7) other teenagers might think badly of you; (8) your teachers might think badly of you; (9) you might think badly of yourself.

Table 9–4 reports the percentage of students in six different high schools who indicated they would probably or definitely worry about each of these nine potential consequences. Nearly all the students indicated they would worry about their parents' reaction, and between 79 and

TABLE 9–4 *Perceived Costs of Labeling, by School Setting and Year*
(Percentage Answering "Yes" and "Definitely Yes")

| | Small Town | | | | | | Urban | | | | |
| | Mining | | Tourist | | Farm | | Public | | Public | | Parochial | |
	1974	1975	1974	1975	1974	1975	1974	1975	1974	1975	1974	1975
Hurt	6	8	2	12	10	10	9	8	9	10	10	13
Kids	25	28	31	44	45	38	33	36	29	32	30	34
Teachers	44	39	44	58	54	44	41	42	40	39	47	48
Reformatory	50	51	51	67	52	57	49	42	47	51	52	54
Self	52	58	63	67	66	61	63	65	65	64	60	59
Probation	54	48	49	53	54	53	49	48	48	46	56	54
College	64	61	72	61	73	60	58	65	59	70	63	75
Job	83	82	85	84	80	82	82	82	79	82	84	87
Parents	90	88	86	92	91	88	90	90	88	90	96	94

Source: Reprinted from "The Social Meaning of Sanctions" by Gary Jensen
and Maynard Erickson in *Crime, Law and Sanctions* edited by Marvin
Krohn and Ronald L. Akers by permission of the publisher, Sage Publications, Inc. Copyright 1978.

87 percent indicated they would worry about a record keeping them from
getting a good job. Between 58 and 75 percent would worry about a record
keeping them out of college. Relatively few students worried about the
reactions of peers, and the least concern was expressed over the possibility of being hurt by the police. The possibilities of being sent to a reformatory or put on probation worried about half of the students. With regard
to the reactions of significant reference persons or groups, parental reaction was of more concern than either teacher reaction or the reactions of
other teenagers. It does not appear that the potential reaction of peers to
labeling is of much concern to teenagers. Next to parental reaction, the
potential costs in terms of future occupational and educational goals
seem to be foremost in students' minds.

There are some interesting variations in these perceived ramifications
of labeling. For each of the nine concerns, females were found to be
significantly more concerned than males. Girls were especially more concerned than boys over parental reaction and over the possibility that they
might think badly of themselves. Similarly, youths who wanted to go to
college were obviously more concerned about jeopardizing their plans
than were those who did not plan to go to college. Students who were
doing well in school worried more about teacher reaction than students
who were not faring well. Students with delinquent friends worried less
about the reactions of other teenagers than did students with no delinquent friends. In short, the nature and degree of concern about the possible ramifications of labeling is related to a person's attachments, commitments, and beliefs. Furthermore, the study indicated that those who are

not worried about such costs are the most likely to commit delinquent acts.

What relevance do such observations have for labeling and deterrence among juveniles? For one thing, it appears that those who anticipate stigmatic consequences as a result of official labeling are the least likely to engage in behavior that is liable to labeling. In contrast those most likely to commit delinquent acts are those for whom labeling may be socially meaningless. Similarly, those most likely to be *persistently* or *repeatedly* involved in delinquency are the very youths for whom labeling or official processing generates relatively little concern. If this interpretation is correct, then we would expect that official labeling would *neither* specifically deter *nor* reinforce involvement in delinquency but would instead be a rather meaningless experience. Labeling does not constitute a "dramatization of evil" when there is no audience, no drama, and no shared definition of evil. Thus, if a study of the effects of labeling is based on a sample that includes a sizable proportion of youths who accord little significance to official labels, the variable of actual application of labels is likely to be of little consequence in the study. On the other hand, a sample that includes youths who accord legitimacy to official labels might find the experience traumatic and stigmatizing. Moreover, those who find the experience stigmatizing might actually be deterred from further delinquency to avoid further stigmatization.

The study of the social meaning of sanctions suggests a possible labeling paradox: Those most likely to be affected by labels are those least likely to do things that make them liable to labeling; those who do accord stigmatic significance to labels but become the victims of labeling are likely to refrain from further acts to avoid further stigmatization. Such speculation does not rule out the possibility of labeling effects. For example, if a delinquent record is a source of status or reputation in a particular group or social setting, then labeling could lead to an increase in delinquent behavior through processes of social reinforcement. Similarly, if the labeling experience undermines tenuous "stakes in conformity," or becomes the "last straw" for already shaky bonds between a youth and parents or school, then it could increase the chances of further violations.

The study of the social meaning of sanctions may provide clues as to why some categories of youth are less likely than others to go on to adult crime. For example, the study of delinquent and criminal careers mentioned earlier (Shannon, 1976) revealed that 78 percent of white males who acquired records before age eighteen acquired a record after that age. About 48 percent of the white females who had been labeled as juveniles subsequently acquired records as adults. Thus, the majority of white girls who were labeled did *not* go on to acquire records as adults. Yet, over three-fourths of the labeled males did acquire records as adults. Why are girls less likely to acquire subsequent records than boys? As we noted earlier, the answer may have nothing to do with labeling or deterrent effects, but the hypothesis that females are more likely than males to be deterred by labeling is at least tenable. At the very minimum, we should be studying the variable meaning of sanctions or labels in different groups as the possible source of answers concerning the effects of different reactions to delinquency.

Jensen and Erickson's findings regarding the meaning of the labeling process for high school students are also relevant to the study of general deterrence and to some of the sociological positions taken on that issue. At the beginning of this chapter, we cited Edwin Sutherland's claim from over half of a century ago that "not the fear of legal penalties but the fear of loss of status in the group is the effective deterrent." For adolescents, that statement should be somewhat revised: Apprehension, adjudication, and legal penalties are feared most when they are perceived to entail loss of status, opportunity, and self-respect. Fear of loss of status and loss of opportunity are important barriers to delinquency. It is when such losses are perceived to flow from apprehension and labeling that the justice system may have its greatest deterrent impact.

SUMMARY

In this chapter we examined labeling theory and deterrence theory—two divergent points of view about the impact of the law on the social problems that the law is intended to solve. From a deterrence perspective, the criminalization of an activity is supposed to reduce the involvement of those punished (specific deterrence) and inhibit involvement in the rest of the populace (general deterrence). Labeling theorists have challenged such notions, arguing that criminalization can transform minor problems into major ones by creating new dimensions of the problem (general labeling effects) and by increasing the criminal involvement of those labeled or punished (specific labeling effects).

Research on issues of general deterrence has progressed from the study of the issue of capital punishment to the study of the relationship between perceived risk of punishment and self-reported delinquent behavior. At present, there is still no evidence that capital punishment has ever had a general deterrent impact on criminal homicide or on other capital crimes. However, research of several different types (laboratory, field, and natural experiments; analyses of police, court, and corrections statistics for states; and survey studies) has tended to support the conclusion that the greater the threat of punishment for crime and delinquency, the lower the involvement in crime and delinquency. Several issues concerning that relationship (causal order, spuriousness, variations by offense) have yet to be resolved. However, there is evidence of an *association* of the type predicted by the deterrence perspective.

Labeling theorists are often unclear about whether the law and its enforcement increase the magnitude of the specific activity toward which they are directed or add new dimensions to the total problem. Their arguments seem to apply best to the latter possibility, although even arguments about the "secondary" effects of drug legislation have been challenged by critics of the labeling perspective. Since arguments about secondary effects are often matters of historical conjecture based on impressionistic evidence, we may never arrive at a resolution to the debate. We can say that there is evidence that property crime is greater for narcotic addicts than for nonaddicts and that it is greater during periods of daily narcotics use than at other times. It appears that addiction reinforces criminal involvement although many addicts would have been involved despite their addiction. However, the larger issues of the impact of the law and its enforcement on the total crime problem, the delinquency problem, and even problems involving so-called victimless crimes are still subject to debate.

The situation is comparably complex and confusing when we consider issues of specific deterrence versus specific labeling effects. There are bits and pieces of research consistent with both arguments. Clarification of the impact of labeling experiences may evolve from greater attention to a variety of issues that deterrence researchers and labeling theorists have raised concerning the social meaning of sanctions. Both labeling theorists and deterrence theorists have suggested that the consequences of labeling vary depending on characteristics of the authority applying labels, the meaning of such experiences in the social world of different youths, and a variety of other circumstances that shape the relevance of legal sanctions in different environments.

REFERENCES

Ageton, S. S., and D. S. Elliott. 1974. "The Effects of Legal Processing on Delinquent Orientations." *Social Problems* 22 (October):87–100.

Andenaes, J. 1971. "Deterrence and Specific Offenses." *University of Chicago Law Review* 38:537–53.

Atunes, G., and L. Hunt. 1973. "The Impact of Certainty and Severity of Punishment on Levels of Crime in American States: An Extended Analysis." *Journal of Criminal Law and Criminology* 64 (4):486–93.

Bailey, W. C., and R. P. Lott. 1976. "Crime, Punishment and Personality: An Examination of the Deterrence Question." *Journal of Criminal Law and Criminology* 67 (March):99–109.

Beccaria, C. 1767. *On Crimes and Punishments.* Translated by Henry Paolucci. Indianapolis, Ind.: Bobbs-Merrill, 1963.

Bowers, W. J. 1974. *Executions in America.* Lexington, Mass.: D. C. Heath.

Chambliss, W. T. 1967. "Types of Deviance and Effectiveness of Legal Sanctions." *Wisconsin Law Review* (Summer):703–19.

Davis, E. 1973. "Victimless Crime: The Case for Continued Enforcement." *Police Science and Administration* 1:11–20.

Ehrlich, I. 1975. "The Deterrent Effect of Capital Punishment: A Question of Life and Death." *American Economic Review* 65:397.

Erickson, M. L., J. P. Gibbs, and G. F. Jensen. 1977. "Deterrence and the Perceived Certainty of Legal Punishment." *American Sociological Review* 42 (April): 305–17.

Fisher, S. 1972. "Stigma and Deviant Careers in School." *Social Problems* 20 (Summer):78–83.

Forst, B. 1976. "The Deterrent Effect of Capital Punishment: A Cross-State Analysis of the 1960s." Mimeographed.

Foster, J. D., S. Dinitz, and W. C. Reckless. 1972. "Perceptions of Stigma following Public Intervention for Delinquent Behavior." *Social Problems* 20 (Fall):202–09.

Geerken, M., and W. R. Gove. 1977. "Deterrence, Overload and Incapacitation: An Empirical Evaluation." *Social Forces* 56 (December):424–47.

Geis, G., et al. 1976. "Reported Consequences of Decriminalization of Consensual Adult Homosexuality in Seven American States." *Journal of Homosexuality* 1 (Summer):419–26.

Gibbs, J. P. 1968. "Crime, Punishment and Deterrence." *Southwestern Social Science Quarterly* 48 (March):515–30.

———. 1975. *Crime, Punishment and Deterrence.* New York: Elsevier.

Giordano, P. C. 1976. "The Sense of Injustice: An Analysis of Juveniles' Reactions to the Justice System." *Criminology* 14 (May):93–112.

Gold, M. 1970. *Delinquent Behavior in an American City.* Belmont, Calif.: Brooks/Cole.

Gold, M., and J. R. Williams. 1969. "National Study of the Aftermath of Apprehension." *Prospectus* 3:3.

Goode, E. 1972. *Drugs in American Society.* New York: Alfred A. Knopf. Copyright © 1972 by Alfred A. Knopf, Inc.

Gould, L. C. 1969. "Who Defines Delinquency?: A Comparison of Self-Reported and Officially Reported Indices of Delinquency for Three Racial Groups." *Social Problems* 16 (Winter):325–36.

Grasmick, H. G., and H. Milligan, Jr. 1976. "Deterrence Theory Approach to Socioeconomic Demographic Correlates of Crime." *Social Science Quarterly* 57 (December):608–17.

Greenberg, S. W., and F. Adler. 1974. "Crime and Addiction: An Empirical Analysis of the Literature, 1920–1973. *Contemporary Drug Problems* 3:221–69.

Hepburn, J. R. 1977. "The Impact of Police Intervention upon Juvenile Delinquents." *Criminology* 15 (August):235–62.

Jensen, G. F. 1969. " 'Crime Doesn't Pay': Correlates of a Shared Misunderstanding." *Social Problems* 17 (Fall):189–201.

———. 1972. "Delinquency and Adolescent Self-Conceptions: A Study of the Personal Relevance of Infraction." *Social Problems* 20 (Summer):84–103.

———. Forthcoming. "Delinquency and Identity: A Reexamination of Findings." *Criminology.*

Jensen, G. F., and M. L. Erickson. 1978. "The Social Meaning of Sanctions." In M. Krohn and R. Akers, eds., *Crime, Law and Sanctions: Theoretical Perspectives.* Beverly Hills, Calif.: Sage.

Jensen, G. F., M. L. Erickson, and J. P. Gibbs. 1978. "Perceived Risk of Punishment and Self-Reported Delinquency." *Social Forces* 57 (September):57–78.

Kraut, R. E. 1976. "Deterrent and Definitional Influences on Shoplifting." *Social Problems* 23 (February):358–68.

Law Enforcement Assistance Administration, National Criminal Justice Information and Statistics Services. 1977. *Capital Punishment.* Washington, D.C.: U.S. Government Printing Office.

Lemert, E. M. 1967. *Human Deviance, Social Problems, and Social Control.* Englewood Cliffs, N.J.: Prentice-Hall.

Matza, D. 1964. *Delinquency and Drift.* New York: John Wiley.

McAuliffe, W. 1975. "Beyond Secondary Deviance: Negative Labelling and Its Effects on the Heroin Addict." In W. Gove, ed., *The Labelling of Deviance.* New York: John Wiley.

McEachern, A. W. 1968. "The Juvenile Probation System." *American Behavioral Scientist* 11 (3):1.

McGlothlin, W. H., M. D. Anglin, and B. D. Wilson. 1978. "Narcotic Addiction and Crime." *Criminology* 16 (November):293–315.

Meade, A. C. 1974. "The Labeling Approach to Delinquency: State of the Theory as a Function of Method." *Social Forces* 53 (September):83–91.

Minor, W. 1976. "A Deterrence-Control Theory of Crime." Paper presented at American Society of Criminology annual meeting. Tucson, Ariz.

O'Donnell, J. A. 1967. "The Rise and Decline of a Subculture." *Social Problems* 15 (1):73–84.

President's Commission on Law Enforcement and Administration of Justice. 1967. *Task Force Report: Juvenile Delinquency and Youth Crime.* Washington, D.C.: U.S. Government Printing Office.

Rose, A. 1968. "Law and the Causation of Social Problems." *Social Problems* 16 (1):33–43. Copyright 1968 by the Society for the Study of Social Problems. Reprinted by permission.

Savitz, L. 1958. "A Study of Capital Punishment." *Journal of Criminal Law, Criminology and Police Science* 49:338.

Schuessler, K. F. 1952. "The Deterrent Influence of the Death Penalty." *Annals of the American Academy of Political and Social Science* 284 (November): 54–62.

Schur, E. 1965. *Crimes without Victims: Deviant Behavior and Public Policy.* Englewood Cliffs, N.J.: Prentice-Hall.

———. 1969a. *Our Criminal Society.* Englewood Cliffs, N.J.: Prentice-Hall.

———. 1969b. "Reactions to Deviance: A Critical Assessment." *American Journal of Sociology* 75 (November):309–22.

———. 1973. *Radical Non-Intervention: Rethinking the Delinquency Problem.* Englewood Cliffs, N.J.: Prentice-Hall.

Schwartz, R. D., and S. Orleans. 1967. "On Legal Sanctions." *University of Chicago Law Review* 34 (Winter):274–300.

Sellin, T. 1967. *Capital Punishment.* New York: Harper & Row.

Shannon, L. 1976. "Predicting Adult Careers from Juvenile Careers." Paper presented at Pacific Sociological Association annual meeting. San Diego, Calif.

Silberman, M. 1976. "Toward a Theory of Criminal Deterrence." *American Sociological Review* 41 (June):442–61.

Sutherland, E. 1924. *Principles of Criminology.* Philadelphia: J. B. Lippincott.

Tannenbaum, F. 1938. *Crime and the Community.* New York: Columbia University Press.

Thornberry, T. P. 1971. Punishment and Crime: The Effect of Legal Dispositions on Subsequent Criminal Behavior. Ph.D. dissertation, University of Pennsylvania.

Thorsell, B. A., and L. W. Klemke. 1972. "The Labelling Process: Reinforcement and Deterrent?" *Law and Society Review* 7 (Spring):372–92.

Tittle, C. R. 1975. "Deterrents or Labelling?" *Social Forces* 53 (March):399–410.

———. 1977. "Sanction Fear and the Maintenance of Social Order." *Social Forces* 55 (March):579–96.

Tittle, C. R., and A. R. Rowe. 1973. "Moral Appeal, Sanction Threat and Deviance: An Experimental Test." *Social Problems* 20 (Spring):488–98.

Waldo, G. P., and T. G. Chiricos. 1972. "Perceived Penal Sanction and Self-Reported Criminality: A Neglected Approach to Deterrence Research." *Social Problems* 19 (Spring):522–40.

Wilson, J. Q. 1975. *Thinking about Crime.* New York: Basic Books.

Zeisel, H. 1976. "The Deterrent Effect of the Death Penalty: Facts v. Faiths." In P. Kurland, ed., *The Supreme Court Review.* Chicago: University of Chicago Press. Copyright 1976 by the University of Chicago Press.

Zimring, F. E., and G. Hawkins. 1973. *Deterrence: The Legal Threat in Crime Control.* Chicago: University of Chicago Press.

10.
INSTITUTIONALIZATION
AND ALTERNATIVES

If it were the wish and aim of magistrates to effect the destruction present and failure of young delinquents, they could not devise a more effectual method than to confine them so long in our prisons, those seats and seminaries . . . of idleness and every vice.
—John Howard, *The State of Prisons in England and Wales,* 1780:13

INSTITUTIONALIZATION: THE CONTINUING CONTROVERSY

In this chapter we will examine a controversial aspect of the juvenile justice system—the institutional treatment of juvenile offenders. Although it was a subject of debate, one rationale for the establishment of the juvenile court was to remove adolescents from the presumably corrupting influence of the adult criminal courts and the horrors of jails and prisons. Children were not to be punished or imprisoned; rather, they were to be placed in a therapeutic milieu that would foster positive, constructive change. Whether there is any difference between the adult and juvenile justice systems, other than the substitution of the words *reform school* for *prison* and *treatment* for *punishment,* is a matter of continuing controversy. The push to provide alternatives to imprisonment for juvenile offenders is central to contemporary efforts at reform. Many observers feel that the juvenile reform school is a relic of the past. However, we must now face the task of critically assessing "new" modes of treatment in contrast to the traditional responses that so many have come to view as failures.

THE RISK OF IMPRISONMENT

In Chapter 9 we summarized the results of a survey in which high school students were asked how much each of several different potential consequences of being caught and taken to juvenile court would worry them (see Table 9–4). One of those potential consequences was "being sent to a reformatory." Around one-half of the total sample indicated they would worry about such a possibility (57 percent of the girls and 49 percent of the boys). In yet another high school, students were asked to estimate the probability of their "ending up in jail" if they were picked up for (1) marijuana use, (2) drunkenness, or (3) the use of such illicit drugs as heroin and cocaine. With regard to marijuana use, only a small proportion (6 percent) thought they would probably be caught by the police; about 25 percent of the students thought that if they were caught, they would end up in jail. About 6 percent thought they would be caught for drunkenness, and about 16 percent thought they would go to jail if caught. For the use of hard drugs, about 23 percent thought they would probably get caught, and 58 percent thought they would end up in jail if they were caught. In sum, the possibility of some form of confinement or imprisonment for breaking the law is a concern for a sizable number of youths, although for many offenses they correctly perceive that their actual chances of such a happening are small.

While variable from one jurisdiction to another, the actual chances of imprisonment or confinement for a juvenile or criminal offense are extremely slight. Consider, for example, Table 10-1, which is derived from a juvenile court report for Pima County, Arizona. Pima County encompasses the city of Tucson and has one of the highest crime rates in the FBI's *Uniform Crime Reports*. One possible outcome of a juvenile court case in that jurisdiction is for the juvenile to be remanded to the state's Department of Corrections for placement in some form of correctional facility. In 1968, out of thousands of cases processed, 139 boys and 66 girls were committed to the Department of Corrections. By 1975 the numbers were down to 16 boys out of 6,924 cases processed and 2 girls out of 2,512 cases. The actual chances, then, of being turned over to the Department of Corrections were about 2 in 1,000 for boys and less than 1 in 1,000 for girls. This particular jurisdiction had such a low rate because of the philosophy of a juvenile court judge (appointed in 1973), who believed in imprisonment only if there is absolutely no alternative. Similarly, national statistics show that of some 1.7 million juveniles arrested

TABLE 10-1 *Commitments to the Department of Corrections, by Sex, 1968–1976*

Year	Boys	Girls	Total
1968	139	66	205
1969	192	88	280
1970	136	82	218
1971	125	51	176
1972	52	20	72
1973	13	7	20
1974	33	4	37
1975	16	2	18
1976	12	4	16

Source: Pima County Juvenile Court. *Annual Report.* Tucson, Ariz.: Pima County Juvenile Court Center, 1976.

in 1975, slightly less than 47,000 were placed in any type of confinement. This means that on the average only 1 out of every 36 arrested juveniles is placed in a detention or correctional facility.

Of course to be sent to an institution, a case has to proceed through a number of earlier "decision points." Figure 10–1 was prepared by the Female Offender Resource Center and summarizes major stages in the adjudication of a juvenile. A large proportion of cases drops out at each stage so that only a small proportion of juveniles processed ends up in one or another form of custody. The study by Williams and Gold (1972) that we referred to in Chapter 4 indicated that although 88 percent of the youths interviewed had done something against the law, only 22 percent had ever had a contact with the police and less than 2 percent had ever been "under judicial consideration." Of youths processed by the court, only a small fraction ends up being confined in some type of institution. As one study of a metropolitan court explained this situation, "The court is extremely reluctant to incarcerate any delinquent (feeling that to commit any youth to reform school is to write him off as hopeless) despite persistent pressure from various primary institutions to dispose of cases in this way" (Emerson, 1969:272). In 1975, at the preliminary stage of *detention* (holding a youth while waiting for a hearing), about eleven thousand youths were being held in detention in the United States out of over one million cases handled by the juvenile court. Moreover, most detention cases are held for only a matter of days. These observations are important as a prelude to any statement concerning the use of imprisonment or confinement of juvenile delinquents in the United States.

Whether in reference to prisons, reformatories, training schools, or reform schools, "imprisonment," "institutionalization," or "incarceration" as means of dealing with crime and delinquency have been under attack for centuries. The quotation heading this chapter, which condemns confinement in prisons as an ineffective and counterproductive method of handling delinquents, was published two hundred years ago. Schlossman's analysis of juvenile justice (1977) identifies the shift from an emphasis on the reformatory to an emphasis on probation (or dealing with delinquent youth in their homes) as the distinguishing characteristic of the juvenile court movement at the turn of the century. Disenchantment with imprisonment as a means of correcting behavior was also central to the President's Commission on Law Enforcement and Administration of Justice (1967).

However, there are periodic attacks on antiinstitutional correctional philosophies as well. A 1977 *National Enquirer* poll, although obviously not a representative sample of the American public, suggested that there is a sizable number of disgruntled citizens who advocate a "get-tough" policy and who would like to see more juvenile delinquents "taken off the streets." The dominant correctional ideology in the juvenile justice

FIGURE 10−1 *Decision Points within the Juvenile
Justice System*

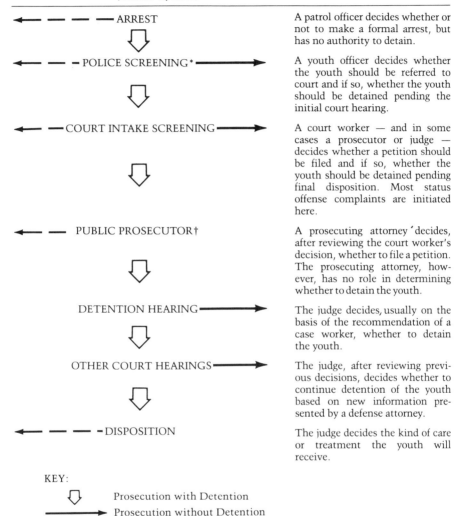

← − − − −ARREST	A patrol officer decides whether or not to make a formal arrest, but has no authority to detain.
← − − − POLICE SCREENING* ————▶	A youth officer decides whether the youth should be referred to court and if so, whether the youth should be detained pending the initial court hearing.
← − −COURT INTAKE SCREENING ————▶	A court worker — and in some cases a prosecutor or judge — decides whether a petition should be filed and if so, whether the youth should be detained pending final disposition. Most status offense complaints are initiated here.
← − − PUBLIC PROSECUTOR†	A prosecuting attorney ´decides, after reviewing the court worker's decision, whether to file a petition. The prosecuting attorney, however, has no role in determining whether to detain the youth.
DETENTION HEARING————▶	The judge decides, usually on the basis of the recommendation of a case worker, whether to detain the youth.
OTHER COURT HEARINGS————▶	The judge, after reviewing previous decisions, decides whether to continue detention of the youth based on new information presented by a defense attorney.
← − − − DISPOSITION	The judge decides the kind of care or treatment the youth will receive.

KEY:

⇩   Prosecution with Detention

————▶   Prosecution without Detention

← − −   Dismissal or Diversion

*This stage is omitted in some jurisdictions, particularly in small communities that cannot afford a special youth officer. It may be handled by a social service employee rather than a police employee.

†The prosecutor has authority to override decisions to dismiss or to prosecute based on social reasons. The authority exists in only two states.

Source: Female Offender Resource Center. *Little Sisters and the Law*, p. 5. Washington, D.C.: U.S. Department of Justice, 1977.

system emphasizes community treatment and diversion (see Chapter 11), yet consensus is far from complete. Various judges and citizen groups continue to advocate the swift, certain, and severe application of punishment, including imprisonment.

DEVELOPMENT OF THE PRISON

Since "de-institutionalization," "diversion," and "community treatment" have constituted the major themes in reform philosophies for a considerable span of time, it is easy to overlook the fact that institutions variably called penitentiaries, correctional centers, prisons, training schools, and reformatories were also products of efforts at penal reform. The innovative reforms and "steps forward" of one era may come to be viewed as the failures and archaic boondoggles of another. The use of imprisonment as a tool for correcting, deterring, or punishing offenders was itself an aspect of various efforts at reform.

In historical context, imprisonment was often viewed as a benevolent alternative to corporal ("bodily") and capital punishment. One historical overview of corrections in America (Carter, McGee, and Nelson, 1975) has described the rise of the use of incarceration as a phase in "the continued search for alternatives to brutality." Until the 1800s, the major means of punishment took the form of flogging, mutilation, branding, torture, banishment, removal to penal colonies, or some form of restitution for the damage or harm done to the victim and the state. Imprisonment was typically a prelude to the real punishment, not the punishment or means of correction itself. It was also used as a penalty for political prisoners of high rank and as a means of coercing payment of debts (Johnston, 1973).

Schrag (1971) has noted that jails were used in England in the twelfth century to detain the accused while they awaited trial and to punish offenders as well. "Houses of correction" and "workhouses" were established in Europe for minor offenders, beggars, and vagabonds beginning in the sixteenth century and were widespread by the seventeenth century. Such houses were not specifically designed to deal with criminals but were repositories for an assortment of minor offenders, the destitute, and the unemployed (Sykes, 1978). Execution, corporal punishment, and banishment were the preferred methods of handling serious criminals (Fox, 1972).

In the American colonies, jails and houses of correction were erected along European lines shortly after the establishment of each colony. The jail was used primarily for individuals awaiting trial, and houses of correction were institutions for drunkards and vagrants. The conditions in early American jails (and in their European counterparts) were deemed appalling. The following is an account of the conditions in the Walnut Street Jail in Philadelphia shortly after the Revolutionary War:

> It is represented as a scene of promiscuous and unrestricted intercourse, and universal riot and debauchery. There was no labor, no separation of those accused, but yet untried, nor even of those confined for debt only, from convicts sentenced for the foulest crimes; no separation of color, age or sex, by day or night; the prisoners lying promiscuously on the floor, most of them without anything like bed or bedding. As soon as the sexes were placed in different wings, which was the first reform made in the prison, of thirty or forty women then confined there, all but four or five immediately left it; it having been a common practice, it is said, for women to cause themselves to be arrested for fictitious debts, that they might share in the orgies of the place. Intoxicating liquors abounded, and indeed were freely sold at a bar kept by one of the officers of the prison. Intercourse between the convicts and persons without was hardly restricted. Prisoners tried and acquited were still detained till they should pay jail fees to the keeper; and the custom of garnish was established and unquestioned; that is the custom of stripping every newcomer of his outer clothing, to be sold for liquor, unless redeemed by the payment of a sum of money to be applied to the same object. It need hardly be added, that there was no attempt to give any kind of instruction and no religious service whatsoever. (Gray, 1847:15–16)

The conditions of jails and houses of correction in both Europe and America prompted efforts at reform, which in America led to the development of the "penitentiary" in the late 1700s. The very word *penitentiary* is a clue to the religious origins of the institution. The Walnut Street Jail described above became the first institution based on the Quaker idea that restraint and isolation would lead inmates to reflect on the error of their ways and do penance for their sins. Rather than flogging, physically branding, or inflicting pain, imprisonment itself—with its deprivation of freedom, restraint, and solitude—was to be both punishment and the means to personal reform. In Quaker philosophy, sin and crime were synonymous. Life in an austere and vigorously disciplined environment, meditation, and Bible reading would strengthen the moral and spiritual fibers of the inmates. To facilitate penitence, inmates were kept in single cells, were not allowed contact with other inmates, and were even made to carry out their assigned work in isolation. This conception of the penitentiary came to be known as the "Pennsylvania system."

A second school of corrections arose in New York state in the early 1800s and became known as the "Auburn system." The hallmark of the Auburn system was silence. Inmates worked together during the day but were kept in solitary confinement at night. Although there was contact, rules requiring silence were strictly enforced. Prisoners worked in common workshops and ate in a common dining hall but were not allowed to communicate. The Auburn system became the dominant penal system in America, primarily because it was economical and secondarily because of concern over the psychological impact of isolation. The Pennsylvania system called for individual confinement, which entailed the construction of separate living quarters for each inmate. In contrast, the Auburn system's architectural design was more economical, requiring only common work areas and small solitary cells for sleeping. Prisons such as Sing Sing, built in 1825, followed the Auburn model. The Pennsylvania system was ultimately abandoned in the United States, although European penologists who studied the two systems preferred the Pennsylvania system as a model for prisons in their countries (Fox, 1972).

Although proponents of each of these systems cast aspersions on the other, both systems were based on a similar philosophy. Each emphasized rigid discipline, restraint, isolation, and work as the means to personal reform. At about the same time, a somewhat different correctional philosophy was being implemented in Australia, Austria, Spain, and Ireland (Sykes, 1978:470; Sutherland and Cressey, 1978:525). In Australia Alexander Maconochie, superintendent of a penal colony, devised the "mark system." Under this system, inmates had to earn their release through hard work and good behavior. Prisoners could work their way to the issuance of a "ticket of leave" that was tantamount to parole. If the prisoner successfully completed his parole period, he was granted a conditional pardon and finally transported back to England as a free man. This progressive method of liberation was imported to Ireland where it became known as the "Irish system." The essence of the Irish system was the use of an indeterminate sentence (that was, length of confinement depended on progress made by the inmate) and the "mark" whereby prisoners could gain their release. Marks were awarded for "good behavior." Upon earning a set number of marks, the prisoner was eligible for parole.

The Irish system was hailed in this country as the most progressive penal model to date. Its philosophy became the underlying correctional philosophy of prison organization in the United States. In 1870 the National Prison Association was founded under the leadership of Enoch Wines, considered the foremost authority on prisons in the latter part of the nineteenth century (Platt, 1969). Out of the reform efforts of Wines and his organization, a new penal system emerged. Established for offenders between the ages of sixteen and thirty, the Elmira Reformatory in New York opened in 1876. (This reformatory was not, however, the first institution set up to remove young offenders from adult prisons.) The Elmira Reformatory combined the central features of the Irish system with a strong emphasis on rehabilitation through education and trade training. The goal was not punishment, but treatment and reform. However, according to Sutherland and Cressey (1978), the "treatment" at Elmira was so severe and the use of corporal punishment so frequent that convicted offenders pleaded with judges to be sentenced to the outmoded Auburn Prison rather than the Elmira Reformatory.

The Society for the Prevention of Pauperism was formed in 1817 for the purpose of finding "a practical measure for the cure of pauperism and the diminution of crime" (Dean and Reppucci, 1974). New York City was particularly beset with a problem of pauperism and the problems associated with it. Immigrants coming to this country were often stranded in New York City, and the children of destitute families were seen as prime candidates for crime. The Society for the Prevention of Pauperism selected the problem of juvenile delinquency as its major focus.

In 1825 the New York House of Refuge opened as a full-time residence for delinquent, dependent, and neglected children. It was the first attempt to provide separate facilities for young offenders and thereby remove them from the contaminating influence of adult prisons. In 1826 the House of Reformation in Boston was established, followed in 1828 by the opening of the Philadelphia House of Refuge. These early institutions, which were supported by private funds, developed many of the principles of "treatment and rehabilitation" that would characterize the philosophy of the juvenile court as it emerged at the start of the twentieth century. Unfortunately, despite the rhetoric of the early house of refuge movement, the administrators of these institutions utilized two basic models: one drawn from the public school system, which called for education and discipline, and the other based on the state penitentiary system, which utilized a strict regimen, physical labor, and corporal punishment (Schlossmann, 1977). In institutions for juveniles—variously known as houses of refuge, reformatories, industrial schools, and training schools—coercion, restraint, and discipline, masked only by the penal reformers' predeliction for euphemism, became an integral part of the "treatment." The enlightened ideology of the reformatory movement gave way to the stark reality of overcrowding, inadequate financial resources, mismanagement, and disillusioned staff. The line of demarcation between juvenile institutions and adult prisons became extremely tenuous.

The house of refuge actually came to parallel the adult penitentiary, as did the Elmira Reformatory. These products of the reformatory movement came under attack in the 1850s by "antiinstitutionalists," such as Charles Loring Brace and Samuel Gridley Home, who felt that the best means of reformation was the family. The family, according to Brace, was "God's reformatory." The antiinstitutionalists' critiques and proposals facilitated the development in America of the family reform school, an organizational model that was growing in popularity in Germany and France. The family reform school actually represented a compromise between the antiinstitutionalists' ideas and the realities of an already existing "institutional establishment" (Schlossman, 1977:49). Steven Schlossman has described the system as follows:

> To Americans the essence of the family design was a format whereby anywhere from one to three dozen inmates with similar personality traits were placed in separate small homes or cottages under the supervision,

ideally, of a surrogate father and mother. Each family lived, worked, and attended school together, meeting with other inmates only on infrequent ceremonial occasions. This residential arrangement contrasted sharply with the Jacksonian refuge, where children of different ages and dispositions slept in cells or barracks-like dormitories, performed identical tasks according to a uniform schedule, and possessed no close authority figure to appeal to for personal assistance or comfort. (1977:49)

Following the development of the family reform school, the next major events in the evolution of juvenile justice and corrections were the "Progressive era" and the "juvenile court movement" that took place during that era. As we noted in Chapter 2, there has been considerable debate about whether the label *progressive* was deserved and whether the accomplishments of that era were in fact progressive. The most recent analyses of the juvenile court movement in the United States and Canada (Schlossman, 1977; Finestone, 1976; Hagan and Leon, 1977) tend to agree that the central and most significant aspect of the movement was its emphasis on probation. Institutional placement was retained as a disposition for some offenders, but "treatment" of the youth and his or her family in the community was the philosophical emphasis.

It is not clear, however, whether this ideology had any real consequences for the probability that a youth might be imprisoned. For instance, in his historical analysis of the juvenile court movement in Chicago (Cook County), Anthony Platt argued that "Cook County juvenile court's early records show that institutional commitment was a basic tenet of the child-saving philosophy" (1969:140). Platt noted that one-third of all juveniles charged with delinquency were sent to a state reformatory. He also contended that delinquents were increasingly committed to institutions. In contrast, Schlossman's analysis of the juvenile court system in the neighboring state of Wisconsin led him to the following conclusions:

Probation accounted for the great majority of dispositions, . . . with the modal period of supervision running about one and a half years. The heavy reliance on probation, especially for male delinquents, is confirmed by records showing a rather small number of commitments to the state reform school at Waukesha during this period. . . . Between 1905 and 1916, the average number of youths committed each year was only thirty. Moreover, although the number of reformatory committals varied from year to year, it clearly did not increase at a rate proportional to rising case intake in the court. Indeed, if anything, it decreased. For example, in 1906, 55 boys were committed to the reformatory, out of 536 new delinquency cases; in 1911, 15 boys were committed out of 705. To sum up, the odds of being committed to a reformatory for boys charged with delinquency in the Progressive era were rather small. Despite increases in intake, the court's reliance on long-term committals actually diminished after 1905. (1977:155)

Schlossman went on to warn that these observations do not necessarily mean that the use of *confinement* declined, since large numbers of children were held in detention centers before, during, and sometimes after their hearings. The proportion of persons detained actually increased during that time. Schlossman argued that detention centers developed into children's jails that allowed institutional control and incapacitation in a system that emphasized probation.

Thus, by the early 1900s four basic dimensions of juvenile justice and institutional confinement had been established: (1) prisonlike training schools, (2) family-cottage reform schools, (3) the heavy use of probation, and (4) detention facilities for youthful offenders.

THE CONTEMPORARY SCENE

Although now used in a minority of cases, some form of institutional confinement and imprisonment has persisted as one possible outcome of the official processing of juveniles. However, since the establishment of the juvenile court, there has been a proliferation in the types of juvenile facilities available. For example, by 1975 there were 2,151 public and private juvenile detention and correctional facilities operating in the United States. Approximately 3 out of every 5 juvenile facilities are privately operated, with state or local governments accounting for the remaining portion. Collectively, these facilities house just under 75,000 juveniles.

Table 10–2 lists the types of public and private facilities in the United States and the number of juveniles detained in each in 1975. As the table shows, both the public and private sector are involved in the institutional care of juvenile delinquents. Slightly over 40 percent of all facilities and 63 percent of all juvenile offenders are in public institutions. The vast majority of these juveniles is placed in training schools, formerly called reformatories. Detention facilities, which provide temporary care for juveniles who are awaiting court disposition or transfer to another jurisdiction, account for the next largest proportion. In the private sector, the bulk of the juveniles is placed on ranches, forestry camps, or farms. These placement settings are long-term residential facilities that are not, however, as restrictive as training schools. The second most frequently used private placement is the halfway house or group home, which is also a long-term residential facility but allows juveniles the opportunity to maintain extensive contacts in the community by attending school or securing employment. Generally, because of the greater number of facilities in the private sector and fewer placements at these establishments, the private sector maintains smaller residential facilities than the public sector.

TABLE 10-2 *Juvenile Detention and Correctional Facilities*

Type of Facility	No. of Facilities	% of Total	No. of Juveniles	% of Total
Public Institutions				
Detention	347	16.1	11,089	14.9
Shelter	23	1.0	200	0.3
Reception or diagnostic center	17	0.8	1,436	1.9
Training school	189	8.8	26,748	36.0
Ranch, forestry camp, and farm	103	4.8	5,385	7.3
Halfway house and group home	195	9.1	2,122	2.9
Total	874	40.6	46,980	63.3
Private Institutions				
Short-term	66	3.1	830	1.1
Training school	65	3.0	3,660	4.9
Ranch, forestry camp, and farm	295	13.7	13,094	17.6
Halfway house and group home	851	39.6	9,706	13.1
Total	1277	59.4	27,290	36.7
Total, All Institutions	2151	100.0	74,270	100.0

Source: U.S. Department of Justice. *Children in Custody: Advance Report
on the Juvenile Detention and Correctional Facility Census of 1975.*
Washington, D.C.: U.S. Government Printing Office, 1975.

According to the Department of Justice, the annual expenditure in 1975 for both private and public correctional facilities amounted to nearly $868 million. The per capita operating expenditure in public institutions was $11,471, as compared to $9,518 for private institutions. The use of an average per capita expense is slightly misleading because of the wide divergence among states in operating expenditures in the public sector. For example, per capita expenditures for private institutions ranged from a low of $2,136 in North Carolina to a high of $15,189 in Wisconsin. For public institutions, the range varied from a low of $3,900 in Mississippi to a high of $24,656 for Alaska (U.S. Department of Justice, 1975).

On the surface, it appears that private institutions are a better investment than public institutions because of their smaller size and lower operating costs. However, as shown in Table 10–3, a higher percentage of placements in private institutions consists of youths who are not adjudicated delinquents. In contrast, nearly three-quarters of all juveniles placed in public institutions *are* adjudicated delinquents—that is, juveniles who, as the result of formal judicial proceedings, have been categorized as delinquent. Usually the status of adjudicated delinquent implies the commission of a criminal offense, although in some states the violation of probation by an adjudicated status offender is deemed a delinquent act. Of all juveniles placed in private institutions, only 36 percent fall into the category of adjudicated delinquent. The next largest categories of

TABLE 10–3   *Detention Status of Juveniles Held at Public and Private Institutions*

Detention Status	No. of Juveniles	% of Juveniles
Public Institutions		
Adjudicated delinquent	34,107	72.6
Persons in need of supervision	4,494	9.6
Held pending court disposition	7,011	14.9
Awaiting transfer to another jurisdiction	392	0.8
Voluntary admission	516	1.1
Dependent and neglected	451	1.0
Other	9	0.0
Total	46,980	100.0
Private Institutions		
Adjudicated delinquent	9,809	36.0
Persons in need of supervision	4,316	15.8
Held pending court disposition	529	1.9
Voluntary admission	5,879	21.5
Dependent and neglected	4,844	17.8
Other	1,913	7.0
Total	27,290	100.0

Source: U.S. Department of Justice. *Children in Custody: Advance Report on the Juvenile Detention and Correctional Facility Census of 1975.* Washington, D.C.: U.S. Government Printing Office, 1975.

juvenile placements in private facilities are (1) voluntary admissions without a court hearing; (2) dependency and neglect cases (for example, improper care by parents or guardian); and (3) "PINS" cases, which is a catchall category for juveniles who are "persons in need of supervision." This last category is not necessarily synonymous with status offenses because status offenders (that is, juveniles who have committed an offense that would not be a crime for an adult) can be adjudicated delinquent, while juveniles whose offenses are of a criminal nature can be declared PINS cases by a juvenile judge. However, it is usually the case that "persons in need of supervision" are noncriminal offenders. Thus, approximately two-thirds of the clientele placed in some form of private juvenile institution are there for reasons other than commission of a crime.

In Table 10–4 we have listed the average lengths of stay at the various types of juvenile correctional facilities. The average stay at temporary care facilities ranges from less than two weeks at detention centers to more than seven weeks at reception or diagnostic centers. Like the jail for adults, the detention facility is the most common type of residential facility for juveniles. It tends to have the smallest capacity and shortest stay of any facility in the juvenile justice system. "Shelter" facilities

TABLE 10-4 *Average Length of Stay for Juvenile Offenders, by Type of Facility*

Type of Facility	Average Length of Stay
Detention	11 days
Shelter	20 days
Reception or diagnostic center	51 days
All temporary care facilities	14 days
Training school	8.7 months
Ranch, forestry camp, and farm	6.6 months
Halfway house and group home	7.2 months
All correctional facilities	7.8 months

Source: U.S. Department of Justice. *Children in Custody: A Report on the Juvenile Detention and Correctional Facility Census of 1973.* Washington, D.C.: U.S. Government Printing Office, 1973.

provide temporary care for juveniles awaiting court disposition, as do detention centers, but shelters are not primarily designed for incarceration. In addition to providing a temporary residence for runaways, shelters provide a broad spectrum of welfare services to dependent and neglected children. However, as seen in Table 10–2, in the United States in 1975, there were only twenty-three shelter facilities, housing 200 children. The third type of short-term juvenile facility is the reception or diagnostic center. Juveniles who have been adjudicated delinquents are sent for an average of seven weeks to reception or diagnostic centers where they are screened for assignment to treatment programs. There were only seventeen such facilities operated by state governments in 1975.

Of the long-term facilities, halfway houses and group homes are the most numerous, with 195 of them in the public sector and 851 in the private sector in 1975. They are also the least physically restrictive facilities. They are generally located in residential neighborhoods and afford maximum contact between the juvenile and the community by allowing juveniles to maintain school or employment ties. Almost all halfway houses and group homes are designed to hold fewer than twenty-five juveniles, and in many instances the number of residents is less than ten. The most popular form of rehabilitation or treatment calls for a family-like setting with house parents and a manageable number of house residents. The traditional juvenile dormitory, or "warehouse" model, is gradually being eclipsed by the family model. Indeed, the redesign of one of the best-known residential facilities for delinquents, orphans, and neglected youth—Boy's Town in Omaha, Nebraska—calls for the exclusive utilization of small, family settings, rather than the massive dormitories of the traditional institutional model. Although a wide range of juvenile facilities has emerged and the family model has grown in popularity, the training school still maintains its dominance in the juvenile justice system, and for that reason we will consider it in greater detail.

THE TRAINING SCHOOL

Training schools handle more juvenile offenders than any other type of facility. The average length of stay in a training school is nearly nine months, the longest of any juvenile correctional facility. In 1975 training schools housed 26,748 offenders in 189 public institutions and 3,660 offenders in 65 private institutions. Three-quarters of these facilities are designed to hold a minimum of 100 juveniles, and 11 have a capacity of 500 or more. The physical configuration of a training school is often severely restricting and represents the most severe form of juvenile incarceration. However, as Charles Unkovich and William Ducsay have warned us, "It is quite misleading to think of them as homogenous or even as uniformly punitively motivated institutions" (1969:47). According to the Children's Bureau and the National Association of Training Schools, the major functions of such institutions are custody, treatment, and education. The Children's Bureau has described these functions as follows:

> The prime function of a training school is to re-educate and train the child to become a responsible, well-adjusted citizen. . . . The training schools must be essentially treatment institutions with an integrated professional service wherein the disciplines of education, casework, group work, psychology, psychiatry, medicine, nursing, vocational rehabilitation and religion all play an important role. Through such an integrated program the child is expected to learn self-discipline, to accept more responsibility and act and react in a more socially acceptable manner. (1975:3)

Although the philosophy expressed by the Children's Bureau calls for a dynamic, resocializing environment, several overviews of training schools agree that they are like miniature prisons that may exacerbate rather than eliminate delinquent problems. In its criticism of the traditional system of handling adolescents in juvenile institutions, the President's Task Force on Corrections stated: "Mass handling, countless ways of humiliating the inmate in order to make him subservient to rules and orders, special rules of behavior designed to maintain social distance between keepers and inmates, frisking of inmates, regimented movement to work, eat, play, drab prison clothing and similar aspects of daily life, all tend to depersonalize the inmate and reinforce his belief that authority is to be opposed, not cooperated with" (President's Commission on Law Enforcement and Administration of Justice, 1967:142).

Some descriptions of juvenile institutions suggest that these facilities may not differ significantly from adult prisons. For instance, in his study of a cottage type of residential treatment center in New York, Howard Polsky (1962) found a stratification system based on toughness and manipulative abilities. The social hierarchy was so pervasive and the code of conduct so strongly enforced that Polsky concluded that the cottage system was culturally and organizationally "delinquent-bound." He found the correctional system to be a vacuum in which the authoritarianism and toughness of the juvenile peer group pervaded the entire living pattern. Polsky's research suggested that the lifestyle in the cottage system tends to sabotage the system's treatment programs and that juvenile institutions may suffer from the same "prisonization" effects as adult penitentiaries.

Many training schools have made a concerted effort to move away from the traditional custodial approach toward a treatment orientation. However, many have been caught in a "custody-treatment" dilemma. Some of the staff function as guards or custodians, while others are responsible for treatment programs. Invariably, animosity arises between the "watchdogs," who have no formal training or expertise, and the "social workers," who have extensive training and whose views differ from those of the custodial staff. The conflict that is generated between the custodial and treatment staff may have repercussions for the juvenile inmates themselves.

David Street and several colleagues have carried out research relevant to the diversity of juvenile institutions and the relevance of that diversity to the perspectives and social relations of juvenile inmates (Street, 1965; Zald and Street, 1964; Street, Vinter, and Perrow, 1966). They studied four different institutions, nicknamed "Dick," "Mixter," "Milton," and "Inland":

Dick (Discipline)—a large (200–250 inmates) public institution which had no treatment program, whose staff felt no lack because of this, and which concentrated on custody, hard work, and discipline.

Mixter (Mixed Goals)—a very large (375–420 inmates) public institution with poorly integrated "mixed goals" of custody and treatment. Some treatment was attempted, but this was segregated from the rest of the activities, and for most boys the environment was characterized by surveillance, frequent use of negative sanctions, and other corollaries of an emphasis on custody.

Milton (Milieu Therapy)—a fairly large (160–190 inmates) public institution using not only individual therapy but a range of other treatment techniques. This institution resembled Mixter in its bifurcation between treatment and containment staffs and activities, but by and large the clinicians were in control, used treatment criteria, and influenced the non-professional staff to allow the inmates considerable freedom.

Inland (Individual Therapy)—a small (60–75 inmates) private "residential treatment center" in which the clinicians were virtually in complete control, allowing much freedom to the inmates while stressing the use of psychotherapeutic techniques in an attempt to bring about major personality change. (Street, 1965:43)

The treatment-oriented institutions were characterized by a higher staff-inmate ratio and contact. Staff at these institutions viewed the organization's goals as rehabilitation and attitudinal change through close, trusting relationships. In contrast, staff in custodially oriented settings stressed order, discipline, immediate response to staff, and isolation.

In analyzing data from questionnaires completed by inmates, Street and his colleagues found several differences among inmates in the different institutions. First, inmates in the treatment settings expressed more positive attitudes toward the institution and its staff and more positive "images of self-change" than inmates in custodial institutions. Second, as summarized in Figure 10–2, length of stay in the custodial institutions was associated with an increasing proportion of inmates expressing negative attitudes, while in the treatment-oriented institutions length of stay was associated with increasing proportions of inmates expressing positive attitudes. Third, Street and his colleagues found that inmate groups in treatment settings more often encourage positive attitudes than do inmate groups in custodial institutions.

In sum, the image of juvenile institutions as junior prisons that generate hostility, opposition, and bitterness ignores the variability in juvenile institutions and the apparent impact of different organizational goals on inmates, as well as on correctional personnel. Since at the time of Street's research at least 50 percent of all public institutions were estimated to be basically custodial (Janowitz, 1966:xi) and about 25 percent treatment-oriented, it is not surprising that most contemporary overviews stressed the opposition-generating aspects of juvenile institutions. We should note, however, that the type of research undertaken by Street and his colleagues does not tell us whether certain types of institutions increase or decrease the chances of committing further offenses (recidivism). Of course, whether we believe such an outcome is important depends on our conception of the function that such institutions are supposed to serve.

OBJECTIVES OF REACTIONS TO DELINQUENCY

What are the objectives of any reaction to crime or delinquency? We use the neutral term *reaction* here because such words as *punishment, treatment,* or *correction* tend to imply that some sort of choice about the major objective has already been made. If we viewed the intended functions of a reaction to crime or delinquency as revenge or deterrence, then we might have called this section "The Objectives of Punishment." On the other hand, if we believed that changing the offender should be the major objective, we might have referred to the objectives of treatment, reform, or correction. Similarly, the names given to an institution may convey a sense of the purpose of that institution's founders. The word *prison* carries with it a connotation of punishment, as compared to *correctional center.* The label *reformatory* implies that reform is the institution's main objective, just as *training school* implies an emphasis

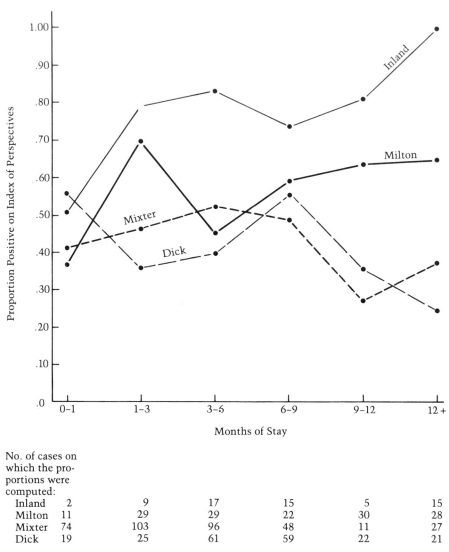

FIGURE 10-2 *Proportion of Inmates with Positive Attitudes, by Length of Stay in Different Types of Institutions*

No. of cases on which the proportions were computed:						
Inland	2	9	17	15	5	15
Milton	11	29	29	22	30	28
Mixter	74	103	96	48	11	27
Dick	19	25	61	59	22	21

Source: David Street. "The Inmate Group in Custodial and Treatment Settings." *American Sociological Review* 30 (February 1965):50.

on learning and *penitentiary* implies an emphasis on penitence. The point is that the words we use in discussing reactions to crime and delinquency reflect our choice of objectives.

Today, the words *treatment, reform, training, correction,* and *rehabili-*

tation are so commonly used that we may lose sight of the fact that several different types of objectives have been used as the rationale for certain reactions to delinquency. Herbert Packer (1968) has outlined two historically developed justifications for reactions to crime: retribution or revenge, and the utilitarian view of prevention. Retribution or revenge, a position that is akin to vengeance, is an emotive response to an act of crime. Although it may be an irrational and nonproductive way of reacting to crime, it resolves the act of wrongdoing insofar as it allows the victim or society to "get even" with the offender. This nonutilitarian position has little, if anything, to do with treating the offender or with protecting society. The second type of justification, the utilitarian prevention of further occurrences of criminal behavior, was heralded as a "rational" approach to crime control in that its objective was the greatest happiness for the greatest number with a minimal infliction of suffering. The objective of prevention can be further amplified to include *incapacitation, deterrence,* and *reformation.*

As we noted in Chapter 9, *incapacitation* refers to the prevention of further offenses through the isolation or confinement of the offender. It is the heart of the "let's-get-them-off-the-streets" philosophy and is based on the idea that society has the right to restrain an offender to prevent him or her from doing further harm. Obviously, capital punishment is the ultimate form of incapacitation. Whether contemporary forms of imprisonment are incapacitating depends on one's view of who is to be protected since inmates inflict a considerable amount of harm on one another.

Another objective of reactions to crime and delinquency has been *deterrence,* which has already been discussed extensively in Chapter 9. From a deterrence perspective, reactions should either deter the individual from further offenses (specific deterrence) or inhibit other potential offenders (general deterrence). The inhibition of offenses as a result of *fear of punishment* is the defining element of a deterrent effect, as opposed to incapacitation or to the inhibition of further offenses because of some change in the offender's perspectives, abilities, or personality.

Inhibition of offenses because of change in the offender is central to *reformation,* or rehabilitation, as an objective of reactions to crime and delinquency. One of the difficulties of using recidivism as a measure of rehabilitation is that a low recidivism rate may mean that offenders committed no future offenses (or fewer offenses) as a result of fear of further treatment or imprisonment. This effect would more properly be considered a deterrent effect than a rehabilitative one. Moreover, a juvenile might be rehabilitated in the area of drug use but might not be deterred from shoplifting. The meaning of rehabilitation has never been clearly defined, but it supposedly entails some form of change in the offender that inhibits subsequent offenses and that is the effect of treatment rather than of specific deterrence.

IMPACT OF CORRECTIONAL EFFORTS

Have any of the efforts to save, treat, rehabilitate, or deter youths from further offenses been successful? To answer such a question is far more difficult than most people initially anticipate. Critics often refer to custodial institutions and traditional training schools as "schools for crime." In *Radical Non-Intervention*, Edwin Schur has stated such a view as a matter of fact:

> There is now widespread recognition that the legal processing of juveniles, whatever it is called and however it is described, is in fact significantly punitive and potentially stigmatizing. This first became clear in the commitment to institutions, which function as "schools for crime." (1973:127)

However, whether institutions function as schools for crime is not as clear and unequivocably accepted as critics have implied.

Since one avowed purpose of institutionalization is to prevent antisocial behavior by reforming individual offenders, critics of the juvenile system frequently cite recidivism rates as evidence that the system is failing. Recidivism rates are arrived at by counting the number of convicted offenders who return to criminal activities. The overall recidivism rate for juvenile institutions is said to be about 50 percent. In the early 1960s Robert Beverly and Evelyn Guttmann (1962) examined the parole performance of juveniles released from California training schools during the first fifteen months of their release. They found marked variation of parole violation from one institution to another. While the rate for all paroled juveniles was 47 percent, the rate ranged from a low of 36 percent to a high of 60 percent. Beverly and Guttmann also found recidivism rates to vary in a single institution from one year to the next.

Do such recidivism rates actually indicate failure of the correctional system? The answer to such a question requires *a basis of comparison.* One relevant comparison might be between the delinquent or criminal behavior of institutionalized offenders and the delinquent or criminal behavior of those who have *never* been caught or punished. A 50 percent recidivism rate might be low compared to the actual crime rate of those who have avoided punishment, or it might be high. However, in actual research the comparisons are between institutionalized offenders and those in other treatment programs, rather than between the institutionalized and the nonapprehended. The difficulty with many of these research comparisons is that persons sent to institutions may have been those most likely to persist in committing offenses, regardless of whether or not they had been institutionalized. Yet even given these problems, which should stack things in favor of a higher recidivism rate for the institutionalized, the evidence on the issue is such that we cannot glibly and unquestioningly accept the argument that institutions are "schools for crime." For example, Thornberry's study (1971), which we described in Chapter 9, found that youths who had been institutionalized had lower subsequent involvement in delinquency than youths who had received less severe dispositions.

Currently there is a pervasive disenchantment with the practice of imprisonment. Protests against the institutionalization of juveniles in particular became a salient issue in the mid-1970s. Yet the truth of the matter is that the impact of imprisonment remains unknown. Glaser (1964) has argued that we do not have very accurate information on the proportion of imprisoned criminals who return to crime. Furthermore, even the accurate identification of the recidivism rate for this group would still not be sufficient evidence to render a judgment since there is no information on comparable offenders who were not imprisoned. In his study of recidivism, Glaser found that over a four-year period 35 percent of adult offenders released from federal prisons could be classified as clear failures. He also found that 52 percent had no further criminal record and that another 13 percent were marginally successful in that they were subsequently convicted of misdemeanors, but no felonies. Thus, Glaser's data do not support the charge that prisons are a total failure.

In a study of juveniles arrested in Newark, New Jersey, Horwitz and Wasserman (1977) examined the percentages of recidivists in terms of the types of dispositions they had received (see Table 10–5). In all instances, females were less likely than males to be rearrested (within two years of their disposition), and none of the five females who had been institutionalized were rearrested. Even though the personal backgrounds of those institutionalized suggested that they should have a higher recidivism rate than those receiving less severe dispositions, the data did not show that that group had a higher recidivism rate than the group who had been put on probation. In fact, when Horwitz and Wasserman took school background and relationships with parents into account, they found that those who had received the least severe dispositions had a higher recidivism rate than those who had been institutionalized. Continued involvement in delinquency or crime appeared to be the product of social circumstances that facilitate such behavior, rather than the product of institutionalization.

TABLE 10–5 *Recidivists, by Disposition and Sex*

Disposition	% of Males	% of Females
Less than probation	55	28
Probation	92	59
Institutionalization	85	0

Source: Data from A. Horwitz and M. Wasserman. "A Cross-Sectional and Longitudinal Study of the Labeling Perspective." Paper presented at American Society of Criminology annual meeting. Atlanta, Ga., 1977.

In an article entitled "Prisons and Rehabilitation: The Inevitability of Disfavor," Charles Tittle (1974) argued that even with regard to adult corrections, the evidence that institutions are the "schools for crime" is weak and that it is possible to muster evidence to the contrary. He summarized the situation as follows:

> The fact is, it cannot be concluded with confidence, either from recidivism data or research on institutional living, that prisons fail in their rehabilitative efforts, and certainly not that prisons are "schools for crime." The evidence does suggest that many incarcerees are not rehabilitated (however one defines that term), but the evidence can just as easily be interpreted to suggest that many others are rehabilitated. In fact, if taken at face value, much of the data, particularly that concerning recidivism, would demonstrate that prisons do a remarkably good rehabilitative job. Consider in this regard that (1) only 16 percent of the evaluation studies reviewed by Logan concludes that the outcome of correctional application was a "failure," while 44 percent concluded that the degree of success was at least "good," . . . (2) recommitment figures indicate that the majority do not return to prison, . . . (3) dispositional data show that most parolees do not return to serious crime, . . . and (4) the FBI follow-up suggests that far more than half are not reconvicted of another crime. . . . The point is not that the data show that incarceration leads to rehabilitation, but rather that they do not demonstrate a failure to rehabilitate. Yet almost everybody continues to assert in the strongest possible terms that prisons are failures and that rehabilitation is not occurring. (1974:390)

Tittle contended that the persistent belief in prison failure may stem from uncritical acceptance of "authoritative" claims, sheer speculation concerning the increase in crime, and the view that anything short of 100 percent success is failure. However, he suggested that the most important factor is that a belief in prison failure is functional for a wide range of people and groups, including law enforcement personnel and prison officials. It can be used—and is used—as a justification for budgetary pleas and bureaucratic expansion. It can be also cited as evidence of corruption and injustice and as evidence of the failure of "law-and-order" tactics.

In short, the view of institutions as schools for crime is no better substantiated than a view of imprisonment as a specific deterrent or as a setting for reformation. Acceptance of one or another position appears to be more a function of ideology than of evidence. However, regardless of its basis in fact or fiction, the view of confinement in prisons, training schools, or reformatories as an inappropriate and counterproductive force has generated considerable correctional experimentation. As we will discuss in the next section, assessing the success or failure of these experimental programs is no easy matter, and the case for their success, relative to the success of institutionalization or total nonintervention, is subject to debate.

EVALUATION OF TREATMENT PROGRAMS

Evaluation research generally addresses two broad considerations: program *effectiveness* — the ability of a program to meet its stated goals and objectives; and program *efficiency* — the utilization of resources in the goal attainment process (Adams, 1974). The assessment of program effectiveness, which is aimed at determining the results of a particular program or policy, requires that the research design approximate the controlled experiment through the use of comparison groups. The assessment of efficiency involves a consideration of expenditures in relation to payoff. James Q. Wilson (1975) has recounted the efforts of the New York City Police Department to curb the rising rate of subway robberies. In 1965 police patrols in New York subways were substantially increased. A police officer was assigned to every subway train and to every station during the peak hours for felony offenses. From one perspective, this saturation approach proved a remarkable success: The robberies immediately dropped and continued to remain low. However, the deterrent effect of this police patrol program was computed to be approximately $35,000 per deterred felony. In terms of effectiveness, the program was relatively successful, but the resources expended were enormous.

In addition to the basic considerations of program effectiveness and efficiency, evaluation of treatment programs involves a host of other methodological issues. The simplest but most perplexing issue is how to establish a basis of comparison. In the parlance of the scientific method, the researcher needs an experimental group and a control group. Ideally, individuals would be randomly assigned to one of two groups, with the experimental group receiving some form of treatment and the control group receiving no treatment. As simple as this design is, there are serious ethical questions in applying it. It is often ethically impossible to randomly assign one juvenile offender to an institution as part of a treatment strategy and another to a control group that simply sends the offender home.

LaMar Empey and Maynard Erickson (1972) have described the difficulty of implementing an experimental design in the study of a nonresidential treatment approach. Their experiment in Provo, Utah, called for random assignment of boys either to a traditional institutional setting or to a probation alternative. In the interest of science, the juvenile judge initially expressed willingness to participate in the experiment. However, once the program got underway, the judge was reluctant to commit boys to institutions. The judicial decision process inevitably diverted offenders from institutions because of beliefs about the harmful effects of institutionalization. From a scientific perspective, these harmful effects, if they do exist, need to be catalogued and analyzed. However, from a legal and ethical perspective, the random assignment of a boy to an institution or to probation becomes an issue of civil rights since it tampers with the guarantees of the Eighth Amendment. Some studies have succeeded in assigning subjects to experimental and control groups, but faulty randomization procedures resulting in selection bias have generated concern about their results.

Correctional research must also confront the question: "How are the outcomes to be measured and evaluated?" Stated another way, what constitutes a success or a failure? Lerman (1968) examined the California Youth Authority's Community Treatment Project and found that the experimental and control organizations reacted to offenses differently. Boys placed in an experimental group who committed a new offense were often given a "second chance," whereas subjects in control groups who broke the law were summarily issued a revocation of probation. The criterion for failure was vastly different between the two groups, which produced the misleading conclusion that the success rate of the community treatment approach was significantly higher than the success rate of the traditional institutional approach.

Several reviews of treatment literature have commented on both the quality and the results of treatment studies. By far the most controversial review in recent years has been the report submitted by Lipton, Martinson, and Wilks (1975) to the Governor's Special Committee on Criminal Offenders in New York. In a six-month search for available reports on attempts at rehabilitation from 1945 through 1967, Lipton, Martinson, and Wilks found 231 studies that met a minimum set of standards for a methodologically adequate study. Perhaps the most telling statement about the methodological adequacy of such research is Martinson's observation that "it is just possible that some of our treatment programs *are* working to some extent, but that our research is so bad that it is incapable of telling" (1974:48). This comment was merely a cautionary note to Martinson's more substantive conclusion that the best studies available "give us very little reason to hope that we have in fact found a sure way of reducing recidivism through rehabilitation. This is not to say that we found no instances of success or partial success; it is only to say that these instances have been isolated, producing no clear pattern to indicate the efficacy of any particular method of treatment" (1974:49). For purposes of formulating policy, Martinson concentrated on *methods of treatment*. For a treatment program to have policy implications, he believed that it should be generally applicable, should be amenable to implementation in new settings, and should rely on something other than "exceptional" personnel. Martinson did cite particular programs that appeared to be effective. However, he noted that the determinants of success of those programs did not seem to be the method of treatment per se, but the coincidence of exceptional personnel, subjects amenable to treatment, and enthusiasm for the program.

CORRECTIONAL EXPERIMENTATION: SOME EXAMPLES

Even as the review by Lipton, Martinson, and Wilks was published it was outdated, not necessarily in terms of the conclusions reached but in terms of the programs evaluated. The field of juvenile corrections is presently experiencing rapid change in practice and philosophy as new strategies of treatment emerge and public criticism of present policies mounts. Any discussion of correctional experimentation currently in vogue quickly becomes dated as innovations are added and other approaches are discarded. However, for heuristic purposes, we will identify certain underlying typologies in correctional experimentation and briefly assess some specific programs.

One dimension that can be utilized in classifying correctional programs is the specific *focus* of the treatment effort. If personal maladjustments are viewed as the source of criminal and delinquent activity, then the eradication or modification of individual traits is likely to be the focus of treatment. Programs oriented toward change in the individual seek to promote healthy personality development through various approaches, including psychiatry, education, social work, recreation, and medical treatment. Correctional programs reflecting this ideological position are quite characteristic of efforts to rehabilitate juveniles.

A second targeted population is not the individual offender, but the delinquent group. As we noted in chapters 6 and 7, several sociological perspectives emphasize a view of delinquency as a group phenomenon. Correctional programs sensitive to the group context of delinquent behavior see antisocial behavior emanating not from individual personality conflicts, but from within delinquent groups. Such programs focus on treatment of the delinquent within the social climate of the peer group.

A third approach to corrections focuses on the broadest possible range of factors that influences delinquent behavior—namely, the environment. The environment-oriented perspective sees the catalyzing forces behind crime and delinquency as deficiencies in the sociocultural world that surrounds groups and individuals. When embodied in an institutional program, this treatment approach is called "milieu therapy." Milieu therapy attempts to use every aspect of the inmates' environment as part of the treatment program (Martinson, 1974:33). It is also the basis for a variety of new programs, such as the "teaching-family" program (which provides a surrogate family, with house parents serving as role models) and related behavior modification programs. When extended beyond the confines of the institutional setting, milieu therapy becomes the most global and most ambitious of the three focuses of treatment because it calls for a restructuring of relationships between the subjects in such a program and agencies and groups in the community.

In addition to the specific focus of treatment, a second major dimension in correctional experimentation is the *locus* of treatment. There is often a natural affinity between the treatment subject (that is, the individual, group, or environment) and the setting where the treatment is to be administered. One can identify three discrete treatment settings: full-time placement, part-time placement, and nonplacement. The first type of placement, which is referred to as "residential treatment," entails confinement to a facility for a period of time. In actual operation, residential treatment is a form of incarceration, although the emphasis may be on the administration of treatment programs rather than on custodial care.

The second level of placement falls in between the rigid control of full-time residential treatment and the relative freedom of nonresidential treatment. For lack of a better term, we refer to this type of placement simply as "semiresidential treatment." This level of treatment includes settings that range from a single-family residence in a middle-class neighborhood where the residents form a substitute family to an institutional setting where inhabitants adhere to a set routine. In either type of setting, the residents are allowed the freedom to maintain contact with the community by attending school, working, and participating in recreational activities.

The third level of placement is really no placement at all. The juvenile offender is allowed to remain in the community, typically with his or her family, but must maintain contact with a juvenile justice agency. The type of contact involved in nonresidential treatment varies from a highly intensive daily "dosage" of the treatment regime to a sporadic or casual contact with a representative of a treatment program. Obviously, nonresidential treatment is the least restrictive type of treatment setting in that it allows the juvenile to maintain total contact with the local community.

For the sake of illustration, but at the risk of oversimplification, we have attempted to classify certain experimental efforts in terms of the scope and breadth of the focus of treatment and the degree of confinement involved. Table 10–6 illustrates the differences among the specific programs that we will assess. In addition, the table gives us an idea of the *directions* of correctional experimentation. The key concepts in juvenile justice in the 1970s and on into the 1980s have been the diversion of offenders away from institutional settings and the modification of both institutional and community environments. Of course, these themes have been reiterated periodically throughout the history of juvenile and adult corrections. Moreover, the juvenile justice system, because of economic necessity as well as correctional philosophy, has tended to "divert" most cases throughout its history. However, it was not until the 1970s that a concerted national effort made diversion an organized, programmatic response to juvenile delinquency. In sum, correctional philos-

TABLE 10–6   *Correctional Treatment Approaches*

Degree of Confinement	Focus		
	Individual	Group	Environment
Totally residential	Juvenile institutions California Youth Authority experiments	Highfields Minnesota Training School	Project CASE Project ACE
Semiresidential	Most halfway houses	Silverlake Experiment	Teaching-family model
Nonresidential	California Community Treatment Program	Provo Experiment	Project New Pride Chicago Area Project

ophy and organized efforts have been moving toward the proliferation of nonresidential alternatives. In addition, the failure or limited success of programs oriented toward the individual, coupled with the input of behavioral psychology and sociological theories, has led to a growing emphasis on the modification of total learning environments. Let us now examine the results of some specific programs that have embodied these key concepts.

Treating the Individual in Total Confinement

The study of diversity in juvenile institutions by Street, Vinter, and Perrow (1966) suggested that juvenile inmates' attitudes and attitudinal changes varied by type of institution, with inmates in treatment-oriented institutions exhibiting the most positive orientations and change. However, we do not know whether these attitudinal differences affected recidivism, nor do we know whether characteristics of inmates in the different institutions or characteristics of the institutional programs themselves accounted for these differences. Neither do we know what particular types of treatment programs (if any) might have made a difference.

Research on the recidivism rates of youths receiving some form of individualized treatment within an institutional context has yielded confusing and far from promising results. The California Youth Authority's Community Treatment Project used personality assessment techniques in setting up treatment plans geared specifically to the needs of individual offenders. A study of a California treatment program that used psychodynamically oriented individual counseling found no improvement in recidivism rates (California Department of Corrections, 1958). Evaluations of psychotherapy for young male offenders (Guttmann, 1963) and female offenders (Adams, 1959, 1961b) in California institutions produced the same findings. Two studies have suggested, however, that subjects who are deemed "amenable" to individual psychotherapeutic treatment have lower recidivism rates than nontreated subjects, but that the rates of subjects who are "nonamenable" to treatment are higher than the rates of the nontreated (Adams, 1961a). In yet another study, Karl Jesness (1970) classified delinquents into "maturity types," such as asocial, conformist, manipulative, and neurotic. He then randomly assigned one group to an experimental program that formulated a specific treatment according to the needs of the individual and the other group to a traditional institutional program. After both groups of juveniles were released back into the community, Jesness found their recidivism rates virtually identical. Moreover, traditional individual and group counseling methods appear to be no more promising with adults (Kassebaum, Ward, and Wilner, 1971) than they are with juveniles (Martinson, 1974). Martinson has qualified this generally negative conclusion with the observation that such programs may work when they are new, when subjects are deemed amenable to treatment, or when therapists are chosen for special qualities of empathy and warmth.

Treating the Group in Total Confinement

One of the earliest alternatives to the traditional institutionalization of juvenile offenders was "therapeutic" treatment in the context of the peer group. The goal of this type of group therapy is to help deviant groups develop new social norms. The goal is achieved by guiding the development of groups within the institution and by allowing the group to put pressure on its members to accept new values. The setting for such a treatment program has usually been a small residential institution, which could also be regarded as a therapeutic mileu. This type of group therapy experience is referred to as "guided group interaction" (GGI). Such programs see the group as the crucial factor in adolescent rehabilitation. According to the Center for Studies of Crime and Delinquency:

> GGI programs involve the delinquent in frequent and intensive group discussions of their own and other members' current problems and experiences. Based on the theory that antisocial youth behavior receives the support and approval of the delinquent peer group, and that substituting acceptable norms for delinquent values and attitudes also requires the support of the peer group, these programs encourage the development of a group culture and the acceptance by members of responsibility for helping and controlling one another. As the group culture develops and the group begins to accept greater responsibility, the staff group leader allows the group a greater degree of decision-making power. Over time, the group's responsibility may extend to decisions involving disciplinary measures imposed on a member or determination of a member's readiness for release. (Public Health Service, n.d.:3)

The best-known residential GGI program is Highfields, which began in 1950 in New Jersey. The Highfields program provides a highly supervised setting. It is limited to serving approximately twenty boys, aged sixteen and seventeen, who have not been previously committed to a correctional institution. During the day, the boys work at a nearby mental hospital as orderlies. They are not permitted to attend school. In the evening, two groups of ten boys each meet for "guided group interaction" sessions. Highfields has a short-term treatment approach that normally does not exceed three months.

The Highfields program was first evaluated by McCorkle, Elias, and Bixby (1959), who reported that the recidivism rate for Highfields "graduates" was only 18 percent, as compared to a 33 percent rate for reformatory inmates. Ashley Weeks (1963) compared a sample of reformatory parolees with Highfields parolees and found the recidivism rate for the reformatory group to be 63 percent, as compared to 47 percent for the Highfields group. On the surface, the Highfields program seemed to be a successful treatment approach. However, critical examinations of the data have shown the program's results to be far less convincing than originally concluded. For example, Paul Lerman (1968) noted that 18 percent of the cases from Highfields were "in-program" failures who did not complete the program. When this group was added to the group whose recidivism rates were studied, the evidence in favor of the effectiveness of the Highfields program was reduced, although a difference still persisted. The results of the Highfields program appear promising, but they are controversial on methodological grounds since youths were not randomly assigned to one or another program.

In 1968 the Minnesota Training School at Red Wing adopted the Highfields' GGI technique in a large institutional setting of over six hundred confined juveniles. This institution's adoption of a new correctional philosophy was precipitated by severe discipline problems that had created a nearly explosive atmosphere. An immediate decision was made to pattern Red Wing after the GGI approach but to leave certain traditional programs, such as academic and vocational education, intact. The new approach was received with great enthusiasm, and the internal conflict at this institution subsided. It has also been claimed that the GGI approach greatly reduced recidivism rates, dramatically altered behavioral problems and plummeting staff morale, and resulted in the active participation of the entire institution in a far more meaningful program. Unfortunately no empirical data have been released, and the claims of success are thus far unsubstantiated.

Treating the Environment in a Totally Residential Setting

Current environmentally oriented programs in totally residential settings tend to be based on *behavior modification* techniques derived from

Skinnerian operant conditioning theory and, more recently, from social learning theory (see Chapter 5). A major characteristic of behavior modification programs is the systematic manipulation of the environment to create a potential for changing behavior. Project CASE (Contingencies Applicable to Special Education) was a one-year demonstration program for juvenile offenders who were school failures. The project's design included a special environment aimed at expanding the social and academic repertoires of the residents and a token economy that rewarded the boys for academic competence and punished them for academic lethargy. The results of this treatment approach were a significant increase in grade levels as measured by the Stanford Achievement Test. There was also a mean increase of 12.5 points in IQ scores after ten months in the program.

A second example of a behavioral program in an institutional setting is Project ACE (Applied Contingency Environment) at the Maryland Training School for Boys. This institution provides cottage housing and a school program for about three hundred delinquent youths. Project ACE was introduced in two cottages that housed the institution's most belligerent inmates. The project involved the identification of target behaviors (breaking windows or chairs, assaultive behavior, poor school performance) and the establishment of a point economy system. Appropriate reinforcers were applied by allowing the subjects access to a "point-spending room" and to a game room. In the spending room, subjects were allowed to convert accumulated points into tangible goods, such as candy, soda, and grooming articles. Unfortunately no data are available on the effectiveness of Project ACE. However, personal observations suggest that the project created an air of normality at the Maryland Training School.

Treating the Individual in a Semiresidential Setting

The "halfway house" is a temporary residence for offenders and is usually located in a community. The resident at a halfway house is generally given certain freedoms that are not possible in totally residential institutions. These freedoms include access to community-based employment, education, and recreation. Private charitable organizations began operating halfway houses for offenders in the nineteenth century, and governmental agencies began establishing such programs in the 1950s. One of the purposes of the halfway house is to provide a transitional setting that will reduce recidivism, which tends to be inordinately high during the early stages of release. Thalheimer has described the functions and purposes of a halfway house in the following manner:

> The very name halfway house suggests its position in the corrections world; halfway-in, a more structured environment than probation and paroles; halfway-out, a less structured environment than institutions. As

halfway-in houses they represent a last stop before incarceration for probationers and parolees having faced revocation; as halfway-out houses, they provide services to probationers and parolees leaving institutions. Halfway houses also provide a residential alternative to jail or outright release for accused offenders awaiting trial or convicted offenders awaiting sentencing. (1975:1)

Depending on the particular halfway house in question, treatment may consist of the provision of an informal familylike atmosphere, formalized group therapy (such as guided group interaction), or individual consultation. Because of the divergent approaches involved, it is difficult to assess the effectiveness of halfway houses. At present, we do not know whether individual or group treatment programs in halfway houses reduce recidivism. The effect of halfway houses as a component of the correctional system has yet to be demonstrated.

Treating the Group in a Semiresidential Setting

The Silverlake Experiment, which was conducted in Los Angeles between 1964 and 1968 by LaMar Empey and Steven Lubeck (1971), is an example of a partially residential, group-oriented program. This project dealt with delinquent youths at Boy's Republic, a private residential treatment facility. Some boys were randomly assigned to a special community-based treatment program, while others were placed in the regular regimen of institutional care at Boy's Republic. The experimental group, which consisted of no more than twenty boys, resided in a residential home located in a middle-class neighborhood during the week and returned home on weekends. The boys in this group attended high school and had the assistance of a tutor. They also attended daily group meetings that were conducted along the lines of guided group interaction. The experiment lasted for three years, with an additional year devoted to the collection of follow-up data.

The overall results indicated no significant difference between the experimental and control group in relative frequency of arrest during the twelve months following release. During that period, there was a 73 percent reduction in the volume of delinquency committed by the experimental subjects and a 71 percent reduction in the volume of delinquency committed by the control group. Although the program failed to show positive results, the Silverlake Experiment remains as one of the most careful and sophisticated studies of community-based treatment.

Treating the Environment in a Semiresidential Setting

The traditional institutional approach of providing "warehouses" for juvenile offenders has given way in many settings to smaller, familylike living quarters. A dramatic example of this changing strategy occurred at

"Boy's Town" in Omaha, Nebraska. In 1967 Boy's Town developed a new program called the "teaching-family model," which entails the placement of youthful offenders in a familylike environment where they learn new skills and behaviors. The "family" is composed of a husband and wife, who are known as "teaching parents," and five to ten adolescents. The youths and the teaching parents live together as a family for approximately one year. Depending on a particular youth's needs, the teaching parents attempt to instill new academic, vocational, social, and family-living skills. The motivation for establishing and maintaining new behavioral responses is based in part on a token economy, or point system. Individuals earn points for behaviors deemed desirable and may exchange the accumulated points for tangible goods or privileges. As a youth progresses in the teaching-family program, these motivational aids are gradually reduced. We will discuss the relative success of such a behavior modification approach later in this chapter.

Treating the Individual in a Nonresidential Setting

One of the most highly acclaimed rehabilitation programs is the Community Treatment Program in California (Warren and Palmer, 1966; Palmer, 1971). In this experiment, youths who would ordinarily have been sent to California Youth Authority training schools were assigned to an experimental program and returned to their community for intensive treatment. Each member of the experimental group was diagnosed and classified on a scale of interpersonal maturity. The range varied from "least maturity" to "extreme social maturity," a status achieved by few individuals. Within each maturity, or "I-level," classification, there were further subclassifications that described the subject's set—that is, the way a delinquent responds to his or her perceptions of the world. Thus, other categories within each I-level indicated whether responses were passive or aggressive, conforming or manipulative, neurotic, acting-out, or culturally identifying. The control group was assigned to one of the traditional institutions of the California Youth Authority.

The initial findings of this project purportedly demonstrated greater success for the community-based program than for institutionalization (Warren, 1969; Palmer, 1971). After fifteen months in the community, the experimental subjects had a parole violation rate of 28 percent, as compared to 52 percent for the control subjects. After two years, the parole violation rate was 38 percent for the experimental subjects and 61 percent for the controls. However, Paul Lerman (1975) concluded that the most dramatic finding was that this project changed the *parole officer's behavior* rather than the youth's behavior. Lerman noted that the *number of reported offenses* for the experimental and control groups after fifteen months of community exposure was essentially the same, but that the *reactions* to these offenses were vastly different. Those juveniles who were part of the experimental group were recommended for fewer parole revocations than were members of the control group. A pronounced bias existed, which gave juveniles in the Community Treatment Program a second chance. In fact, the experimental subjects had committed an average of 2.81 offenses in the follow-up period, as compared to 1.61 for the control group. However, it is conceivable that parole officers of the experimental subjects were more informed of their clients' delinquent behaviors than were the parole officers of the control subjects; thus, detection may have been more probable for the experimental group. These problems make definite conclusions about either the success or failure of the program impossible.

Treating the Group in a Nonresidential Setting

The basic principles of the Highfields project (GGI) were expanded upon in a nonresidential setting in Provo, Utah, beginning in 1959 (Empey and Erickson, 1972). This program was conveniently centered in the city of Provo so that the program's participants could reside at home. Each day, following school or work, the boys went to the center for guided group interaction sessions. The control groups were to be a random selection of adjudicated youths placed on probation in the community and youths committed to the state training school. However, once the program was underway, the juvenile judge decided against committing boys to the training school, and a new sample of youths drawn from other Utah counties and committed to the state training school had to be utilized.

Analysis of the program results showed that the experimental group did not have a significantly higher success rate than the probation control group. After the first year of the program, the recidivism rates of the experimental group and the probation group were virtually the same—approximately 50 percent. The differences between these two groups did not change appreciably over a four-year period. At the end of that time, both groups exhibited a recidivism rate of around 60 percent. However, the institutional control group had a higher recidivism rate after one year (60 percent) than either the experimental or probation group. In addition, its rate increased to nearly 80 percent by the fourth year. These results appear to demonstrate that institutionalization is ineffective in comparison to two noninstitutional alternatives. However, because the incarcerated youths were not entirely comparable to the experimental or probation control group, caution must be exercised in interpreting these findings.

Treating the Environment in a Nonresidential Setting

The objective of a totally nonresidential, environmentally oriented program is to alter the community environment and the experiences encountered by offenders. Perhaps the most notable example of an environmental program is the Chicago Area Project (Kobrin, 1959). This project was instituted in the 1930s by Clifford Shaw in Chicago neighborhoods where a disproportionately large number of delinquents resided. An effort was made to effect changes in the social environments of these neighborhoods by providing residents with the tools to develop a sense of neighborhood cohesiveness and by establishing local self-help enterprises. The Chicago Area Project had the dual objective of preventing delinquency and rehabilitating parolees in neighborhoods with high crime rates. The core aim of this program was a revitalization of neighborhood identity and pride. Shaw emphasized that if there is to be any sense of permanency to environmental change, the desire for change must come from within the local community. Kobrin, a colleague of Shaw and McKay, has cited evidence that the project contributed to the reduction of delinquency. However, Kobrin has also noted the difficulty inherent in evaluating such a program. Critics of this type of environmental approach have argued that the Chicago Area Project did not in any way alter such basic problems as poverty, slum dwellings, unemployment, and alienation and, as a result, was nothing more than window dressing.

Project New Pride in Denver, Colorado, is a comprehensive community-based program for adjudicated juveniles. It attempts to prepare an individual to confront problems in his or her own environment and thereby to change the environment. The areas of service include academic education, counseling, employment, and cultural education. After this project had been operating for twelve months, a control group had a 32 percent recidivism rate, while New Pride clients had a 27 percent recidivism rate. Although evaluation of this program is still in the preliminary stages of analysis, Project New Pride also appears to have improved employment opportunities and academic performance (Blew, McGillis, and Bryant, 1977).

BEHAVIOR MODIFICATION

Since it is rapidly becoming the most popular correctional technique in the United States, behavior modification deserves some additional comment. The term *behavior modification* has been used to refer to a variety of techniques aimed at altering behavior. These techniques range from "aversive conditioning" (where pleasant or unpleasant stimuli are coupled with certain forms of behavior or situations) to psychosurgery, chemotherapy, and electroshock therapy. However, the most widespread form of behavior modification (and the most likely referent for the term) uses principles of operant learning theory in the attempt to change behavior. Programs that utilize this approach are based on the premise that behavior is controlled by its consequences. In this view, deviant behavior is learned and maintained in the same way as any other behavior. "Both deviant and nondeviant behavior are conceptualized as 'normal,' that is, the same basic laws and principles are assumed to underlie all forms of human behavior" (Milan and McKee, 1974:746). Because it is based on conditioning theory, behavior modification attempts to replace undesirable behavior with adaptive alternatives learned through the use of positive and negative reinforcement. If positive behavior is adequately rewarded, then it will be maintained, and, conversely, if negative behavior is not rewarded, then it will gradually subside.

While such programs are growing in popularity, there is also growing concern over the legal aspects of behavior modification and the rights of experimental subjects. For example, David Wexler (1973) has noted that many behavior modification programs initially deprive inmates of privileges and basic necessities to make rewards for appropriate behavior more valuable. The Supreme Court (*Wyatt* v. *Stickney*) has specifically addressed the legal and ethical issues involved in behavior modification programs and has enumerated certain rights of inmates: the right to the least restrictive conditions necessary for treatment; the right not to be subjected to experimental research without consent; the right not to be subjected to such treatment procedures as lobotomy, shock therapy, or adversive conditioning without express and informed consent. Wexler has asserted that this Court decision guarantees a certain minimal level of rights and greatly restricts the deprivation of rewards in a token economy system. Presumably the legal issues involved in behavior modification in nonresidential or semiresidential community-based programs are not quite as complex as in institutions, provided that the element of voluntarism is present.

Behavior modification programs were not included in Lipton, Martinson, and Wilks's review of the treatment literature since they did not come into vogue until the late 1960s. It appears, however, that their inclusion would not have greatly modified the conclusions of that review. Institutionally based behavior modification has not been found to be more effective than traditional institutionalization (Braukmann and Fixsen, 1975; Jesness et al. 1972), and in some instances, such programs have produced higher recidivism rates than nontreatment programs (Ross, 1974; Wolfred, 1974).

Braukmann and Fixsen (1975) have surveyed the many studies and reports that focus on this mode of treatment in the community. Typically, community-based behavior modification programs occur in group homes that utilize the teaching-family model developed at Achievement Place in Lawrence, Kansas. Most evaluation studies appear to support the notion that behavior modification programs may offer a viable alternative to incarceration or traditional treatment. Unfortunately, far too many of these studies are lacking in rigorous scientific evaluation techniques, and their findings are therefore tentative at best. For example, many studies are based on extremely small samples. The results from Project CASE were derived from a total sample of forty-one youths during the program phase and twenty-seven during the follow-up period (Cohen and Filipczak, 1971). An evaluation of Achievement Place was based on eighteen youths (Kirigan et al., 1974). Many studies do not employ control groups, and so it is uncertain whether the results obtained are attributable to treatment or to some other variable. In those studies that have utilized control groups, Braukmann and Fixsen (1975) found that there was neither random assignment nor matching of subjects. Finally, there has been almost no reporting of long-term results. Until such follow-up is accomplished, the results of behavior modification programs, which presently appear promising, will remain uncertain.

WHERE DO WE GO FROM HERE?

We began this chapter with the observation that confinement in some type of institution is a rare outcome in the processing of juveniles and that the philosophy of juvenile justice since the turn of the century has emphasized noninstitutional alternatives. This emphasis grew during the 1970s and will continue on into the 1980s. It is evidenced by the proliferation of camps, halfway houses, group homes, and nonresidential programs and by the abandonment of large centralized training schools (Carter, McGee, and Nelson, 1975:33). The rationale for providing alternatives to institutionalization has been that institutions, whether they are called training schools, reformatories, or industrial schools, are schools for crime and that they generate a higher recidivism rate than noninstitutional alternatives. Yet after decades of research, all we can say is that the pursuit of noninstitutional alternatives is not likely to increase recidivism among delinquent youth.

Such conclusions have led some policy evaluators to propose that we modify our criteria for evaluating the "effectiveness" of a treatment policy. One advantage to some noninstitutional treatment alternatives is cost. Empey and Erickson (1972) estimated that at the time of their study in Provo, Utah, the cost of handling a case in their program was one-tenth the cost per case in a reformatory; yet their cases appeared to do better than the training school's cases. Of course, ordinary probation cases did just as well as Empey and Erickson's subjects, and probation may have been even cheaper. Some of these cost benefits may disappear as states set a certain dollar amount per month per case, regardless of whether the case is handled in a training school or in a less institutional alternative. Even with the equalization of state support, programs that can operate out of existing houses and structures should require less capital outlay than institutions.

Another criteria for evaluating treatment programs is the morale and attitudes of the juveniles processed. Paul Lerman (1968:63) has asked, "Given the fact that social work is still unable to influence appreciably the rates of failure of institutions for court sentenced delinquents, should not ways be sought to make the total criminal-delinquent system more humane?" Even if we cannot lower recidivism in treatment-oriented institutions (Street, Vinter, and Perrow, 1966), we can consider the positive feelings and self-images of institutionalized juveniles as worthwhile ends in and of their own right. Lerman has also suggested that since shorter sentences and community-based treatment do not seem to *increase* recidivism rates, such policies could be pursued on humanitarian grounds.

Another proposal in response to current treatment research has been that we shift our attention away from recidivism to the impact (and costs) of programs on the *crime rate* in general. Robert Martinson has noted that the emphasis on rehabilitation has overshadowed other possible criteria for assessing programs, such as *general deterrence* and *incapacitation.* Martinson pointed out that a particular treatment policy might generate lower recidivism rates and yet contribute to a community's crime rate by allowing free movement of offenders and reducing fear of punishment among nonoffenders. Such possibilities are the basis for growing criticism of studies that use recidivism as the sole criterion for evaluating the effects of treatment programs (Martinson, 1976; Wilson, 1975).

Another response to the evaluations of treatment programs has been to argue that different types of treatment may have different consequences for different types of offenders. Ted Palmer (1976) has stated that the main question in treatment should be: "Which methods work best for *which* types of offenders, and under *what* conditions or in what types of settings?" There was some controversial support for this argument in the evaluations of the California Community Treatment Program. The support was controversial in that (1) different studies using similar classifications of types of offenders have yielded different results (Guttmann, 1963; Adams, 1961a) and (2) the major research cited as support for this argument has been challenged on methodological grounds (see Lerman, 1968).

A common sociological response to treatment research has been to question the basic view of treatment programs that offenders can be changed through what typically amounts to a minor legal intervention in their lives. Sociologists have argued that rather than attempting to reform the offender, we should institute basic social reforms to modify conditions that are conducive to crime and delinquency. The underlying principles of behavior modification suggest a supportive argument for the sociologists' case: If people are responsive to *new* contingencies of reinforcement and punishment in a correctional program, they will also be responsive to the contingencies operating in the outside world after release. Such observations, together with the question of whether treatment is any more effective than doing nothing and with concern over possible labeling effects, have led sociologists to propose policies that combine *radical nonintervention* with efforts at social reform (see Schur, 1973). These two emphases are reflected in the diversion and prevention programs that we will discuss in chapters 11 and 12.

SUMMARY

In this chapter we summarized the history and current status of the institutionalization of juvenile offenders. While the risk of apprehension for a delinquent offense is quite low and the proportion of juveniles who are eventually sent to some type of correctional facility is small, the use of institutionalization as a form of treatment or rehabilitation is under a barrage of criticism. Ironically, the use of imprisonment itself was originally viewed as a humane alternative to physical punishment. Moreover, the imprisonment or confinement of offenders came to be viewed as a means of changing or "reforming" people, rather than as simply a means of punishment. The reformatory emerged as the symbol of correctional philosophy in the United States but was attacked in the 1850s by antiinstitutionalists. While the juvenile court movement was characterized by an antiinstitutional ideology, it did not abolish institutions and in fact led to an increasing use of a new form of confinement—the detention center. The necessity of institutionalizing juveniles is still under attack, with the popular image of training schools being that they are "schools for crime." This image has not been totally supported by research, but neither has the efficacy of confinement been clearly demonstrated.

The current alternatives to institutionalization are too numerous to recount, ranging from formal, intensive group sessions to bland periods of probation, which many feel is tantamount to doing nothing. Concern over the quality of the evaluation of these new programs has become a stumbling block to acceptance of the "new" as "better." Many programs have not been evaluated at all, and the design of the evaluations of others has been so weak that the results are practically worthless. Some programs have been found to produce positive results, but these results have often been attributable to the staff or the subjects, rather than to the treatment itself. Our excursion through the various correctional treatment strategies that have been employed suggests that some may be promising, but that in general we are left with more questions than answers.

In any measurement of program effectiveness, we are suddenly confronted by a very complex question: What is meant by *success?* Such concepts as rehabilitation, reintegration, recidivism, and deterrence are often cited as possible goals, but these concepts are ill-defined. Some critics say that *anything* is better than the current practice of confining juveniles in institutions and that if they are nothing else, some of the new alternatives are at least more efficient in terms of cost, as well as more humane. However, critics are increasingly challenging the notion that alternative programs are the direction for juvenile justice reform. Radical critics of correctional efforts have increasingly advocated policies of minimal intervention, tolerance, and basic social change. Scholars with a more conservative bent have advocated a return to an emphasis on punishment as a general deterrent.

REFERENCES

Adams, S. 1959. "Effectiveness of the Youth Authority Special Treatment Program: First Interim Report." Research report no. 5. Sacramento: California Youth Authority.

———. 1961a. "Effectiveness of Interview Therapy with Older Youth Authority Wards: An Interim Evaluation of the PICO Project." Research report no. 20 (January 20). Sacramento: California Youth Authority.

———. 1961b. "Assessment of the Psychiatric Treatment Program: Phase 1, Third Interim Report." Research report no. 21 (January 31). Sacramento: California Youth Authority.

———. 1974. "Measurement of Effectiveness and Efficiency in Corrections." In D. Glaser, *Handbook of Criminology.* Chicago: Rand McNally.

Beverly, R. F., and E. S. Guttmann. 1962. *An Analysis of Parole Performance by Institution of Release 1956–1960.* Sacramento: State of California.

Blew, C. H., D. McGillis, and G. Bryant. 1977. *Project New Pride.* Washington, D.C.: U.S. Government Printing Office.

Braukmann, C. J., and D. L. Fixsen. 1975. "Behavior Modification with Delinquents." In M. Hersen, R. Eisler, and P. M. Miller, eds., *Progress in Behavior Modification.* New York: Academic Press.

California Department of Corrections. 1958. "Intensive Treatment Program: Second Annual Report." Prepared by H. B. Bradley and J. D. Williams (December 1). Sacramento. Mimeographed.

Carter, R. M., R. A. McGee, and E. K. Nelson. 1975. *Corrections in America.* Philadelphia: J. B. Lippincott.

Children's Bureau. 1975. *Institutions Serving Delinquent Children.* Washington, D.C.: U.S. Government Printing Office.

Cohen, H. L., and J. Filipczak. 1971. *A New Learning Environment.* San Francisco: Jossey-Bass.

Dean, C. W., and N. D. Reppucci. 1974. "Juvenile Correctional Institutions." In D. Glaser, ed., *Handbook of Criminology.* Chicago: Rand McNally.

Emerson, R. M. 1969. *Judging Delinquents.* Chicago: Aldine.

Empey, L. T., and M. L. Erickson. 1972. *The Provo Experiment.* Lexington, Mass.: Lexington Books.

Empey, L. T., and S. G. Lubeck. 1971. *The Silverlake Experiment.* Chicago: Aldine.

Female Offender Resource Center. 1977. *Little Sisters and the Law.* Washington, D.C.: U.S. Department of Justice.

Finestone, H. 1976. *Victims of Change.* Westport, Conn.: Greenwood Press.

Fox, V. 1972. *Introduction to Corrections.* Englewood Cliffs, N.J.: Prentice-Hall.

Glaser, D. 1964. *The Effectiveness of a Prison and Parole System.* Indianapolis, Ind.: Bobbs-Merrill.

Gray, F. C. 1847. *Prison Discipline in America.* London: J. Murray.

Guttmann, E. S. 1963. "Effects of Short-Term Psychiatric Treatment on Boys in Two California Youth Authority Institutions." Research report no. 36 (December). Sacramento: California Youth Authority.

Hagan, J., and J. Leon. 1977. "Rediscovering Delinquency: Social History, Political Ideology and the Sociology of Law." *American Sociological Review* 42 (August):587–98.

Horwitz, A., and M. Wasserman. 1977. "A Cross-Sectional and Longitudinal Study of the Labeling Perspective." Paper presented at American Society of Criminology annual meeting. Atlanta, Ga.

Howard, J. 1780. *The State of Prisons in England and Wales,* 2nd ed. London: Cadell and Conant.

Janowitz, M. 1966. Foreword to Street, Vinter, and Perrow, *Organization for Treatment.*

Jesness, K. F. 1970. "The Preston Typology Study." *Youth Authority Quarterly* 23 (Winter):26–38.

Jesness, K. F., et al. 1972. *The Youth Center Research Project.* Sacramento: California Youth Authority.

Johnston, N. 1973. *The Human Cage: A Brief History of Prison Architecture.* New York: Walker.

Kassebaum, G., D. Ward, and D. Wilner. 1971. *Prison Treatment and Parole Survival: An Empirical Assessment.* New York: John Wiley.

Kirigan, K. A., et al. 1974. *Overall Evaluation of the Achievement Place Program.* Lawrence: University of Kansas Printing Service.

Kobrin, S. 1959. "The Chicago Area Project—A 25 Year Assessment." *Annals of the American Academy of Political and Social Science* 322 (March):20–29.

Lerman, P. 1968. "Evaluative Studies of Institutions for Delinquents: Implications for Research and Social Policy." *Social Work* 13 (July):55–64.

———. 1975. *Community Treatment and Social Control.* Chicago: University of Chicago Press.

Lipton, D., R. Martinson, and J. Wilks. 1975. *The Effectiveness of Correctional Treatment: A Survey of Treatment Evaluation Studies.* New York: Praeger.

Martinson, R. 1974. "What Works?—Questions and Answers about Prison Reform." *Public Interest* 35 (Spring):22–54.

———. 1976. "California Research at the Crossroads." *Crime and Delinquency* (April):180–91.

McCorkle, L. W., A. Elias, and F. L. Bixby, 1959. *The Highfields Story.* New York: Holt, Rinehart and Winston.

Milan, M. A., and J. McKee. 1974. "Behavior Modification: Principles and Applications in Corrections." In D. Glaser, *Handbook of Criminology.* Chicago: Rand McNally.

Packer, H. 1968. *The Limits of Criminal Sanction.* Palo Alto, Calif.: Stanford University Press.

Palmer, T. B. 1971. "California's Community Treatment Program for Delinquent Adolescents." *Journal of Research in Crime and Delinquency* 8 (January): 74–92.

———. 1976. "Martinson Revisited." In M. Matlin, ed., *Rehabilitation, Recidivism and Research*. Hackensack, N.J.: National Council on Crime and Delinquency.

Pima County Juvenile Court. 1976. *Annual Report*. Tucson, Ariz.: Pima County Juvenile Court Center.

Platt, A. 1969. *The Child Savers*. Chicago: University of Chicago Press.

Polsky, H. W. 1962. *Cottage Six*. New York: Russell Sage Foundation.

President's Commission on Law Enforcement and Administration of Justice. 1967. *Task Force Report: Corrections*. Washington, D.C.: U.S. Government Printing Office.

Public Health Service. N.d. *Community Based Correctional Programs: Models and Practices*. Publication no. 2130. Washington, D.C.: U.S. Government Printing Office.

Ross, R. R. 1974. "Behavior Modification in an Institution for Female Adolescent Offenders." Report to the Ontario Mental Health Foundation. Toronto.

Schlossman, S. L. 1977. *Love and the American Delinquent*. Chicago: University of Chicago Press. Copyright 1977 by the University of Chicago Press.

Schrag, C. 1971. *Criminal Justice: American Style*. Washington, D.C.: U.S. Government Printing Office.

Schur, E. 1973. *Radical Non-Intervention: Rethinking the Delinquency Problem*. Englewood Cliffs, N.J.: Prentice-Hall. Copyright 1973. Reprinted by permission of Prentice-Hall, Inc., Englewood Cliffs, N.J.

Street, D. 1965. "The Inmate Group in Custodial and Treatment Settings." *American Sociological Review* 30 (February):40–55.

Street, D., R. D. Vinter, and C. Perrow. 1966. *Organization for Treatment*. New York: Free Press.

Sutherland, E. H., and D. R. Cressey. 1978. *Criminology*, 10th ed. Philadelphia: J. B. Lippincott.

Sykes, G. 1978. *Criminology*. New York: Harcourt Brace Jovanovich.

Thalheimer, D. J. 1975. *Cost Analyses of Correctional Standards: Halfway Houses*, vol. 2. Washington, D.C.: Law Enforcement Assistance Administration, U.S. Department of Justice.

Thornberry, T. P. 1971. "Punishment and Crime: The Effect of Legal Dispositions on Subsequent Criminal Behavior." Ph.D. dissertation. University of Pennsylvania.

Tittle, C. R. 1974. "Prisons and Rehabilitation: The Inevitability of Disfavor." *Social Problems* 21 (3):385–95. Copyright 1974 by the Society for the Study of Social Problems. Reprinted by permission.

Unkovich, C. M., and W. J. Ducsay. 1969. "The Objectives of Training Schools for Delinquents." *Federal Probation* 33 (March):49–52.

U.S. Department of Justice. 1973. *Children in Custody: A Report on the Juvenile Detention and Correctional Facility Census of 1973*. Washington, D.C.: U.S. Government Printing Office.

———. 1975. *Children in Custody: Advance Report on the Juvenile Detention and Correctional Facility Census of 1975*. Washington, D.C.: U.S. Government Printing Office.

Warren, M. Q. 1969. "The Case for Differential Treatment of Delinquents." *Annals of the American Academy of Political and Social Science* 38:47–59.

Warren, M. Q., and T. B. Palmer. 1966. *The Community Treatment Project after Five Years.* Sacramento: California Youth Authority.

Weeks, H. A. 1963. *Youthful Offenders at Highfields.* Ann Arbor: University of Michigan Press.

Wexler, D. 1973. "Token and Taboo: Behavior Modification, Token Economics, and the Law." *California Law Review* 61:81–109.

Williams, J. R., and M. Gold. 1972. "From Delinquent Behavior to Official Delinquency." *Social Problems* 20 (Fall):209–29.

Wilson, J. Q. 1975. *Thinking about Crime.* New York: Basic Books.

Wolfred, T. R. 1974. "Institutional Treatment for Adolescents: The Crisis Care Center." Unpublished manuscript. University of Illinois.

Zald, M. N., and D. Street. 1964. "Custody and Treatment in Juvenile Institutions." *Crime and Delinquency* 10 (July):249–56.

11.
DIVERSION

Does clubbing a man reform him? Does brutal treatment elevate his thoughts? Does handcuffing him fill him with good resolves? Stop right here, and for a moment imagine yourself forced to submit to being handcuffed, and see what kind of feelings will be aroused in you. Submission to that one act of degradation prepares many a young man for a career of crime. It destroys the self-respect of others, and makes them the easy victim of crime.
—John P. Altgeld, *Our Penal Machinery and Its Victims,* 1884

DIVERSION AND THE JUVENILE COURT

A common lament about the juvenile justice system is that it has become an institution for handling society's rejects. In the words of Robert Emerson (1969), the juvenile justice system is the "dumping ground" for problem youth. Juvenile court personnel are expected to deal with adolescent problems that range from serious criminal behavior to such relatively minor behavioral problems as loitering, curfew violations, and the possession of tobacco. Confronted with such a vast array of problems, the juvenile court is more akin to a social welfare agency than a court of law. Sociologists have been critical of the practice of funneling so many adolescent problems into the juvenile court. As we noted in Chapter 2, sociologist Edwin Lemert (1967) has advocated a philosophy of "judicious nonintervention," arguing that the juvenile court should be an agency of last resort for children, to be used only when all other remedies have been exhausted. In devoting time and attention to relatively petty behavioral problems, the juvenile court is less able to deal with far more serious matters. Thus, critics call for limiting the activities of the juvenile court to a narrower range of adolescent misconduct. Out of the criticism of the juvenile justice system has come a concerted effort to develop techniques for sidestepping the system. This new orientation or philosophy for handling certain types of juvenile offenders is called *diversion.*

Despite the recent popularity of the term *diversion* in the field of juvenile justice, the concern about creating alternative strategies for dealing with juvenile offenders is not a new one. As we have noted several times, one rationale for the creation of the juvenile court system in the late nineteenth century was the perceived need to deal with juvenile offenders in a noncriminal setting. Thus, one of the first attempts at juvenile diversion was the creation of the juvenile court in Cook County, Illinois, in 1899. In the poignant quote that begins this chapter, Governor

John Altgeld of Illinois was referring to the lack of special consideration for juveniles in the criminal code of the nineteenth century. In a popular pamphlet published in 1884 entitled *Our Penal Machinery and Its Victims,* Governor Altgeld described the criminal justice system as a "crushing process." His forceful indictment of the inhumane treatment of offenders was a catalyzing force in the development of the juvenile court in Illinois. Similarly, in his treatise on prisons, Enoch Wines (1880), a nineteenth century penologist, stated that "human justice is a clumsy machine and often deserves the punishment which it inflicts." Wines advocated a reformatory system for juveniles that would reflect the conditions of home life rather than the harsh and punitive aspects of the penitentiary. The advent of the juvenile justice system may have represented certain regressive and politically motivated social policies, as Anthony Platt's study of the juvenile court contends (1969); however, there is also evidence that the emergence of the juvenile court represented a perceived need to divert juveniles from the adult criminal justice system and a basic opposition to institutional modes of treatment (see Hagan and Leon, 1977; Schlossman, 1977).

More recently, the view that juvenile offenders should be diverted not only from institutions, but from the *juvenile court* as well, has been gaining support. The 1967 report of the President's Commission on Law Enforcement and Administration of Justice was highly critical of the juvenile justice system. It called for the utilization of alternative programs so that contact with the juvenile justice system could be minimized:

> The formal sanctioning system and pronouncement of delinquency should be used only as a last resort. In place of the formal system, dispositional alternatives to adjudication must be developed for dealing with juveniles, including agencies to provide and coordinate services and procedures to achieve necessary control without unnecessary stigma. Alternatives already available, such as those related to court intake, should be narrowed, with greater emphasis upon consensual and informal means of meeting the problems of difficult children. (1967b)

This commission advocated limiting the jurisdiction of the juvenile court to criminal cases involving juvenile offenders.

In the 1970s the diversion philosophy received national prominence when the Law Enforcement Assistance Administration granted awards to state and local municipalities for developing diversion programs. The need for alternative methods of handling juvenile offenders was viewed both as a matter of justice and equity and as a matter of pressing economic necessity. Perhaps the greatest catalyzing force in advancing the concept of diversion was the passage of the Juvenile Justice and Delinquency Prevention Act of 1974, which underwrote an $8.5 million program for the development of model juvenile diversion programs across the nation. In enacting this law, Congress stated that present juvenile

programs have not responded to the problems of juvenile offenders. Moreover, Congress declared that "the devastating failures of the juvenile justice system" demand technical expertise and adequate resources to deal
comprehensively with "the crisis of delinquency."

The first step in the implementation of this law was the establishment
of the Deinstitutionalization of Status Offenders (DSO) Project, which
was funded by an additional $8.5 million and was to deal only with
juveniles arrested for status offenses. The DSO Project proposed to
develop and implement means of diverting juveniles from the traditional
juvenile justice and correctional system. From the viewpoint of social
science, an important innovation in this legislation was its stipulation
that all juvenile delinquency programs assisted under this act be *evaluated* to determine their results and effectiveness. It is hoped that this
strong emphasis on evaluation and on the dissemination of pertinent
findings will provide a wealth of scientific information. It will take years
of research to determine the effectiveness of these programs, but the
current policy of diverting status offenders from the juvenile court in the
funded demonstration areas has already been acclaimed as a significant
advance for the legal rights of juveniles.

RATIONALES FOR DIVERSION

The support for a diversion philosophy is very strong among juvenile
court personnel and sociologists. However, the support is not as yet based
on any clearly demonstrated advantages. Rather, the alleged failure of
treatment and imprisonment, the popularity of the labeling perspective
on deviance, a growing concern for children's rights, economic considerations, professionalization and bureaucratization of the police, and criticisms of the use of detention—all seem to have encouraged a commitment to developing and implementing diversion policies. As we will note
later, this commitment has not yet resulted in a clear delineation of the
exact nature and meaning of diversion, nor has it resulted in a clear
specification of the relationship of diversion to past policies.

Theoretical Precedents

When the members of the President's Commission on Law Enforcement and Administration of Justice advocated diversion, they made specific reference to the dangers of stigmatization and contamination
believed to be inherent in the labeling and mass processing of juveniles.
In doing so, they were drawing on two prominent sociological perspectives on delinquency—labeling and differential association. According to
the tenets of labeling theory, juveniles who are processed through the
juvenile justice system may become what they are labeled. Diversion

policies would presumably avoid or minimize the stigma of being labeled a delinquent by diverting certain categories of juvenile offenders out of the court system.

Similarly, advocates of differential association theory assume that crime, like other behavior, is learned in social interaction. By associating with persons whose attitudes favor law violation, an individual comes to learn those attitudes and gradually becomes a lawbreaker himself. From the perspective of differential association theory, the juvenile justice system creates more delinquency by introducing nondelinquents to the infectious values of "hard-core" delinquents. Differential association theorists would lobby for diversion that prevents any fraternization of "predelinquents" with "lawbreakers."

Juvenile Rights and Due Process

Another underlying theme in the development of a diversion philosophy has been a concern for the clarification of children's rights and the extension of guarantees of "due process of law" to persons being processed through the juvenile justice system. Several critics of juvenile justice have taken the position that the denial of certain rights of due process and the processing of juveniles for trivial and often unspecified transgressions may contribute to a "sense of injustice" (Matza, 1964) and may undermine respect for the legal system (Schur, 1973:130). A concern for juvenile rights and due process is central to arguments of judicious nonintervention or radical nonintervention in the lives of the young.

Edwin Schur has proposed a policy that stresses the narrowing of the range of activities for which an adolescent can be brought to the attention of the juvenile court. Schur's policy is one of nonintervention:

> Basically radical non-intervention implies policies that accommodate society to the widest possible diversity of behaviors and attitudes, rather than forcing as many individuals as possible to "adjust" to supposedly common societal standards. This does not mean that anything goes, that all behavior is socially acceptable. But delinquency policy has proscribed youthful behavior well beyond what is required to maintain a smooth-running society or to protect others from youthful depredations. Thus, the basic injunction for public policy becomes: *leave kids alone wherever possible.* (1973:154–55)

This noninterventionist strategy calls not only for mechanisms to divert juveniles away from the courts but also for thoroughgoing reform in the structure and values of our society. Immediate priorities involve what Schur describes as a return to the "rule of law"—that is, implementation of due process of law. The vagueness of delinquency statutes, which allows enormous degrees of discretion to be vested in juvenile court officials, ultimately invites discrimination and injustice. Those concerned about the rights of juveniles argue that juvenile statutes should clearly delineate what kinds of behavior are legally proscribed and should set explicit penalties for law violations. In this regard, the practices of the juvenile court should reflect the judicial nature of a criminal proceeding with all the accoutrements of the guarantees found in the Bill of Rights.

Economics

Depending on the type of diversion program that is implemented, removing juveniles from the juvenile justice system could save billions of dollars. The Commonwealth of Massachusetts found that the cost for each institutionalized offender amounted to $11,500 a year and that the recidivism rate was 80 percent (Ohlin, Coates, and Miller, 1974). According to statistics that we cited in the last chapter, detention and correctional facilities cost the taxpayers $868 million in 1975. This figure represents an increase of nearly 100 percent since 1970. The average cost of maintaining various types of facilities, such as temporary care facilities and correctional facilities, was about $7,000 per offender in 1971 but had increased to over $10,000 by 1975. Furthermore, with offenders under the age of eighteen accounting for nearly 30 percent of all arrests, dealing with the increasing volume of juvenile offenders has taken up a significant proportion of law enforcement personnel's time. According to the *Uniform Crime Reports* for 1977, 1,782,049 juveniles were taken into custody, and 57 percent of these alleged offenders were referred to either a juvenile or an adult court. We also know from *Juvenile Court Statistics* for 1972 that the juvenile courts in the United States received a total of 1,112,500 delinquency cases, of which 41 percent, or 461,300, resulted in a judicial hearing. By removing a significant number of juvenile offenders from the formal system, diversion might serve the lofty ideals of human justice, as well as the mundane need for economic retrenchment.

One plausible solution in checking the growing volume of cases being funneled into the juvenile justice system would be to divert noncriminal offenses to alternative programs. Presumably, diversion programs would significantly reduce the amount of time that law enforcement agencies must spend reacting to minor offenses and would free up the system to direct its activities to serious offenses. Furthermore, community-based alternative programs may provide far more appropriate treatment for a condition that is often precipitated by conditions in the local community. Diversion could accomplish two things: It could allow for a more judicious handling of noncriminal behavioral problems, and it could enable the juvenile justice system to assume the posture of a court of law that deals with serious criminal matters.

The Professionalization of Police Work

People in many occupations in the United States have been seeking the status of a "professional" or attempting to "professionalize" their jobs. In an article entitled "The Professionalization of Everyone?" Harold Wilensky (1964) argued that the degree of professionalization is measured not merely by the degree of technical competence, adherence to rules and regulations, and rigid educational standards, but also by the degree of adherence to a service ideal. According to Wilensky, a craftsman who has gone to a trade school, served an apprenticeship, and become a highly competent technician would nonetheless be a nonprofessional if he lacked a moral commitment to serve the best interest of his client. Thus, professionalism entails the notion of putting service to clients above the demands of profit, personal reputation, and personal sentiment.

In *The Police and the Public* (1971), Albert J. Reiss, Jr., has expounded upon Wilensky's discussion of professionalization. Reiss sees police work as one of the few occupations that includes all the essential elements of a profession. The police in the United States are constantly required to make decisions involving technical and moral judgments that may greatly affect the fate of various people. They are sworn to enforce the law impartially and to exercise discretion in the application of just standards. Reiss has underscored the professional nature of police work:

> Duty perhaps means more to the police than it does to those who work in occupations that lay more legitimate claims to the status of professions. Policing is one of the few "moral call" occupations. Police are duty bound to come when and where called, regardless of who calls them. Like clergymen, they serve others in matters of moral crisis and dilemma. But, as in the military, they must be prepared to follow orders and give their lives in the line of duty. (1971:183)

It has been argued that diversion programs can contribute to the growing professionalization of police departments by demanding the universal application of explicit, legitimate criteria in the decision to arrest, detain, or divert. Formal diversion programs can be developed for specific types of offenders, and police discretion can be channeled or directed according to clearly delineated standards. Removal of certain categories of noncriminal behavioral problems from the domain of the juvenile justice system would introduce structural and procedural regularity and would greatly enhance the emerging professional stance of police work.

The Attack on Detention

One of the major concerns among the advocates of diversion is keeping more juveniles out of detention or jail than has been the case in the past. Juvenile detention is the practice of holding juveniles in secure custody pending court disposition for offenses that range from abandonment by parents, incorrigibility, and running away from home to such serious offenses as homicide, rape, burglary, and aggravated assault. Persons involved in the less serious offenses are often referred to as "PINS," "MINS," or "CINS," meaning persons, minors, or children "in need of supervision." Many persons who are designated as PINS cases are dealt with informally but are in need of some temporary care until suitable placement can be found. Those juveniles charged with criminal acts may also be placed in a detention facility as a measure of public protection and to prevent the offender from absconding before the juvenile court can review the case.

In counties where no detention facility is available, the only alternative is often the local jail or an adult penal institution. According to a 1973 Senate subcommittee that investigated the detention and jailing of juveniles, over 100,000 youths annually spend at least twenty-four hours incarcerated in a jail or a police lockup. A special LEAA jail survey, entitled the 1970 *National Jail Census* (Law Enforcement Assistance Administration, 1971), found that on a single day surveyed (March 15, 1970), 7,800 juveniles were held in about 4,000 adult jails. The survey did not include the jails of all states, nor did it include jails that do not have authority to hold prisoners for more than forty-eight hours. If it had, the total number of juveniles in adult jails would have been larger. Of these 7,800 juveniles in adult jails, two-thirds were being held for a court appearance and the remaining third were serving sentences, were awaiting transfer to some other jurisdiction, or were neglected children with no other facility available.

Although the chances of confinement may be quite rare relative to the total volume of juvenile delinquency in the United States, critics of the treatment of youth see incarceration in jails even for a short time as an arbitrary and inappropriate response to youthful offenders. Consider the following excerpts from the hearings before a Senate subcommittee that was investigating juvenile delinquency:

Senator Bayh: Here we are in the age of relative enlightenment, and yet despite the enlightenment which exists in many parts of our society, we are incarcerating more and more young people in adult jails than we did in previous years.

Mrs. Sarri, Project Coordinator, National Assessment of Juvenile Corrections: Yes, in this one State, which is an urban, Middle Western State, it appears that between 1968 and 1972, if we can trust the data, that it went from 10,000 to 25,000 children in jail per year in that 4-year period of time. So, that represents a substantial increase, and at a time 75 years after the founding of the juvenile court, which was established to remove children from the adult criminal justice system, we in fact, have a very, very large number of youths in jail.

A recent survey in Illinois done by Mattick indicated there are also serious problems in trying to separate juveniles from adults. Many States require that there be separate facilities. If children are to be held in adult jails that there be separate facilities for juveniles and adults. In the Mattick survey of 160 jails in Illinois, he found 142 of those jails held juveniles but only 9 out of 142, in fact, had facilities for the segregation of juveniles from adult offenders. So, there is more fiction than fact if we look at the survey that Mattick completed and there is no reason to believe that the Illinois survey represents a deviant case as far as the other States are concerned.

Now, another problem is the fact that those children who are held in jail are very frequently not children who would represent any kind of serious danger for the community. A recent survey in upper New York State . . . indicated that 43 percent of the children who were held in jail were what we call status offenders. . . .

[Another survey] noted that the number of prior court contacts was more highly correlated with detention and jail than the type of offense that led to the particular holding at that point in time. Those who were charged with crimes against persons were more likely to be detained than those who committed property or victimless crimes, but the people who committed crimes against persons were detained less than juveniles who committed status offenses.

Senator Bayh: Let me explore the distinction. You are saying that someone could get involved in a crime involving an attack on a person, like a mugging, and be treated less severely than someone who dropped out of school or who wouldn't attend school regularly or who ran away?

Mrs. Sarri: Right. A Western State survey which was completed last year indicated that dependent and neglected children were held in jail when necessary in more than 50 percent of the counties in that State and, furthermore, more than half of the jails reported they placed juveniles in jail as a deterrent even though there was not any formal charge. (Committee on the Judiciary, U.S. Senate, 1973:7–9)

Although most states have laws forbidding the use of jails for juvenile detention, the LEAA *National Jail Census* and the testimony given before the Senate's Committee on the Judiciary point to flagrant violations of the laws. A report by the Department of Health, Education, and Welfare recognized that "with few exceptions, individual counties do not have a sufficient number of detention cases to justify maintaining a detention service" (Downey, 1970). Some 93 percent of the country's juvenile court jurisdictions, serving 44 percent of the overall population, have no special facilities to detain children. Thus, despite the laudable intent of the law, counties without juvenile detention facilities often have no choice but to send juveniles to jails or adult institutions.

Detention statistics are difficult to obtain. From the detention information that certain jurisdictions do maintain, it is virtually impossible to assemble comparable statistics because of the wide variation among jurisdictions in recording the data. The National Council on Crime and Delinquency found that the detention rates in eleven counties in California ranged from 19 percent to 66 percent. A study of juvenile detention in eleven states also found substantial variation in detention rates (Ferster, Snethen, and Courtless, 1969). Table 11–1 indicates the percentage of juvenile detention by offense for the six major metropolitan areas and five counties included in the latter study. As Table 11–1 confirms, there is no

TABLE 11–1 *Percentage Detained, by Offense*

Offense	Locality										
	A	B	C	D	E	F	G	H	I	J	K
Against persons	24.9	8.8	17.6	8.1	N/A	5.2	1.6	1.0	3.0	6.1	3.0
Against property	45.5	19.1	31.1	20.0	N/A	22.3	15.1	24.0	36.7	32.9	32.0
Conduct[a]	9.9	15.0	6.9	N/A	N/A	N/A	8.2	8.1	9.5	12.2	15.0
Status	16.5	32.3	23.0	64.2	21.8	54.3	68.5	65.2	32.5	38.6	45.0
Traffic	N/A	0.4	0.8	N/A	N/A	N/A	N/A	1.0	1.7	1.4	3.0
All others	3.3	24.4	20.7	7.6	N/A	18.2	6.6	0.8	16.6	8.8	2.0

Source: E. Z. Ferster, E. N. Snethen, and T. F. Courtless. "Juvenile Detention: Protection, Prevention or Punishment." *Fordham Law Review* 37 (December 1969):161–96.

[a]Examples of conduct offenses include being drunk and disorderly, disturbing the peace, and creating mischief.

apparent pattern to detention rates other than that the highest rates are usually not for the most serious offenses.

The President's Commission on Law Enforcement and Administration of Justice, which studied the issue of corrections in the United States, concluded its section on juvenile detention with the following statement:

> Confusion and misuse pervade detention. It has come to be used by police and probation officers as a disposition; judges use it for punishment, protection, storage and lack of other facilities. More than in any other phase of the correctional process, the use of detention is colored by rationalization, duplicity, and double talk, generally unchallenged because it is always easy to make a case for detaining on the grounds of the child's offenses or the demands of the public as interpreted by the police or the press. Detention too often serves as storage, a means of delaying action. It protects the police, the probation officer and the judge from criticism in the event that a released child commits another law violation while awaiting court hearing. It removes from the probation officer its obligation to help parents assume responsiblity for supervising their child in his own home and to help the child assume responsibility for his own behavior in the community. (1967a:129)

Accurate data on the length of detention stays are simply not available at the present time. In some jurisdictions, detention may be overnight or two or three days at the most while other jurisdictions routinely detain juveniles for several weeks. In some instances, a lengthy period of detention may be indicated because the child constitutes a clear threat to the community or because the probability that the child will run away is extremely high. In other cases, detention becomes a matter of convenience, of diagnostic study, or of "teaching kids a lesson." The National Council on Crime and Delinquency (President's Commission on Law Enforcement and Administration of Justice, 1967a) found that the range of detention was from one day to sixty-eight days, with the average being six days for jails, eighteen days for detention facilities, and twenty-eight days for other types of facilities. Only three states prescribe a hearing within a specified period of time after detention; a few others specify that priority in the scheduling of adjudicatory hearings is to be given to detained juveniles. Some states limit the length of detention but also allow renewals of detention with no apparent limits on the renewals. A substantial number of juveniles are detained for longer than two-week periods, with the District of Columbia detaining nearly 70 percent for more than two weeks and 30 percent for more than two months (Ferster, Snethen, and Courtless, 1969). The National Council on Crime and Delinquency concluded that long periods of detention usually stem from the misconceptions of juvenile judges that

> these [detention] facilities are all-purpose institutions for (1) meeting health or mental needs, (2) punishment or treatment in lieu of a training school commitment, (3) retarded children until a State institution can

receive them, (4) pregnant girls until they can be placed prior to delivery, (5) brain-injured children involved in delinquency, (6) protection from irate parents who might harm the child, (7) a material witness in an adult case, (8) giving the delinquent "short sharp shock" treatment, (9) educational purposes ("He'll have to go to school in detention"), (10) therapy, (11) "ethical and moral" training, (12) lodging until an appropriate foster home or institution turns up. (President's Commission on Law Enforcement and Administration of Justice, 1967a:129)

Some jurisdictions require detention hearings after the juvenile court intake officer makes a decision to detain a juvenile. For example, the rules of procedure for the juvenile court system in Arizona specify that no child may be detained for more than twenty-four hours without a formal detention hearing and that if a detention hearing is not held within the time specified, the child must be released to the custody of his or her parents or guardians. Many jurisdictions do not require detention hearings, thereby granting the police or probation officer full authority in what should be exclusively a court prerogative. The National Council on Crime and Delinquency found that police often made the decision about whether a juvenile would be detained, even though such action was prohibited by statute in the particular state under study. In most cases, the juvenile judge routinely endorses the decisions of police officers.

The National Council recommended using an alternative method of juvenile court decision making that would involve a "consent decree" rather than formal adjudication. A consent decree would entail a conference conducted by the intake officer, the juvenile, his or her parents, and an attorney. Such negotiations would seem to be appropriate when adjudication appears unnecessary, but some form of intervention does seem necessary. Upon conclusion of the negotiations, all the parties involved would agree to a tentative plan of action. Should the negotiations fail or the consent decree be violated, standard juvenile court procedures ranging from dismissal to formal adjudication would still be available. A consent decree arrived at by all parties involved is seen as a further protection of the legal rights of juveniles and as a way of lessening the need for detention.

As laudable as this consent decree process may be, it is doubtful whether it actually protects the rights of juveniles. One problem is the informality of the entire proceeding and the lack of formal legitimization by a juvenile judge. A second problem is that it could violate the double jeopardy provision of the Fifth Amendment by allowing a juvenile to be subject to an unofficial hearing and informal settlement, as well as to a formal court hearing for the same offense. In addition to these problems, it is doubtful whether the consent decree represents any significant savings in time.

The Juvenile Justice and Delinquency Prevention Act of 1974 stipulates that states receiving federal funds under this act must agree to remove all status offenders from institutional confinement, whether confinement is in a detention or jail facility. The movement to implement a diversion process requires a reduction in the role of the juvenile court system in dealing with youth problems. Avoiding detention is a prime aim of that movement.

THE MEANING OF DIVERSION

As we have just seen, a wide range of forces has combined to make *diversion* the key word in juvenile justice for the 1980s. However, at present, the word has no one precise meaning. Diversion can refer simply to the act of deflecting juveniles away from the juvenile justice system. In many other instances, it implies the development of alternative strategies or programs for dealing with juveniles outside of the formal processing mechanisms of the juvenile court. These alternative strategies range from informal, "field adjustment" strategies to sophisticated, formalized treatment programs that may be as institutionalized as the juvenile justice system except that they are not administered by a formal agency of social control. Finally, to make matters even more confusing, some juvenile justice agencies use the term *diversion* to refer to formal actions taken by the juvenile court that attempt to "minimize penetration into the juvenile justice system" (Cressey and McDermott, 1973). In this instance, the "diverted" juvenile actually remains within the formal system, but attempts are made to reduce the exposure of the offender to the juvenile court process. This type of diversion may take the form of an official or semiofficial program in which the standard procedures of the juvenile justice system are somewhat modified or altered. Thus, as simple as the word *diversion* may be, the actual implementation of diversion may entail radically different alternatives.

Klein (1976) has suggested that the term *diversion* should refer only to the process of turning alleged juvenile offenders away from the formal juvenile justice system. According to this definition, diversion does not require that specific alternatives be prescribed, only that the juvenile not enter the official system. The term *referral* is used to describe the process by which a juvenile who is diverted from the formal system is placed in a program that is not directly related to the juvenile justice system. Thus, a juvenile can be *diverted* from the juvenile justice system but may or may not be *referred* to a specific agency or program.

Discretionary Points of Diversion

Not only do we encounter difficulty in providing one concrete definition of diversion, but we also have difficulty in specifying the precise moment when diversion has officially or unofficially occurred. Cases may be diverted officially or unofficially at a number of points. For example, of the 2,170,193 juveniles taken into custody in 1977, 44 percent were released by law enforcement officers, 47 percent were referred to juvenile court, 2.5 percent were referred to a welfare agency, 2 percent were referred to some other police agency, and 4 percent were remanded to criminal court (Federal Bureau of Investigation, 1978). Thus, we see that a great deal of diversion occurs before cases enter the juvenile justice system. What we do not know is how many cases of police contact in the field result in no arrest or no official police action. This type of contact could also be defined as diversion. Similarly, of those cases disposed of by the juvenile court, growing numbers of them are being handled in a non-judicial fashion that represents another type of diversion. The discretion of citizens in lodging complaints can result in yet another kind of diversion. Let us examine four points at which discretion can result in diversion.

1. *Citizen Discretion.* Before a juvenile offender is even brought to the attention of the police or the juvenile justice system, the offense must be known. Despite the popular image of the active and aggressive nature of police work, Black and Reiss (1970) have argued that most police operations are "reactive"—that is, the vast majority of police work is initiated through citizen complaints (see Chapter 3). Crime detection depends primarily on citizen action and police reaction. After monitoring telephone calls to police stations, Black and Reiss concluded that 78 percent of police and juvenile encounters are initiated by citizens, while the remaining 22 percent are initiated by police. Thus, the community at large has a significant input into the official rate of juvenile delinquency, and the standards of the public contribute more to the official creation of juvenile delinquents than do the standards of the police officer on patrol. In sum, a type of unofficial or informal diversion can occur as the result of citizens' discretion in lodging complaints.

2. *Police Discretion.* Discretion is based on a personal judgment that is influenced by practical skills, experience, information, and—often—ambiguity. The police exercise enormous discretion in enforcing the law, and the decision to arrest is highly influenced by personal judgment. In his field studies, Black (1971) observed that the police released approximately half of the persons they suspected of committing a crime; 58 percent of the felony encounters and 44 percent of the misdemeanor encounters resulted in an arrest. Black also found that police discretion is strongly influenced by the preference of the citizen complainant. When the citizen expressed a preference for arrest, the police made an arrest in roughly 65 percent of those situations. When the expressed preference was for no arrest, the police made an arrest in only 10 percent of those

encounters. When the expressed preference was for an arrest, the police arrested 75 percent of those alleged offenders.

Bittner (1967) discussed the role of police as "law officers" and "peace officers." As law officers, the police are seen as functionaries of the court and, as such, are constrained in their activities. The role of peace officer encompasses a wide range of occupational duties not directly related to making arrests and generally without specified structure. This role receives only casual attention by the police, and while it is directed to the maintenance of peace and order, it covers a large residual category of aiding, informing, directing, admonishing, disciplining, counseling, and all other activities that do not focus on making an arrest. It is in the role of peace officer that the police exercise the greatest amount of discretion. The experienced police officer who can "play it by ear" has many options open during encounters with juveniles. Indeed, an actual arrest may be the last option that a police officer uses when he or she confronts a juvenile. Depending on the organizational structure of the police department, a juvenile suspected of committing an offense may be turned over to a special police youth squad that deals exclusively with juvenile matters. In other instances, a police officer may call the encounter a "field contact," which serves as an accounting device for police work but does not constitute a lawful arrest. In many other instances, police are encouraged to utilize the services of nonlegal agencies or institutions, such as counseling centers, health clinics, or shelter care facilities. Informal diversion practices by the police can effectively screen out certain types of juvenile offenders well before any formal diversion action is called for by the juvenile justice system.

3. *Juvenile Court Intake Discretion.* The function of juvenile court intake is to screen out cases that do not warrant a petition. This kind of nonjudicial handling of juvenile cases masks varying levels of official reaction. For example, although the juvenile intake officer may not file a petition for a juvenile offender, he or she may utilize informal adjustment procedures or may attempt to satisfy the complainant by a less formal remedy than juvenile court adjudication. In its *Legislative Guide*, the Children's Bureau (1969) recognized the need for some method of adjustment at the point of intake other than a simple court referral or outright dismissal. The Children's Bureau recommended unambiguous procedures for these informal adjustments. In practice, however, intake dispositions often include informal probationary periods of "grounding." Behavioral expectations during this period of informal supervision normally include regular attendance at school (in some instances even church), conventional dress, restricted hours for leaving the house, and curtailment of social interaction with friends. Advocates of the use of informal probation argue that it avoids the evils of formal adjudication, saves time, and is more economical. Opponents of this practice argue that

it is too informal and that the rights of juveniles are too easily subject to abuse or disregard.

Whichever perspective on informal probation one wishes to take, one still has to recognize that diversion can occur at the point of intake without any official policy or formal procedure being utilized. Depending on the resources available in the community, the intake officer may decide to remove juveniles from the juvenile justice system and refer them to alternative services in the community. One can refer to this process as diversion, deinstitutionalization, or "alternative encapsulation" (Klein et al., 1976). Whatever the term used to describe it, the opportunity to turn young offenders away from the juvenile justice system has long been part of the juvenile court.

4. *Judicial Discretion.* Juvenile judges are formally granted an enormous range of discretionary power in dealing with youthful offenders. The glaring lack of statutory prescriptions in delinquency matters results in a greater opportunity for judicial discretion at the juvenile level than at the adult level. There is very little review of judicial discretion, and because of the essentially hidden nature of juvenile cases, even less is known of juvenile judicial decisions than of adult ones. That there is considerable variability in the sentencing practices of judges has been demonstrated for many years. This variability may be partially attributable to the varying structure of the court system. In some jurisdictions, the juvenile court is a separate court; in others, juvenile jurisdiction comes under a family court; in still others, it is part of the probate court (Rubin, 1976). In addition, as the President's Commision on Law Enforcement and Administration of Justice has pointed out, judges are not uniformly qualified. The commission found that nearly half did not have a college degree, some 20 percent had not even attended college, and about 20 percent were not members of the bar (President's Commission on Law Enforcement and Administration of Justice, 1967b:607). In short, the lack of standardization in the judicial posture of the juvenile courts produces variable and ambiguous results. The distinction between a new approach called "diversion" and "old-fashioned" discretion becomes blurred when the end result is the same and only the label changes.

Diversion as a Formal Policy

While cases may be diverted at a number of points, diversion as a formally prescribed policy or process normally begins at the point of intake. A juvenile is referred to the juvenile court either physically (actually brought to the intake facility) or through a process known as a "paper referral" (that is, the juvenile is to appear sometime in the future at the intake facility but is released in the meantime). The function of the juvenile intake unit is to screen out certain types of cases before they are submitted for a judicial hearing. It is also up to the intake officer to decide whether a juvenile is to be detained or released to his or her parent. Ideally, diversion at this intake stage would follow prescribed procedures and clearly delineated criteria. Juveniles charged with certain types of offenses would qualify for diversion programs and would advance no further into the juvenile justice system. Of course, we have to recognize that some jurisdictions have no intake personnel and that the intake function in these jurisdictions is performed outside of the juvenile system. When that is the case, the police generally are delegated the responsibility for intake, and diversion can occur even before contact with the juvenile court is made.

As a guide to actual policy, Edwin Lemert has recommended the following as "minimal" considerations for the construction of a diversion program:

1. Diversion should be closely articulated with the workings of the juvenile justice system because that's what it is about.

2. Police should become the chief source of referrals to diversion agencies because that's where most official processing starts.

3. There should be positive gains to police from their making referrals.

4. Diversion agencies in large cities probably are best located near schools but not in them.

5. Serious truancy and cases of aggravated disciplinary problems should be referred routinely to diversion agencies. No school should be allowed to dismiss or suspend a child without finding that provision has been made for his continuing education or employment.

6. In unfit home cases, absence of home care, incorrigibility complaints by parents or school authorities, and moral danger cases, the police, sheriff's departments, district attorneys, and probation departments should be compelled to find that no agency exists or none is willing to accept the cases before referring them to juvenile court or filing petitions.

7. Diversion agencies should reserve the right to reject cases but should not refer cases to the police or juvenile court. (1971:94)

Reflected in Lemert's proposal is the idea that some juvenile offenses are readily categorized as suitable for diversion. Cases involving status offenses are cited as prime candidates for deflection from the official court process and assignment to some diversion program or procedure. However, difficulty immediately arises since there is no standardized definition of status offense other than its reference to "noncriminal" offenses. Several jurisdictions define some relatively serious acts as status offenses. In these instances, certain types of drug possession, health, welfare, and morals violations, and the nebulous category of incorrigible behavior may, as status offenses, mask serious offenses that are not appropriate for diversion. Thus, in many instances, even if the intake worker had mandatory, clearly delineated criteria to follow, the final determination regarding diversion could still be quite arbitrary.

A comparison of police arrest or field contact forms with intake forms at juvenile courts will often reveal glaring discrepancies. In a study of one diversion project, it was found that juveniles diverted from the court were routinely charged at intake with a "health, welfare, and morals violation" whenever the police arrest was for any type of drug violation, which included the possession of tobacco, alcohol, marijuana, amphetamines, barbiturates, and other types of illegal drugs. It was also found that many minor and some major personal offenses were "adjusted" at the point of intake and classified as "incorrigible behavior" when in fact the arrest sheet indicated that the initial offense was disorderly conduct, malicious mischief, vandalism, joyriding, or shoplifting. The very existence and proliferation of diversion programs may encourage such adjustments for the sake of utilizing and supporting diversion.

Other issues involved in making decisions about diversion are discrimination and arbitrary discretion. The President's Commission on Law Enforcement and Administration of Justice pointed out the extremely subjective nature of intake decision making. In *Juvenile Delinquency and Youth Crime* (1967b), the commission condemned the use of social factors, such as race, ethnicity, and social class, and attitudes, such as "deviant," "hostile," "remorseful," and "cooperative," in the intake screening of clients. One study of juvenile court intake criteria found that in addition to the severity of the offense, prior referrals to the juvenile court were used extensively at the intake evaluation of clients, as were the strengths and weaknesses of the home and school life, the youth's attitude toward authority, and, in some instances, the youth's church attendance (Ferster, Courtless, and Snethen, 1970). It was also found that the case load facing the juvenile court can become a critical variable in determining whether a youth is diverted. The availability of diversion programs has had the effect of granting law enforcement officials more discretion at the point of intake, as well as at other points in the judicial process. Discretion can be an invaluable tool for the individualization of justice and often is a principle source of creativeness in the administration of justice. However, it can and does allow discrimination and inequitable treatment as well.

Legal, Paralegal, and Nonlegal Diversion

Rutherford and McDermott (1976) set forth a diversion typology based on the legal standing of programs in relation to the juvenile justice system. This framework is helpful for grappling with the definitional issues of diversion and for specifying the types of diversion programs that can be developed.

1. *Legal Diversion.* The first type of diversion discussed by Rutherford and McDermott is legal diversion. Legal diversion is usually administered by one of the formal social control agencies—most often the police or the juvenile court probation staff—and represents a process of minimizing the penetration into the juvenile justice system. It may entail informal encounters on the street or formalized programs, but in either case the objective of legal diversion is to divert the juvenile offender from the normal judicial process by creating alternative routes. The critical difference between this approach to diversion and other types that will be discussed is that a program of legal diversion is administered by a formal social control agency and thus reflects a strong element of formal legal sanctioning. For example, police in some jurisdictions initiate diversion for minors who, although they need help, do not require official referral to the juvenile system. Services range from counseling by police officers to placement in special programs provided by the community. Informal probation is another example of legal diversion. It operates within the confines of the juvenile justice system but allows court personnel the discretion of placing certain types of juvenile offenders in a probation program. Informal probation may range from a warning or reprimand to formal placement in a treatment program. The advantage of both these approaches to diversion is that the juvenile offender is diverted from the formal legal process and alternative, nonlegal strategies can be developed in the community to render service to juveniles in need of help.

The major shortcoming of legal diversion is that because such programs are administered and often staffed by formal social control agencies, they may inadvertently "widen the net." The attempt to remove young offenders from one process by channeling them into another that is basically no different from the first is hardly an advancement for juvenile rights. Klein et al. (1976) reported that one administrator of a diversion program estimated that 75 percent of cases referred to the program by the police were of the type that would normally have been released. There is also the danger that diversion programs may spotlight many first offenders who, without the existence of the programs, would be released but who now become pawns of a new social service system. Legal diversion can have all the trappings of institutionalization or legal sanctioning even though it comes under the guise of diversion.

2. *Paralegal Diversion.* Paralegal diversion exists outside of the formal organizational structure of the juvenile justice system but has formal ties with the legal system. These ties can take a number of forms; the two most common are financial support and administrative control. Other ties may be less explicit, but careful examination of a paralegal program often reveals organizational similarity and even personnel overlap with the juvenile justice system. Paralegal programs often develop directly

from the organizational needs of the juvenile justice system, and many, if not all, clients of paralegal programs are referred by the formal social control agency. Numerous private youth programs exist at the pleasure of the parent organization, the juvenile court; in these instances, the line of demarcation between the private and public sector becomes tenuous.

The *youth service bureau* is an example of a paralegal diversion program. The state of California pioneered in legislation for the establishment and founding of these bureaus, and some 170 of them now exist throughout the country. Because these bureaus vary tremendously from one jurisdiction to another in both the scope and nature of the service provided, it is virtually impossible to define them. The California Department of Youth Authority has described the youth service bureau as follows:

> The Youth Service Bureau is a place in the community to which
> delinquent-prone youths can be referred by parents, law enforcement agen-
> cies, the schools, etc. It should have a wide range of services reflecting the
> coordination and integration of important public and private prevention
> resources existing in the community. . . . The Youth Service Bureau con-
> cept asks those agencies, organizations, and individuals in a community
> who are involved in delinquency prevention to inventory, organize, and
> coordinate their resources in an exploration of new avenues of referral,
> education, and treatment adapted to meet the unique problems repre-
> sented by delinquency in their community. (1968:1)

The concept of a youth service bureau was initially suggested in 1967 by the task force report of the President's Commission on Law Enforcement and Administration of Justice (1967b). Such a bureau was to be a non-authoritarian social service agency serving delinquents and nondelinquents. The Department of Health, Education, and Welfare has estimated that some 50,000 minors have been diverted from the juvenile justice system into approximately 170 youth service bureaus, with another 150,000 juveniles who were not involved with the juvenile justice system receiving some form of service from a youth service bureau.

Despite the intuitive appeal of youth service bureaus, they have been the target of strong criticism. Howlett has argued that the creation of a diversion program through youth service bureaus may be a counterproductive endeavor: "In attempting to identify and treat the most menial forms of deviance, many of which neither require nor are amenable to treatment, the community may bind itself to its own inability to tolerate, absorb, or modify its concept of deviance" (1973:485). Most bureaus have not been in operation long enough to permit a meaningful evaluation of their effectiveness. However, they have the potential of creating a serious problem by violating the rights of juveniles.

3. *Nonlegal Diversion.* Nonlegal diversion programs operate totally outside the context of the juvenile justice system, and participation in

their activities is voluntary. The fundamental difference between nonlegal and paralegal or legal diversion programs is the absence of authority or control by social control agents. The client volunteers and participates in the nonlegal program because the program provides a meaningful service that meets his or her needs. In many instances, nonlegal diversion programs perform an advocacy role in attempting to guarantee the juvenile's freedom of choice. Such programs also maintain a strict posture of independence from the formal juvenile justice machinery, especially in the area of funding. Of course, many of these nonlegal programs become highly vulnerable to criticism and can be co-opted if they accept funds from certain sources.

"Schools for dropouts" exemplify a type of nonlegal diversion program that has appeared in some areas of the country. These schools or educational enrichment programs attempt to rescue the dropout from the frustration of boredom, unemployment, and low educational achievement by offering a learning experience geared to the needs of each client. Such educational programs may offer radically different curricula to stimulate the intellectual curiosity of confirmed school failures. Mandatory attendance, discipline, grades, and lesson plans may become of secondary importance, with informality, creativity, and flexibility receiving primary emphasis. Community interest and support often wanes when reports are released indicating that such schools have a high absentee rate and that the core of the curriculum is not intellectually overpowering. Yet, such innovative educational centers may accomplish a great deal with a certain forgotten or discarded segment of the school dropout population. A cursory examination of this type of nonlegal diversion program shows these educational enrichment centers to be relatively short-lived. They are often forced to buckle under to the bureaucratic demands of the traditional educational system.

EVALUATION OF DIVERSION PROGRAMS

A common observation concerning criminal and juvenile justice research is that most evaluations are scientifically inadequate. For example, in *The Effectiveness of Correctional Treatment* (1975), Lipton, Martinson, and Wilks discussed the difficulties encountered in assessing the rehabilitation research conducted between 1945 and 1967. Their only requirements for a methodologically adequate piece of research were that it use a control group and that it have some objective measure of the treatment effect. Out of the thousands of studies that had been conducted, Lipton, Martinson, and Wilks found only 231 acceptable ones. Since diversion is a relatively new approach to juvenile justice, very few studies have focused upon it. Many of the studies that have focused on diversion take the form of a narrative description, rather than a vigorous, scientific evaluation of the diversion process.

One problem in attempting to summarize evaluation studies of diversion programs is that there is no one precise definition of diversion. For some, diversion is simply the removal of juvenile offenders from the juvenile justice process. For others, it refers to the minimization of penetration into the system. For yet others, it means referring a juvenile to some form of community treatment. Furthermore, can one equate informal and unstructured diversion that occurs outside the official system with "official" diversion that occurs within the juvenile justice system? The diversion philosophy is so popular that a wide variety of different programs are lumped together as examples of the diversion movement. Research is handicapped by an absence of precise operational definitions and pronounced ambiguity about the meaning of diversion.

Like all evaluation research, evaluations of diversion programs must grapple with the problem of establishing criteria of success or failure. Usually the dependent variable in evaluation research is recidivism or a renewed contact with the criminal justice system. Recidivism is a particularly difficult concept to measure. Generally, it entails determining the number of new arrests incurred by the individuals in question. The first problem with using arrest data as a measure of success or failure is that an arrest does not constitute a finding of guilt. Second, a significant number of criminal offenses are not known to the police, and recidivism rates are thereby artificially deflated. Third, the subsequent offense committed may be totally different from the original offense so that one ends by comparing apples to oranges.

Glaser (1964) has argued that recidivism should not be treated as a simple dichotomy of success or failure. In evaluating the rehabilitative effects of any program, Glaser has suggested using four *degrees* of recidivism: (1) clear reformation—no apparent new crimes, no association with criminals, and relative order and stability in the ex-offenders' personal lives; (2) marginal reformation—no return to prison, but commission of minor crimes, some association with criminals, and inability to hold a steady job; (3) marginal failure—return to prison for parole violation or for commission of minor crimes; and (4) clear recidivism—return to prison for commission of a major crime.

In addition to adopting a sufficiently sophisticated notion of recidivism, evaluation research needs to be sensitive to such issues as *effectiveness, efficiency, due process of law,* and *system impact.* Effectiveness refers to the outcome of the program—whether the diversion process can demonstrate a reduction of juvenile crime, reintegration into the community, and some form of rehabilitation. The resources expended in bringing about this change are subsumed under the category of efficiency. A program may prove effective, but its efficiency, or social costs, may be prohibitive. Similarly, a diversion program may be highly effective and efficient but may constitute a grave infringement on the rights or dignity of an individual and thus result in a serious violation of due process of law. The diversion model of due process of law deliberately erects barriers or stumbling blocks to ensure that the justice system does not have total autonomy. Finally, when segments of the justice system and the community are interrelated, diversion may have a systemwide impact. A diversion program's repercussions for the police, schools, jobs, city budgets, and taxes can affect interpretations of the program's success or failure. With these problems in mind, let us now consider the scarce and limited data available on diversion programs.

Research Findings

1. *New Jersey Juvenile Conference Committees.* This diversion project grew out of a plan devised in 1945 for committees of representative citizens to hear complaints against children and to work out a solution by mutual agreement between the parties involved—the juvenile and his or her parent and the complainant. This kind of dispute settlement for minor behavioral problems proved so successful that the New Jersey Supreme Court encouraged the adoption of a statewide rule in 1953 to allow these citizens' committees to convene in each municipality. This type of diversion is voluntary in that if any of the parties object to submitting the dispute to such arbitration, the citizens' committee has no power to act. However, a study of this diversion program found that the citizens' committees looked and acted more like formal courts than benign arbitration boards. The committees often made decisions on matters over which they had no jurisdiction (for example, hearing serious criminal violations, "ordering" terms of probation, assessing fines, and calling for psychiatric examinations). There is also strong evidence that a disproportionate number of white, middle-class juveniles were diverted to these citizens' committees, while low-status or minority youth were sent to the juvenile court (Goff, 1966).

2. *Sacramento County 601 Diversion Project.* Under Section 601 of the California Welfare and Institutions Code, youths referred to the juvenile court for status offenses were randomly assigned to a unit where they received short-term, family-crisis therapy administered at intake by specially trained probation officers. The control group received only traditional probation treatment. This program was technically not a true diversion project since the juvenile court was highly involved in the project. However, it did represent an alternative approach to the traditional procedures of the juvenile court. During the first nine months of the project, 2.2 percent of the project cases were referred to court, in

contrast to 21.3 percent of the control group. A seven-month follow-up revealed that 36 percent of the project youth were subsequently rearrested, as compared to 46 percent of the control group. Criminal violations accounted for 18 percent of the recidivism of project clients, while for the control group criminal violations accounted for 31 percent of recidivism. On the surface, this project appears to have been successful, but a seven-month follow-up is unduly short. Furthermore, it might have been extremely informative had a third group been entirely diverted from the court process and a comparison made between this group and the other two groups (Thorton, Barrett, and Musolf, 1972).

3. *Project Crossroads.* This study, conducted under the auspices of the U.S. Department of Labor, involved the diversion and referral of first-time juvenile offenders and a comparison with a control group of traditionally processed juvenile offenders. The latter group was further divided into those who were screened from court processing and those who were adjudicated. The results of this project showed that during a fifteen-month follow-up period, 31 percent of the diverted and referred group were rearrested, while 44 percent of the screened group and 47 percent of the adjudicated cases were rearrested. The conclusion of the study was that diversion accompanied by some form of referral for services was more effective than the traditional mode of processing or the type of screening that typically took place (Leiber, 1971).

4. *Los Angeles County Diversion Study.* Malcolm Klein (1975) has attempted to evaluate four dispositional alternatives for juvenile offenders: counsel and release, referral to community agencies with purchase of services, referral to community agencies without purchase of services, and petition. Despite this study's establishment of a carefully structured system to ensure random assignment to one of the four conditions, police involved in the study began assigning certain youths to dispositions they considered appropriate. In addition to this distortion of the research design, the actual number of juveniles assigned to each of the four dispositional categories was considerably lower than expected, which placed severe limitations on the subsequent analysis. Klein's most dramatic finding was that juveniles whose cases received further action (through petition and the two types of referral to community agencies) had higher recidivism rates over a six-month period than juveniles who were counseled and released. However, Klein indicated that according to self-report data, the counseled and released group committed as many delinquent acts as did the youths in the three other dispositional categories. Apparently the greater involvement of the three groups in the juvenile justice system and referral process resulted in high visibility of the deviant acts that these youth subsequently committed.

5. *Juvenile Referral Project.* Suzanne Lincoln (1975) evaluated a pilot diversion project in a large West Coast police agency. This diversion program referred juveniles to ten community agencies for such social services as health care, counseling, recreational opportunities, and employment assistance. The referred offenders were matched with nontreated juveniles. Nearly half of the nontreated control group was counseled and released, whereas all members of the experimental group received some form of treatment. A follow-up investigation using police records was conducted one year later. The two groups differed in the average number of offenses committed during the one-year follow-up period: Diverted juveniles averaged 1.7 offenses, while the nontreated juveniles averaged 1.1 offenses. Lincoln also found that the diverted group scored higher in the commission of three or more new offenses. On the basis of these findings, Lincoln concluded that the referral process increased rather than decreased recidivism rates. Thus, a diversion program may have the effect of widening the net of the justice system by reacting to behavioral problems that would have been dismissed or ignored had the program not existed.

6. *Deinstitutionalization of Status Offenders Project (DSO).* The most comprehensive study of diversion has been the DSO Project funded by the Law Enforcement Assistance Administration. The project operated in several regions of the country. Although the findings of DSO are only preliminary, they present a number of problems relevant to the evaluation of diversion. The avowed purpose of DSO was to divert status offenders from the juvenile court system. Initially, it was naively assumed that "pure" status offenders would be the prime candidates for diversion. However, self-report surveys of these status offenders revealed that only 8 percent were in fact pure status offenders, while over 88 percent were a mixed category of status, misdemeanor, and felony offenders. Furthermore, less than 1 percent were "pure" felony or misdemeanor offenders. These findings suggest two observations: (1) Juvenile offenders do not "specialize" in one type of offense. (2) "Offense" and "offender" are not interchangeable—that is, a *status offender* has very likely committed a *variety of offenses.* While a diversion program may divert a case because the specific offense under consideration is a status offense, the offender is most likely to have committed other offenses as well. With or without diversion programs, the juvenile court will be confronted by offenders who have committed a mixed bag of offenses.

Another way of looking at the same problem is to examine the number of offenses committed by juveniles in terms of arrest status. Table 11–2 summarizes the average number of self-reported offenses by level of contact with the police, ranging from no arrest to five or more arrests. The first row of Table 11–2 shows that many youths with no arrest records do

TABLE 11-2 Self-Reported Offenses, by Arrest Status

Arrest Status	Average No. of Status Offenses	Average No. of Misdemeanor Offenses	Average No. of Felony Offenses	Average No. of All Offenses
No arrests (N=237)	3.960	1.542	.936	1.988
One arrest: status (N=60)	4.868	1.762	1.233	2.433
One arrest: misdemeanor (N=18)	4.758	2.016	1.164	2.448
One arrest: felony (N=15)	4.392	2.962	1.894	2.910
Two arrests (N=57)	4.494	1.995	1.309	2.424
Three arrests (N=35)	5.441	2.544	1.575	2.963
Four arrests (N=26)	5.077	2.985	2.242	3.194
Five or more arrests (N=52)	5.653	3.211	1.926	3.379

Source: Dean G. Rojek. "Juvenile Diversion: Preliminary Evaluation Issues."
Unpublished manuscript. University of Georgia, 1979.

report that they have violated the law. Juveniles involved in the DSO Project who had no arrests self-reported committing nearly 4 status offenses, 1.5 misdemeanors, and about 1 felony during the preceding six months. Moreover, a juvenile arrested for a status offense did not differ appreciably in self-reports of past offenses from a one-time misdemeanant or felony offender. As the number of arrests increases to five or more, the mean violation rates increase only slightly. Overall, Table 11–2 suggests that regardless of the seriousness of the offense that precipitated the arrest, the violation rates for all types of offenders are remarkably similar. Hence, in diverting a juvenile apprehended for a status offense, we may be ignoring the possibility that the juvenile is also a felony offender.

A final observation stemming from the DSO Project has to do with diversion as a "nip-it-in-the-bud" program. Many advocates of a diversion philosophy argue that by dealing with today's status offender, we deter tomorrow's felony offender. This argument presumes an escalation of offenses from status offenses to misdemeanors to felonies. Diversion is often justified as a first-offender program that treats the potential delinquent when the problem first arises. In Figure 11–1 we have attempted to delineate a career history for persons with multiple arrests to see whether there is a progression from status offenses to more serious criminal offenses. A total of 1,250 juvenile offenders were randomly selected for this purpose (Rojek, 1979). Some 4 percent of the juveniles referred to juvenile court did not have an arrest record, and 62 percent had only one arrest. This means that two-thirds of the sample would be irrelevant to a discussion of offense escalation. Of the remaining 34 percent, who had two or more arrests, 12 percent had "static careers"—that is, there was no change in the seriousness of offense from one arrest to the next. The remaining juveniles, who had changing career histories were classified as having escalating careers, de-escalating careers, or erratic careers. As can be seen in Figure 11–1, only fourteen offenders out of the entire population fit the escalation pattern, progressing from a less serious to a more serious offense. The overwhelming majority of those with changing career patterns had erratic, or random, careers. No clear or discernable offense pattern arose for most offenders. Thus, actual offense patterns quite rarely substantiate the "escalation" rationale behind diversion programs for status offenders.

In sum, the DSO Project suggested that many of the assumptions of the movement to divert status offenders are overly simplistic and imply a far easier and more significant impact than may actually be the case. The alleged target of diversion, the pure status offender, is quite rare. Moreover, substantiation of the assumption that deviant careers develop as status offenses escalate to more serious offenses is, in reality, also quite rare. These observations do not mean that diversion is or will be a failure.

FIGURE 11–1 *Deviant Careers of Juveniles Referred to Juvenile Court (Pima County, Arizona)*

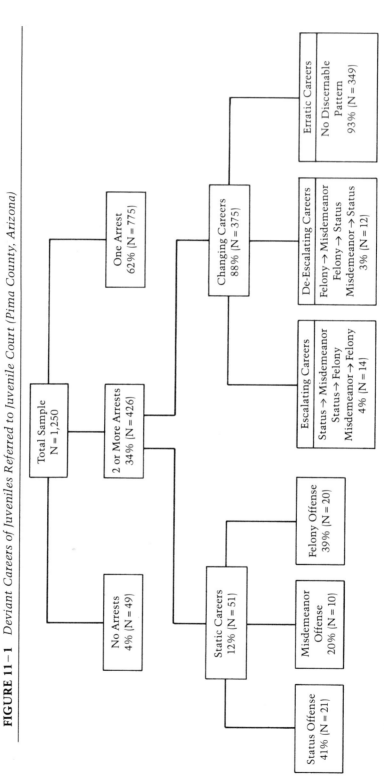

Source: Dean G. Rojek. "Juvenile Diversion: Preliminary Evaluation Issues." Unpublished manuscript. University of Georgia, 1979.

Rather, they force us to recognize the complexities in transforming a simple and "obvious" proposal into an operating program.

ASSESSMENT OF THE EVIDENCE: DIVERSION AS AN IDEOLOGY

Martinson's quip in defense of his review of treatment programs looms as a possible epitaph for diversion: "The history of correction is a graveyard of abandoned fads" (1976:181). To date, the evidence for or against diversion is not overwhelmingly compelling, but the final verdict is not in. While there is considerable agreement in principle about diverting youths from the juvenile justice system, no systematic body of findings has yet identified the efficacy of different diversion approaches or even the advantage of diversion over traditional modes of handling youthful offenders.

A major problem confronting evaluation research is the ambiguity that shrouds the concept of diversion. Similarly, it is not clear what yardstick is appropriate in defining the success or failure of diversion. Recidivism measures may reveal more about the agents of social control than they do about the offenders themselves. New measures may have to be formulated to grapple with issues of efficiency, justice, humaneness, and effectiveness. The first round of evidence has produced anything but a clear verdict for or against diversion. However, what sketchy evidence we do have seems to indicate that diversion may not win the case as the new champion of juvenile justice. Indeed, the transient nature of juvenile reform measures leads one to believe that the courtroom may be empty before the jury turns in the final verdict.

As we noted earlier, the proponents of diversion draw on labeling theory in arguing that juvenile court proceedings stigmatize youth and help reinforce deviant careers. The initial movement for formal diversion of juveniles from the court machinery emerged at a time when empirical investigations of the labeling perspective were favorable. Dramatic findings and support for the labeling perspective were provided in studies conducted by Scheff (1966) on mental illness and Schwartz and Skolnick (1964) on the impact of involvement in the criminal justice system on employment opportunities, and by the highly acclaimed reader edited by Rubinton and Weinburg (1968). Early research on the labeling approach was, however, less than systematic. Although these studies examined selective dimensions of labeling theory, a thorough assessment was lacking. More recent studies of the assertions of labeling theorists have seriously questioned and challenged many of the earlier conclusions (see Chapter 9). In view of these recent criticisms, the ideology of diversion is in the uncomfortable position of having its underpinnings weakened, if not totally dislodged.

Correctional administrators are continually faced with a history of failure and are constantly seeking ways of developing more effective strategies of prevention or rehabilitation. At the very outset of their discussion of diversion projects, Cressey and McDermott made the following observation:

> Only a few years ago, most American chief probation officers and other juvenile justice administrators used the words "research" and "breakthrough" constantly if they wanted good marks from their superiors and their colleagues. In large cities especially, ratings of "excellent" went to the men who frequently used this rhetoric and who developed the corresponding research programs. Now the word is "diversion" and it is diversion programs that win accolades. (1973:1)

There is intuitive appeal for change, experimentation, and innovation, particularly in the area of delinquency control and prevention. However, far too many social programs are implemented with undue frenzy and speed only to be discarded for the next public policy fad. Etzioni, in discussing the "modern" approach in many community mental health programs, stated:

> Once in a while there erupts a "new approach" that catches the imagination of the media, policy-makers, and many an expert, and hurriedly affects the well-being of hundreds of thousands of people and the allocation of millions of tax dollars. With little experimentation, whole agencies are disbanded, dismembered or subsumed. New bureaucracies, centers and services are created and sources of laws enacted and hundreds of regulations issued. Then, a few years following a major overhaul, it is discovered that the fashionable new policy's merits were poorly documented, its flaws unanticipated and its glamour chiefly the result of its novel contrast to the preceding battle-scarred and weary programs. (1976:10)

Criminologists have often been appalled at the myth of the United States criminal justice system. Despite the glamour and prestige that the media accord the judiciary, the image is eclipsed by the process of plea bargaining, outmaneuvered by enterprising defense attorneys or prosecuting attorneys, and, perhaps most disturbing of all, outmuscled by administrative bureaucracies. The fact of the matter is that the courts are inundated with cases and that administrative agencies are responsible for more and more of the judicial decision making and arbitration. In the area of juvenile justice, nonjudicial avenues are rapidly increasing. Although these avenues may represent a proper delegation of authority by the court, they are also usurping a considerable share of judicial decision making. Formal diversion programs are, by virtue of definition, channeling cases to nonjudicial agencies that are charged with the duty of treating or rendering services to nonadjudicated juveniles.

But what course of action is available for these nonjudicial agencies if a juvenile refuses services or does not fully comply with the demands of the program? How voluntary should diversion referral practices be? Klein et al. (1976) have argued that too many of the clients referred to diversion programs are first offenders who have not committed serious crimes and would normally be released by the police. With the availability of diversion programs that allow referral for services, the total number of juvenile offenders receiving some form of treatment can increase significantly. Once again, the growth of administrative agencies can be enhanced by diversion. As Cressey and McDermott concluded:

> So far as we know, no one has shown that the juvenile offender and his family perceived their handling as materially different under the auspices of a diversion unit than under a more traditional juvenile justice agency. The question is rarely formulated, let alone asked. It is probably that the juvenile does not discriminate as readily as the intake officer between such realities as counseling, informal probation, regular probation and coercion. It seems plausible that if an act of diversion were truly successful in an individual case the subject of the act would perceive that something positive had entered his life and something negative had gone away. (1973:34)

As we have pointed out throughout this chapter, the idea of diversion is anything but a new, revolutionary approach to juvenile justice. The very existence of the juvenile court is predicated on the need to divert youthful offenders from the criminal courts. The juvenile reform movement at the end of the nineteenth century argued vociferously for the need to reduce the harmful effects of arrest, court appearance, and incarceration. Although that movement did not fully recognize the tenets of labeling theory, it did regard the development of informal, closed hearings and the destruction of a juvenile's court record upon reaching the age of majority as attempts to reduce the stigma of the criminal justice process. Interestingly, some one hundred years later, the same arguments are being used to advance the cause of diversion. Our observations are not an attempt to denigrate the diversion movement or to prophesize its failure. Rather, they are a plea that we avoid merely relabeling old problems with new words. With the emergence of the juvenile court in 1889 a new vocabulary entered the scene: *adjudication* rather than *trial*, *disposition* instead of *finding of guilt, homes for wayward youth* rather than *prison*. The same pitfall may arise again with diversion: *crisis intervention* instead of *juvenile court intake, referral for services* rather than *sentence, clients* rather than *children in custody*.

SUMMARY

One of the rationales for the creation of the juvenile court was the perceived need to divert juveniles from the adult criminal justice system. Moreover, the central elements of juvenile justice were to be treatment in the community and a minimal use of confinement. Many critics have challenged whether these goals have been realized. In the 1960s a renewed interest in "diversion" developed. It emphasized minimal processing of juvenile status offenders and the development of new programs into which juvenile offenders could be diverted. Labeling theory and differential association theory provided a theoretical basis for a renewed diversion philosophy. That philosophy was also facilitated by concerns for due process of law, a lessening of the burden on the juvenile court, and the provision of more definite guidelines for police decision making. The use of detention before trial has been increasingly challenged as just another form of imprisonment that can contribute to the escalation of deviant careers.

Although it has become a rallying point for juvenile justice reform, diversion has no clear, precise, consensual definition. Actually, cases are continually diverted by citizens, the police, intake officers, and judges. However, diversion has come to refer to definite policies or programs for minimizing the court processing of certain types of offenders by returning them to their homes or referring them to other agencies at the intake stage. The shape, size, and operational characteristics of a diversion program are contingent upon the resource base of the community. Obviously not all communities are able to provide shelter care homes, counseling programs, educational alternatives, or other types of services for youthful offenders. The degree of sophistication and comprehensiveness of any diversion program is highly dependent on what the community can provide. Moreover, diversion programs can exhibit variable degrees of legal autonomy from the juvenile court.

Evaluations of programs emerging as part of the diversion movement have yielded inconsistent results, with some signs of success and some signs of failure. While the scarcity of studies makes it impossible to reach any definite conclusions, bits and pieces of evidence seem to call for a far more precise delineation of the concept of diversion. There is some evidence that diversion programs can increase the amount of attention paid to offenders who, without the existence of diversion programs, would have been sent home by the juvenile court. To survive, programs must have clients, and they thus begin competing with one another for their share of the clients. Proponents of nonintervention and diversion typically qualify their recommendation that juveniles be "left alone" with the caveat "whenever possible." If the status offender is the obvious candidate for diversion, then some decision has to be made about "mixed" offenders, since the pure status offender is quite rare. Preliminary evidence suggests that the presumed escalation from status offenses to more serious offenses can also be challenged as a rationale for diversion. In sum, the diversion movement, like other reform movements, has gained a momentum that far surpasses either evidence or systematic specification. The idea that we should leave kids alone whenever possible has not been accompanied by a delineation of when it is possible to leave them alone. Rather than leaving them alone, diversion can increase intervention. We may soon see the beginnings of a movement to divert youths from diversion.

REFERENCES

Altgeld, J. P. 1884. *Our Penal Machinery and Its Victims.* Chicago: Jansen and McClurg.

Bittner, E. 1967. "The Police on Skid-Row: A Study of Peace-Keeping." *American Sociological Review* 32 (October):669–715.

Black, D. J. 1971. "The Social Organization of Arrest." *Stanford Law Review* 23 (June):1104–09.

Black, D. J., and A. Reiss, Jr. 1970. "Police Control of Juveniles." *American Sociological Review* 35 (February):63–77.

California Department of Youth Authority. 1968. *Youth Service Bureaus: Standards and Guidelines.* Sacramento: California Department of Youth Authority.

Children's Bureau. 1969. *Legislative Guide for Drafting Family and Juvenile Court Acts.* Washington, D.C.: U.S. Department of Health, Education, and Welfare, Publication no. 472.

Committee on the Judiciary, U.S. Senate. 1973. *The Detention and Jailing of Juveniles.* Hearings before the Subcommittee to Investigate Juvenile Delinquency, 93rd Cong. 1st sess. Washington, D.C.: U.S. Government Printing Office.

Cressey, D., and R. McDermott. 1973. *Diversion from the Juvenile Justice System.* Ann Arbor, Mich.: National Assessment of Juvenile Corrections.

Downey, J. 1970. *State Responsibility for Juvenile Detention Care.* U.S. Department of Health, Education, and Welfare. Washington, D.C.: U.S. Government Printing Office.

Emerson, R. M. 1969. *Judging Delinquents.* Chicago: Aldine.

Etzioni, A. 1976. "Deinstitutionalization: A Public Policy Fashion." *Evaluation* 3:9–10. Reprinted from *Evaluation* © 1976 by permission of the copyright holder, Minneapolis Medical Research Foundation, Inc.

Federal Bureau of Investigation. 1978. *Uniform Crime Reports, 1977.* Washington, D.C.: U.S. Government Printing Office.

Ferster, E. Z., T. F. Courtless, and E. N. Snethen. 1970. "Separating Official and Unofficial Delinquents: Juvenile Court Intake." *Iowa Law Review* 55 (April):864–93.

Ferster, E. Z., E. N. Snethen, and T. F. Courtless. 1969. "Juvenile Detention: Protection, Prevention or Punishment." *Fordham Law Review* 37 (December):161–96.

Glaser, D. 1964. *The Effectiveness of a Prison and Parole System.* Indianapolis, Ind.: Bobbs-Merrill.

Goff, D. 1966. *Report on the New Jersey Supreme Court's Committee on Juvenile Conference Committees.* Trenton: New Jersey Department of Youth Services.

Hagan, J., and J. Leon. 1977. "Rediscovering Delinquency: Social History, Political Ideology and the Sociology of Law." *American Sociological Review* 42 (August):587–98.

Howlett, F. W. 1973. "Is the Youth Service Bureau All It's Cracked Up to Be?" *Crime and Delinquency* 19 (October):488–92.

Klein, M. W. 1975. "Alternative Dispositions for Juvenile Offenders: An Assessment for the Juvenile Referral and Resource Development Program." University of Southern California. Mimeographed.

———. 1976. "Issues and Realities in Police Diversion Programs." *Crime and Delinquency* 22 (October):421–27.

Klein, M. W., et al. 1976. "The Explosion in Police Diversion Programs: Evaluating the Structural Dimensions of a Social Fad." In M. W. Klein, ed., *The Juvenile Justice System.* Beverly Hills, Calif.: Sage.

Law Enforcement Assistance Administration. 1971. *1970 National Jail Census.* Washington, D.C.: U.S. Government Printing Office.

Leiber, Leon. 1971. *Project Crossroads: A Final Report to the Manpower Administration.* Washington, D.C.: U.S. Department of Labor.

Lemert, E. M. 1967. "The Juvenile Court—Quest and Realities." In President's Commission on Law Enforcement, *Juvenile Delinquency.*

———. 1971. *Instead of Court: Diversion in Juvenile Justice.* Rockville, Md.: National Institute of Mental Health.

Lincoln, S. 1975. "Juvenile Diversion, Referral and Recidivism." In R. Carter and M. Klein, eds., *Police Diversion of Juvenile Offenders.* Englewood Cliffs, N.J.: Prentice-Hall.

Lipton, D., R. Martinson, and J. Wilks. 1975. *The Effectiveness of Correctional Treatment: A Survey of Treatment Evaluation Studies.* New York: Praeger.

Martinson, R. 1976. "California Research at the Crossroads." *Crime and Delinquency* 22 (April):180–91.

Matza, D. 1964. *Delinquency and Drift.* New York: John Wiley.

Ohlin, L. E., R. B. Coates, and A. D. Miller. 1974. "Radical Correctional Reform: A Case Study of the Massachusetts Youth Correctional System." *Harvard Educational Review* 44 (February):74–111.

Platt, A. 1969. *The Child Savers.* Chicago: University of Chicago Press.

President's Commission of Law Enforcement and Administration of Justice. 1967a. *Task Force Report: Corrections.* Washington, D.C.: U.S. Government Printing Office.

———. 1967b. *Task Force Report: Juvenile Delinquency and Youth Crime.* Washington, D.C.: U.S. Government Printing Office.

Reiss, A. J., Jr. 1971. *The Police and the Public.* New Haven, Conn.: Yale University Press.

Rojek, D. G. 1979. "Juvenile Diversion: Preliminary Evaluation Issues." Unpublished manuscript. University of Georgia.

Rubin, H. T. 1976. *The Courts: Fulcrum of the Justice System.* Pacific Palisades, Calif.: Goodyear.

Rubinton, E., and M. Weinburg. 1968. *Deviance: The Interactionist Perspective.* New York: Macmillan.

Rutherford, A., and R. McDermott. 1976. *Juvenile Diversion: Phase I Summary Report.* Washington, D.C.: National Institute of Law Enforcement and Criminal Justice.

Scheff, T. 1966. *Being Mentally Ill: A Sociological Theory.* Chicago: Aldine.

Schlossman, S. L. 1977. *Love and the American Delinquent.* Chicago: University of Chicago Press.

Schur, E. M. 1973. *Radical Non-intervention: Rethinking the Delinquency Problem.* Englewood Cliffs, N.J.: Prentice-Hall. Copyright © 1973. Reprinted by permission of Prentice-Hall, Inc. Englewood Cliffs, N.J.

Schwartz, R., and J. Skolnick. 1964. "Two Studies of Legal Stigma." *Social Problems* 10 (Fall):133–42.

Thorton, W., E. Barrett, and L. Musolf. 1972. *The Sacramento County Probation Department 601 Diversion Project.* Sacramento, Calif.: Sacramento County Probation Department.

Wilensky, H. 1964. "The Professionalization of Everyone?" *American Journal of Sociology* 70 (September):137–58.

Wines, E. C. 1880. *The State of Prisons and of Child-Saving Institutions in the Civilized World.* Cambridge, Mass.: Harvard University Press.

12.
PREVENTION:
DILEMMAS OF
CHOICE, CHANGE,
AND CONTROL

We have come of late to the realization that the pace of achievement in domestic programs ranges chiefly from the slow to the crablike—two steps backward for every step forward—and the suspicion is growing that there is something basically wrong with most of these programs. A nagging feeling persists that maybe something even more basic than the lack of funds or will is at stake. Consequently, social scientists like myself have begun to reexamine our core assumption that man can be taught almost anything and quite readily. We are now confronting the uncomfortable possibility that human beings are not very easily changed after all.

—Amitai Etzioni, "Human Beings Are Not Very Easy to Change After All"

PREVENTION REVISITED

As we have seen in the last several chapters, no particular response to delinquency has had significant rehabilitative or deterrent consequences relative to alternative responses or, for that matter, relative to doing nothing. Yet the impulse to have a policy, "to do something," is quite strong and persistent in America. Even diversion, which could have developed into a true "let-them-alone" policy, has developed into a hodgepodge of alternative programs that attempt to do everything from teaching good grooming to providing treatments indistinguishable from traditional juvenile court programs.

Another response to the growing awareness that treatment or correctional programs do not appear to be the answer to the delinquency problem has been a renewed interest in *prevention.* Whereas efforts to correct and rehabilitate focus on changing the offender "after the fact," the emphasis in prevention is on changing conditions thought to be conducive to delinquency. These conditions range from characteristics of individuals to the certainty, severity, and speed of law enforcement to the basic features of our social and cultural system.

Of course, the term *prevention,* like the terms *rehabilitation, deterrence,* and *diversion,* has no one, unambiguous, consensual definition. At one time or another, virtually all attempts to *inhibit* the delinquent activity of offenders or potential offenders have been referred to as prevention programs. For example, a review of literature by Wright and Dixon (1977) revealed that of 350 research reports using the words *delinquency prevention* (or their equivalent), a large number were actually programs involving juvenile court probation and differential parole treatment. In many instances, the court or police were the referral agencies, and participation in the program was a disposition for juveniles processed by the juvenile justice system. However, the arguments for prevention are typically presented in the context of the failure of correctional programs. In our discussion, we will use the term *prevention* only in reference to efforts to inhibit delinquency in the populace in general, rather than in reference to programs that constitute a disposition for offenders.

An orientation toward prevention is by no means new. It has been proposed periodically for centuries. A prevention philosophy has been central to social reform movements throughout American history, although with considerable variation in views about what needed to be reformed and how change should be accomplished. It has also been central to sociological positions on crime and delinquency. Consider, for example, the following paragraphs from Edwin Sutherland's 1924 edition of *Criminology:*

> Two methods of reducing the frequency of crimes have been suggested and tried. One is the method of treatment, the other is the method of prevention. The conventional policy has been to punish those who are convicted of crimes, on the hypothesis that this both reforms those who are punished and deters others from crimes in the future. Also, according to this hypothesis, crime rates can be reduced by increasing the severity, certainty, and speed of punishment.
>
> Methods of reformation have been suggested and tried, also. These have been in the form of probation, educational work in prisons, and parole supervision. These methods, like the methods of punishment, have not been notably successful in reducing crime rates.
>
> Prevention is a logical policy to use in dealing with crime. Punishment and other methods of treatment are, at best, methods of defense. It is futile to take individual after individual out of the situations which produce criminals and permit the situations to remain as they were. A case of delinquency is more than a physiological act of an individual. It involves a whole network of social relations. If we deal with his set of social relations we shall be working to prevent crime. It has become a commonplace in medicine that prevention is better than cure. The same superiority exists in the field of crime. (1924:613–14)

Arguments over half a century later are much the same. According to C. R. Jeffrey, "Crime cannot be controlled through measures designated for the individual offender, but can be controlled only through the manipulation of the environment where crimes occur" (1971:19). Jeffrey illustrated his argument by comparing the treatment of crime to the futility of trying to eradicate yellow fever without eliminating the swamps where the mosquitoes that carry the disease flourish. The presumed superiority of preventive approaches is that efforts are directed at the fundamental social conditions or personal maladjustments that are seen as the "seedbed" of crime.

Every criminology text written by sociologists advocates an emphasis on prevention in one form or another. This point of view flows quite naturally from the sociological emphasis on the social and cultural circumstances that facilitate crime and delinquency. It is a quite common sociological belief that if the circumstances that encourage delinquency can be identified, then those circumstances can be modified to discourage delinquency. (We refer to it as a "belief" because, as we will discuss later, there is a huge gap between the identification of "causes" of delinquency and the development of prevention strategies consistent with those causes.)

Although the concept of prevention is by no means new, we do find references to the emphasis on prevention as "revolutionary." Martin, Fitzpatrick, and Gould observed that "a revolution is stirring in national thinking about crime and delinquency. Instead of the old emphasis on changing the individual offender, the new movement stresses changing the manner in which various institutions, including courts and correctional agencies, relate to him" (1970:3). Others (Wheeler, Cottrell, and Romasco, 1967) have noted that the Juvenile Delinquency and Youth Offenses Control Act of 1961 was the first major federal effort to prevent delinquency. Moreover, the series of "task force" reports compiled by the President's Commission on Law Enforcement and Administration of Justice during the Johnson administration placed a strong emphasis on prevention. Several of these reports pointed toward conditions in the community as direct contributors to delinquency and crime that would continue to make a contribution despite changes in law enforcement or correctional efforts. For example, the President's Commission expressed doubts "that even a vastly improved criminal justice system can substantially reduce crime if society fails to make it possible for each of its citizens to feel a personal stake in it—in the good life that it can provide and in the law and order that are prerequisite to such a life" (1967:58). The notion of preventing crime before it starts was given strong emphasis: "Once a juvenile is apprehended by the police and referred to the juvenile court, the community has already failed" (1967:58).

Drawing on the task force reports, Congress passed the Juvenile Delinquency Prevention and Control Act of 1968, which was intended to implement many of the reports' recommendations. In 1972 the Juvenile Delinquency Prevention Act was passed in an attempt to spur the creation of youth service bureaus. The Juvenile Justice Act of 1974 created a new office of Juvenile Justice and Delinquency Prevention in the Law Enforcement Assistance Administration. Its goal was to develop prevention programs and to divert juveniles from the juvenile justice system. Thus, an orientation toward prevention, which was consistent with Lyndon Johnson's "Great Society" programs of the 1960s, received considerable governmental support. Several prominent sociologists who served on the President's Commission on Law Enforcement and Administration of Justice played an important role in the development of this orientation.

However, some critics (for example, Platt, 1970) have argued that the preventions programs that have been proposed focus on short-range goals and improved means of controlling youth, rather than on basic social reform.

PREVENTION EXPERIMENTS

As we noted above, the term *delinquency prevention* is often loosely used. As a result, many correctional experiments, such as those we discussed in Chapter 10, are included in comprehensive reviews of the prevention literature. Such reviews suggest that the vast majority of reports on programs that aspire to delinquency prevention provide *no* data on program effectiveness. Wright and Dixon (1977) found that of the 350 reports they examined, only 96 contained any type of empirical data. After evaluating the reports that did provide some empirical data, they concluded that "most were of low validity" and of little utility for decision makers. In view of the methodological limitations of these studies and the results reported, Wright and Dixon could find no particular prevention strategy that could be "definitely recommended." Their ultimate conclusions and recommendations for further research were quite similar to the reviews of correctional experimentation that we summarized in Chapter 10:

> We conclude that changing or preventing certain kinds of behavior is a difficult task, that positive results are probably related to quality and quantity of intervention, that any one intervention strategy is probably going to be differentially effective given a heterogeneous population, that theory-based strategies are going to be in a better position to profit from evaluations than are atheoretical strategies, and that sound research design is needed if we wish to be able to attribute changes in delinquency rates to prevention efforts. (Wright and Dixon, 1977:60)

Given these sorts of observations (which by now are beginning to sound familiar), one impulse might be to end the chapter here, deeming prevention, together with most other historical themes, a lost cause. However, if we are to gain any insight into what circumstances might account for the failure of so many prevention programs, we need to consider several of them in detail. For the same reason, we also need to consider the observations of proponents and opponents of various strategies.

Early Identification and Intensive Treatment

Jackson Toby (1965) has observed that one argument concerning delinquency prevention that seems on the surface to be "breathtakingly plausible" involves *early identification and intensive treatment.*

According to this argument, delinquency can be prevented by developing techniques to identify those who are headed for trouble and providing some form of treatment that would prevent such predictions from coming true. Such a possibility has been the dream of a variety of scholars. It received a brief flurry of publicity as a proposal for "ending violent crime in the United States within a decade" that was submitted to President Nixon by Dr. Arnold Hutschnecker, a physician and personal confidant of the president. As reported in the *National Observer:*

> Hutschnecker's "plan is to test all 6, 7 and 8-year old children for possible criminal tendencies, then mobilize a nationwide network of remedial care for those deemed likely to become dangerously violent.
>
> Emotionally disturbed children would attend special, after-school classes and receive guidance from trained psychologists. More severe cases would receive special therapy to curb their aggressive tendencies. Severely disturbed, hard-core criminals over the age of 16 would be placed in special camps to undergo group activities supervised by trained counselors and psychologists. . . ."
>
> As the doctor explains his plan's rationale, "I was thinking like a physician: Why wait until an illness breaks out? Why not prevent it? And the thought came to me: Why not start with the young children?". . .
>
> "The aim," he continued, "is to prevent the child with the delinquent character structure from being allowed to grow into a full fledged, teen-age delinquent or adult criminal. The sooner this destructive trend is recognized and reversed, the better the chances for the prevention of crime and the cure of the individual." (Lanoutte, 1970:7)*

This type of strategy was explored in at least three different studies carried out in the late 1930s through the early 1950s. One such study, carried out in St. Paul, Minnesota, from 1937 to 1943, claimed success. However, since success was judged by treatment staff themselves and the study lacked a control group with which to compare the treatment group, the claim of success actually tells us nothing about the objective impact of the program (Hakeem, 1957–58). From the standpoint of evaluation, the Cambridge-Somerville Youth Study in Massachusetts was a much better designed program. Instituted in 1936, the study continued for nine years as a child guidance program aimed at preventing delinquent behavior. In this experiment, teachers and police officers identified two groups of boys: "difficult boys," who were viewed as potential delinquents, and "average boys," who were viewed as having no predisposition to delinquency. By a random process, about half of the predelinquent boys were assigned to an experimental group, while the other half were assigned to a control group. The experimental group received family guidance, individual counseling, tutoring, medical care, and recreational services. The control group received no special treatment. Follow-up studies indicated no significant differences between the experimental and control groups, and the prevention program was thus seen as relatively ineffective. In fact, evaluations of the Cambridge-Somerville experiment suggested possible "boomerang" effects (or what contemporary theorists might call "labeling effects") in that a slightly greater proportion of the treatment group (41 percent) than of the control group (37 percent) was subsequently convicted of at least one major crime in a state or federal court.

One response to such negative results has been to question the "intensity" of treatment. William and Joan McCord (1959) indicated that only 12 of 253 treatment cases in the Cambridge-Somerville Youth Study received what they would consider intensive treatment (remaining in the program at least two years, seeing the counselor at least once a week, having a close relationship with the counselor, and so on). Furthermore, the McCords reported, the 12 youths who did receive intensive treatment did better than controls. However, these 12 cases may have been errors of prediction at the outset and may not have become delinquent even without treatment. Overall, the Cambridge-Somerville experiment did not succeed in preventing delinquency.

The New York City Youth Board Prediction Study yielded similar results. In this study, social workers made predictions of delinquency for first graders on the basis of home visits in two neighborhoods that had high delinquency rates. Although characteristics of the child's home situation were the basis for predictions, the treatment program that was implemented provided individual psychiatric treatment in a clinic setting. Treatment was administered by a team of psychologists, psychiatrists, and social workers. After a four-year period, no differences were found in the delinquency of the treatment and control groups (Toby, 1965:168).

Michael Hakeem (1957–58) and Jackson Toby (1965), who have critically analyzed such programs, have outlined several problems with early identification and intensive treatment strategies. Hakeem argued that the projective techniques that psychiatrists often use for early identification (such as Rorschach "inkblot" test) are notoriously unreliable and that many of the symptoms of future delinquency may also be symptoms of future, more conventional accomplishments:

> Suppose a child were discovered to evince a bothersome quantum of aggression, a characteristic which many clinicians insist is one of the cardinal signs of predelinquency. Should measures be taken to reduce the aggression? But aggression is not a trait that eventuates only in wanton rape and plunder. It can be quite handy in managing a corporation. Some generals have been aggressive. Some aggressive people have become noted explorers. Some have gone into medicine and law. Some have specialized in psychiatry. Some have entered teaching, as any student and any faculty member could attest. Aggression can find many happy uses. (1957–58:200)

In a more detailed critique, Jackson Toby identified several problems with early identification and intensive treatment strategies. For one thing, although measurable characteristics of individuals and their social circumstances may be predictive of subsequent delinquency, the predictions are only probabilistic. In analyzing both the Cambridge-Somerville and the New York Youth Board studies, Toby found that delinquency was overpredicted relative to actual outcomes. In the Cambridge-Somerville study, only 114 of 305 boys who were viewed as headed for delinquency actually fulfilled the prediction. In the New York study, between 65 and 75 percent of those thought to be headed for delinquency had not acquired records seven years later. However, as Toby pointed out, even if we arrive at more accurate prediction that takes into account other contingencies at later stages of a youth's life, we still do not know "what kind of intensive treatment should be given" (1965:175). We also do not know how intensive "intensive treatment" should be or how early it should start. Moreover, we do not know how to avoid possible boomerang effects stemming from stigmatic experiences and potentially self-fulfilling prophecies of future trouble.

Total Community Casework Experiments

Sociologists have quite commonly attributed the failure of psychiatrically and individually oriented prevention strategies to their focus on treating the *individual.* John Martin (1961) argued that the basic flaw with "individual-centered techniques" is that "such efforts fail to come to grips with the underlying social and cultural conditions giving rise to delinquency." Similarly, Edwin Schur maintained that "our overall crime picture massively reflects conditions that require collective social solutions" and that "social reform, not individual counseling, must have the highest priority in our program to reduce crime problems" (1969:15).

Somewhere between the two poles of individual treatment and basic social reform are action programs that attempt to strengthen or reorganize certain social relationships in neighborhoods or areas of the city. This type of prevention program tries to overcome factors in the youth's immediate environment that are seen as contributing to delinquent behavior in the neighborhood or community. Perhaps the best-known prevention program of this type is the Chicago Area Project. Developed by Clifford R. Shaw, the project was based on social disorganization theory (see chapters 6 and 8). It attributed delinquency to a lack of neighborhood cohesiveness and viewed self-help enterprises on the part of residents of areas with high crime rates as the key to prevention. Indigenous community leaders were to serve as conventional role models for youngsters in such areas in the hope of facilitating the growth of an antidelinquent culture.

Measuring the effectiveness of a program like the Chicago Area Project is extremely difficult—if not impossible. Delinquency statistics declined in three out of the four communities where the project was implemented, but since the project had no control groups, its findings were inconclusive. However, the project did pay sufficient attention to the organization, development, and implementation of the area projects to provide some clues as to the conditions under which a total community strategy might be feasible. One analyst (Finestone, 1976) noted that ironically it was in communities or neighborhoods with high delinquency rates that the Chicago Area Project had the most difficulty establishing local community committees or organizations concerned with the welfare of the area. On the other hand, the project was quite successful in facilitating the development of active, strong community committees in areas with low rates of delinquency. As Finestone observed:

> Where the disorder characterizing a community was so great as to preclude the existence of established institutions with a stake in the area, the area project idea tended to become more form than substance. In retrospect it is unrealistic to have expected the area projects to be able to develop effective community organizations out of whole cloth. (1976:148)

The very problems that sustained a high rate of delinquency limited the possibility of implementing change.

While the Chicago Area Project could not demonstrate a preventive impact on delinquency, it did stimulate many ideas on how to facilitate evaluation. These ideas were implemented in subsequent projects. One such project was a "total community" delinquency program carried out in a lower-class district of Boston from 1954 to 1957 (Miller, 1962). Known as the Midcity Project, it was concerned with developing and strengthening local citizens' groups and organizing relationships among agencies and institutions involving youth. The project also provided an intensive program of psychiatrically oriented casework for "chronic problem families" and assigned professionally trained adult workers to work with street gangs in certain areas of the city. The worker's goal was to help the street gang move in the direction of conventional, rather than delinquent, activities. Workers also acted as intermediaries between adult institutions and gang members. The project used psychiatric clinics, family service agencies, and group therapy sessions when cases or situations were felt to require such a response. A variety of techniques was viewed as valuable for testing what Walter Miller called the "synergism" concept—the idea that the application of a diverse set of procedures in concert might be more effective than distinct programs operating individually (1962:189).

Given the Midcity Project's intensity and diversity of programs, the ultimate conclusions concerning delinquency prevention generated by this project were surprising. The evaluation of the project, which used a variety of different measures of delinquency, concluded that there was no significant inhibition of either illegal or immoral behavior resulting from this prevention program. In the words of Walter Miller, "All major measures of violative behavior . . . provide consistent support for a finding of 'negligible impact'" (1962:187). As a qualification to this finding, Miller observed that the project, which had been instituted in response to concern over "rampant gang violence," did appear to mollify those fears and to "calm" the adult community. Moreover, the project did establish new local organizations that survived the project. Miller further noted that there was considerable variability in the responses of different neighborhood groups.

In 1962 a smaller-scale project designed to prevent delinquency among "high-risk" black youths was implemented in Seattle's central area. Whereas the Midcity Project worked with existing gangs, the workers in the Seattle Delinquency Control Project were each assigned a set of youths whom they subsequently attempted to organize into groups. The caseworkers, who were trained male social workers, worked with the boys, their families, and the schools. Berleman and Steinburn (1967) evaluated the impact of the program by comparing an experimental group of high-risk boys with a control group of high-risk boys. Cases had been randomly assigned to either group. They also compared the experimental and control groups with boys who refused to participate and with a set of "low-risk" boys. One interesting finding was that at all points in time examined, boys who refused to participate had the highest scores in terms of combined indexes of school and police disciplinary records. There were no significant differences between the experimental or treatment group and the control group. Disciplinary scores for the treatment group appeared to decrease over time as compared to increases in the other groups, but the differences were too small to be reliable. The treatment group's improvement disappeared after termination of service.

Youth Service Bureaus and the Neighborhood Youth Corps

A third type of prevention strategy includes a broad range of services for juveniles. The 1967 report of the President's Commission on Law Enforcement and Administration of Justice recommended the creation of youth service bureaus to reduce the role of the juvenile court and to act as central coordinators of various community services for juveniles. The concept of youth service bureaus is not totally clear and precise. Originally they were to be diversion agencies for arrested children, but most youth service bureaus receive referrals from nonlegal and nonjudicial agencies. Kenneth Polk (1971) observed that the functions of a youth service bureau are extremely varied and imprecise, dealing with a wide range of behavioral problems. Until the youth service bureau is defined and standardized, it will be difficult to assess its impact on delinquency prevention.

The Neighborhood Youth Corps, operated under the Department of Labor, employs youngsters living in low-income families and provides them with income, work experience, counseling, and remedial education.

Gerald Robin summarized the rationale for Neighborhood Youth Corps programs as follows:

> The dialogue supporting such programs has increasingly emphasized their contribution toward reducing delinquency and youth crime by inculcating more positive and socially acceptable attitudes and values in the youths and by constructively occupying leisure time through employment activities, thereby reducing the inclination and opportunity of its recipients to engage in behavior which would make them objects of law enforcement attention. (1969:323)

Robin reported on evaluations of two such programs. One was a Neighborhood Youth Corps program in Cincinnati that provided jobs to students from poor families. Participants were allowed to work up to fifteen hours per week during the school year and thirty-two hours per week during the summer at a rate of $1.25 per hour, which was the minimum wage in 1966. The work projects were generally sponsored by school boards and educational institutions. The participants were directed by a work supervisor and assigned to counselors who were to help with any problems. Since there was a large waiting list of equally qualified applicants, the researchers were able to select enrollees randomly, thus creating a control group "of unassailable quality" (Robin, 1969:323). The experimental group was comprised of actively enrolled youths, and the control group consisted of eligible youths who had not been accepted into the program. The other program evaluated was a Neighborhood Youth Corps project in Detroit.

Robin examined offense records for the control group and for enrollees both during and after participation in the program. His findings illustrate the importance of having a control group for comparison. During participation in the Cincinnati Neighborhood Youth Corps program, there was a 33 percent reduction in the proportion of year-round male enrollees with police contacts. This is a type of finding that could easily be reported to the public and funding agencies as evidence of success. However, the presence of a control group allowed a comparison with those youths who did not make it into the program. The startling finding was that for the control group, the reduction was 39 percent. Comparisons of the program enrollees with the control groups indicated that participation in the Neighborhood Youth Corps in Cincinnati and in Detroit neither reduced delinquency during the program relative to nonparticipation nor prevented subsequent delinquency. These findings were true for both males and females. Robin concluded: "Assuming that police contacts are a valid index of variation in illegal behavior, then the putative importance of anti-poverty programs that consist largely of the creation of work opportunities in reducing criminality among juveniles and young people may be more illusive than real" (1969:331). A study of the impact of a work program in the central area of Seattle supported Robin's conclusion (Hackler, 1966).

School-Based Programs

The programs that we have just described were based in the community and worked with a variety of institutions, including schools. Other delinquency prevention programs have been specifically based in the school. The most ambitious study of a school-based program was carried out in Columbus, Ohio, and has been documented by Walter Reckless and Simon Dinitz (1972). This particular experiment was based on ideas developed by Reckless and others to the effect that a boy's "self-image" is an important determinant of how he behaves. From such a perspective, a "good self-concept" insulates a youth from pressures and pulls that are conducive to delinquency, while a "poor self-concept" increases susceptibility to such forces. Hence, the experiment sought to develop special teaching programs that would provide attractive conventional role models and, to use Reckless and Dinitz's words, "beef up" the self-concepts of youths who otherwise appeared to be headed for delinquent involvement.

The subjects were incoming seventh-grade boys. They were divided into three subgroups: (1) randomly selected "bad" boys (predicted by sixth-grade teachers or principals to be headed for delinquency) who were assigned to all-male experimental classes; (2) "bad" boys in regular classes; and (3) a sample of "good" boys in regular classes. A select group of teachers was given special training that was intended to facilitate their becoming role models for the experimental youths. The program attempted to improve the boys' reading and to implement a disciplinary system based on respect for the rights of others. Finally, the program developed special educational materials to present conventional role models to the treatment group.

Over three school years, 1,726 boys were studied. A large volume of data was compiled on each case, with the following results: There were no significant differences between the control group and the experimental subjects in (1) school performances, (2) police contacts, (3) changes in self-concept, and (4) perceptions of law, police, courts, school, teachers, and education. When interviewed, both teachers and students were enthusiastic about the program, but despite this enthusiasm, experimental subjects did not differ from controls on a single outcome variable.

The Minnesota Youth Advocate Program was a school-oriented program designed to prevent delinquency by assisting returnees from correctional institutions to resume their educations (Higgins, 1978). It was called a "youth advocate" program because it involved assigning adults to advocate, or "go to bat," for delinquent youths with the aim of facilitating their return to school. The advocates also provided services to youths on probation and to "predelinquent" youths. Advocates spent much of their time counseling and "rapping" with their clients, taking them to job interviews, resolving disputes with adults, and acting as resource persons in the development of other programs for youths. All advocates had backgrounds as teachers, school social workers, or counselors.

Evaluation of this program required a "quasi-experimental" design. In a true experimental design, the experimental group and the control group would have been created by random assignment to help insure that the two groups were comparable on all characteristics except treatment versus nontreatment. The research staff had no control over the placement of returnees in this program nor over the creation of a program itself in a particular locale. Since random assignment was not possible, the next best procedure was to match cases as closely as possible and then assess whether the treatment cases did better than their nontreated matches. Thus, Paul Higgins (1978) compared returnees from correctional institutions who were served by the advocate program with returnees who were not served. The areas in which the schools encompassing both the experimental and control groups were located were deemed "roughly comparable in 'socio-educational' disadvantagement." Higgins examined school attendance, grades, offenses, and commitments to correctional institutions. In comparing data for experimentals and controls during participation with data before release from correctional institutions, Higgins found no evidence that the returnees with advocates improved any more than the returnees without advocates. However, in a follow-up analysis, Higgins found that more returnees with advocates than those without remained in school and that control returnees were more likely to end up back in a correctional institution. This difference may have resulted from the greater likelihood that experimental returnees would enroll in one of Minnesota's "alternative" schools (special private schools for difficult or poorly achieving adolescents). That greater likelihood was apparently the result of the youth advocates' urgings. The alternative schools had flexible curricula, relatively democratic procedures, liberal attendance requirements, and informal teaching. Higgins concluded that the Minnesota Youth Advocate Program "seems to have had a small favorable impact on adjustment," which was most prominent at the end of the follow-up period. Of course, since this study did not have a true experimental design, its findings are inconclusive.

AN OVERVIEW: FACTORS IN FAILURE

By now the quote at the beginning of this chapter—"human beings are not very easily changed after all"—no doubt seems like an understatement. In general, evaluations of correctional and juvenile justice experimentation lead to the same conclusion. Prevention strategies that treat individuals, attempt to organize communities, or provide jobs or special education have not been found to reduce or prevent delinquency. Although the Minnesota Youth Advocate Program may have made some small difference, the evaluation of the program did not have the best possible design. Studies that have randomly assigned subjects to experimental and control groups have yielded the most discouraging results of all.

But why do these experimental programs fail? Most of them seemed to make good sense to one or another set of delinquency theorists. If we consider the observations of the prevention researchers themselves, we can find some common themes regarding experimental failures. One recurrent theme is: "The theory is still good, but we need to do what we did with more resources, greater intensity, and for a longer period of time." For example, Reckless and Dinitz concluded that one of the lessons they learned from their prevention program was that they needed to develop more effective methods of presenting role models and of training effective project teachers. Thus, they wrote "There is reason to suspect that the exposure to role-model internalization was not intensive enough" (1972:158). The McCords (1959) felt the same way in their reevaluation of the Cambridge-Somerville Youth Study. However, it is hard to imagine creating more intensive prevention programs than those that have already been attempted. The Boston Midcity Project was no loose, haphazard program; yet it had no significant impact. Reckless and Dinitz's program appears to have been carried out with considerable intensity and to have generated enthusiasm among teachers and students; yet it made no difference. Gerald Robin found the lack of preventive effect in the Neighborhood Youth Corps programs a "somewhat unexpected finding if for no reason other than that the program utilized approximately 1,000 hours of what would otherwise have been leisure time and therefore opportunity for misbehavior" (1969:327). Unless the researchers' own descriptions of their programs are misleading, it is hard to believe that more of the same in bigger doses will make the difference.

If the failure of these programs is a problem of intensity, then we have to face the fact (or propose some way to overcome it) that there are political, social, and cultural forces that limit the implementation of prevention programs of any greater intensity than those described above. In fact, the circumstances that limit more intense intervention are quite commonly mentioned as problems in implementing several of the programs that have been tried. In evaluating the Minnesota Youth Advocate Program, Higgins observed that the funding and ultimate demise of this program was determined by lobbying efforts and conflicts between advocates and school principals, rather than by any evidence of the program's success or failure. Advocates were "going to bat" for youths whom some school principals did not particularly want to see back in school. However, when advocates began encouraging their clients to enroll in private schools, they generated complaints that funds for public schools were being threatened. Very few school principals supported the program.

It often appears that delinquency persists because of the reluctance of many people, groups, and organizations to accommodate to changes that might reduce delinquency. Some action programs require a redistribution of power—the "haves" yielding some decision-making power to the "have-nots." It is at this juncture in implementing a new policy that change falls short. For instance, a few years ago one of the authors was involved in a Headstart program for Mexican-American children. One of the fundamental goals of the program was to involve parents. Not only was the child to receive some preparation for a school career, but also, and more importantly, local residents were to be organized to deal with specific community concerns. Something akin to a PTA (Parent-Teacher Association) was to be created. This group was to include parents, teachers, and school officials. It was, however, to act as an advisory group and deal with a wider array of issues than is normally accorded a PTA organization.

One problem that arose in the course of the program was the daily diet of "Anglo" food for Mexican-American children who were unaccustomed and unreceptive to this type of food. The advisory council recommended that these children be gradually introduced to new foods lest they refuse to eat altogether. Unfortunately, the school administration insisted that the food was wholesome and the menus carefully prepared. It did not matter that many of these children were not eating these "nutritious" meals because they had never been introduced to such foods. The issue was recast into a power struggle between "professional" school administrators and "ill-informed" parents.

A second confrontation between the advisory board and the school administration concerned the timing of morning bus pickups. Most of the parents were farm workers who began work between six and seven o'clock in the morning. The advisory council suggested that an earlier bus schedule be improvised to pick up children whose parents had to leave them home alone. The school administration pointed out the disruptive nature of such a bus schedule, stressing that it would necessitate the total revision of bus routes. Again, this suggestion was rejected because it involved the alteration of the "normal" routine.

Eventually the advisory council fell into performing perfunctory chores and never achieved the decision-making role that it was initially intended to have. The school administration was so recalcitrant that even the slightest suggestion was viewed as a threat to its power. Delinquency prevention programs are often confronted with the same dilemma: The solution of a delinquency problem may require the redistribution of power or resources; this in turn proves to be too threatening to the powers that be, and nothing of substance is altered.

In addition, internal problems in the implementation of a prevention program may reflect the fact that the program is operating as a minor force in a large social, political, and economic setting. For example, Finestone observed that in the Chicago Area Project some community committees began to "distance themselves" from the delinquency issue and that some committee members did not want to associate with persons with delinquent or criminal backgrounds (1976:137). Moreover, some community workers attained a "kind of vested interest" in their local organization and began molding the organizations around themselves. On an even broader scale, Walter Miller (1958) found that a major impediment to delinquency prevention was "inter-institutional conflict." Describing the early years of the Midcity Project, Miller wrote that the executive board "became a battleground for its component organizations." Different groups, organizations, and agencies involved and concerned with delinquency had quite different philosophies concerning *etiology* (causes), *disposition* of offenders, *approach priority*, appropriate *organizational method*, and the proper *status of personnel*. Miller concluded that such conflict is a major source of difficulty in implementing and carrying out delinquency prevention programs.

We also have to question some of the underlying assumptions of delinquency prevention programs. We have already cited the rationale behind the Neighborhood Youth Corps programs that the services provided would take up time, as well as inspire new attachments, commitments, or attitudes. However, as we noted in Chapter 6, occupying a youth's time does not appear to be an important barrier to delinquency. Delinquent activities are episodic, situational, and require very little time. Moreover, it may be that the types of activities provided by the Neighborhood Youth Corps do not inspire "more positive and socially acceptable attitudes and values" as intended. Too often the work is "busy work" or work that would not get done by anyone else at that wage. For example, one of the authors was called upon to provide work for Neighborhood Youth Corps enrollees on a research project where extra help was not really needed. However, the Youth Corps staff was desperate for placements. Hence, the only work available was provided, and it was busy work. Moreover, the youths in the program had come to view the money they received as a gift that would be awarded regardless of the quantity or quality of their work. The money was the major incentive for participating in the program since the jobs generally available would hardly generate enthusiasm and commitment.

We also should add that some of our own research has shown spending money to be significantly and *positively* related to many types of delinquency. We found that students who were in the top half of their high school in terms of spending money were significantly more likely to report alcohol and marijuana use, experimentation with more serious drugs, and a variety of "hell-raising" activities, such as joyriding, dragging, and vandalism. Moreover, this effect persisted regardless of parental social status (Jensen, 1979). No matter what the parents' social standing, the adolescent with more spending money was freer to engage in delinquent activity than the adolescent with less money. As we noted in Chapter 7, having a car also appears to increase the freedom to commit delinquent acts. The point here is not that paying disadvantaged youths is bad or wrong. Given the larger economic system and the larger social world of a program's participants, any delinquency prevention program would probably flounder at the outset without monetary incentives. However, it should be recognized that some aspects of a program may *increase* the probability of some forms of delinquency, countervailing any other preventive potential.

Overall it appears that the major limitation on both the implementation and potential effectiveness of prevention programs is that the wider system—the real world—"will have its way." It might generate optimism and make us feel better to argue (1) that prevention strategies purporting to be comprehensive must be directed at fairly massive kinds of environmental change and (2) that rather than focusing on individual delinquents or potential delinquents, delinquency prevention must call for an alteration of those factors in the environment that contribute to delinquent behavior. However, the fact of the matter is that if small-scale change has met with such resistance, it is doubtful that prevention programs on a wider scale will ever be mounted successfully.

SOCIAL SCIENCE AND POLICY IMPLICATIONS

At the beginning of this book, we noted that one of the most common questions students expect to have answered in criminology and delinquency classes is: "What can we do about it?" Given our credentials as social scientists, we are expected to provide answers that are backed up by adequate, verifiable evidence. On the basis of past organized attempts "to do something about it," the only scientific answer possible is that means of preventing delinquency have not yet been found. Moreover, in considering "what can be done," it is vital that we recognize the limits of social science research for making statements about what "ought" to be done.

One important aspect of social science research that limits its utility for answering questions about what can and ought to be done is its focus on *natural variations* in characteristics of the social world. Findings concerning the relationships currently existing between one characteristic of the social world in its natural variations and delinquency or crime may have no bearing on *new* proposals and policies. For example, there is still no good evidence that capital punishment as *historically* used had a deterrent effect. However, such a finding does not necessarily apply to capital punishment used *differently* (for example, with greater certainty or more swiftly). There is mounting evidence that *existing* variations in gun control laws make no difference for rates of firearm violence, but such findings do not necessarily mean that *proposed* controls would be ineffective.

When we consider radical proposals for reform, we can say very little about their probability of success or failure on the basis of research findings. It *might* be true, as several theorists have argued, that a basic change in our economic arrangements (for example, from modern capitalism to socialism) would reduce some forms of crime. But how are we to test that theory? We might study existing societies and economic arrangements, except for the fact that we do not have reliable comparative data on crime and delinquency. In any case, such theories are rarely couched in terms of existing examples. Proposals for change that go beyond existing variations always sound the most promising, and their arguments "ring true" for many of us. However, we cannot look to current scientific research for confirmation.

Although not necessarily an insurmountable problem, there are definite limitations on our knowledge of the full repercussions of policies that have already been implemented. For example, Robert Martinson has criticized Stuart Palmer and the "California research tradition" for its emphasis on recidivism. Martinson has labeled this approach "recidivism-only" research. He gives the following example of the problem as he sees it:

> Suppose Palmer knew a truly effective "community treatment" method and could demonstrate that this "intervention" reduced recidivism by, say, ten percentage points. The administrators in California then release 10,000 persons, who are given the "treatment." It works. Their recidivism rates are ten percentage points below their expected rates. My neighbors in the 20th precinct can no longer afford to be polite; they are too busy avoiding hoodlums and ducking bullets. They keep insisting that there is a gaping hole in my logic when I say that the above program has "reduced recidivism" at "no additional risk" to the public. "Whaddayamean? You got 10,000 of these guys out here committing crimes when they could have been in prison. You may have reduced this here recidivism rate with your treatment, but the overall crime rate could have gone up couldn't it?" Well, Dr. Palmer, couldn't it? I have no hesitation in saying that you don't know, nor does anyone else, including me. (1976:74)

We can ask similar questions about the policy implications of some of the research findings that we summarized in Chapter 7. Use of "tracking" in schools appears to increase the chances of failure, troublemaking, and delinquency for youths in the less prestigious tracks. Therefore, if we did away with tracking, we would lower the delinquency rate. But would we? We noted in Chapter 7 that schools *with* tracking systems might have lower delinquency rates than schools *without* tracking. We simply do not know what the actual repercussions would be. Suppose, for example, that youths in the more prestigious track have lower delinquency rates *because they are in that track,* and suppose the prestigious track's insulating quality stems from the fact that it is limited to certain students. Abolishing tracking could increase rather than decrease delinquency. In sum, there is still a huge gap between research findings and policy proposals that can be stated with an aura of scientific certitude.

In *Thinking About Crime* (1975), James Q. Wilson contended that sociological research on "causes" tends to concentrate on conditions that cannot be readily manipulated or that have little relevance for policy. Wilson described sociologists' findings of differences in crime and delinquency by age and gender as "theoretically important," but of little relevance to policy makers because "men cannot be changed into women or made to skip over the adolescent years" (1975:55). Wilson argued that sociological theory and research has concentrated on social conditions "which cannot be easily and deliberately altered" (1975:53). Such conditions include relationships within the family, attitudes, and values.

The retort to Wilson's criticism is that conditions that *are* easily changed as a result of policy are likely to have little or no consequence for crime and delinquency. Moreover, it is not entirely true that findings concerning basic demographic variations have no policy implications. Rather, the implications that they do have would not seem reasonable to Wilson, or to many other people. For instance, we could propose a nationwide program beginning in the primary grades to encourage boys to be more like girls. Research findings do make this a policy implication, but it is one that would be considered "unreasonable" and certainly would not be easily implemented.

In fact, Wilson's very definition of policy analysis would put a large number of potential manipulations of features of American life outside the realm of policy:

> Policy analysis, as opposed to causal analysis, begins with a very different perspective. It asks not what is the "cause" of a problem, but what is the condition one wants to bring into being, what measure do we have that will tell us when that condition exists, and what policy tools does a government (in our case, a democratic and libertarian government) possess that might, when applied, produce at reasonable cost a desired alteration in the present condition or progress toward the desired condition? In this case, the desired condition is a reduction in specified forms of crime. The government has at its disposal certain—rather few, in fact—policy instruments: It can redistribute money, create (or stimulate the creation of) jobs, hire persons who offer advice, hire persons who practice surveillance and detection, build detention facilities, illuminate public streets, alter (within a range) the price of drugs and alcohol, require citizens to install alarm systems, and so on. It can, in short, manage to a degree money, prices and technology, and it can hire people who can provide either simple (e.g., custodial) or complex (e.g., counseling) services. (1975:59)

Wilson's definition of policy analysis builds in limitations on the amount of change and the means of implementing change that qualify a proposal as a *policy* proposal. In sum, it is not so much that sociological theory and research have no policy implications, but that their implications are not "realistic" given current social reality. Yet, it is the same social reality that is under attack as the source of many social problems. What one views as realistic or reasonable may very well depend on how well one has benefited from that reality. The failure of so many policies that use existing tools at a reasonable cost has become an argument for seemingly unreasonable proposals.

From his studies of low crime rates in Switzerland, Marshall Clinard (1978) arrived at several policy implications that would be deemed "unreasonable." For example, he proposed limiting cities in the United States to under 500,000 population. He also cited Switzerland's mandatory military participation as a factor that kept the youth crime rate down and suggested that a policy of mandatory service might have the same effect in the United States. He noted that political decentralization is another characteristic of Swiss society that may account for the low crime rate. Recommendations to decentralize the United States Government along Swiss lines would be deemed unreasonable in terms of Wilson's definition of policy analysis, as would proposals by radical criminologists that we actively work to change our political economy by revolutionary action if necessary.

In short, with growing pressure for social scientists to make their work relevant to *policy*, we have to be careful that we do not so restrict the term that nothing new can be proposed. In fact, it may very well be the case that research that is carried out to test theories or extend our knowledge with *little concern* for policy implications is potentially more valuable than research directly tied to policy issues. Why? Because research tied to "policy issues" has been limited to policy as it has been defined by governments, bureaucrats, and politicians. In this sense, both conservative and radical proposals share something in common. In his radical critique of "child-saving" movements and government programs for preventing delinquency, Anthony Platt (1970) argued that contemporary policies are based on a belief in "the benevolence of government" and differ from earlier child-saving movements mainly in the sense that it is now specialists, professionals, and persons in the child-saving bureaucracy itself who are defining directions, goals, and the limits of policy. We need people who study the social world without being bound to bureaucratic proclamations about what is and is not "reasonable." We need to learn what they discover for good or ill if we are to control our own lives.

CHOICES: ASSESSING YOUR OWN VALUES, BELIEFS, AND COMMITMENTS

We are rapidly coming to a close in this chapter on prevention and, as of yet, have not actually answered the question of how we can prevent delinquency. Despite the intuitive appeal of listing a series of recommendations for someone "out there" to act on, we need to consider our *own* stake in this matter. Obviously, there are any number of alternatives that could be selected for a nationwide delinquency prevention program. The problem we immediately confront is how to develop a plan that is tempered by objectivity and enlightened reason when we lack conclusive scientific evidence that our plan will work. Overcoming personal bias, prejudice, or even ignorance while we collectively fashion a plan of action that may fail is no simple matter. Furthermore, any set of far-reaching proposals that calls for a significant alteration of the social structure very quickly becomes an intensely personal matter. The price of eradicating crime and delinquency may be too painful for us to bear. It is relatively simple to suggest changes in the lives of other people, but far more difficult to alter our own lifestyle. Before we commit society to a plan of action, we need to judiciously assess our own contribution to the problem and to the solution. Grappling with choices is what delinquency prevention is all about.

A "War on Crime"

It should be clear by now that the ability of traditional criminal or juvenile justice policy to effectively "solve" the problem of delinquency in the United States has inherent limitations. But while there may be a lack of consensus in the body politic as to a course of action, a sizable, or at least vocal, segment of the public clamors for something to be done, something that uses existing tools at a reasonable cost. It is conceivable that crime could be significantly reduced by restricting individual liberties and allowing the criminal justice system far greater authority. We noted in Chapter 9 that some research findings are consistent with the view that stiffer law enforcement *might* reduce delinquency; such findings are viewed by Wilson and others as having reasonable policy implications. Moreover, nighttime burglaries and robberies might be drastically reduced by a simple decree of martial law prohibiting anyone to be on the streets from 6:00 P.M. to 6:00 A.M. Indeed, a blanket restriction requiring everyone to remain home twenty-four hours a day might be even better! However, in this case, the cure could be far worse than the perceived problem. Similarly, as technology improves in the areas of electronic detection, surveillance devices, computer systems, and communications hardware, the right to privacy becomes increasingly threatened.

In contemplating "what to do" about crime and delinquency, each of us must come to grips with the trade-offs involved in preserving individual freedom and controlling crime. The safeguards contained in the Bill of Rights apply to the innocent as well as the guilty. Before we unleash criminal justice agencies in a "war on crime," each of us should consider the costs involved. Not all of us will agree. If we choose to live in a democratic society, then we must limit the effectiveness of the police and provide a degree of freedom to deviate. "Cracking down on crime" can potentially lead to a crackdown on personal liberty. Thus, as part of the price we must pay for individual freedom, we may have to allow crime and delinquency to remain high.

Revolution

Current radical theorists, drawing heavily on types of sociological theory called *conflict theory* and *Marxian theory*, argue that delinquency is the product of the perpetual class struggle in capitalist societies. The ruling class creates the conditions out of which delinquency arises, and nothing short of revolution will alter the situation. For instance, the Schwendingers (1976) see the core of the delinquency problem as the *marginalization of youth.* Capitalism is viewed as a "criminogenic" system that perpetuates inequities based on age, sex, race, and occupation. Thus, merely "tinkering" with the system by investing time and resources into rehabilitation, diversion, or prevention will not rectify the delinquency problem. Once children are freed from the evils of class struggles and reintegrated into the mainstream of life, the cooperative instincts of the young will become dominant, and a society free of crime and delinquency will emerge. The prescriptions for this revolution are stated in the following manner by Richard Quinney, one of America's most prolific, radical criminologists:

> Our task as students is to consider the alternatives to the capitalist legal order. Further study of crime and justice in America must be devoted to the contradictions of the existing system. At this advanced stage of capitalist development, law is little more than a repressive instrument of manipulation and control. We must make others aware of the current meaning of crime and justice in America. The objective is to move beyond the existing order. And this means ultimately that we engage in socialist revolution. (1974:25)

While the goals of a truly liberated society are clearly articulated by radical theorists, the means of attaining a classless state are uncertain, and its idyllic functioning is even more ambiguous. Chambliss and Mankoff have stated that "the ultimate test of a theory's utility is not its logical structure or its 'fit' with empirical data but its ability to create workable recipes for changing the existing set of social conditions" (1976:3). Yet that is the precise bone of contention—what are those "workable recipes"? A search of the literature that expounds the radical doctrine does not clearly articulate any plan of action. One rationale for this lack of articulation is as follows:

> We cannot present a blueprint or an exact specification of how a socialist "utopia" would work; nor should we attempt to do so, since constructing imaginary utopias bears little relation to the actual task of building a decent society. Any *real* alternative to capitalism will be historically

linked to the forces and movements generated by the contradictions of capitalist society itself. New institutions which liberate rather than oppress can only be created by real people confronting concrete problems in their lives and developing new means to overcome oppression. The political movements arising from capitalism's contradictions therefore constitute the only means for society to move from its present condition to a new and more decent form, and only out of these movements will humane as well as practical new institutions be generated. (Edwards, Reich, and Weisskopf, 1974:433)

The authors of this statement go on to say that they can explain the values and goals that would characterize a "decent" society, but a blueprint of how a socialist society would work is not available.

The common criticism of such a utopian vision is that it entails a strong element of faith. There is no scientific evidence that a truly liberated society is possible or that the elimination of class interests would solve the crime problem. Thus, despite its acrid comments on delinquency policy, the radical perspective does not give us a particularly clear plan of action. On the other hand, faith and utopian vision are no worse than disillusionment, pessimism, and apathy. Again, it is your choice.

Reform of Social Institutions

Recognizing that our specific proposals *may* have all sorts of unintended consequences and *may* end up making no difference, we may still choose to pursue change in certain institutions. There are, in fact, certain institutions that each of us has an opportunity to change. Wilson may be correct in arguing that "no one knows how a government might restore affection, stability, and fair discipline to a family" (1975:54). Nonetheless, your understanding of findings concerning the family may determine the style of family life you choose. Many parents avoid feelings of guilt by viewing their children's problems as the responsibility of the government or the school, even though what goes on in the family and in parent-child relationships appears *directly* relevant to an understanding of delinquency. It is possible for you to make a difference for the probability of delinquency through interventions in your own family life. Sociological research on the family is relevant to "policies of parenting," whether the government is involved or not.

Moreover, there is considerable evidence that school achievement and school experiences are associated with delinquency. Certain organizational characteristics of schools are suspect as contributing to delinquency (see Chapter 7). As criminologists, we do not know how to improve achievement, but pursuing that goal may have great potential for reducing delinquency. We have already noted that we do not know what the full repercussions of changing school organizational structure would be. However, it certainly appears worthwhile to encourage further research on the variable arrangements that already exist and to foster experimentation with alternative systems. Such efforts will meet with resistance, but resistance is one price of freedom and diversity.

We commented in Chapter 8 on the common sociological view that organized religion and the church are irrelevant to modern life. However, the findings on that point are not consistent. There is evidence that when a church takes clear and definite stands, it can have a definite impact on values and attitudes, and even on delinquent behavior. Obviously, when no stands are taken, or when the church and its members come to view their religion as a superficial aspect of their lives, the church is likely to have superficial consequences.

Juvenile Justice

Even though the research on alternative reactions to delinquency does not clearly answer all questions, some rather radical alternative plans have not turned out to be as unreasonable as many feared. For example, in a concerted effort to de-institutionalize the treatment and care of troubled youth, Massachusetts began closing its training schools in the early 1970s. The Department of Youth Services in that state was spending some $11,500 per child, and yet recidivism was approaching 80 percent (Bakal, 1973). A series of reports, exposés, and investigations revealed that enormous sums of money were being spent on a system that simply was not working. The governor of Massachusetts appointed a new commissioner, Dr. Jerome Miller, to head the Department of Youth Services. Between 1970 and 1972, Dr. Miller closed all residential institutions funded by the Department of Youth Services, and new community-based alternatives were developed. The twelve hundred youths normally committed each year to the care of the Department of Youth Services were placed in small community-based residential or nonresidential programs. Fewer than 5 percent of these youths required the secure surroundings of a training school. Services for these offenders were purchased from a private organization.

Although the evaluation of the Massachusetts experiment is not complete, preliminary results are encouraging. The rate of institutionalization in Massachusetts is 2.1 per 100,000 population, while the average rate for the United States is 17.8 (Ohlin et al., n.d.). However, there is no evidence that the crime rate has changed significantly as a result of this change in the juvenile justice system. The evidence to date also shows that Massachusetts has spent significantly less per capita for correctional programs than most other states but ranks very high in expenditures for community-based programs. Thus, funds that are normally allocated for institutional care can be redirected to fund a wide range of youth service programs. As a result of such a policy, the Massachusetts Department of Youth Services has changed its posture from a custodial and punitive agency to that of a youth advocacy bureau.

Other states are observing the Massachusetts experiment closely. Several have already made initial overtures to de-institutionalize their juvenile justice systems. The enormous cost involved in supporting the juvenile justice system and the questionable impact it has on juvenile offenders may precipitate a taxpayers' revolt. Governmental agencies can no longer, with impunity, make any and all funding requests. Hence, new alternatives, such as prevention programs, may be seen as face-saving gestures or as serious efforts to grapple with fundamental causes.

Tolerance

Edwin Schur popularized the notion of *radical nonintervention,* which "implies policies that accommodate society to the widest possible diversity of behaviors and attitudes, rather than forcing . . . individuals to 'adjust' to supposedly common societal standards" (1973:154). How radical this proposal really is, is a matter of conjecture, but the gist of Schur's argument is that children ought to be diverted away from the juvenile justice system. In Schur's view, the standards governing youthful behavior are far more rigorous than is necessary. Therefore, his dictum is "leave kids alone wherever possible" (1973:155). This kind of "true" diversion has not really been tested and deserves exploration.

Edwin Lemert (1967) coined the phrase *judicious nonintervention.* He asserted that the juvenile court should be considered a court of last resort, to be used only after all alternatives have been exhausted. This line of reasoning parallels the concerns of many criminologists who are critical of the overextension of criminal law. It is their belief that the law should not be used by those trying to enforce disputed moral standards of minor significance. The Wolfenden committee studied the problem of prostitution and homosexuality in Great Britain. It concluded that there need to be precise limitations on the scope of criminal law and that behaviors involving consenting adults do not fall within that scope: "Unless a deliberate attempt is to be made by society, acting through the agency of the law, to equate the sphere of crime with the sphere of sin, there must remain a realm of private morality and immorality which is in brief and crude terms, not the law's business" (Committee on Homosexual Offenses and Prostitution, 1964:23).

There are parallels between the Wolfenden committee's report and arguments that we must learn to tolerate a wider range of adolescent behavior. In the first place, we need to rank juvenile offenses so that we can arrive at some sense of what is more serious and what is less serious. Far too often the juvenile justice system has been accused of having a "shotgun" approach—spreading energy too thinly over far too many problem areas. Certain petty problems could be resolved in noncriminal arenas or perhaps simply ignored. To steal a phrase from the Wolfenden committee, certain forms of adolescent behavior are "not the law's business." This is not to say that they should be ignored or condoned but simply that there are more appropriate ways of handling many forms of annoying behavior than "calling the cops."

Personal Reform

Our own behavior is another factor relevant to delinquency, and it provides us with yet another choice. We may all accept the view that parents and other adults set the example for children, or that fathers and mothers have a high probability of being role models for their children. At the same time, however, we should recognize that every child growing up in the United States is likely to have been told, "Do as I say! Not as I do!" What is too readily forgotten is that what parents *do* is correlated with what their children *do,* regardless of the convenient caveat. Moreover, the saying itself reflects one of the underlying candidates as a cause of delinquency—hypocrisy.

Most social science research has concentrated on the relationship between the behavior of peers and involvement in delinquency. Parents are presumed to be fairly conventional in terms of the values they endorse and their attitudes toward lawbreaking. Travis Hirschi (1969) accurately argued that an Oliver Twist-Fagin pattern of adult socialization of the young into delinquency is rare. However, adults and parents can facilitate delinquency in more subtle ways. Consider, for example, the "Soap Box Derby scandal" of 1974. The fourteen-year-old winner was disqualified for using an electromagnet to get a head start on the competition. As Richard Woodley (1974) pointed out, "The befouling of the venerable Derby was not, to be sure, the idea of the children who aspired to its crown, but of the adults who guided the innocents in the childhood game." The adult in this case was merely trying to "even the odds" since cheating was seen as pervasive in the Soap Box Derby. The view that "everybody does it" and that to win or survive you have to break rules was communicated quite clearly in the course of a very conventional, adult-influenced activity.

The relationship between parental behavior and the behavior of juveniles is quite apparent in the area of drug use. Erich Goode has noted that there is a *generational continuity* to drug use: "Parents who use legal drugs—cigarettes, alcohol, and prescription drugs such as barbiturates and amphetamines—are more likely to have children who use illegal drugs, marijuana included" (1972:34). The generational link between parental drug use and juvenile drug use appears to be indirect, with cigarettes and alcohol the intermediary drugs.

In one of the authors' studies in a middle-class high school in Tucson, Arizona, parental drug use was found to be significantly related to juvenile tobacco use, drinking, drunkenness, marijuana use, and use of amphetamines, barbiturates, and sleeping pills (Jensen, 1979). Use of drugs by friends was also related to all these forms of juvenile drug use. In addition, friends' drug use was related to juvenile use of narcotics, LSD, and cocaine. However, the greatest levels of drug use tended to occur among students whose friends *and* parents used drugs. For example, only 4 percent of the students whose friends and parents did not drink had been drunk in the year preceding the survey (according to their own self-reports), as compared to 68 percent of students whose parents and friends did drink. In short, what parents are perceived to do is correlated with what their children do.

The Soap Box Derby scandal can be viewed in the context of the attitudes of high school students toward the law. When students in the Tucson study were asked to give their opinion about whether "it's O.K. to break the law if you can get away with it," the vast majority disagreed (76 percent). Only 8 percent agreed and the other 16 percent were uncertain. In contrast, when asked to comment on the statement "To get what you want in this world you have to do some things that are against the law," 28 percent agreed and 23 percent were uncertain. When students in four other southern Arizona communities were given these statements, their responses were quite similar. Such findings seem to reflect an ambivalence in the adult world that one generation helps to perpetuate in the next. The law is something we ought to obey but may have to ignore if it gets in the way of success. This point of view was not independently invented by wayward youth. Since the correlation between adult attitudes and conduct and juvenile attitudes and conduct is a naturally occurring correlation, and one over which adults potentially have some degree of control, changes in adult behavior may have great potential for preventing delinquency.

RESPONSES TO DELINQUENCY

In Chapter 1 we cited several traditional rationales for spending an inordinate amount of time studying delinquency, including the view that juveniles account for an inordinate amount of crime in America. The presidential task force reports on the problems of delinquency and youth crime, which we have alluded to several times, were composed during a period when the crime rate was climbing dramatically. Black Americans were rioting and protesting injustice in America. Students were protesting the war in Vietnam. The post–World War II "baby boom" was passing through adolescence into young adulthood and was swelling educational institutions. Girls were no longer "acting like girls" and were beginning to account for an increasing share of the delinquency problem. From claims of presidential task force reports and the popular press, it appeared that young people were getting "out of hand," and there were so many of them it was hard not to notice.

However, survey data show no evidence of significant increases in self-reported delinquency during the 1960s, and victimization data show some modest increases and decreases during the 1970s. In fact, by the late 1970s several different bodies of data suggested a leveling or decline in crime and delinquency. By then, the baby boom of the late 1940s and early 1950s was moving into the "over-thirty crowd." The average American woman is currently bearing 1.9 children, somewhat less than the 2.1 required for zero poulation growth. Demographers estimate it will take fifty years before this declining birth rate stems the overall growth rate. However, changes in the age structure of American society are already occurring. The increase in the older age categories could inflate the incidence of crimes committed by adults, and the crime picture could alter dramatically as we become a more aged population. Midlife crimes, alcoholism, and white-collar crime could be to the 1980s and 1990s what the delinquency problem has been to the 1960s and 1970s.

If the recent respite from perpetually increasing delinquency and crime turns out to be more than temporary, will there be a decline in public concern about juvenile delinquency? Will attention shift elsewhere? The sociological issue to be addressed in responding to these questions is the correlation (or lack of it) between perceptions of social problems and the actual magnitude of the problem. Consider, for example, Marshall Clinard's study of crime and delinquency in Switzerland (1978). Clinard found that a majority of household residents in Zurich believed that major crimes had been increasing. Women and older persons were more likely to perceive increases than were males and younger persons. However, official statistics revealed few significant increases in recorded crime in Switzerland. Moreover, while the majority of respondents felt crime had increased, 61 percent felt crime had remained the same in their neighborhoods. The Swiss seemed to believe that crime was increasing even though the official crime rate remained constant.

In his analysis of perceptions of crime and criminals in the United States, John Conklin suggested that one source of disparity between responses to crime and actual crime is the tendency to respond to *numbers* of events rather than rates (1975:22). The number of offenses may increase, and yet the rate may stay the same because of increases in population. For example, 200 offenses in a population of 2,000 yields a crime rate of 100 offenses per 1,000 people. If the population increased to 4,000 and the number of offenses increased to 400, the rate would be the same—100 per 1,000 people. However, there are 200 more offenses. In other words, although the *crime rate* has remained the same, the *number* of offenses has increased. To the degree that people respond to numbers with no real knowledge of rates, crime and delinquency may be viewed as increasing even during periods of declining rates.

Public perception of social problems can also reflect media coverage of issues. F. James Davis (1952), who studied the relationship between crime news in Colorado newspapers and actual crime rates, reported little correspondence between the two. Moreover, he found public opinions about crime to be more a function of news coverage of crime than of actual crime. One of the most recent considerations of this topic has been Mark Fishman's study "Crime Waves as Ideology" (1978). Fishman noted that in 1976 New York City supposedly experienced a major crime wave that involved violence against the elderly. All three daily newspapers and five television stations reported on this upsurge in crime. However, Fishman's conclusion was: "It is doubtful that there really was a crime wave or any surge in violence against elderly people" (1978:532). He noted that police statistics did not reveal a crime wave and that homicides involving the elderly had actually declined. Moreover, the elderly did not appear to have been "singled out" by criminals in that victimization seemed to have increased for all age categories. Fishman concluded that the crime wave began as a "theme" that journalists hit upon in selecting news. Once some incident is cited as an instance of a particular problem, other incidents become "news" because they fit the emerging theme. Fishman stated that "each use of the theme confirms and justifies its prior uses" (1978:538). Thus, although in Chapter 8 we found little evidence that violence or pornography in the media cause crime or delinquency, there is some indication that media content may shape the public image of social problems.

Another finding concerning public reaction to crime and delinquency, which should help us understand our own feelings about social problems, is the tendency to attribute problems to groups we do not like or to "outsiders." John Conklin (1975) reported that the vast majority of the people he studied in two eastern communities believed crimes in their area could be attributed to outsiders. Clinard's study in Switzerland yielded similar results, with two-thirds of respondents in Zurich and Stuttgart attributing neighborhood crimes to persons from outside their neighborhoods. Of course, these perceptions may be accurate. However, there is evidence to the contrary. One study (Montgomery, 1973) found that while the residents of a particular area attributed crime and delinquency to outsiders, over three-fourths of all arrests and over 90 percent of arrests of juveniles in the area involved residents. Conklin noted that evidence of exaggerated beliefs in the culpability of the outsider can be found in studies of alcoholics and in studies of residents of housing projects. The outsider is more suspect than the actual evidence justifies.

In short, our responses to delinquency and crime are not necessarily based on the actual magnitude and objective nature of the problem. When we stand back and take an objective look at ourselves, our institutions, and our society, we discover that the very problem that we intermittently abhor and want to do "something" about may be facilitated by characteristics of our society, institutions, and selves that we do not "really" want to change.

Commenting on the prospects for reducing delinquency, Jackson Toby concluded:

> Adolescent delinquency may be part of the price industrial societies pay for their affluence, their freedom from oppressive social controls, and their willingness to give young people a relatively long period of preparation for adult responsibilities. This does not mean that high rates of delinquency are inevitable, but it suggests that panaceas are unlikely. The lowering of delinquency rates will come about only if the fuller participation of youth in major institutions becomes a priority value—important enough to justify large expenditures not only for the education and job-training of intellectually marginal youth but also for the development of the civic, marital, and aesthetic potentialities of all adolescents. (1963:25)

Delinquency is shaped and facilitated by aspects of the social world that each of us helps to create and sustain. We may not do so consciously or intentionally since we are each also constrained by the social world. However, an understanding of the forces that shape delinquency and of reactions to delinquency should help us understand ourselves and our own role in the problem. Such understanding does not provide clear and certain answers to the choices we must make, which is why this chapter is subtitled "Dilemmas of Choice, Change, and Control."

If you choose to view delinquency as a serious problem and *if* you want to advocate doing "something" about it, then it is important to learn what has been tried and to consider alternatives in view of past failures. If previous prevention designs did not work because they were not intensive enough or because of vested interests and political limitations, then you will have to overcome such limitations and try these designs again. If they failed because they did not change society sufficiently, then you may choose to alter the system radically and hope for the best. There will be risks and costs involved and no scientific research to tell you with certainty what the rewards and costs of alternative utopias will be. To paraphrase one author (Empey, 1974), they may all turn out to be "fugitive utopias." If you feel that you are a source of the problem, then try to gain control over your own behavior and recognize the consequences of your own actions and inactions. If you feel you need to know more before deciding what to do, then pursue such knowledge and support others in that pursuit. Existing knowledge is a risky and an uncertain guide. It can help you narrow your options, but it also leaves you in the age-old human position of making choices with no guarantee of success.

REFERENCES

Bakal, Y. 1973. "Closing Massachusetts' Institutions: A Case Study." In Y. Bakal, ed., *Closing Correctional Institutions.* Lexington, Mass.: Lexington Books.

Berleman, W. C., and T. W. Steinburn. 1967. "The Execution and Evaluation of a Delinquency Prevention Program." *Social Problems* 14 (Spring):413–23.

Chambliss, W. J., and M. Mankoff. 1976. *Whose Law? What Order?* New York: John Wiley.

Clinard, M. B. 1978. *Cities with Little Crime: The Case of Switzerland.* Cambridge: Cambridge University Press.

Committee on Homosexual Offenses and Prostitution. 1964. *The Wolfenden Report.* New York: Lancer Books.

Conklin, J. 1975. *The Impact of Crime.* New York: Macmillan.

Davis, F. J. 1952. "Crime News in Colorado Newspapers." *American Journal of Sociology* 57 (January):325–30.

Edwards, R. C., M. Reich, and T. E. Weisskopf. 1974. "Toward a Socialist Alternative." In Quinney, *Criminal Justice.*

Empey, L. T. 1974. "Crime Prevention: The Fugitive Utopia." In D. Glaser, ed., *Handbook of Criminology.* Chicago: Rand McNally.

Etzioni, A. 1972. "Human Beings Are Not Very Easy to Change After All." *Saturday Review* (June):45–47. Copyright 1972 by *Saturday Review.* All rights reserved.

Finestone, H. 1976. *Victims of Change.* Westport, Conn.: Greenwood Press. Reprinted by permission of the publisher, Greenwood Press, Inc., Westport, Conn.

Fishman, M. 1978. "Crime Waves as Ideology." *Social Problems* 25 (June):531–43.

Goode, E. 1972. *Drugs in American Society.* New York: Alfred A. Knopf.

Hackler, J. C. 1966. "Boys, Blisters and the Behavior—The Impact of a Work Program in an Urban Central Area." *The Journal of Research in Crime and Delinquency* 3 (July):155–64.

Hakeem, M. 1957–58. "A Critique of the Psychiatric Approach to the Prevention of Juvenile Delinquency." *Social Problems* 5 (Winter):194–206. Copyright 1957 by the Society for the Study of Social Problems. Reprinted by permission.

Higgins, P. S. 1978. "Evaluation and Case Study of a School-Based Delinquency Prevention Program." *Evaluation Quarterly* 2 (May):215–34.

Hirschi, T. 1969. *Causes of Delinquency.* Berkeley: University of California Press.

Jeffrey, C. R. 1971. *Crime Prevention through Environmental Design.* Beverly Hills, Calif.: Sage.

Jensen, G. 1979. *Final Report: Delinquency in a Middle Class School.* National Institute of Mental Health. Washington, D.C.

Lanoutte, W. J. 1970. "Doctor, a Nixon Friend, Says 'It Will Be Done.'" *National Observer* 9 (May 4):7.

Lemert, E. 1967. "The Juvenile Court—Quest and Realities." In President's Commission on Law Enforcement and Administration of Justice, *Task Force Report: Juvenile Delinquency and Youth Crime.* Washington, D.C.: U.S. Government Printing Office.

Martin, J. M. 1961. "Three Approaches to Delinquency Prevention: A Critique." *Crime and Delinquency* 7 (January):16–24.

Martin, J. M., J. P. Fitzpatrick, and R. E. Gould. 1970. *The Analysis of Delinquent Behavior, A Structural Approach.* New York: Random House.

Martinson, R. 1976. "California Research at the Crossroads." In R. Martinson, T. Palmer, and S. Adams, eds., *Rehabilitation, Recidivism and Research.* Hackensack, N.J.: National Council on Crime and Delinquency.

McCord, J., and W. McCord. 1959. "A Follow-Up Report on the Cambridge-Somerville Youth Study." *Annals of the American Academy of Political and Social Science* 322 (March):89–98.

Miller, W. B. 1958. "Inter-Institutional Conflict as a Major Impediment to Delin-quency Prevention." *Human Organization* 17 (Fall):20–23.

———. 1962. "The Impact of a 'Total Community' Delinquency Control Project." *Social Problems* 10 (Fall):168–91.

Montgomery, P. 1973. "Its Crime Indigenous to Westchester." *New York Times,* May 13:43.

Ohlin, L., et al. N.d. *Juvenile Correctional Reform in Massachusetts.* Washing-ton, D.C.: U.S. Government Printing Office.

Platt, A. 1970. "Saving and Controlling Delinquent Youth: A Critique." *Issues in Criminology* 5 (Winter):1–24.

Polk, K. 1971. "Delinquency Prevention and the Youth Service Bureau." *Criminal Law Bulletin* 7 (July–August):490–511.

President's Commission on Law Enforcement and Administration of Justice. 1967. *The Challenge of Crime in a Free Society.* Washington, D.C.: U.S. Gov-ernment Printing Office.

Quinney, R., ed. 1974. *Criminal Justice in America.* Boston: Little, Brown.

Reckless, W. C., and S. Dinitz. 1972. *The Prevention of Juvenile Delinquency: An Experiment.* Columbus: Ohio University Press.

Robin, G. D. 1969. "Anti-Poverty Programs and Delinquency." *Journal of Crimi-nal Law, Criminology and Police Science* 60 (Fall):323–31.

Schur, E. 1969. *Our Criminal Society.* Englewood Cliffs, N.J.: Prentice-Hall.

———. 1973. *Radical Non-Intervention: Rethinking the Delinquency Problem.* Englewood Cliffs, N.J.: Prentice-Hall.

Schwendinger, H., and J. R. Schwendinger. 1976. "Marginal Youth and Social Policy." *Social Problems* 24 (December):84–91.

Sutherland, E. 1924. *Principles of Criminology.* Philadelphia: J. B. Lippincott.

Toby, J. 1963. "The Prospects for Reducing Delinquency Rates in Industrial Societies." *Federal Probation* 27 (December):23–25.

———. 1965. "An Evaluation of Early Identification and Intensive Treatment Programs for Predelinquents." *Social Problems* 13 (Fall):160–75.

Wheeler, S. L., S. Cottrell, Jr., and A. Romasco. 1967. "Juvenile Delinquency: Its Prevention and Control." In President's Commission on Law Enforcement and Administration of Justice, *Juvenile Delinquency and Youth Crime.* Washing-ton, D.C.: U.S. Government Printing Office.

Wilson, J. Q. 1975. *Thinking about Crime.* New York: Vintage Books.

Woodley, R. 1974. "How to Win in the Soap Box Derby." *Harper's Magazine* 249 (August):62–69.

Wright, W. E., and M. C. Dixon. 1977. "Community Prevention and Treatment of Juvenile Delinquency." *Journal of Research in Crime and Delinquency* 14 (January):35–67.

INDEX OF NAMES

Teevan, J. J., 238, 249
Tennenbaum, D. J., 145, 154
Tennyson, R. A., 176, 189
Terry, R. M., 77, 78, 79, 80, 85
Thalheimer, D. J., 318, 329
Thomas, W. I., 163, 189
Thompson, R. J., 218, 225
Thornberry, T., 76, 78, 85, 276, 277, 280, 288, 308, 329
Thorndike, R. L., 208, 225
Thorsell, B. A., 281, 288
Thorton, W., 354, 365
Thrasher, F. M., 15, 20, 228, 251
Tiffany, P., 39, 47
Tittle, C. R., 72, 74, 85, 102, 105, 120, 265, 266, 281, 288, 310, 329
Toby, J., 166, 189, 218, 225, 371, 373, 374, 396, 398
Trasler, G., 148, 150, 154

Unkovich, C. M., 303, 329

van den Berghe, P., 140, 154
Villemez, W. J., 72, 74, 85, 102, 105, 120
Vinter, R. D., 304, 315, 325, 329
Volkman, A. P., 146, 154
Voltaire, 128
Voss, H. L., 94, 119, 176, 177, 178, 182, 183, 187, 189, 206, 215, 222

Waldo, G. P., 145, 154, 184, 189, 266, 288
Walters, R. H., 179, 187
Ward, D., 316, 328
Warren, M. Q., 320, 330
Wasserman, M., 309, 328
Weaver, C. N., 69, 83
Weber, J. R., 31, 32, 38, 41, 46
Weber, M., 229
Weeks, H. A., 317, 330
Weinburg, M., 359, 364
Weiner, N. L., 77, 85
Weisskopf, T. E., 389, 397

Wenninger, E. D., 99, 119
Werthman, F., 234, 251
West, D. J., 209, 225
Westley, W., 212, 222
Wexler, D., 323, 330
Whatmore, P. B., 137, 154
Wheeler, S. L., 370, 398
White, M., 184, 187, 231, 232, 248
Wigmore, J. H., 3, 19
Wilensky, H., 337, 365
Wilkinson, K., 193, 225
Wilks, J., 312, 313, 323, 328, 351, 364
Williams, J. R., 5, 20, 73, 85, 101, 102, 104, 120, 276, 286, 292, 330
Willie, C. V., 77, 85
Wilner, D., 316, 328
Wilson, A. B., 214, 215, 225, 234, 251
Wilson, B. D., 272, 287
Wilson, J. Q., 12, 20, 63, 77, 78, 85, 242, 251, 272, 288, 311, 325, 330, 385, 389, 398
Wines, E. C., 296, 333, 365
Wise, N. B., 100, 120
Witkin, H., 138, 154
Witmore, H. L., 89, 120
Wolfgang, M., 5, 20, 65, 69, 73, 85, 204, 209, 225
Wolfred, T. R., 323, 330
Woodley, R., 392, 398
Wright, W. E., 368, 371, 398
Wrong, D., 179, 189

Yablonsky, L., 158, 166, 178, 189, 192, 218, 225, 229, 249
Yinger, M., 168, 173, 189

Zald, M. N., 304, 330
Zeisel, H., 263, 265, 288
Zimring, F. E., 264, 288
Znaniecki, F., 163, 189
Zola, I., 198, 199, 200, 224

INDEX OF SUBJECTS

Biological causes
    atavism, 129–131
    body type (somatotypes), 134, 135
    chromosomal abnormalities, 137–138
    health, 135
    gender, 140
    sociological view, 139–140
    twin studies, 136–137
Black youth, 68–69, 75–78, 82, 101–102,
    114–115, 117, 196–197, 219
Body type, 134
Boston midcity project, 380, 382
Boys Town, 302, 320
Breed v. Jones, 37
Broken homes, 195–197, 220

California Youth Authority Community
    Treatment Project, 312, 315, 320–321
Cambridge-Somerville Youth Study, 372,
    380
Capital punishment, 260–263
Causal questions
    association, 125–126
    causal order, 127–128
    individual and probabilistic causation,
        124–125
    intervening processes, 128
    nonspuriousness, 127
Child abuse, 11
Childhood, 22–24, 28
Child-saving movement, 25
Children's Aid Society, 27
Children's Bureau, 303, 345
Children's rights, 43–44, 335–336
Chicago area project, 322, 374–375, 382
Chicano youth, 69, 101, 117
Chromosomal abnormalities, 137–138
Church attendance, 230, 246
Classical school, 128, 131, 255–256, 257
Clearance rates, 54
Comic books, 234–235
Commitment, 181
Commitment to peers, 215–217, 221
Communal bonds, 241–246, 247
Community size
    and official delinquency, 65–66
    and self-reported delinquency, 99–100
    and victimization, 133
Community treatment, 28, 320–322
Complainants, 52–53
Compulsive masculinity, 196–197
Compulsory education, 24–25
Conflict theory, 388
Consent decree, 342
Constitutional psychology, 133–134
Containment theory, 164
Contraculture, 156, 160–161, 168, 173,
    175–176
Cost of crime, 7
Criminal families, 135–136
Cultural conflict theory, 150–151,
    169–171, 177–179, 194, 212–213, 234

Darwinian theory, 129

Deinstitutionalization of Status Offenders
    (DSO) project, 334, 355–359
Defensible space, 245
Delinquency law
    common law, 29, 39
    continuing controversy, 43–44
    current statutes, 39
    definition of delinquent, 39
    delinquent act, 40
    dependent child, 39, 40
    detention, 299, 334, 337–343
    incorrigible child, 40–41
    labeling theory, 273–274
    legal precedent, 25–26, 29–30, 32, 35,
        37
    status offences, 40–41
Delinquent
    act, 39–40
    as myth, 88–89
    behavior, 156–157, 159
    careers, 269, 277–278, 283–284,
        357–358
    gangs, 156–159
    subcultures, 156, 159, 161, 167–168,
        169–174
Dependent child, 39, 40
Deterrence, 255, 257–268
    absolute, 259
    and criminological theory, 257
    capital punishment, 260–263
    general, 258, 325
    general preventive effects, 258
    incapacitation, 258, 264, 325
    marginal efficacy, 277
    overload, 264
    perception, 266–268
    restrictive, 259
    socialization, 258
    specific, 258, 259
Diagnostic centers, 302
Differential association, 145–150, 170,
    334–335
Direct parental control, 181–182, 201
Direct supervision and control, 201
Discretion, 52–53, 343–346
Discrimination
    gender, 79–80, 82
    race, 75–78, 82
    social class, 78–79, 82
Distribution of delinquency, 5, 54–56
    among groups, 66–74, 81–82,
        100–105, 113–115, 117–118
    space, 65–66, 81, 98–100, 113, 117
    time, 57–64, 81, 97–98, 111–113, 118
Diversion
    discretion, 343–346
    evaluation, 351–353
    ideology, 359–361
    policy, 346–348
    rationales, 334–343
    status offenders, 355–358
    types, 348–350
    youth service bureaus, 350
Dramatization of evil, 273, 283

Swiss society, 243

Teaching-family model, 320
Techniques of neutralization, 165–166
Television violence, 235–238, 246–247
Theories
  biological, 128–140
  psychological, 140–151
  sociological, 150–184
Ties to parents, 200
Time trends, 57–64, 81, 97–98,
  111–113, 118
Token economies, 320
Tracking in schools, 206–208, 384
Training schools, 28, 303–305, 308
Treatment, 311–315
  behavior modification, 322–324
  community, 28, 320–322
  guided group interaction, 316–317, 321
  half-way houses, 299, 302, 318–319
  milieu therapy, 313
  psychotherapy, 315–316
Twin studies, 136–137
Types of delinquent offenses, 184, 264

Uniform Crime Reports, 5, 7, 53–54, 336
  crimes known, 57
  serious crime index, 53–54
Urban-rural differences, 65–66

Value consensus, 165
Value stretch, 176
Victimization surveys, 51, 89, 105–116
  characteristics of offenders, 113–115
  characteristics of victims, 115–116
  in-person interviews, 106
  mail-back questionnaires, 106
  problems with, 106, 110
  spatial distribution, 113
  students as victims, 210
  telephone, 106
  victim-offender relationships, 116

White collar crime, 9–10
Wolfenden Committee, 391
Work, 181
Writ of Habeas Corpus, 34
Wyatt v. Stickney, 323

Youth Service Bureau, 350, 376